Guide to the Irish Companies Acts 1990

GUIDE
to the
IRISH COMPANIES
ACTS 1990

Michael Phelan

Gill and Macmillan

Published in Ireland by
Gill and Macmillan Ltd
Goldenbridge
Dublin 8
with associated companies in
Auckland, Delhi, Gaborone, Hamburg, Harare,
Hong Kong, Johannesburg, Kuala Lumpur, Lagos, London,
Manzini, Melbourne, Mexico City, Nairobi,
New York, Singapore, Tokyo
© Michael Phelan 1991
Designed by Maurren Kelly
Print origination by
Seton Music Graphics Ltd, Bantry, Co. Cork
Printed by Billing & Sons Ltd, Worcester

British Library Cataloguing in Publication Data
Phelan, Michael B.
Guide to the Irish Companies Acts 1990.
I. Title
346.417
ISBN 0-7171-1908-4

CONTENTS

PREFACE

The Companies Acts of 1990 had a very lengthy gestation period. As far back as 1981 this legislation was promised, but it was not until 1987 that the legislation was published. During the summer of 1990 the Goodman group of companies had financial difficulties, and the new court protection provisions were hurriedly enacted by recalling the Oireachtas from its summer recess. This legislation became the Companies (Amendment) Act, 1990; the remainder of the legislation was enacted in December 1990 and became known as the Companies Act, 1990.

The Acts are complex pieces of legislation, with many technical provisions; and much study and monitoring by company administrators, advisers, directors and others associated with companies will be required to ensure that they comply with the numerous requirements and obligations. I hope that this work, by supplying an annotation for each section, will provide a comprehensive guide and reference to the new legislation.

I would like to thank Éamonn Ó Raghallaigh, Daniel Healy and Ray Bowman for their assistance, encouragement, comments and suggestions in the preparation of this work.

The book is dedicated to my sons, Rory and Dónal, who were patient and understanding during the evenings when I disappeared to work on this text.

Every effort has been made to ensure that the information and commentary in this book is accurate. However, no responsibility, legal or otherwise, is accepted by the publishers or myself for any error, omissions or otherwise in the information in this book.

TABLE OF CASES

THE COMPANIES ACT, 1990

1
PRELIMINARY

SECTION 1

Short title, collective citation and construction

(1) This Act may be cited as the Companies Act, 1990.

(2) This Act and the Companies Acts, 1963 to 1986, may be cited together as the Companies Acts, 1963 to 1990.

(3) The Companies Acts, 1963 to 1986, and this Act shall be construed together as one Act.

General Note

Subsection (3) provides that this Act shall be construed with the other companies legislation, namely:

- Companies Act, 1963
- Companies (Amendment) Act, 1977
- Companies (Amendment) Act, 1982
- Companies (Amendment) Act, 1983
- Companies (Amendment) Act, 1986

SECTION 2

Commencement

This Act shall come into operation on such day or days as may be fixed therefor by order or orders of the Minister, either generally or with reference to a particular purpose or provision, and different days may be so fixed for different purposes and different provisions of this Act.

General Note

On 27 December 1990 the following provisions came into effect under SI 336 of 1990:

Part	Sections
I	1–5
V	107–121
IX	180 (except subsections (1) (*g*), (2), and (3)), 181
XII	235, 238–240, 242, 244, 245, 247

SI 337 of 1990—the Companies (Stock Exchange) Regulations, 1990—confirmed the Irish Unit of the International Stock Exchange of the United Kingdom and the Republic of Ireland as a recognised stock exchange for the purposes of the Act.

On 1 February 1990 the following provisions came into operation under SI 10 of 1991:

Part	Sections
II	15, 16, 19–21, 23, 24
III	25–27, 29–49, 52
XII	243
XIII	252–262

On 1 July 1991 the following sections came into effect under SI 117 of 1991:

Part	Sections
I	6 (insofar as it repeals sections 147, 163, 165–173, 294, 296, 380 and 385 of, and the seventh and tenth schedules to, the Companies Act, 1963)
II	7–14, 17, 18, 22
III	28, 50, 51 (other than subsection (8) of section 185 of the Companies Act, 1963)
X	182–186, 190, 193–198, 201–205
XI	206–234
XII	241, 246

On 1 August 1991 the following sections came into effect under SI 117 of 1991:

Part	Sections
I	Subsection (1) of section 6 (insofar as it repeals section 184 of the Companies Act, 1963), and subsection (2)
IV	53–106
VI	122–148
VII	149–169
VIII	170–179
IX	180 (1) (*g*), (2) and (3)
XII	236, 237, 250, 251

On 19 June 1991 section 110 of the Companies Act, 1990, was modified by SI 151 of 1991, as follows:

'A person shall be regarded as having entered in good faith into a transaction to which subsection (2) (*b*) of section 110 of the Companies Act, 1990, relates if he enters in good faith into—

(*a*) an agreement to underwrite securities, or

(*b*) an agreement, in advance of dealing facilities being provided by a recognised stock exchange for securities, to acquire or subscribe for a specified number of those securities, or

(*c*) negotiations with a view to an agreement referred to in paragraph (*a*) or (*b*), or

(*d*) a transaction in accordance with his obligations under an agreement referred to in paragraph (*a*) or (*b*).

SECTION 3

Interpretation

(1) In this Act, unless the context otherwise requires—

"books and documents" and "books or documents" include accounts, deeds, writings and records made in any other manner;

"child" includes a step-child and an adopted child and "son", "daughter" and "parent" shall be construed accordingly;

"the Companies Acts" means the Companies Act, 1963, and every enactment (including this Act) which is to be construed as one with that Act;

"connected person" has the meaning assigned to it by section 26;

"contravention" includes failure to comply;

"daily default fine" has the meaning assigned to it by section 240 (6);

"the Minister" means the Minister for Industry and Commerce;

"prescribe" means prescribe by regulations;

"the Principal Act" means the Companies Act, 1963;

"recognised stock exchange" has the meaning assigned to it by subsection (2);

"related company" has the meaning assigned to it by section 140;

"shadow director" has the meaning assigned to it by section 27.

(2) (*a*) A recognised stock exchange for the purposes of any provision of the Companies Acts is an exchange prescribed by the Minister for the purposes of that section.
(*b*) The definition of "recognised stock exchange" in paragraph (*a*) is in substitution for the definition in section 2 (1) of the Principal Act.

(3) The Minister may make regulations in relation to any matter referred to in this Act as prescribed or to be prescribed.

(4) In this Act—

(*a*) a reference to a Part or section is to a Part or section of this Act unless it is indicated that a reference to some other enactment is intended;
(*b*) a reference to a subsection, paragraph or subparagraph is to the subsection, paragraph or subparagraph of the provision in which the reference occurs, unless it is indicated that reference to some other provision is intended; and
(*c*) a reference to any other enactment shall, unless the context otherwise requires, be construed as a reference to that enactment as amended by or under any other enactment, including this Act.

Definitions

'books and documents' has the same meaning as 'book and paper' in the Companies Act, 1963, section 2. It has a similar definition in the UK Companies Act, 1985, section 744. In the *Seanad Debates* (vol. 121, no. 3, at 252–256) the Minister stated that the definition 'books and documents' was construed to include computerised records.

'child': the term 'child' is not defined as a minor child, and it must be assumed it would have the meaning of a person under eighteen years of age: Age of Minority Act, 1985, section 2.

'Companies Acts': Companies Act, 1990, section 3.

'connected person': Companies Act, 1990, section 26.

'contravention': Companies Act, 1990, section 3.

'daily default fine': Companies Act, 1990, section 240.

'Minister': Companies Act, 1990, section 3.

'prescribe': Companies Act, 1990, section 3.

'Principal Act': Companies Act, 1990, section 3.

'related company': Companies Act, 1990, section 140.

'recognised stock exchange': Companies Act, 1990, section 3 (2).

'shadow director': Companies Act, 1990, section 27.

General Note

(2) This subsection provides that the term 'recognised stock exchange' shall have the meaning prescribed in section 2 (1) of the Companies Act, 1963, as amended.

(3) The Minister for Industry and Commerce may make regulations on any matter in this Act.

SECTION 4
Periods of time.

(1) Where the time limited by any provision of this Act for the doing of anything expires on a Saturday, Sunday or public holiday, the time so limited shall extend to and the thing may be done on the first following day that is not a Saturday, Sunday or public holiday.

(2) Where in this Act anything is required or allowed to be done within a number of days not exceeding six a day that is a Saturday, Sunday or public holiday shall not be reckoned in computing that number.

General Note

This section provides that in relation to periods of time, any requirements relate only to normal working days, and in the calculation of a period of time Saturdays and Sundays are to be excluded. This is to ensure that only normal business days are included in calculations for normal periods of time.

SECTION 5
Orders

The Minister may by order revoke or amend an order made by him under any provision of this Act, other than section 2.

Definitions

'*Minister*': Companies Act, 1990, section 3.

General Note

This section empowers the Minister to revoke any order made by him under the Act.

SECTION 6
Repeals

(1) The following provisions of the Principal Act are hereby repealed—sections 147, 162 (inserted by section 6 of the Companies (Amendment) Act, 1982), 163, 165 to 173, 184, 294, 296, 380 and 385, and the Seventh and Tenth Schedules.

(2) The following provisions are also hereby repealed—

(a) Regulation 8 of the European Communities (Companies) Regulations, 1973,
(b) section 6 of the Companies (Amendment) Act, 1977, and
(c) section 21 of the Companies (Amendment) Act, 1986.

Definitions

'*Principal Act*': Companies Act, 1990, section 3.

General Note

(1) The provisions repealed include:

Section 147	(Keeping of books of account)
Section 162	(Qualification for appointment of auditor)
Section 163	(Auditor's report and right of access to books and to attend and be heard at general meetings)
Section 165–173	(Inspection)
Section 184	(Power of court to restrain certain persons from acting as directors of or managing companies)
Section 294	(Alteration or falsification of books)
Section 296	(Liability where proper books of account not kept)
Section 380	(Penalty for false statements)
Section 385	(Summary proceedings)
Seventh schedule	(Matters to be expressly stated in auditor's report)
Tenth schedule	(Provisions referred to in section 380)

The provisions repealed are re-enacted in amended form in part II: Investigations (sections 7–23 inclusive).

(2) The following provisions are repealed:

European Communities (Companies) Regulations, 1973, regulation 8.

Companies (Amendment) Act, 1977, section 6.

Companies (Amendment) Act, 1986, section 21.

The objective of the repeal is to rationalise and extend the application of certain of the provisions of the Companies Acts to unregistered companies.

2
INVESTIGATIONS

Part II of the Act deals with investigations, and in general strengthens the provisions of the Companies Act, 1963, in relation to the investigation of a company's affairs.

The main changes imposed by this part are the moving of the role of appointing inspectors from the Minister for Industry and Commerce to the High Court. The investigation itself will be under the supervision of the court. There is a new power to enable the Minister to request information directly from companies in certain circumstances without the need to launch a formal investigation of its affairs. The Minister may also ascertain the true ownership of limited companies.

The purpose of the change was to make it easier to appoint an inspector to examine the affairs of a company. Under the procedure introduced by the Companies Act, 1963, the Minister appointed an inspector, and there was a question about the constitutionality of the section, with the result that it was only used on two occasions. The transfer of the power to the court should now make it easier to appoint an inspector to undertake an investigation.

SECTION 7
Investigation of company's affairs

(1) The court may appoint one or more competent inspectors to investigate the affairs of a company in order to enquire into matters specified by the court and to report thereon in such manner as the court directs—

(a) in the case of a company having a share capital, on the application either of not less than 100 members or of a member or members holding not less than one-tenth of the paid up share capital of the company;

(b) in the case of a company not having a share capital, on the application of not less than one-fifth in number of the persons on the company's register of members;

(c) in any case, on the application of the company;

(d) in any case, on the application of a director of the company;

(e) in any case, on the application of a creditor of the company.

(2) The application shall be supported by such evidence as the court may require, including such evidence as may be prescribed.

(3) Where an application is made under this section, the court may require the applicant or applicants to give security, to an amount not less than £500 and not exceeding £100,000, for payment of the costs of the investigation.

(4) Where the court appoints an inspector under this section or section 8, it may, from time to time, give such directions as it thinks fit, whether to the inspector or otherwise, with a view to ensuring that the investigation is carried out as quickly and as inexpensively as possible.

Definitions

'company': Companies Act, 1963, section 2.
'court' : Companies Act, 1990, section 235.
'director': Companies Act, 1963, section 2.
'prescribe' : Companies Act, 1990, section 3.

General Note

This section is a substitution for section 165 of the Companies Act, 1963, the main change being the transfer from the Minister to the court of the function of appointing inspectors, and the provision of security for payment of the costs of the investigation.

(1) The court may appoint inspectors to investigate the affairs of a company in order to enquire into matters specified by the court

(*a*) where there is an application from not fewer than 100 members or members holding not less than 10 per cent of the paid-up share capital of the company,

(*b*) if the company has not got a share capital (for example a company limited by guarantee not having a share capital), on the application of not less than 20 per cent of the members registered in the register of members of the company (it should be noted that the subsection refers to 'registered holders', therefore if there are shareholders who are not yet registered they have not got the power to vote),

(*c*) where there is an application from the company,

(*d*) where there is an application by a director of a company (this is to facilitate a non-executive director who could petition the court for the appointment of an investigator), or

(*e*) where any creditor makes an application to the court (note that there is no limitation on the amount owed by a creditor before being allowed to make such an application).

(2) The application should be supported by such evidence as may be required by the court.

(3) The High Court may require an application for an investigation to be supported by evidence. This is to ensure that the application is reasonable and not a frivolous or mischievous one; and it should be remembered that the court will require the security of not less than £500 and not more than £100,000 referred to in subsection (3) to be provided. The purpose of this security is to rule out mischievous claims or actions.

(4) Where a court appoints an inspector it may give such directions as it thinks fit to ensure that the investigation is carried out as quickly and as cheaply as possible.

SECTION 8
Investigation of company's affairs on application of Minister

(1) Without prejudice to its powers under section 7, the court may on the application of the Minister appoint one or more competent inspectors to investigate the affairs of a company and to report thereon in such manner as the court shall direct, if the court is satisfied that there are circumstances suggesting—

(a) that its affairs are being or have been conducted with intent to defraud its creditors or the creditors of any other person or otherwise for a fraudulent or unlawful purpose or in an unlawful manner or in a manner which is unfairly prejudicial to some part of its members, or that any actual or proposed act or omission of the company (including an act or omission on its behalf) is or would be so prejudicial, or that it was formed for any fraudulent or unlawful purpose; or

(b) that persons connected with its formation or the management of its affairs have in connection therewith been guilty of fraud, misfeasance or other misconduct towards it or towards its members; or

(c) that its members have not been given all the information relating to its affairs which they might reasonably expect.

(2) (a) The power conferred by section 7 or this section shall be exercisable with respect to a body corporate notwithstanding that it is in course of being wound up.

(b) The reference in subsection (1) (a) to the members of a company shall have effect as if it included a reference to any person who is not a member but to whom shares in the company have been transferred or transmitted by operation of law.

Definitions

'*body corporate*': Companies Act, 1963, section 2 (3).

'*company*': Companies Act, 1963, section 2.

'*court*': Companies Act, 1990, section 235.

'*Minister*': Companies Act, 1990, section 3.

General Note

This section is substituted for section 166 of the Companies Act, 1963, and allows the Minister to apply to the High Court to appoint inspectors to investigate the affairs of a company. It also widens the range of circumstances in which inspectors may be appointed. The expression 'the affairs of the company' was interpreted by Justice Phillismore in *R.* v. *Board of Trade, exp. St. Martin Preserving Co. Ltd.* [1965] 1 QB 603, 613 as to include the company's 'goodwill, its profits or losses, its contracts and assets including its shareholding in and ability to control the affairs of a subsidiary and perhaps in the latter regard a sub-subsidiary.'

(1) The Minister may apply to the High Court to appoint one or more competent inspectors to investigate the affairs of a company. The court may appoint inspectors where it is satisfied that there are grounds suggesting

(*a*) that the affairs of the company have been or are being conducted with intent to defraud its creditors, or creditors of any other person, or for a fraudulent or unlawful purpose or in an unlawful manner or in a manner that is unfairly prejudicial to some part of its members, or that the company was formed for any fraudulent or unlawful purpose,

(*b*) that persons who have been connected with the formation or management of the company's affairs have been guilty of fraud, misfeasance or other misconduct towards the shareholders, or

(*c*) that relevant and important information that members might reasonably expect to receive has been withheld from them.

(2) The powers conferred by section 7 and this section may be exercised even if the company is in the course of being wound up. For the purposes of this section a 'member' will be construed to include a person who is not a member but to whom shares have been transferred or transmitted by operation of law.

SECTION 9
Power of inspectors to extend investigation into affairs of related companies.

If an inspector appointed under section 7 or 8 to investigate the affairs of a company thinks it necessary for the purposes of his investigation to investigate also the affairs of any other body corporate which is related to such company, he shall, with the approval of the court, have power so to do, and shall report on the affairs of the other body corporate so far as he thinks the results of his investigation thereof are relevant to the investigation of the affairs of the first-mentioned company.

Definitions

'*body corporate*': Companies Act, 1963, section 2 (3).
'*company*': Companies Act, 1963, section 2.
'*court*': Companies Act, 1990, section 235.

General Note

This section replaces section 167 of the Companies Act, 1963, and substitutes the High Court for the Minister for Industry and Commerce in relation to the appointment of inspectors to investigate a company's affairs. It provides that the inspector may extend any investigation into a company's affairs to any other body corporate that is related to such company; this must, however, be with the court's approval. The inspector will then report on the affairs of all the companies so investigated by him.

SECTION 10
Production of documents and evidence on investigation.

(1) It shall be the duty of all officers and agents of the company and of all officers and agents of any other body corporate whose affairs are investigated by virtue of section 9 to produce to the inspectors all books and documents of or relating to the company, or, as the case may be, the other body corporate which are in their custody or power, to attend before the inspectors when required so to do and otherwise to give to the inspectors all assistance in connection with the investigation which they are reasonably able to give.

(2) If the inspectors consider that a person other than an officer or agent of the company or other body corporate is or may be in possession of any information concerning its affairs, they may require that person to produce to them any books or documents in his custody or power relating to the company or other body corporate, to attend before them and otherwise to give them all assistance in connection with the investigation which he is reasonably able to give; and it shall be the duty of that person to comply with the requirement.

(3) If an inspector has reasonable grounds for believing that a director of the company or other body corporate whose affairs the inspector is investigating maintains or has maintained a bank account of any description, whether alone or jointly with another person and whether in the State or elsewhere, into or out of which there has been paid—

(*a*) any money which has resulted from or been used in the financing of any transaction, arrangement or agreement—
(i) particulars of which have not been disclosed in a note to the accounts of any company for any financial year as required by section 41; or
(ii) in respect of which any amount outstanding was not included in the aggregate amounts outstanding in respect of certain transactions, arrangements or agreements as required by section 43 to be disclosed in a note to the accounts of any company for any financial year; or
(iii) particulars of which were not included in any register of certain transactions, arrangements and agreements as required by section 44; or
(*b*) any money which has been in any way connected with any act or omission, or series of acts or omissions, which on the part of that director constituted misconduct (whether fraudulent or not) towards that company or body corporate or its members;

the inspector may require the director to produce to him all documents in the director's possession, or under his control, relating to that bank account; and in this subsection "bank account" includes an account with any person exempt by virtue of section 7 (4) of the Central Bank Act, 1971, from the requirement of holding a licence under section 9 of that Act, and "director" includes any present or past director or any person connected, within the meaning of section 26, with such director, and any present or past shadow director.

(4) An inspector may examine on oath, either by word of mouth or on written interrogatories, the officers and agents of the company or other body corporate and such person as is mentioned in subsection (2) in relation to its affairs and may—

(*a*) administer an oath accordingly,
(*b*) reduce the answers of such person to writing and require him to sign them.

(5) If any officer or agent of the company or other body corporate or any such person as is mentioned in subsection (2) refuses to produce to the inspectors any book or document which it is his duty under this section so to produce,

refuses to attend before the inspectors when required so to do or refuses to answer any question which is put to him by the inspectors with respect to the affairs of the company or other body corporate as the case may be, the inspectors may certify the refusal under their hand to the court, and the court may thereupon enquire into the case and, after hearing any witnesses who may be produced against or on behalf of the alleged offender and any statement which may be offered in defence, punish the offender in like manner as if he had been guilty of contempt of court.

(6) Without prejudice to its power under subsection (5), the court may, after a hearing under that subsection, make any order or direction it thinks fit, including a direction to the person concerned to attend or re-attend before the inspector or produce particular books or documents or answer particular questions put to him by the inspector, or a direction that the person concerned need not produce a particular book or document or answer a particular question put to him by the inspector.

(7) In this section, any reference to officers or to agents shall include past, as well as present, officers or agents, as the case may be, and "agents", in relation to a company or other body corporate, shall include the bankers and solicitors of the company or other body corporate and any persons employed by the company or other body corporate as auditors, whether those persons are or are not officers of the company or other body corporate.

Definitions

'agent': Companies Act, 1990, section 10.

'bank account': Companies Act, 1990, section 10.

'body corporate': Companies Act, 1963, section 2 (3).

'books and documents': Companies Act, 1990, section 3.

'company': Companies Act, 1963, section 2.

'director': Companies Act, 1963, section 2.

'officer': Companies Act, 1963, section 2.

'shadow director': Companies Act, 1990, section 3.

General Note

This section replaces section 168 of the Companies Act, 1963, and broadens the inspectors' powers in relation to the evidence that they may require and the persons whom they may examine and obtain information from.

(1) It is the duty of the officers and agents of the company to produce all books and documents in their custody to the inspectors and to attend before the inspectors when required and to give them all the assistance that may be reasonably required to help them in the investigation of the company's affairs.

(2) If the inspectors consider that any person other than an officer or agent is in possession of any information concerning the company's affairs they may require and can compel such person to produce any books or documents in his custody and to assist them in their inspection.

(3) If an inspector has reasonable grounds for believing that a director of the company or any other body corporate being investigated has or had a bank account that has been used in the financing of or involved in a transaction that has not been disclosed in a note in the company accounts or included in the accounts or omitted, irrespective of the reason, he may compel that person to produce all documents in his possession or under his control relating to that bank account. The subsection has been extended to include bodies such as building societies, the Post Office Savings Bank, the Agricultural Credit Corporation, trustee savings banks and other deposit-taking institutions that would not be regarded as 'licensed banks' in the strict sense of the term. Likewise, the term 'director' has been extended to include a past or present director or a shadow director.

(4) The inspector has power to examine any person under oath, either orally or by written interrogatories, in relation to the company's affairs.

(5) If anyone who is required to attend for examination refuses to attend, produce the books and documents that they are required to produce or refuses to answer the questions of the inspector relating to the affairs of the company under investigation the inspector may certify the refusal under hand to the High Court, and, after hearing evidence of witnesses and making any enquiries it considers fit, the court can punish the offender for contempt of court. There is no reference in section 240 to a penalty for contempt of court; at common law, punishment for criminal contempt is at the discretion of the court.

(6) The court in addition to the remedy of contempt of court will have other remedies available to it, including obliging the person to attend or re-attend before the inspector, producing books or documents, or answering particular questions put to him by the inspector.

(7) References to 'officers' and 'agents' include past as well as present officers and agents. An 'agent' is defined so as to include bankers, solicitors and auditors of the company.

SECTION 11
Inspectors'
reports.

(1) Inspectors appointed under section 7 or 8 may, and if so directed by the court shall, make interim reports to the court and on the conclusion of the investigation, shall make a final report to the court.

(2) Notwithstanding anything contained in subsection (1), an inspector appointed under section 7 or 8 may at any time in the course of his investigation, without the necessity of making an interim report, inform the court of matters coming to his knowledge as a result of the investigation tending to show that an offence has been committed.

(3) Where inspectors were appointed under section 7 or 8, the court shall furnish a copy of every report of theirs to the Minister and the court may, if it thinks fit—

(a) forward a copy of any report made by the inspectors to the company's registered office,

(b) furnish a copy on request and payment of the prescribed fee to—
(i) any member of the company or other body corporate which is the subject of the report;
(ii) any person whose conduct is referred to in the report;
(iii) the auditors of that company or body corporate;
(iv) the applicants for the investigation;
(v) any other person (including an employee) whose financial interests appear to the court to be affected by the matters dealt with in the report whether as a creditor of the company or body corporate or otherwise;
(vi) the Central Bank, in any case in which the report of the inspectors relates, wholly or partly, to the affairs of the holder of a licence under section 9 of the Central Bank Act, 1971; and

(c) cause any such report to be printed and published.

(4) Where the court so thinks proper it may direct that a particular part of a report made by virtue of this section be omitted from a copy forwarded or furnished under subsection (3) (a) or (b), or from the report as printed and published under subsection (3) (c).

Definitions

'*auditor*': this is not defined in the Companies Acts; but see the UK case *R.* v. *Shacter* [1960] 2 QB 252.

'*body corporate*': Companies Act, 1963, section 2 (3).

'*company*': Companies Act, 1963, section 2.

'*court*': Companies Act, 1990, section 235.

'*Minister*': Companies Act, 1990, section 3.

General Note

This section replaces section 169 of the Companies Act, 1963, and clarifies the position regarding the inspectors' powers and making information available to the court on an informal basis. It also gives the court greater discretion than previously enjoyed by the Minister regarding those to whom copies of the report can be made available.

(1) The inspectors can make interim reports either at their own discretion or at the request of the court, and they will also make a final report to the court at the conclusion of their investigation.

(2) The inspectors may also inform the court, without having to prepare a report, of matters coming to their knowledge tending to show that an offence has been committed.

(3) The court will give a copy of every report to the Minister and at its discretion can send a copy to the company at its registered office. The court may send a copy to the Central Bank, which may have an interest in the matter as the supervisory authority concerned in financial matters. The report may also be published for the general public. The court may at its discretion furnish a copy of the report on request and on payment of a prescribed fee to

(*a*) any member of the company or other body corporate that is referred to in the report,

(*b*) anyone whose conduct is referred to in the report,

(*c*) the auditors of the company,

(*d*) applicants for the investigation,

(*e*) any other person whose financial interests in the opinion of the court would be affected by matters referred to in the report, or

(*f*) the Central Bank in a case where there is a reference to a holder of a licence under section 9 of the Central Bank Act, 1971.

(4) The court can demand that a particular part of a report be omitted from a copy furnished or printed or published.

SECTION 12
Proceedings on inspectors' report.

(1) Having considered a report made under section 11, the court may make such order as it deems fit in relation to matters arising from that report including—

(*a*) an order of its own motion for the winding up of a body corporate, or

(*b*) an order for the purpose of remedying any disability suffered by any person whose interests were adversely affected by the conduct of the affairs of the company, provided that, in making any such order, the court shall have regard to the interests of any other person who may be adversely affected by the order.

(2) If, in the case of any body corporate liable to be wound up under the Companies Acts, it appears to the Minister from—

(*a*) any report made under section 11 as a result of an application by the Minister under section 8, or

(*b*) any report made by inspectors appointed by the Minister under this Act, or

(*c*) any information or document obtained by the Minister under this Part,

that a petition should be presented for the winding up of the body, the Minister may, unless the body is already being wound up by the court, present a petition for it to be so wound up if the court thinks it just and equitable for it to be so wound up.

Definitions

'body corporate': Companies Act, 1963, section 2 (3).
'court': Companies Act, 1990, section 235.
'Minister': Companies Act, 1990, section 3.

General Note

This section replaces section 170 of the Companies Act, 1963, and gives the Minister wider powers than he had under the 1963 Act to petition the court to have a company wound up after an investigation has been completed, as well as giving the court powers to do as it seems fit after an investigation is completed.

(1) The court has the power to make such orders as it considers appropriate after considering the inspectors' report, including an order for the winding up of a company or an order to remedy a disability suffered by any person whose interests have been adversely affected by the conduct of the company's affairs. The court will take into account the interests of any other person who may be adversely affected by the order.

(2) The Minister has the power after considering the inspectors' report to present a petition to the court to wind up a company, and it will be wound up if it is considered just and equitable to do so.

SECTION 13
Expenses of investigation of company's affairs.

(1) The expenses of and incidental to an investigation by an inspector appointed by the court under the foregoing provisions of this Act shall be defrayed in the first instance by the Minister for Justice but the court may direct that any person being—

(*a*) a body corportate dealt with in the report, or
(*b*) the applicant or applicants for the investigation,

shall be liable, to such extent as the court may direct, to repay the Minister for Justice, provided that no such liability on the part of the applicant or applicants shall exceed in the aggregate £100,000.

(2) Without prejudice to subsection (1), any person who is—

(*a*) convicted on indictment of an offence on a prosecution instituted as a result of an investigation,
(*b*) ordered to pay damages or restore any property in proceedings brought as a result of an investigation, or
(*c*) awarded damages or to whom property is restored in proceedings brought as a result of an investigation,

may, in the same proceedings, be ordered to repay all or part of the expenses referred to in subsection (1) to the Minister for Justice or to any person on whom liability has been imposed by the court under that subsection, provided that, in the case of a person to whom paragraph (*c*) relates, the court shall not order payment in excess of one-tenth of the amount of the damages awarded or of the value of the property restored, as the case may be, and any such order shall not be executed until the person concerned has received his damages or the property has been restored, as the case may be.

(3) The report of an inspector may, if he thinks fit, and shall, if the court so directs, include a recommendation as to the directions (if any) which he thinks appropriate, in the light of his investigation, to be given under subsection (1).

Definitions

'body corporate': Companies Act, 1963, section 2 (3).
'court': Companies Act, 1990, section 235.

General Note

This section replaces section 171 of the Companies Act, 1963, and provides that if a person other than an applicant for an investigation fails to pay expenses for which he is liable under the section, the court may require the applicants to meet the deficiency (if any) from the security given by them.

(1) The expenses of the investigation will be paid by the Minister for Justice, but he may recoup them from any company dealt with in the report, as decided by the court. Likewise, if the court decides, the applicant or person who applied for the investigation may be held liable to pay if so decided by the court, up to a maximum aggregate of £100,000.

(2) The court may order any person convicted on indictment of an offence as a result of the prosecution to pay damages or restore property or order any person awarded damages or to whom property is restored to repay all or part of the expenses. The court will not order payments in excess of 10 per cent of the amount of the damages awarded or value of the property restored, and such order will not be executed until the person concerned has received his damages or the property has been restored.

(3) The inspectors may make a recommendation as to the directions on liability for expenses in their report. This will include such a recommendation if they are directed to do so by the court.

(4) Any liability to pay the expenses will be a liability to indemnify all persons against liability under subsection (1) (*b*) and (*c*) and any contribution from any other person liable under this section in proportion to their liabilities.

SECTION 14
Appointment and powers of inspectors to investigate ownership of company.

(1) The Minister may, subject to subsection (2), appoint one or more competent inspectors to investigate and report on the membership of any company and otherwise with respect to the company for the purpose of determining the true persons who are or have been financially interested in the success or failure (real or apparent) of the company or able to control or materially to influence the policy of the company.

(2) An appointment may be made by the Minister if he is of the opinion that there are circumstances suggesting that it is necessary—

(a) for the effective administration of the law relating to companies;
(b) for the effective discharge by the Minister of his functions under any enactment; or
(c) in the public interest.

(3) The appointment of an inspector under this section may define the scope of his investigation, whether as respects the matters or the period to which it is to extend or otherwise, and in particular may limit the investigation to matters connected with particular shares or debentures.

(4) Subject to the terms of an inspector's appointment his powers shall extend to the investigation of any circumstances suggesting the existence of an arrangement or understanding which, though not legally binding, is or was observed or likely to be observed in practice and which is relevant to the purposes of his investigation.

(5) For the purposes of any investigation under this section, sections 9 to 11, except section 10 (3), shall apply with the necessary modifications of references to the affairs of the company or to those of any other body corporate, so, however, that—

(a) the said sections shall apply in relation to all persons who are or have been, or whom the inspector has reasonable cause to believe to be or have been, financially interested in the success or failure or the apparent success or failure of the company or any other body corporate whose membership is investigated with that of the company, or able to control or materially to influence the policy thereof, including persons concerned only on behalf of others and to any other person whom the inspector has reasonable cause to believe possesses information relevant to the investigation, as they apply in relation to officers and agents of the company or of the other body corporate, as the case may be;
(b) if the Minister is of opinion that there is good reason for not divulging any part of a report made by virtue of this section he may disclose the report with the omission of that part; and may cause to be kept by the registrar of companies a copy of the report with that part omitted or, in the case of any other such report, a copy of the whole report; and
(c) for references to the court (except in section 10 (5) and (6)), there shall be substituted references to the Minister.

Definitions

'*body corporate*': Companies Act, 1963, section 2 (3).
'*company*': Companies Act, 1963, section 2.
'*court*': Companies Act, 1990, section 235.
'*debenture*': Companies Act, 1963, section 2.

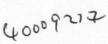

'*Minister*': Companies Act, 1990, section 3.
'*officer*': Companies Act, 1963, section 2.
'*registrar of companies*': Companies Act, 1963, section 2.
'*share*': Companies Act, 1963, section 2.

General Note

This section gives the Minister the power to appoint inspectors to investigate the ownership of a company.

(1) The Minister has the power to appoint inspectors to investigate the membership of the company so as to determine who owns or controls the company or is in a position 'materially to influence the policy of the company'. This would entitle the inspector to try to determine who the true owners are even if the shares are not legally held by them.

(2) The inspectors can be appointed by the Minister if he is of the opinion that it is in the public interest, if there are circumstances that warrant it so as to enable him to discharge his duties under the Companies Acts, or if it is necessary for the effective administration of company law.

(3) The appointment of the inspectors may specify the extent of the investigation and may limit it to matters connected with particular shares or debentures of the company.

(4) The terms of an inspector's appointment will allow his powers to extend to circumstances that suggest the 'existence of an arrangement or understanding' that is likely to be observed in practice even though it may not be legally binding, if it would be relevant to the investigation.

(5) The inspectors will have the power to extend the investigation into related companies where the circumstances warrant. The investigation may apply to persons who the inspector has reasonable cause to believe may have been financially interested in the success or failure or the 'apparent success or failure' of the company or who are able to control or 'materially to influence' the policy. Nowhere in the legislation is there any attempt to define 'apparent', 'control', or 'materially', and this will be a subjective view of the inspector. However, the aggrieved person may contest the view in court. If the inspector has reasonable cause to believe that a person has information relevant to the investigation he may require that person to provide the information.

SECTION 15

Power to require information as to persons interested in shares or debentures.

(1) Where it appears to the Minister that it is necessary—

(a) for the effective administration of the law relating to companies;

(b) for the effective discharge by the Minister of his functions under any enactment; or

(c) in the public interest;

to investigate the ownership of any shares in or debentures of a company and that it is unnecessary to appoint an inspector for the purpose, he may require any person whom he has reasonable cause to believe to have or to be able to obtain any information as to the present and past interests in those shares or debentures and the names and addresses of the persons interested and of any persons who act or have acted on their behalf in relation to the shares or debentures to give any such information to the Minister.

(2) For the purposes of this section a person shall be deemed to have an interest in a share or debenture if he has any right to acquire or dispose of the share or debenture or any interest therein or to vote in respect thereof or if his consent is necessary for the exercise of any of the rights of other persons interested therein or if the other persons interested therein can be required or are accustomed to exercise their rights in accordance with his instructions.

(3) Any person who fails to give any information required of him under this section or who in giving any such information makes any statement which he knows to be false in a material particular, or recklessly makes any statement which is false in a material particular, shall be guilty of an offence.

Definitions

'*debenture*': Companies Act, 1963, section 2.

'*Minister*': Companies Act, 1990, section 3

'*share*': Companies Act, 1963, section 2.

General Note

The Minister may in certain circumstances require the production of information on the ownership of shares without having to appoint inspectors. These circumstances are where it is necessary for the effective administration of company law, or the effective discharge of the Minister's functions under legislation, or where the Minister is of the opinion that it is 'in the public interest'. This is a less expensive and faster method of investigation than a formal case where inspectors are appointed.

(1) The Minister may investigate the ownership of shares or debentures if it is necessary

(a) for the effective administration of company law,

(b) for the effective discharge of the Minister's functions under statute, or

(c) in the public interest.

The Minister can require any person who he has reasonable cause to believe has or is able to obtain any information on the present or past interests in the shares or debentures to give any such information to the Minister.

(2) A person is deemed to have an interest in a share or debenture if he has the right to acquire or dispose of any share or debenture, any interest in it, or the right to vote the shares, or if that person can instruct other persons to vote or exercise rights in the shares or debentures.

(3) If any person fails to give information required of him or knowingly gives false information, or recklessly makes any statement that is false in a material way, he will be guilty of an offence and under section 240 can be fined up to £1,000 or imprisoned for a period of up to one year on summary conviction. On conviction on indictment he can be fined up to £10,000 or imprisoned for a period of up to three years.

SECTION 16
Power to impose restrictions on shares or debentures.

(1) Where in connection with an investigation or enquiry under section 14 or 15 it appears to the Minister that there is difficulty in finding out the relevant facts about any shares (whether issued or to be issued), the Minister may by notice in writing direct that the shares shall until further notice be subject to the restrictions imposed by this section.

(2) So long as a direction under subsection (1) in respect of any shares is in force—

(a) any transfer of those shares, or in the case of unissued shares any transfer of the right to be issued therewith and any issue thereof, shall be void;
(b) no voting rights shall be exercisable in respect of those shares;
(c) no further shares shall be issued in right of those shares or in pursuance of any offer made to the holder thereof; and
(d) except in a liquidation, no payment shall be made of any sums due from the company on those shares, whether in respect of capital or otherwise.

(3) Where shares are subject to the restrictions imposed by subsection (2) (a) any agreement to transfer the shares or in the case of unissued shares the right to be issued with the shares shall be void except an agreement to sell the shares pursuant to subsection (6) (b).

(4) Where shares are subject to the restrictions imposed by subsection (2) (c) or (2) (d) any agreement to transfer any right to be issued with other shares in right of those shares or to receive any payment on those shares (otherwise than in a liquidation) shall be void except an agreement to transfer any such right on the sale of the shares pursuant to subsection (6) (b).

(5) Where the Minister directs that shares shall be subject to the said restrictions, or refuses to direct that shares shall cease to be subject thereto, any person aggrieved thereby may apply to the court for an order that the shares shall cease to be subject thereto.

(6) Subject to subsections (7) and (13), an order of the court or a direction of the Minister that shares shall cease to be subject to the restrictions imposed by this section may be made only if—

(a) the court or, as the case may be, the Minister is satisfied that the relevant facts about the shares have been disclosed to the company and no unfair advantage had accrued to any person as a result of the earlier failure to make that disclosure; or

(b) the shares are to be sold and the court or the Minister approves the sale.

(7) Where any shares in a company are subject to the restrictions imposed by this section, the court may on the application of the Minister or the company order the shares to be sold, subject to the approval of the court as to the sale, and may also direct that the shares shall cease to be subject to those restrictions.

(8) Where an order has been made under subsection (7) then, on application of the Minister, the company, the person appointed by or in pursuance of the order to effect the sale or any person interested in the shares, the court may make such further order relating to the sale or to the transfer of the shares as it thinks fit.

(9) Where any shares are sold in pursuance of an order made under subsection (7), the proceeds of sale, less the costs of the sale, shall be paid into court for the benefit of the persons who are beneficially interested in the shares; and any such person may apply to the court for the whole or part of those proceeds to be paid to him.

(10) On an application under subsection (9) the court shall, subject to subsection (11), order the payment to the applicant of the whole of the proceeds of sale together with any interest thereon or, if any other person had a beneficial interest in the shares at the time of their sale, such proportion of those proceeds and interest as is equal to the proportion which the value of the applicant's interest in the shares bears to the total value of the shares.

(11) On granting an application for an order under subsection (7) or (8), the court may order that the costs of the applicant shall be paid out of the proceeds of sale; and, where an order under this subsection is made, the applicant shall be entitled to payment of his costs out of the proceeds of sale before any person interested in the shares in question receives any part of those proceeds.

(12) Any order or direction that shares shall cease to be subject to the said restrictions which is expressed to be made or given with a view to permitting a transfer of those shares or which is made under subsection (7) may continue the restrictions mentioned in subsection (2) (c) and (2) (d) in whole or in part, so far as they relate to any right acquired or offer made before the transfer.

(13) Subsection (6) shall not apply in relation to any order of the court or of the Minister directing that shares shall cease to be subject to any restrictions which have been continued in force in relation to those shares by virtue of subsection (12).

(14) Any person who—

(a) exercises or purports to exercise any right to dispose of any shares which, to his knowledge, are for the time being subject to the said restrictions or of any right to be issued with any such shares; or

(b) votes in respect of any such shares, whether as holder or proxy, or appoints a proxy to vote in respect thereof; or (*c*) being the holder of any such shares, fails to notify of their being subject to the said restrictions any person whom he does not know to be aware of that fact but does know to be entitled, apart from the said restrictions, to vote in respect of those shares whether as holder or proxy; or

(*d*) being the holder of any such shares, or being entitled to any such right as is mentioned in subsection (4) enters into an agreement which is void by virtue of subsection (3) or (4);

shall be guilty of an offence.

(15) Where shares in any company are issued in contravention of the said restrictions, the company and every officer of the company who is in default shall be guilty of an offence.

(16) Summary proceedings shall not be instituted under this section except by or with the consent of the Minister.

(17) This section shall apply in relation to debentures as it applies in relation to shares.

(18) The Minister shall cause notice of any direction given by him under this section—

(*a*) to be sent to the company concerned at its registered office, and

(*b*) to be delivered to the registrar of companies,

(*c*) to be published in *Iris Oifigiúil* and in at least two daily newspapers,

as soon as may be after the direction is given.

Definitions

'company': Companies Act, 1963, section 2.

'court': Companies Act, 1990, section 235.

'Minister': Companies Act, 1990, section 3.

'officer': Companies Act, 1963, section 2.

'registrar of companies': Companies Act, 1963, section 2.

'share': Companies Act, 1963, section 2.

General Note

This section allows the Minister to impose various restrictions on shares and debentures where there is difficulty in uncovering the required information about the shares or debentures in question.

(1) Where the Minister has difficulty in finding out the relevant facts about any shares he may impose restrictions on any relevant shares by notice in writing.

(2) So long as any direction under subsection (1) exists, any transfer of the relevant shares or the transfer of the right to issue unissued shares will be void. It will not be possible for the holders to exercise their voting rights, no further shares can be issued in right of these shares, and no dividends or capital payments can be made on these shares except on liquidation.

(3) Any agreement to transfer shares that are subject to the restriction mentioned in this section will be void, except where there is an agreement to transfer shares that can be transferred by court order or Ministerial approval under subsection (6).

(4) Any agreement to transfer any right where a person is issued with other shares or receives payment for them (except in a liquidation) will be void unless under a court order or with Ministerial approval in accordance with subsection (6).

(5) Where the Minister imposes restrictions on shares or refuses to direct that shares cease to be subject to the restriction, the aggrieved person may apply to the High Court for an order of release.

(6) The court may order or the Minister may direct that the restrictions cease to apply to the particular shares only if
(*a*) the court or the Minister, as the case may be, is satisfied that the relevant facts have been disclosed and no unfair advantage has accrued to anyone because of the earlier failure to disclose, or
(*b*) where any shares are subject to a restriction, the Minister or the company applies to the court for approval to have the shares sold and the court or the Minister directs that the shares cease to be subject to the restrictions.

(7) The court may on the application of the Minister or the company order the shares to be sold. It may also direct that the shares cease to be subject to the restrictions.

(8) The court may make any further order relating to the sale or transfer of shares as it thinks fit.

(9) If any shares are sold under subsection (7) the proceeds of any sale, less the costs of the sale, will be paid into the court for the persons who are beneficially interested in the shares, and such person can apply to have the proceeds paid to him.

(10) The court on application will order the payment of the entire proceeds of sale, together with interest, to the applicant, and if any other person had a beneficial interest in the shares that person is entitled to a proportional payment.

(11) On the granting of an order under subsection (7) the court has the power to order that the costs of the applicant be taken out of the proceeds of the sale, and the applicant would be entitled to his costs before the proceeds are paid out to any interested party.

(12) Any order or direction that the shares cease to be subject to the restrictions with a view to permitting a transfer of shares may continue the restrictions mentioned in subsection (2) (*c*) and (*d*) so far as they relate to any right acquired or offer made before the transfer of the shares.

(13) The provisions of subsection (6) would not apply to any order or direction that the shares cease to be subject to the restrictions.

(14) Any person who tries to get around the restrictions or ignore them in certain ways, such as

(*a*) by exercising or attempting to exercise any right to dispose of any shares that to the person's knowledge are the subject of restrictions,

(*b*) by voting or appointing a proxy to vote over the shares,

(*c*) by failing to notify any person who may be entitled to vote on such shares of the fact that the shares are subject to restrictions, or,

(*d*) if he is the holder of any such shares, by entering into a void agreement mentioned in subsections (3) and (4),

will be guilty of an offence under section 240 and on conviction on a summary offence liable to a fine not exceeding £1,000 or up to twelve months' imprisonment, and on conviction on indictment may be subject to a fine not exceeding £10,000 or imprisonment not exceeding three years.

(15) Where any company issues shares in contravention of the restrictions imposed, the company and every officer of the company who is in default will be guilty of an offence and subject to the penalties set out in section 240.

(16) No summary proceedings can be instituted under this section without the consent of the Minister.

(17) The restrictions in this section on shares apply equally to debentures.

(18) Any direction by the Minister under this section will be published in *Iris Oifigiúil* and in at least two daily newspapers, and a copy sent to the relevant company at its registered office and a copy delivered to the Registrar of Companies.

SECTION 17
Extension of powers of investigation to certain bodies incorporated outside the State.

Sections 8 to 11, 13, 18 and 22 shall apply to all bodies corporate incorporated outside the State which are carrying on business in the State or have at any time carried on business therein as if they were companies registered under the Principal Act, subject to any necessary modifications.

Definitions

'body corporate': Companies Act, 1963, section 2 (3).

'company': Companies Act, 1963, section 2.

General Note

The powers of investigation apply to foreign companies that are carrying on business in the state. For the purposes of the Companies Registration Office these would generally be referred to as 'external companies'.

SECTION 18
Admissibility in evidence of certain matters.

An answer given by a person to a question put to him in exercise of powers conferred by—

(a) section 10;

(b) section 10 as applied by sections 14 and 17; or

(c) rules made in respect of the winding-up of companies whether by the court or voluntarily under section 68 of the Courts of Justice Act, 1936, as extended by section 312 of the Principal Act;

may be used in evidence against him, and a statement required by section 224 of the Principal Act may be used in evidence against any person making or concurring in making it.

Definitions

'Principal Act': Companies Act, 1990, section 3.

General Note

This section makes express statutory provisions for the admissibility in both criminal and civil proceedings of evidence given to inspectors. In addition it provides that a statement of affairs required under section 224 of the Companies Act, 1963, will be admissible in evidence against the person making the statement.

SECTION 19
Power of Minister to require production of documents.

(1) The Minister may, subject to subsection (2), give directions to any body being—

(a) a company formed and registered under the Companies Acts;

(b) an existing company within the meaning of those Acts;

(c) a company to which the Principal Act applies by virtue of section 325 thereof or which is registered under that Act by virtue of Part IX thereof;

(d) a body corporate incorporated in, and having a principal place of business in, the State, being a body to which any of the provisions of the said Act with respect to prospectuses and allotments apply by virtue of section 377 of that Act;

(e) a body corporate incorporated outside the State which is carrying on business in the State or has at any time carried on business therein;

(f) any other body, whether incorporated or not, which is, or appears to the Minister to be, an insurance undertaking to which the Insurance Acts, 1909 to 1990, or regulations on insurance made under the European Communities Act, 1972, would apply, requiring the body, at such time and place as may be specified in the directions, to produce such books or documents as may be so specified, or may at any time, if he thinks there is good reason so to do, authorise any officer of his, on producing (if required so to do) evidence of his authority, to require any such body as aforesaid to produce to him forthwith any books or documents which the officer may specify.

(2) Directions may be given by the Minister if he is of the opinion that there are circumstances suggesting that—

(a) it is necessary to examine the books and documents of the body with a view to determining whether an inspector should be appointed to conduct an investigation of the body under the Companies Acts; or

(b) that the affairs of the body are being or have been conducted with intent to defraud—
(i) its creditors,
(ii) the creditors of any other person, or
(iii) its members; or

(c) that the affairs of the body are being or have been conducted for a fraudulent purpose other than described in paragraph (b); or

(d) that the affairs of the body are being or have been conducted in a manner which is unfairly prejudicial to some part of its members; or

(e) that any actual or proposed act or omission or series of acts or omissions of the body or on behalf of the body are or would be unfairly prejudicial to some part of its members; or

(f) that any actual or proposed act or omission or series of acts or omissions of the body or on behalf of the body are or are likely to be unlawful; or

(g) that the body was formed for any fraudulent purpose; or

(h) that the body was formed for any unlawful purpose.

(3) Where by virtue of subsection (1) the Minister or an officer authorised by the Minister has power to require the production of any books or documents from any body, the Minister or officer shall have the like power to require production of those books or documents from any person who appears to the Minister or officer to be in possession of them; but where any such person claims a lien on books or documents produced by him, the production shall be without prejudice to the lien.

(4) Any power conferred by or by virtue of this section to require a body or other person to produce books or documents shall include power—

(a) if the books or documents are produced—
(i) to take copies of them or extracts from them; and
(ii) to require that person, or any other person who is a present or past officer of, or is or was at any time employed by, the body in question, to provide an explanation of any of them;

(b) if the books or documents are not produced, to require the person who was required to produce them to state, to the best of his knowledge and belief, where they are.

(5) If a requirement to produce books or documents or provide an explanation or make a statement which is imposed by virtue of this section is not complied with, the body or other person on whom the requirement was so imposed shall be guilty of an offence; but where a person is charged with an offence under this subsection in respect of a requirement to produce any books or documents, it shall be a defence to prove that they were not in his possession or under his control and that it was not reasonably practicable for him to comply with the requirement.

(6) A statement made by a person in compliance with a requirement imposed by virtue of this section may be used in evidence against him.

(7) Nothing in this section shall prevent the Minister from authorising a person other than an officer of his to exercise the functions which an officer of his may exercise under this section and, where the Minister so authorises, such person shall have the same rights, duties and obligations as if he were such officer.

Definitions

'*body corporate*': Companies Act, 1963, section 2 (3).
'*books and documents*': Companies Act, 1990, section 3.
'*company*': Companies Act, 1963, section 2.
'*Minister*': Companies Act, 1990, section 3.
'*officer*': Companies Act, 1963, section 2.
'*Principal Act*': Companies Act, 1990, section 3.

General Note

The Minister has the power to require the production of a company's books and papers for inspection. The power can also be used to gather data from a company in relation to which a charge or a request for an investigation has been made.

(1) The Minister may instruct any of the following bodies to produce their records:
- a company formed under the Companies Acts;
- an existing company within the meaning of the Acts, e.g. a company formed under the 1908 or 1959 Acts;
- an external company;
- a body incorporated outside the state but carrying on business in the state;
- a company formed under the Insurance Acts.

(2) The Minister may direct that the records be produced if he is of the opinion that there are circumstances suggesting that
(*a*) it is necessary to examine the records so as to determine whether an inspector should be appointed to investigate the company's affairs,
(*b*) the affairs of the body are being conducted with the intent to defraud the creditors, creditors of any other person, or shareholders,
(*c*) the affairs of the body have been or are being conducted for a fraudulent purpose other than (*b*) above,
(*d*) the affairs are being or have been conducted in a manner that is unfairly prejudicial to some of its members,

(*e*) an act or omission to act would be unfairly prejudicial to the members,

(*f*) an act or omission to act is likely to be unlawful, or

(*g*) the body was formed for a fraudulent or unlawful purpose.

(3) The Minister has the power to require the production of records from any person who appears to be in possession of them, and if there is a lien on them it is without prejudice to the lien.

(4) Any power requiring the production of records includes a power to take copies or extracts of them and to require any person to give explanations, and, if the records are not produced, to require any person to state to the best of his knowledge where they are.

(5) If a person refuses to produce the records that person will be guilty of an offence. A person may use as a defence the fact that the records were not in his possession or under his control and it was not reasonably practicable for him to comply with the requirement.

(6) Any statement made by a person in compliance with this section may be used as evidence in any action against him.

(7) The Minister may authorise a person other than an officer of his to inspect the books or documents of the company concerned. The person who is appointed by the Minister will have the same rights, duties and obligations as if he were an officer.

SECTION 20
Entry and search of premises.

(1) If a District Justice is satisfied on information on oath laid by an officer authorised by the Minister or laid under the authority of the Minister that there are reasonable grounds for suspecting that there are on any premises any books or documents of which production has been required under section 14, 15 or 19, and which have not been produced in compliance with that requirement, the Justice may issue a warrant authorising any member of the Garda Síochána together with any other persons named in the warrant and any other members of the Garda Síochána to enter the premises specified in the information (using such force as is reasonably necessary for the purpose) and to search the premises and take possession of any books or documents appearing to be such books or documents as aforesaid, or to take, in relation to any books or documents so appearing, any other steps which may appear necessary for preserving them and preventing interference with them.

(2) Every warrant issued under this section shall continue in force until the end of the period of one month after the date on which it is issued.

(3) Any books or documents of which possession is taken under this section may be retained for a period of three months or, if within that period there are commenced any such criminal proceedings as are mentioned in section 21 (1) (*a*) or (1) (*b*) (being proceedings to which the books or documents are relevant), until the conclusion of those proceedings.

(4) A person who obstructs the exercise of a right of entry or search conferred by virtue of a warrant issued under this section or who obstructs the exercise of a right so conferred to take possession of any books or documents, shall be guilty of an offence.

Definitions

'*books or documents*': Companies Act, 1990, section 3.
'*Minister*': Companies Act, 1990, section 3.

General Note

This section provides for the right to enter and search a premises and seize any of the books found therein, in order to prevent an inspection under sections 14, 15 or 19 of this Act being frustrated by a failure to produce the books or their removal to another premises.

(1) A district justice may issue a warrant to enter and search premises where there are reasonable grounds for suspecting that certain records are on the premises. The search officers have the right to take possession of records that they suspect are the ones sought by them and to take such steps as may appear necessary to them to preserve and prevent interference with such records.

(2) Every warrant will be valid for a period of one month from the date of issue.

(3) Any records taken may be retained for a period of up to three months, and if criminal proceedings are commenced within that time, until the conclusion of such proceedings.

(4) Anyone who obstructs the entry or search of a premises that is the subject of a warrant will be guilty of an offence under section 240 of the Act.

SECTION 21
Provision for security of information.

(1) No information, book or document relating to a body which has been obtained under section 19 or 20 shall, without the previous consent in writing of that body, be published or disclosed, except to a competent authority, unless the publication or disclosure is required—

(a) with a view to the institution of, or otherwise for the purposes of, any criminal proceedings pursuant to, or arising out of the Companies Acts or any criminal proceedings for an offence entailing misconduct in connection with the management of the body's affairs or misapplication or wrongful retainer of its property;

(b) with a view to the institution of, or otherwise for the purposes of, any criminal proceedings pursuant to or arising out of the Exchange Control Acts, 1954 to 1986, or the Insurance Acts, 1909 to 1990, or regulations on insurance made under the European Communities Act, 1972;

(c) for the purpose of complying with any requirement, or exercising any power, imposed or conferred by this Part with respect to reports made by inspectors appointed thereunder by the court or the Minister;

(d) with a view to the institution by the Minister of proceedings for the winding-up under the Principal Act of the body or otherwise for the purposes of proceedings instituted by him for that purpose;

(e) for the purposes of proceedings under section 20.

(2) A person who publishes or discloses any information, book or document in contravention of this section shall be guilty of an offence.

(3) For the purposes of this section "competent authority" includes—

(a) the Minister,
(b) a person authorised by the Minister,
(c) an inspector appointed under this Act,
(d) the Minister for Finance,
(e) an officer authorised by the Minister for Finance,
(f) any court of competent jurisdiction,
(g) a supervisory authority within the meaning of regulations relating to insurance made under the European Communities Act, 1972, and
(h) the Central Bank.

Definitions

'books or documents': Companies Act, 1990, section 3.
'competent authority': Companies Act, 1990, section 21.
'Minister': Companies Act, 1990, section 3.

General Note

This section provides that information given under section 19 and 20 be treated as confidential.

(1) No information or records relating to any body that has been obtained under sections 19 and 20 will be disclosed without the consent of a competent authority unless publication is done with a view to criminal proceedings for misconduct in connection with the management of the company's affairs, or arising out of the Exchange Control Acts, Insurance Acts, or European Communities Acts, or proceedings for the winding up of the company.

(2) Anyone who publishes or discloses information in contravention will be guilty of an offence under section 240.

(3) 'Competent authority' is defined for the purpose of this section.

SECTION 22
Inspectors' reports to be evidence.

A document purporting to be a copy of a report of an inspector appointed under the provisions of this Part shall be admissible in any civil proceedings as evidence—

(a) of the facts set out therein without further proof unless the contrary is shown, and

(b) of the opinion of the inspector in relation to any matter contained in the report.

General Note

This section re-enacts section 172 of the Companies Act, 1963, and provides that an inspector's report be admissible in legal proceedings as evidence of the facts, without additional proof, unless the contrary is shown, and as evidence of the opinion of the inspector of any matter shown in the report.

SECTION 23
Saving for privileged information.

(1) Nothing in this Part shall compel the disclosure by any person of any information which he would, in the opinion of the court, be entitled to refuse to produce on the grounds of legal professional privilege or authorise the taking of possession of any document containing such information which is in his possession.

(2) The Minister shall not, under section 19, require, or authorise an officer of his to require, the production by a person carrying on the business of banking of a document relating to the affairs of a customer of his unless either it appears to the Minister that it is necessary so to do for the purpose of investigating the affairs of the first-mentioned person or the customer is a person on whom a requirement has been imposed by virtue of that section.

(3) The publication, in pursuance of any provision of this Part, of any report, information, book or document shall be privileged.

Definitions

'books or documents': Companies Act, 1990, section 3.

'court': Companies Act, 1990, section 235.

'Minister': Companies Act, 1990, section 3.

'officer': Companies Act, 1963, section 2.

General Note

This section is designed to protect privileged communications between a lawyer and his client as well as the confidentiality of banking transactions. This exemption for legal professional privilege is similar to that contained in the Companies Act, 1963.

SECTION 24
Power to make supplementary regulations.

(1) If, in any respect, any difficulty arises in bringing any provision of this Part into operation or in relation to the operation of any such provision, the Minister may by regulations do anything which appears to him to be necessary or expedient for removing that difficulty, for bringing the provision into operation, or for securing or facilitating its operation, and any such regulations may modify any provision of this Part so far as may be necessary or expedient for carrying such provision into effect for the purposes aforesaid.

(2) Every regulation made by the Minister under this section shall be laid before each House of the Oireachtas as soon as may be after it is made and, if a resolution annulling the regulation is passed by either House within the next 21 days on which that House has sat after the regulation is laid before it, the regulation shall be annulled accordingly, but without prejudice to the validity of anything previously done thereunder.

Definitions
'Minister': Companies Act, 1990, section 3.

General Note
This section enables the Minister to make regulations to overcome any difficulty that may arise from the implementation of the procedures introduced in part II of the Act.

Any regulation made by the Minister under this section will be laid before each house of the Oireachtas as soon as possible after it is made and will be deemed to be passed if no order annulling it is passed by either house within twenty-one days after the regulation is laid before the house.

3
TRANSACTIONS INVOLVING DIRECTORS

Part III of the Act deals with the detailed provisions on transactions involving directors where a company director might be tempted to put his personal interest before that of the company. The main emphasis is on the question of loans to directors and similar transactions. Subject to certain exceptions, all companies are prohibited from making loans or quasi-loans in excess of 10 per cent of the company's relevant assets to their own directors and members of their families or to other companies in which those persons have a controlling interest. In addition, they will be required to disclose details of any loans made.

If a prohibited transaction is entered into it may be set aside, depending on the circumstances. Furthermore, the director or connected person concerned, together with any other director who authorised the transaction, may have to account to the company for any gain arising or to indemnify the company for any loss incurred. If a transaction is entered into that would be prohibited except that it is below the 10 per cent threshold and the company subsequently becomes insolvent and goes into liquidation, the court may declare that the beneficiary of the transaction is liable for the company's debts if it believes that the transaction contributed to the insolvency of the company.

The part introduces into Irish law the concept of 'shadow director', a person who is deemed to exercise control over the company or gives instructions to the directors. Such a person will be regarded as being a director for the purposes of company law.

It also deals with long-term service agreements entered into by directors and their companies and certain dealings by directors in options in respect of listed shares of their own company.

The sections included in this part of the Act are very complex and require study to interpret them. It is accepted that the provisions in the Companies Act, 1963, on loans to directors were unsatisfactory and have been the subject of abuse over the years. The new provisions will lead to difficulties, in particular with regard to the determination of the limit allowable for the director. The 10 per cent threshold could vary significantly during an accounting period, especially if there are special write-offs or losses incurred that will affect the net asset value of the company.

SECTION 25

Interpretation of Part III.

(1) In this Part, unless the context otherwise requires—

"credit transactions" has the meaning assigned to it by subsection (3);

"guarantee" includes indemnity;

"quasi-loan" has the meaning assigned to it by subsection (2);

"licensed bank" means the holder of a licence under section 9 of the Central Bank Act, 1971.

(2) For the purposes of this Part—

(*a*) a quasi-loan is a transaction under which one party ("the creditor") agrees to pay, or pays otherwise than in pursuance of an agreement, a sum for another ("the borrower") or agrees to reimburse, or reimburses otherwise than in pursuance of an agreement, expenditure incurred by another party for another ("the borrower")—
(i) on terms that the borrower (or a person on his behalf) will reimburse the creditor; or
(ii) in circumstances giving rise to a liability on the borrower to reimburse the creditor;

(*b*) any reference to the person to whom a quasi-loan is made is a reference to the borrower; and

(*c*) the liabilities of a borrower under a quasi-loan include the liabilities of any person who has agreed to reimburse the creditor on behalf of the borrower.

(3) For the purposes of this Part a credit transaction is a transaction under which one party ("the creditor")—

(*a*) supplies any goods or sells any land under a hire-purchase agreement or conditional sale agreement;

(*b*) leases or licenses the use of land or hires goods in return for periodical payments;

(*c*) otherwise disposes of land or supplies goods or services on the understanding that payment (whether in a lump-sum or instalments or by way of periodical payments or otherwise) is to be deferred.

(4) For the purposes of this Part the value of a transaction or arrangement is—

(*a*) in the case of a loan, the principal of the loan;

(*b*) in the case of a quasi-loan, the amount, or maximum amount, which the person to whom the quasi-loan is made is liable to reimburse the creditor;

(*c*) in the case of a transaction or arrangement, other than a loan or quasi-loan or a transaction or arrangement within paragraph (*d*) or (*e*), the price which it is reasonable to expect could be obtained for the goods, land or services to which the transaction or arrangement relates if they had been supplied at the time the transaction or arrangement is entered into in the ordinary course of business and on the same terms (apart from price) as they have been supplied or are to be supplied under the transaction or arrangement in question;

(*d*) in the case of a guarantee or security, the amount guaranteed or secured;

(*e*) in the case of an arrangement to which section 31 (2) or 31 (3) applies the value of the transaction to which the arrangement relates less any amount by which the liabilities under the arrangement or transaction of the person for whom the transaction was made have been reduced.

(5) For the purposes of subsection (4), the value of a transaction or arrangement which is not capable of being expressed as a specific sum of money (because the amount of any liability arising under the transaction is unascertainable, or for any other reason) shall, whether or not any liability under the transaction has been reduced, be deemed to exceed £50,000.

(6) For the purposes of this Part, a transaction or arrangement is made for a person if—

(a) in the case of a loan or quasi-loan, it is made to him;

(b) in the case of a credit transaction, he is the person to whom goods or services are supplied, or land is sold or otherwise disposed of, under the transaction;

(c) in the case of a guarantee or security, it is entered into or provided in connection with a loan or quasi-loan made to him or a credit transaction made for him;

(d) in the case of an arrangement to which section 31 (2) or 31 (3) applies, the transaction to which the arrangement relates was made for him; and

(e) in the case of any other transaction or arrangement for the supply or transfer of goods, land or services (or any interest therein), he is the person to whom the goods, land or services (or the interest) are supplied or transferred.

(7) This Part, except sections 41, 43 and 44, does not apply to arrangements or transactions entered into before the commencement of this section but, for the purposes of determining whether an arrangement is one to which section 31 (2) or 31 (3) applies the transaction to which the arrangement relates shall, if it was entered into before the said commencement, be deemed to have been entered into thereafter.

(8) This Part shall have effect in relation to an arrangement or transaction whether governed by the law of the State or of another country.

Definitions

'auditor': this is not defined in the Companies Acts; but see the UK case *R.* v. *Shacter* [1960] 2 QB 252.

'average number of persons employed': Companies Act, 1990, section 25.

'company': Companies Act, 1963, section 2.

'credit transactions': Companies Act, 1990, section 25.

'guarantee': Companies Act, 1990, section 25.

'licensed bank': Companies Act, 1990, section 25.

'public limited company': Companies (Amendment) Act, 1983, section 2.

'quasi-loan': Companies Act, 1990, section 25.

'relevant annual number': Companies Act, 1990, section 25.

'relevant company': Companies Act, 1990, section 25.

'subsidiary': Companies Act, 1963, section 155.

General Note

This section defines various terms used in the following part concerning transactions involving directors.

(1) Subsection (1) sets out various definitions, which are self-explanatory.

(2) 'Quasi-loan' is defined as a transaction where one party agrees to pay or reimburse the other for expenditure incurred by the other on terms that the borrower or some other person will reimburse the creditor.

(3) 'Credit transaction' is defined.

(4) 'Value of certain transactions' is defined, such as:
- loan: the principal of the loan;
- quasi-loan: the maximum amount for which a person is liable to reimburse the creditor;
- transaction or arrangement other than a loan or quasi-loan or transaction referred to above: the price that it is reasonable to expect the goods, land or services would fetch in the ordinary course of business and on the same terms as those on which they would have been supplied;
- guarantee or security: the amount guaranteed or secured;
- an arrangement to which section 31 applies (prohibitions of loans, etc.): the value of the transaction less any amount by which the liabilities under the arrangement or transaction had been reduced.

(5) For the purposes of subsection (4) the value of a transaction or arrangement that is not capable of being expressed as a specific sum of money (because the amount of the liability is unascertainable), whether or not the liability of the transaction has been reduced, will be deemed to exceed £50,000. This amount is significant, as under section 29 of the Act the approval of the shareholders in general meeting is required for substantial property transactions in excess of £50,000 between a company and its directors.

(6–8) These subsections define when a transaction or arrangement is deemed to have been made. In general a 'transaction' is the particular business conducted between two parties, such as the transfer of the money by way of loan or the granting of a mortgage. An 'arrangement' is wider and may cover a number of transactions and involve a number of parties.

SECTION 26
Connected
persons.

(1) For the purposes of this Part, a person is connected with a director of a company if, but only if, he is—

(a) that director's spouse, parent, brother, sister or child;

(b) a person acting in his capacity as the trustee of any trust, the principal beneficiaries of which are the director, his spouse or any of his children or any body corporate which he controls; or

(c) a partner of that director;

unless that person is also a director of the company.

(2) A body corporate shall also be deemed to be connected with a director of a company if it is controlled by that director.

(3) For the purposes of this section, a director of a company shall be deemed to control a body corporate if, but only if, he is, alone or together with any of the persons referred to in paragraph (a), (b) or (c) of subsection (1), interested in more than one-half of the equity share capital of that body or entitled to exercise or control the exercise of more than one-half of the voting power at any general meeting of that body.

(4) In subsection (3)—

(a) "equity share capital" has the same meaning as in section 155 of the Principal Act; and

(b) references to voting power exercised by a director shall include references to voting power exercised by another body corporate which that director controls.

(5) The provisions of section 54 shall have effect for the purposes of subsection (3) with the substitution of the words "more than half" for the words "one-third or more" in subsections (5) and (6) of that section.

Definitions

'body corporate': Companies Act, 1963, section 2 (3).

'child': Companies Act, 1990, section 3.

'company': Companies Act, 1963, section 2.

'director': Companies Act, 1963, section 2.

'employees share scheme': Companies (Amendment) Act, 1983, section 2.

'equity share capital': Companies Act, 1990, section 26.

General Note

This section defines when a person is to be regarded as a 'connected person' and specifies when a director of a company is to be regarded as associated with or in control of a body corporate.

(1) This subsection defines a connected person as a person connected with a director who is that director's spouse, parent, brother, sister, or child, or a person who acts in the capacity of a trustee of any trust where the beneficiaries include the children or

spouse of the director, or a person connected with the director or any company that he controls as a partner of the director.

(2) This subsection stipulates that a body corporate will be deemed to be connected with a director of the company if it is controlled by him. The circumstances under which 'control' arises are set out in subsection (3).

(3) A director will be regarded as having control of a company if he alone or together with persons specified in subsection (1) (*a*), (*b*) or (*c*) is interested in more than half of the equity share capital or is entitled to exercise or control the exercise of more than half of the voting power at any general meeting of that body.

(4) 'Equity share capital' is defined.

(5) The provisions of section 54 dealing with the nature of an interest concerning the disclosure of an interest in shares will apply in subsection (3) above, substituting 'half' for 'one-third'.

SECTION 27
Shadow directors.

(1) Subject to subsection (2), a person in accordance with whose directions or instructions the directors of a company are accustomed to act (in this Act referred to as "a shadow director") shall be treated for the purposes of this Part as a director of the company unless the directors are accustomed so to act by reason only that they do so on advice given by him in a professional capacity.

(2) A shadow director shall not be guilty of an offence under section 44 (8) by virtue only of subsection (1).

(3) Section 194 of the Principal Act shall apply in relation to a shadow director of a company as it applies in relation to a director of a company, except that the shadow director shall declare his interest, not at a meeting of the directors, but by a notice in writing to the directors which is either—

(*a*) a specific notice given before the date of the meeting at which, if he had been a director, the declaration would be required by subsection (2) of that section to be made; or
(*b*) a notice which under subsection (3) of that section falls to be treated as a sufficient declaration of that interest or would fall to be so treated apart from the proviso;

and section 145 of that Act shall have effect as if the declaration had been made at the meeting in question and had accordingly formed part of the proceedings at that meeting.

Definitions

'*company*': Companies Act, 1963, section 3.
'*director*': Companies Act, 1963, section 2.
'*Principal Act*': Companies Act, 1990, section 3.
'*shadow director*': Companies Act, 1990, section 3.

General Note

The purpose of this section is to extend the prohibitions and duties contained in this part of the Act to persons (referred to as 'shadow directors') who, even though they are not directors, in effect control and direct the company through the nominated directors. A person is regarded as being a shadow director if he is a person on whose instructions the directors are accustomed to act.

(1) A person will be treated as being a shadow director of the company if the directors normally act on his instructions or directions, unless they are accustomed to so acting when such advice is given only in that person's professional capacity. The addition of the phrase 'in a professional capacity' should ensure that lawyers, financial advisers etc. will not be treated as 'shadow directors'.

(2) A shadow director will not be guilty of an offence under section 44 (8) by virtue only of subsection (1) above.

(3) The obligations under section 194 of the Companies Act, 1963, in relation to a duty to disclose his interest in contracts made by the company will also apply to a shadow director, who must disclose the interest by notice in writing to the directors. The form of notice to the directors may be either

(*a*) a specific notice given before the date of the meeting at which, if he had been a director, a declaration would have been made, or

(*b*) a notice that would be regarded as a sufficient declaration of such interest under section 194 (3) of the Companies Act, 1963.

SECTION 28
Contracts of employment of directors.

(1) Subject to subsection (6), a company shall not incorporate in any agreement a term to which this section applies unless the term is first approved by a resolution of the company in general meeting and, in the case of a director of a holding company, by a resolution of that company in general meeting.

(2) This section applies to any term by which a director's employment with the company of which he is the director or, where he is the director of a holding company, his employment within the group is to continue, or may be continued, otherwise than at the instance of the company (whether under the original agreement or under a new agreement entered into in pursuance of the original agreement), for a period exceeding five years during which the employment—

(*a*) cannot be terminated by the company by notice; or
(*b*) can be so terminated only in specified circumstances.

(3) In any case where—

(*a*) a person is or is to be employed with a company under an agreement which cannot be terminated by the company by notice or can be so terminated only in specified circumstances; and

(b) more than six months before the expiration of the period for which he is or is to be so employed, the company enters into a further agreement (otherwise than in pursuance of a right conferred by or by virtue of the original agreement on the other party thereto) under which he is to be employed with the company or, where he is a director of a holding company, within the group,

subsection (2) shall apply as if to the period for which he is to be employed under that further agreement there were added a further period equal to the unexpired period of the original agreement.

(4) A resolution of a company approving a term to which this section applies shall not be passed at a general meeting of the company unless a written memorandum setting out the proposed agreement incorporating the term is available for inspection by members of the company both—

(a) at the registered office of the company for not less than the period of 15 days ending with the date of the meeting; and
(b) at the meeting itself.

(5) A term incorporated in an agreement in contravention of this section shall to the extent that it contravenes this section be void; and that agreement and, in a case where subsection (3) applies, the original agreement shall be deemed to contain a term entitling the company to terminate it at any time by the giving of reasonable notice.

(6) No approval is required to be given under this section by any body corporate unless it is a company within the meaning of the Principal Act or registered under Part IX of that Act or if it is, for the purposes of section 150 of that Act, a wholly owned subsidiary of any body corporate, wherever incorporated.

(7) In this section—

(a) "employment" includes employment under a contract for services; and
(b) "group", in relation to a director of a holding company, means the group which consists of that company and its subsidiaries.

Definitions

'body corporate': Companies Act, 1963, section 2 (3).

'company': Companies Act, 1963, section 2.

'director': Companies Act, 1963, section 2.

'employment': Companies Act, 1990, section 28.

'group': Companies Act, 1990, section 28.

'holding company': Companies Act, 1963, section 155.

'subsidiary': Companies Act, 1963, section 155.

General Note

This section deals with long-term service contracts between a director and the company. Such contracts must be approved by the company in general meeting.

(1) A company cannnot enter into service contracts for more than five years unless the term is first approved by the shareholders in general meeting.

(2) This subsection will apply to any term by which a director's employment with the company of which he is a director—or, where he is a director of the holding company, his employment within the group (which is defined in subsection (7))—is to continue, whether under the original agreement or a revised one, for a period of more than five years. This subsection will apply if the contract cannot be terminated by the company by notice or can be terminated only in specific circumstances.

(3) This subsection prevents new agreements being entered into whose effect would be to extend the period of employment for more than five years from the date at which the further agreement is entered into. Where, for example, after the first year of a five-year contract the director enters into a further four-year contract, approval is required as if the further agreement were for eight years.

(4) A resolution of the company approving a term for a director's service agreement cannot be passed at a general meeting unless a written memorandum setting out the proposed agreement is available for inspection by shareholders at the registered office for a period of not less than fifteen days before the general meeting and at the meeting itself.

(5) If a term is incorporated in a service agreement in contravention of this section, such term will be void and the agreement will be deemed to contain a term entitling the company to terminate the agreement at any time by the giving of reasonable notice.

(6) This section will only apply to bodies corporate within the meaning of the Companies Acts.

(7) The terms 'employment' and 'group' are defined. It should be noted that the term 'employment' is wide enough to bring contracts for service or consultancy contracts within the scope of the section.

SECTION 29
Substantial property transactions involving directors, etc.

(1) Subject to subsections (6), (7) and (8), a company shall not enter into an arrangement—

(*a*) whereby a director of the company or its holding company or a person connected with such a director acquires or is to acquire one or more non-cash assets of the requisite value from the company; or

(*b*) whereby the company acquires or is to acquire one or more non-cash assets of the requisite value from such a director or a person so connected;

unless the arrangement is first approved by a resolution of the company in general meeting and, if the director or connected person is a director of its holding company or a person connected with such a director, by a resolution in general meeting of the holding company.

(2) For the purposes of this section a non-cash asset is of the requisite value if at the time the arrangement in question is entered into its value is not less than £1,000 but, subject to that, exceeds £50,000 or ten per cent of the amount of the company's relevant assets, and for those purposes the amount of a company's relevant assets is—

(a) except in a case falling within paragraph (b), the value of its net assets determined by reference to the accounts prepared and laid in accordance with the requirements of section 148 of the Principal Act in respect of the last preceding financial year in respect of which such accounts were so laid;

(b) where no accounts have been prepared and laid under that section before that time, the amount of its called-up share capital.

(3) An arrangement entered into by a company in contravention of this section and any transaction entered into in pursuance of the arrangement (whether by the company or any other person) shall be voidable at the instance of the company unless—

(a) restitution of any money or any other asset which is the subject-matter of the arrangement or transaction is no longer possible or the company has been indemnified in pursuance of subsection (4) (b) by any other person for the loss or damage suffered by it; or

(b) any rights acquired *bona fide* for value and without actual notice of the contravention by any person who is not a party to the arrangement or transaction would be affected by its avoidance; or

(c) the arrangement is, within a reasonable period, affirmed by the company in general meeting and, if it is an arrangement for the transfer of an asset to or by a director of its holding company or a person who is connected with such a director, is so affirmed with the approval of the holding company given by a resolution in general meeting.

(4) Without prejudice to any liability imposed otherwise than by this subsection, but subject to subsection (5), where an arrangement is entered into with a company by a director of the company or its holding company or a person connected with him in contravention of this section, that director and the person so connected, and any other director of the company who authorised the arrangement or any transaction entered into in pursuance of such an arrangement, shall (whether or not it has been avoided in pursuance of sub-section (3)) be liable—

(a) to account to the company for any gain which he had made directly or indirectly by the arrangement or transaction; and

(b) (jointly and severally with any other person liable under this subsection) to indemnify the company for any loss or damage resulting from the arrangement or transaction.

(5) Where an arrangement is entered into by a company and a person connected with a director of the company or its holding company in contravention of this section, that director shall not be liable under subsection (4) if he shows that he took all reasonable steps to secure the company's compliance with this section and, in any case, a person so connected and any such other director as is mentioned in that subsection shall not be so liable if he shows that, at the time the arrangement was entered into, he did not know the relevant circumstances constituting the contravention.

(6) No approval is required to be given under this section by any body corporate unless it is a company within the meaning of the Principal Act or registered

under Part IX of that Act or, if it is, for the purposes of section 150 of that Act, a wholly owned subsidiary of any body corporate, wherever incorporated.

(7) Subsection (1) shall not apply in relation to any arrangement for the acquisition of a non-cash asset—

(a) if the non-cash asset in question is or is to be acquired by a holding company from any of its wholly owned subsidiaries or from a holding company by any of its wholly owned subsidiaries or by one wholly owned subsidiary of a holding company from another wholly owned subsidiary of that same holding company; or
(b) if the arrangement is entered into by a company which is being wound up unless the winding up is a members' voluntary winding up.

(8) Subsection (1) (a) shall not apply in relation to any arrangement whereby a person acquires or is to acquire an asset from a company of which he is a member if the arrangement is made with that person in his character as such member.

(9) In this section—

(a) "non-cash asset" means any property or interest in property other than cash, and for this purpose "cash" includes foreign currency;
(b) any reference to the acquisition of a non-cash asset includes a reference to the creation or extinction of an estate or interest in, or a right over, any property and also a reference to the discharge of any person's liability other than a liability for a liquidated sum; and
(c) "net assets", in relation to a company, means the aggregate of the company's assets less the aggregate of its liabilities, and for this purpose "liabilities" includes any provision for liabilities or charges within paragraph 70 of the Schedule to the Companies (Amendment) Act, 1986.

Definitions

'body corporate': Companies Act, 1963, section 2 (3).

'called-up share capital': Companies (Amendment) Act, 1983, section 2.

'cash': Companies Act, 1990, section 29.

'company': Companies Act, 1963, section 2.

'director': Companies Act, 1963, section 2.

'holding company': Companies Act, 1963, section 155.

'liabilities': Companies Act, 1990, section 29.

'net assets': Companies Act, 1990, section 29.

'non-cash asset': Companies Act, 1990, section 29.

'person connected': Companies Act, 1990, section 26.

'Principal Act': Companies Act, 1990, section 3.

'subsidiary': Companies Act, 1963, section 155.

General Note

The approval of the shareholders in general meeting is required for substantial property transactions (in excess of £50,000) between a company and its directors. Any such arrangement or transaction entered into by a company in contravention of this section will be voidable unless certain conditions are met.

(1) A company cannot enter into an arrangement where a director acquires non-cash assets exceeding £50,000 or 10 per cent of the relevant assets from the company unless it is first approved by the shareholders in general meeting. The term 'arrangement' is not defined in the Companies Acts, but it is clearly not intended to be confined to a legally enforceable agreement.

(2) The section will apply where the requisite non-cash asset value in the arrangement exceeds £50,000 or 10 per cent of the company's relevant assets if the asset is in excess of £1,000.

(3) Any arrangement entered into by the company will be voidable at the instance of the company if it is in contravention of the section, unless
(*a*) restitution of any money or other asset under the arrangement is no longer possible or the company has been indemnified for loss or damage suffered by it,
(*b*) any rights acquired in good faith for value and without notice of contravention by any party who is not a party to the arrangement would be affected by its avoidance, or
(*c*) the arrangement is approved by the shareholders in general meeting within a reasonable period.

(4) Where an arrangement has been entered into in contravention of this section the director and any person connected and any other director who authorised such arrangement will be liable to account for any gain made directly or indirectly and to indemnify the company for any loss or damage resulting from such arrangement.

(5) Where an arrangement is entered into by a company with a director in contravention of this section that director will not be liable if he shows he has taken all reasonable steps to ensure the company's compliance or was not aware of the relevant circumstances concerning the contravention.

(6) The section only applies to bodies corporate to which the Companies Acts apply.

(7) Subsection (1) will not apply to any arrangement for the acquisition of a non-cash asset where the arrangement is between

a subsidiary and holding company or a company in the process of being wound up, unless it is a members' voluntary winding up.

(8) Subsection (1) (*a*) does not apply where a person is a shareholder of a company and the arrangement for the acquisition of an asset is being made in his character as such shareholder.

(9) 'Net assets' and 'non-cash assets' are defined.

SECTION 30

Penalisation of dealing by director of a company in options to buy or sell certain shares in, or debentures of, the company or associated companies.

(1) A director of a company who buys—

(*a*) a right to call for delivery at a specified price and within a specified time of a specified number of relevant shares or a specified amount of relevant debentures; or

(*b*) a right to make delivery at a specified price and within a specified time of a specified number of relevant shares or a specified amount of relevant debentures; or

(*c*) a right (as he may elect) to call for delivery at a specified price and within a specified time or to make delivery at a specified price and within a specified time of a specified number of relevant shares or a specified amount of relevant debentures;

shall be guilty of an offence.

(2) In subsection (1)—

(*a*) "relevant shares", in relation to a director of a company, means shares in the company or in any other body corporate, being the company's subsidiary or holding company or a subsidiary of the company's holding company, being shares for which dealing facilities are provided by a stock exchange (whether within the State or elsewhere); and

(*b*) "relevant debentures", in relation to a director of a company, means debentures of the company or of any other body corporate, being the company's subsidiary or holding company or a subsidiary of the company's holding company, being debentures as respects which there has been granted such dealing facilities as aforesaid.

(3) Nothing in this section shall be taken to penalise a person who buys a right to subscribe for shares in, or debentures of, a body corporate or buys debentures of a body corporate that confer upon the holder thereof a right to subscribe for, or to convert the debentures (in whole or in part) into, shares of the body.

(4) For the purposes of this section any reference, however expressed, to any price paid, given or received in respect of any interest in shares or debentures shall be construed as including a reference to any consideration other than money given or received in respect of any such interest, and any reference to a specified price includes a reference to a specified price range.

(5) This section shall also apply to any person (not being a director of the company) who—

(*a*) buys a right referred to in subsection (1), and

(*b*) does so on behalf or at the instigation of a director of the company.

Definitions

'body corporate': Companies Act, 1963, section 2 (3).

'company': Companies Act, 1963, section 2.

'debenture': Companies Act, 1963, section 2.

'director': Companies Act, 1963, section 2.

'holding company': Companies Act, 1963, section 155.

'relevant debentures': Companies Act, 1990, section 30.

'relevant shares': Companies Act, 1990, section 30.

'share': Companies Act, 1963, section 2.

'subsidiary': Companies Act, 1963, section 155.

General Note

It is an offence for a director to buy options in listed shares or debentures of a company of which he is associated or of its related companies. This section does not, however, exclude or prevent directors from subscribing for options under an approved share option scheme operated by the company.

(1) Directors are prohibited from buying options in listed shares or debentures of the company, its holding company or its subsidiaries; and if the director does purchase options he will be guilty of an offence and subject to the penalties provided for in section 240 of the Act.

(2) The terms 'relevant shares' and 'relevant debentures' are defined for the purposes of this section.

(3) A director is permitted to purchase shares in or debentures of a company that gives the right to subscribe for or convert such debentures into shares.

(4) Reference to price includes consideration other than money given or recovered in respect of any such interest and covers options that are framed within a specified price range.

(5) The scope of the section is extended to any person who buys options on behalf of or at the instigation of a director of the company concerned.

SECTION 31

Prohibition of loans, etc. to directors and connected persons.

(1) Except as provided by sections 32 to 37, a company shall not—

(a) make a loan or a quasi-loan to a director of the company or of its holding company or to a person connected with such a director;

(b) enter into a credit transaction as creditor for such a director or a person so connected;

(c) enter into a guarantee or provide any security in connection with a loan, quasi-loan or credit transaction made by any other person for such a director or a person so connected.

(2) A company shall not arrange for the assignment to it or the assumption by it of any rights, obligations or liabilities under a transaction which, if it had been entered into by the company, would have contravened subsection (1); but for the purposes of this Part the transaction shall be treated as having been entered into on the date of the arrangement.

(3) A company shall not take part in any arrangement whereby—

(a) another person enters into a transaction which, if it had been entered into by the company, would have contravened subsection (1) or (2); and

(b) that other person, in pursuance of the arrangement, has obtained or is to obtain any benefit from the company or its holding company or a subsidiary of the company or its holding company.

Definitions

'*company*': Companies Act, 1963, section 2.

'*credit transaction*': Companies Act, 1990. section 25.

'*director*': Companies Act, 1963, section 2.

'*guarantee*': Companies Act, 1990, section 25.

'*holding company*': Companies Act, 1963, section 155.

'*quasi-loan*': Companies Act, 1990, section 25.

'*relevant company*': Companies Act, 1990, section 25.

'*subsidiary*': Companies Act, 1963, section 155.

General Note

The rules applicable to 'relevant companies' are wider in that they apply to both quasi-loans and credit transactions in addition to conventional loans. They also apply where the beneficiary is connected with a director. A quasi-loan is a transaction whereby the company incurs a liability or spends money on behalf of a director or connected person in circumstances where the company is to be reimbursed in due course, or personal expenditure incurred on a company credit card.

The prohibition on making loans to directors stipulated by this section is subject to the exceptions set out in sections 32–37 of this Act, which are dealt with individually below.

(1) A company is prohibited from making loans to directors or providing security or guarantees in connection with a loan made to such a director. These provisions apply equally to persons connected with a director.

(2) A company cannot arrange for the assignment to it or the assumption of any liabilities, rights or obligations which if entered into by the company would be in contravention of subsection (1); and for the purposes of this section the transaction is regarded as having been entered into on the date of the arrangement.

(3) A company cannot take part in any arrangement whereby some other person enters into a transaction that would contravene this section if entered into by the company and that other person has obtained a benefit from the company, its holding company or subsidiary in pursuance of the arrangement.

SECTION 32
Arrangements of certain value.

(1) Section 31 shall not prohibit a company from entering into an arrangement with a director or a person connected with a director if—

(a) the value of the arrangement, and
(b) the total amount outstanding under any other arrangements entered into by the company with any director of the company, or any person connected with a director,

together, is less than ten per cent of the company's relevant assets.

(2) For the purposes of this section—

(a) a company enters an arrangement with a person if it makes a loan or quasi-loan to, or enters into a credit transaction as creditor for, that person, and
(b) the amount of a company's relevant assets shall be determined in accordance with section 29 (2).

Definitions
'company': Companies Act, 1963, section 2.
'director': Companies Act, 1963, section 2.
'quasi-loan': Companies Act, 1990, section 25.

General Note
A company will not be prohibited from entering into an arrangement provided the value of the arrangement is less than 10 per cent of the company's relevant assets as determined in accordance with section 29 (2).

(1) A company will not be prohibited from entering into an arrangement with a director or a person connected with a director if the value of the arrangement and the total amount outstanding under any other arrangements entered into by the company do not exceed 10 per cent of the company's relevant assets.

(2) A company is deemed to have entered into an arrangement with a person if it makes a loan or quasi-loan or enters into a credit transaction as creditor for the person; and the amount of the company's relevant assets will be determined in accordance with the provisions of section 29 (2).

SECTION 33
Reduction in amount of company's relevant assets.

(1) This section applies to a company in respect of which the total amount outstanding under any arrangements referred to in section 32 comes to exceed 10 per cent of the company's relevant assets for any reason, but in particular because the value of those assets has fallen.

(2) Where the directors of a company become aware, or ought reasonably to become aware, that there exists a situation referred to in subsection (1), it shall be the duty of the company, its directors and any persons for whom the arrangements referred to in that subsection were made, to amend, within two months, the terms of the arrangements concerned so that the total amount outstanding under the arrangements again falls within the percentage limit referred to in that subsection.

Definitions

'*company*': Companies Act, 1963, section 2.
'*director*': Companies Act, 1963, section 2.

General Note

This section requires the directors of the company to reorganise or renegotiate the loans so that they remain within the 10 per cent limit. It would apply where the 10 per cent limit is breached and not just because the value of the net assets has fallen.

Where the directors become aware or ought to have become aware that there is a situation referred to in subsection (1) it is their duty to ensure that the arrangements are amended within two months, so that the total amount outstanding falls within the percentage limit.

SECTION 34
Inter-company loans in same group.

Where a company is a member of a group of companies, consisting of a holding company and its subsidiaries, section 31 shall not prohibit that company from—

(a) making a loan or quasi-loan to another member of that group; or
(b) entering into a guarantee or providing any security in connection with a loan or quasi-loan made by any person to another member of the group;

by reason only that a director of one member of the group is connected with another.

Definitions

'*company*': Companies Act, 1963, section 2.
'*director*': Companies Act, 1963, section 2.
'*guarantee*': Companies Act, 1990, section 25.
'*holding company*': Companies Act, 1963, section 155.
'*quasi-loan*': Companies Act, 1990, section 25.
'*subsidiary*': Companies Act, 1963, section 155.

General Note

This section provides that the prohibition in section 31 of making loans or providing security will not apply to the making of loans within the group by reason of the fact that a director of one member of the group is connected with some other member of the group. Paragraph (*b*), however, prevents a company from entering into a guarantee or providing any security in connection with a loan or quasi-loan made by any person to another member of the group by reason only that a director of one member of the group is connected with another.

SECTION 35

Transactions with holding company.

Section 31 shall not prohibit a company from—

(*a*) making a loan or quasi-loan to its holding company or entering into a guarantee or providing any security in connection with a loan or quasi-loan made by any person to its holding company;

(*b*) entering into a credit transaction as creditor for its holding company or entering into a guarantee or providing any security in connection with any credit transaction made by any other person for its holding company.

Definitions

'*company*': Companies Act, 1963, section 2.
'*credit transaction*': Companies Act, 1990, section 25.
'*guarantee*': Companies Act, 1990, section 25.
'*holding company*': Companies Act, 1963, section 155.
'*quasi-loan*': Companies Act, 1990, section 25.

General Note

Section 35 provides that the prohibitions imposed by section 31 on the making of loans or provision of other security to directors will not prohibit a company from making a loan or quasi-loan providing any security to its holding company, or from entering into a credit transaction as a creditor for its holding company, or entering into a guarantee or providing security in connection with a credit transaction made by any other person for its holding company.

SECTION 36
Directors'
expenses.

(1) Section 31 shall not prohibit a company from doing anything to provide any of its directors with funds to meet vouched expenditure properly incurred or to be incurred by him for the purposes of the company or the purpose of enabling him properly to perform his duties as an officer of the company or doing anything to enable any of its directors to avoid incurring such expenditure.

(2) Where a company enters into any transaction pursuant to subsection (1), any liability falling on any person arising from any such transaction shall be discharged by him within six months from the date on which it was incurred.

(3) A person who contravenes subsection (2) shall be guilty of an offence.

Definitions

'*company*': Companies Act, 1963, section 2.
'*director*': Companies Act, 1963, section 2.
'*officer*': Companies Act, 1963, section 2.

General Note

Section 36 provides that the prohibitions imposed by section 31 on the making of loans to directors will not prohibit a company from doing anything so as to provide the directors with funds to meet vouched expenditure incurred for the purposes of the company.

(1) A company can reimburse or provide funds to directors to meet vouched expenditure incurred for the purposes of the company so as to enable him to properly perform his duties as a director of the company.

(2) Where a company enters into a transaction in relation to subsection (1), any liability resulting or arising from the transaction must be discharged by him within six months from the date on which it was incurred.

(3) Any person who contravenes subsection (2) will be guilty of an offence and subject to the penalties set out in section 240.

SECTION 37
Business
transactions.

Section 31 shall not prohibit a company from making any loan or quasi-loan or entering into any credit transaction as creditor for any person if—

(a) the company enters into the transaction concerned in the ordinary course of its business; and
(b) the value of the transaction is not greater, and the terms on which it is entered into are no more favourable, in respect of the person for whom the transaction is made, than that or those which—
(i) the company ordinarily offers, or
(ii) it is reasonable to expect the company to have offered,

to or in respect of a person of the same financial standing as that person but unconnected with the company.

Definitions

'company': Companies Act, 1963, section 2.

'credit transaction': Companies Act, 1990, section 25.

'quasi-loan': Companies Act, 1990, section 25.

General Note

Section 37 provides that the prohibitions on making loans to directors under section 31 will not prevent a company from making a loan or quasi-loan or entering into a credit transaction as a creditor for any person if

(*a*) it is entered into in the ordinary course of business by the company, and

(*b*) the terms and value of the transaction are not more favourable than those the company ordinarily offers or is reasonably expected to have offered in respect of a person of the same financial standing as one unconnected with the company.

SECTION 38
Civil remedies for breach of section 31.

(1) Where a company enters into a transaction or arrangement in contravention of section 31 the transaction or arrangement shall be voidable at the instance of the company unless—

(*a*) restitution of any money or any other asset which is the subject matter of the arrangement or transaction is no longer possible, or the company has been indemnified in pursuance of subsection (2) (*b*) for the loss or damage suffered by it; or

(*b*) any rights acquired *bona fide* for value and without actual notice of the contravention by any person other than the person for whom the transaction or arrangement was made would be affected by its avoidance.

(2) Without prejudice to any liability imposed otherwise than by this subsection but subject to subsection (3), where an arrangement or transaction is made by a company for a director of the company or its holding company or person connected with such a director in contravention of section 31, that director and the person so connected and any other director of the company who authorised the transaction or arrangement shall (whether or not it has been avoided in pursuance of subsection (1)) be liable—

(*a*) to account to the company for any gain which he has made directly or indirectly by the arrangement or transaction; and

(*b*) (jointly and severally with any other person liable under this subsection) to indemnify the company for any loss or damage resulting from the arrangement or transaction.

(3) Where an arrangement or transaction is entered into by a company and a person connected with a director of the company or its holding company in contravention of section 31 that director shall not be liable under subsection (2)

if he shows that he took all reasonable steps to secure the company's compliance with that section and, in any case, a person so connected and any such other director as is mentioned in the said subsection (2) shall not be so liable if he shows that, at the time the arrangement or transaction was entered into, he did not know the relevant circumstances constituting the contravention.

Definitions

'company': Companies Act, 1963, section 2.
'director': Companies Act, 1963, section 2.
'holding company': Companies Act, 1963, section 155.
'person connected': Companies Act, 1990, section 26.

General Note

This section deals with civil liabilities for breach of section 31, and a prohibited transaction will be voidable by the company at its option. Where a prohibited transaction is made, the person benefiting, together with any other director who authorised it, will be required to account to the company for any resulting gain and to indemnify the company for any resulting loss or damage.

A person will not, however, be liable to account to or indemnify the company if he can show that he took all reasonable care and steps to ensure that the company had complied with section 31 or if he was unaware of the circumstances constituting a breach of the section.

(1) Any transaction entered into in contravention of section 31 is voidable at the company's option unless restitution is no longer possible or any rights acquired by another person unconnected with the contravention would be affected by its avoidance.

(2) Where any director of the company or a person connected with him has entered into a transaction or arrangement in contravention of section 31, that director and/or person will be liable to the company for any gain made directly or indirectly, or liable for any loss or damage resulting from the transaction.

(3) A director of the company or its holding company or any person connected with a director of the company may not be liable under subsection (2) if he can demonstrate that he took all reasonable steps to secure the company's compliance. Such person will also not be liable if he was not aware of the circumstances leading to the contravention at the time the transaction or arrangement was entered into.

SECTION 39
Personal liability for company debts in certain cases.

(1) If a company is being wound up and is unable to pay its debts, and the court considers that any arrangement of a kind described in section 32 has contributed materially to the company's inability to pay its debts or has substantially impeded the orderly winding up thereof, the court, on the application of the liquidator or any creditor or contributory of the company, may, if it thinks it proper to do so, declare that any person for whose benefit the arrangement was made shall be personally liable, without any limitation of liability, for all, or such part as may be specified by the court, of the debts and other liabilities of the company.

(2) In deciding whether to make a declaration under subsection (1), the court shall have particular regard to whether, and to what extent, any outstanding liabilities arising under any arrangement referred to in that subsection were discharged before the commencement of the winding up.

(3) In deciding the extent of any personal liability under this section, the court shall have particular regard to the extent to which the arrangement in question contributed materially to the company's inability to pay its debts or substantially impeded the orderly winding up of the company.

Definitions

'company': Companies Act, 1963, section 2.

'court': Companies Act, 1990, section 235.

General Note

Section 39 provides that where a company is being wound up and is unable to pay its debts, if any arrangements referred to in section 32 of this Act have materially contributed to the company's inability to pay its debts then on application to the High Court a liquidator or creditor can ask to have any person who is the subject of the arrangement made permanently liable for the debts.

(1) On the application to the High Court by a liquidator or creditor of a company being wound up because of its inability to pay its debts as a result of an arrangement being entered into as referred to in section 32, and where such arrangement has contributed materially to the company's inability to pay its debts, the High Court may declare that any person who has benefited from such an arrangement be held personally liable for all or part of the debt without a limit to the liability as may be specified by the court.

(2) The High Court in deciding to make a declaration as referred to in subsection (1) will take into account the extent to which any of the outstanding liabilities under the arrangement were discharged before the commencement of the winding up.

(3) The court will have particular regard to the extent to which any loans taken out by the director concerned materially affected the company's solvency.

SECTION 40
Criminal penalties for breach of section 31.

(1) An officer of a company who authorises or permits the company to enter into a transaction or arrangement knowing or having reasonable cause to believe that the company was thereby contravening section 31 shall be guilty of an offence.

(2) A person who procures a company to enter into a transaction or arrangement knowing or having reasonable cause to believe that the company was thereby contravening section 31 shall be guilty of an offence.

Definitions

'company': Companies Act, 1963, section 2.
'contravention': Companies Act, 1990, section 3.
'officer': Companies Act, 1963, section 2.

General Note

It is an offence for an officer (which includes a director or secretary) of a company to authorise or permit the company to enter into a transaction or arrangement knowing or having reasonable cause to believe that the company was contravening the prohibitions of section 31. This includes anyone who procures a company to enter into an arrangement or transaction knowing or having reasonable cause to believe that the company would contravene the provisions. Anyone in contravention would be subject to the penalty provisions in section 240.

It is therefore in the interest of officers to ensure that if they dissent from the transaction or the making of a loan, their dissension is recorded in the minutes of the meeting.

SECTION 41
Substantial contracts, etc., with directors and others to be disclosed in accounts.

(1) Subject to subsections (5) and (6) and to section 45, group accounts prepared by a holding company in accordance with the requirements of section 150 of the Principal Act in respect of the relevant period shall contain the particulars specified in section 42 of—

(a) any transaction or arrangement of a kind described in section 31 entered into by the company or by a subsidiary of the company for a person who at any time during the relevant period was a director of the company or its holding company or was connected with such a director;

(b) any agreement by the company or by a subsidiary of the company to enter into any such transaction or arrangement for a person who at any time during the relevant period was a director of the company or its holding company or was connected with such a director;

(c) any other transaction or arrangement with the company or with a subsidiary of the company in which a person who at any time during the relevant period was a director of the company or its holding company had, directly or indirectly, a material interest.

(2) Subject as aforesaid, accounts prepared by any company other than a holding company in respect of the relevant period shall contain the particulars specified in section 42 of—

(a) any transaction or arrangement of a kind described in section 31 entered into by the company for a person who at any time during the relevant period was a director of the company or of its holding company or was connected with such a director;

(b) any agreement by the company to enter into any such transaction or arrangement for a person who at any time during the relevant period was a director of the company or of its holding company or was connected with such a director;

(c) any other transaction or arrangement with the company in which a person who at any time during the relevant period was a director of the company or of its holding company had, directly or indirectly, a material interest.

(3) Particulars which are required by subsection (1) or (2) to be contained in any accounts shall be given by way of notes to those accounts.

(4) Where by virtue of sections 150 (2) and 154 of the Principal Act a company does not produce group accounts in relation to any financial year, subsection (1) shall have effect in relation to the company and that financial year as if the word "group" were omitted.

(5) For the purposes of subsections (1) (c) and (2) (c)—

(a) a transaction or arrangement between a company and a director of the company or of its holding company or a person connected with such a director shall (if it would not otherwise be so treated) be treated as a transaction, arrangement or agreement in which that director is interested; and

(b) an interest in such a transaction or arrangement is not material if in the opinion of the majority of the directors (other than that director) of the company which is preparing the accounts in question it is not material (but without prejudice to the question whether or not such an interest is material in any case where those directors have not considered the matter).

(6) Subsections (1) and (2) do not apply, for the purposes of any accounts prepared by any company which is, or is the holding company of, a licensed bank, in relation to a transaction or arrangement of a kind described in section 31, or an agreement to enter into such a transaction or arrangement, to which that licensed bank is a party.

(7) Subsections (1) and (2) do not apply in relation to the following transactions, arrangements and agreements—

(a) a transaction, arrangement or agreement between one company and another in which a director of the first company or of its subsidiary or holding company is interested only by virtue of his being a director of the other;

(b) a contract of service between a company and one of its directors or a director of its holding company or between a director of a company and any of that company's subsidiaries;

(c) a transaction, arrangement or agreement which was not entered into during the relevant period for the accounts in question and which did not subsist at any time during that period; and

(d) a transaction, arrangement or agreement which was made before the commencement of this section and which does not subsist thereafter.

(8) Subsections (1) and (2) apply whether or not—

(a) the transaction or arrangement was prohibited by section 31;
(b) the person for whom it was made was a director of the company or was connected with a director of the company at the time it was made;
(c) in the case of a transaction or arrangement made by a company which at any time during a relevant period is a subsidiary of another company, it was a subsidiary of that other company at the time the transaction or arrangement was made.

(9) In this section and in sections 43 and 45, "relevant period", in relation to a company, means a financial year of the company ending not earlier than 6 months after the commencement of the section concerned.

Definitions

'*company*': Companies Act, 1963, section 2.

'*director*': Companies Act, 1963, section 2.

'*financial year*': Companies Act, 1963, section 2.

'*group accounts*': Companies Act, 1963, section 2.

'*holding company*': Companies Act, 1963, section 155.

'*licensed bank*': Companies Act, 1990, section 25.

'*Principal Act*': Companies Act, 1990, section 3.

'*relevant period*': Companies Act, 1990, section 41.

'*subsidiary*': Companies Act, 1963, section 155.

General Note

This section describes the types of transaction of which details must be disclosed, the accounts in which they are to be disclosed, and the arrangements and transactions that are exempt from disclosure. The general requirement is for full disclosure of each transaction involved in the company's annual accounts. Previously, disclosure under section 194 of the Companies Act, 1963, only required that a general disclosure be made to the board of directors, whereas under section 41 it is required that a full disclosure be made in the accounts that are sent to all members.

(1) This subsection sets out the details of transactions to be disclosed in group accounts prepared in accordance with section 150 of the Companies Act, 1963. The details that must be disclosed are:

(a) any transaction or arrangement concerning loans to directors of the company or its holding company that are entered into by the company or a subsidiary;

(*b*) any agreement made by the company or a subsidiary entering into a transaction or arrangement for someone who was a director of the company or holding company or connected with it during the relevant period;

(*c*) any other transaction or arrangement with the company or a subsidiary in which a person was a director of the company or its holding company and who had during the relevant period a material interest.

(2) This subsection defines the types of transaction that must be disclosed in the accounts of companies other than a holding company, and covers similar situations referred to in subsection (1).

(3) The details may be disclosed by way of notes to the accounts.

(4) In any financial year where group accounts are not prepared the requirements will apply to the company as if group accounts were prepared.

(5) A transaction between a company and a director of the company or its holding company or a person connected with a company will be treated as a transaction in which a director is interested. An interest in such transaction will not be material if in the opinion of the majority of the directors it is not material.

(6) Subsections (1) and (2) will not apply where it is a transaction to which a licensed bank is a party.

(7) Subsections (1) and (2) will not apply to the following:

(*a*) a transaction, arrangement or agreement between a company and another in which a director is interested only by virtue of being a director of the other;

(*b*) a contract of service between a company, its subsidiary or holding company and a director;

(*c*) a transaction, arrangement or agreement that was not entered into during the accounting period and did not subsist during the accounting period;

(*d*) a transaction, arrangement or agreement made before the commencement of the section and that does not subsist thereafter.

(8) The publication requirements in subsection (1) and (2) apply whether or not

(*a*) the transaction or arrangement was prohibited by section 31, (*b*) the person for whom it was made was a director of the company or connected with a director of the company at the time it was made, or

(*c*) a company was a subsidiary of another company at the time the transaction or arrangement was entered into.

(9) The term 'relevant period' is defined.

SECTION 42
Particulars required to be included in accounts by section 41.

The particulars of a transaction, arrangement or agreement which are required by section 41 to be included in the annual accounts prepared by a company are particulars of the principal terms of the transaction, arrangement or agreement and (without prejudice to the generality of the foregoing provision)—

(*a*) a statement of the fact either that the transaction, arrangement or agreement was made or subsisted, as the case may be, during the financial year in respect of which those accounts are made up;

(*b*) the name of the person for whom it was made, and, where that person is or was connected with a director of the company or of its holding company, the name of that director;

(*c*) in any case where subsection (1) (*c*) or (2) (*c*) of section 41 applies, the name of the director with the material interest and the nature of that interest;

(*d*) in the case of a loan or an agreement for a loan or an arrangement within section 31 (2) or 31 (3) relating to a loan—
(i) the amount of the liability of the person to whom the loan was or was agreed to be made, in respect of principal and interest, at the beginning and at the end of that period;
(ii) the maximum amount of that liability during that period;
(iii) the amount of any interest which, having fallen due, has not been paid; and
(iv) the amount of any provision (within the meaning of the Sixth Schedule to the Principal Act or the Companies (Amendment) Act, 1986) made in respect of any failure or anticipated failure by the borrower to repay the whole or part of the loan or to pay the whole or part of any interest thereon;

(*e*) in the case of a guarantee or security or an arrangement within section 31 (2) relating to a guarantee or security—
(i) the amount for which the company (or its subsidiary) was liable under the guarantee or in respect of the security both at the beginning and at the end of the financial year in question;
(ii) the maximum amount for which the company (or its subsidiary) may become so liable; and
(iii) any amount paid and any liability incurred by the company (or its subsidiary) for the purpose of fulfilling the guarantee or discharging the security (including any loss incurred by reason of the enforcement of the guarantee or security); and

(*f*) in the case of any transaction, arrangement or agreement, other than those mentioned in paragraphs (*d*) and (*e*) the value of the transaction or arrangement or, as the case may be, the value of the transaction or arrangement to which the agreement relates; and

(*g*) in the case of arrangements to which section 32 relates, the aggregate value of such arrangements at the end of the financial year concerned, in relation to any persons specified in that section, expressed as a percentage of the company's relevant assets at that time; and (*h*) any amendment of the terms of any such arrangement in accordance with section 33.

Definitions

'*company*': Companies Act, 1963, section 2.
'*director*': Companies Act, 1963, section 2.
'*financial year*': Companies Act, 1963, section 2.
'*guarantee*': Companies Act, 1990, section 25.
'*holding company*': Companies Act, 1963, section 155.
'*Principal Act*': Companies Act, 1990, section 3.
'*subsidiary*': Companies Act, 1963, section 155.

General Note

This section supplements the requirements of section 41 by specifying the particulars that need to be disclosed. These particulars cover the names of the persons and other companies involved, together with the amounts for which the company could be liable.

The particulars to be disclosed of any such transaction, arrangement or agreement must include the principal terms and include:

(*a*) a statement of the fact that relevant transactions occurred or subsisted during the financial period to which the accounts relate;

(*b*) the name of the person involved or, where the person was connected with a director, the name of the director;

(*c*) the name of any director with a material interest and details of the interest of substantial contracts etc. to which section 41 applies;

(*d*) in the case of loan transactions, details of the amount involved during the financial period, the amount of unpaid interest, and any provision made against the loan in the accounts;

(*e*) in the case where the company has provided a guarantee or other security, the amount of the maximum liability during the period and any amount paid under that security;

(*f*) the value of the transaction or arrangement involved;

(*g*) in the case of an arrangement to which section 32 relates, the aggregate value of the arrangement at the end of the financial year, expressed as a percentage of the company's relevant assets;

(*h*) any amendment to the terms of the arrangement under section 33 (Reduction in amount of company's relevant assets).

SECTION 43
Particulars of amounts outstanding to be included in accounts.

(1) This section applies in relation to the following classes of transactions, arrangements and agreements—

(*a*) loans, guarantees and securities relating to loans, arrangements of a kind described in section 31 (2) or 31 (3) relating to loans, and agreements to enter into any of the foregoing transactions and arrangements;

(*b*) quasi-loans, guarantees and securities relating to quasi-loans, arrangements of a kind described in those subsections relating to quasi-loans and agreements to enter into any of the foregoing transactions and arrangements;

(*c*) credit transactions, guarantees and securities relating to credit transactions and arrangements of a kind described in those subsections relating to credit transactions and agreements to enter into any of the foregoing transactions and arrangements.

(2) The group accounts of a holding company prepared in accordance with the requirements of section 150 of the Principal Act and the accounts of any other company prepared in accordance with the requirements of section 148 of the Principal Act in respect of the relevant period shall contain a statement in relation to transactions, arrangements and agreements made by the company and, in the case of a holding company, by a subsidiary of the company for persons who at any time during the relevant period were officers of the company (but not directors) of the aggregate amounts outstanding at the end of the relevant period under transactions, arrangements and agreements within any paragraph of subsection (1) and the number of officers for whom the transactions, arrangements and agreements falling within each of those paragraphs were made.

(3) Subsection (2) shall not apply, in relation to the accounts prepared by any company in respect of any relevant period, to transactions, arrangements and agreements made by the company or any of its subsidiaries for any officer of the company if the aggregate amount outstanding at the end of that period under the transactions, arrangements and agreements so made for that officer does not exceed £2,500.

(4) Subsection (2) shall not apply in relation to any transaction, arrangement or agreement made by a licensed bank for any of its officers or for any of the officers of its holding company.

(5) The group accounts of a company which is, or is the holding company of, a licensed bank prepared in accordance with the requirements of section 150 of the Principal Act, and the accounts of any other company which is a licensed bank, prepared in accordance with the requirements of section 148 of the Principal Act in respect of the relevant period shall contain a statement in relation to transactions, arrangements or agreements made by the company preparing the accounts, if it is a licensed bank, and (in the case of a holding company) by any of its subsidiaries which is a licensed bank, for persons who at any time during the relevant period were directors of the company, of the aggregate amounts outstanding at the end of the relevant period under transactions, arrangements and agreements within any paragraph of subsection (1) and the number of persons for whom the transactions, arrangements and agreements falling within each of those paragraphs were made.

(6) (*a*) The statement referred to in subsection (5) shall also separately contain the like information as is referred to in that subsection in relation to transactions, arrangements or agreements made for persons who at any

time during the relevant period were connected with a director of the company.

(*b*) A transaction, arrangement or agreement to which paragraph (a) applies need not be included in the statement if—

(i) it is entered into by the company concerned in the ordinary course of its business, and

(ii) its value is not greater, and its terms no more favourable, in respect of the person for whom it is made, than that or those which—

(I) the company ordinarily offers, or

(II) it is reasonable to expect the company to have offered,

to or in respect of a person of the same financial standing but unconnected with the company.

(7) Particulars which are required by subsection (2), (5) or (6) to be contained in any accounts shall be given by way of notes to those accounts.

(8) Where by virtue of sections 150 (2) and 154 of the Principal Act, a company does not produce group accounts in relation to any financial year, subsections (2), (5) and (6) shall have effect in relation to the company and that financial year as if the word "group" were omitted.

(9) Subsections (2), (5) and (6) do not apply in relation to a transaction, arrangement or agreement which was made before the commencement of this section and which does not subsist thereafter.

(10) For the purposes of this section, "amount outstanding" means the amount of the outstanding liabilities of the person for whom the transaction, arrangement or agreement in question was made, or, in the case of a guarantee or security, the amount guaranteed or secured.

Definitions

'amount outstanding': Companies Act, 1990, section 43.

'company': Companies Act, 1963, section 2.

'credit transaction': Companies Act, 1990, section 25.

'director': Companies Act, 1963, section 2.

'financial year': Companies Act, 1963, section 2.

'group accounts': Companies Act, 1963, section 2.

'guarantee': Companies Act, 1990, section 25.

'holding company': Companies Act, 1963, section 25.

'licensed bank': Companies Act, 1990, section 25.

'officer': Companies Act, 1963, section 2.

'Principal Act': Companies Act, 1990, section 3.

'quasi-loan': Companies Act, 1990, section 25.

'relevant period': Companies Act, 1990, section 41.

'subsidiary': Companies Act, 1963, section 155.

General Note

This section requires, in the case of certain transactions, arrangements or agreements entered into with officers of a company who are not directors, that the aggregate of the amount outstanding together with the number of officers involved be disclosed where the amount outstanding exceeds £2,500. In the case of banks, the accounts must disclose the total amount outstanding for transactions or arrangements for directors, and the number of directors involved.

(1) This subsection sets out the classes of transaction to which the section applies. These include loans, guarantees, securities relating to loans, arrangements and agreements to enter into loans.

(2) Group accounts for financial periods ending after 31 July 1991 (being six months after the commencement date of this section) must contain a statement relating to transactions, giving details of the aggregate amounts outstanding at the end of the financial year and the number of officers involved.

(3) Subsection (2) does not apply if the amount outstanding at the end of the period for a particular officer does not exceed £2,500.

(4) Subsection (2) does not apply to transactions made by a licensed bank for any of its officers or officers of its holding company.

(5) The group accounts of a holding company or a company that is a licensed bank and prepares its accounts in accordance with section 150 of the Companies Act, 1963, must give details of the aggregate amount of loans outstanding to officers together with the number of persons involved.

(6) The disclosure referred to in this section also applies to a person who was during the accounting period connected with a director of the company. Furthermore, under subsection (6) a transaction, arrangement or agreement need not be disclosed if entered into by the company in the ordinary course of business and the value and terms are no more favourable than those that the company ordinarily offers or is expected to offer to a person unconnected with the company.

(7) Particulars to be given under subsections (2) or (5) can be made by way of notes to the accounts.

(8–10) These subsections give technical interpretations and assist in explaining the section.

SECTION 44
Further provisions relating to licensed banks.

(1) Subject to section 45, a company which is, or is the holding company of, a licensed bank, shall maintain a register containing a copy of every transaction, arrangement or agreement of which particulars would, but for section 41 (6), be required by subsection (1) or (2) of that section to be disclosed in the company's accounts or group accounts for the current financial year and for each of the preceding ten financial years (but excluding any financial year ending prior to the passing of this Act) or, if such a transaction, arrangement or agreement is not in writing, a written memorandum setting out its terms.

(2) Subsection (1) shall not require a company to keep in its register a copy of any transaction, arrangement or agreement made for a connected person if—

(a) it is entered into in the ordinary course of the company's business, and
(b) its value is not greater, and its terms no more favourable, in respect of the person for whom it is made, than that or those which—
(i) the company ordinarily offers, or
(ii) it is reasonable to expect the company to have offered,

to or in respect of a person of the same financial standing but unconnected with the company.

(3) Subject to section 45, a company which is, or is the holding company of, a licensed bank shall before its annual general meeting make available, at the registered office of the company for not less than the period of 15 days ending with the date of the meeting, for inspection by members of the company a statement containing the particulars of transactions, arrangements and agreements which the company would, but for section 41 (6), be required by subsection (1) or (2) of that section to disclose in its accounts or group accounts for the last complete financial year preceding that meeting and such a statement shall also be made available for inspection by the members at the annual general meeting.

(4) Subsection (3) shall not require the inclusion in the statement of particulars of any transaction, arrangement or agreement if—

(a) it is entered into in the ordinary course of the company's business, and
(b) its value is not greater, and its terms no more favourable, in respect of the person for whom it is made, than that or those which—
(i) the company ordinarily offers, or
(ii) it is reasonable to expect the company to have offered,

to or in respect of a person of the same financial standing but unconnected with the company.

(5) It shall be the duty of the auditors of the company to examine any such statement before it is made available to the members of the company in accordance with subsection (3) and to make a report to the members on that statement; and the report shall be annexed to the statement before it is made so available.

(6) A report under subsection (5) shall state whether in the opinion of the auditors the statement contains the particulars required by subsection (3) and, where their opinion is that it does not, they shall include in the report, so far as they are reasonably able to do so, a statement giving the required particulars.

(7) Subsection (3) shall not apply in relation to a licensed bank which is for the purposes of section 150 of the Principal Act the wholly owned subsidiary of a company incorporated in the State.

(8) Where a company fails to comply with subsection (1) or (3), the company and every person who at the time of that failure is a director of the company shall be guilty of an offence and liable to a fine.

(9) It shall be a defence in proceedings for an offence under subsection (8) for the defendant to prove that he took all reasonable steps for securing compliance with subsection (1) or (3), as the case may be.

Definitions

'auditor': this is not defined in the Companies Acts; but see the UK case *R. v. Shacter* [1960] 2 QB 252.

'company': Companies Act, 1963, section 2.

'director': Companies Act, 1963, section 2.

'financial year': Companies Act, 1963, section 2.

'holding company': Companies Act, 1963, section 155.

'licensed': Companies Act, 1990, section 25.

'person connected': Companies Act, 1990, section 26.

'Principal Act': Companies Act, 1990, section 3.

'quasi-loan': Companies Act, 1990, section 25.

General Note

This section sets out the matters that must be disclosed by licensed banks. The basic requirement is that a bank must keep a register both for the current financial year and the preceding ten financial years of all transactions and arrangements entered into with directors and connected persons. A statement containing these particulars must be available for inspection by shareholders both before and at the annual general meeting. The statement must be examined and reported on by the bank's auditors.

(1) Each licensed bank is required to maintain a register of each transaction, arrangement or agreement with each director or person connected with him, to contain the current financial year's information and that of the previous ten financial years (but excluding any financial year ending before the passing of this Act).

(2) A company need not maintain in its register a copy of any transaction, agreement or arrangement made for a connected person if it is entered into in the ordinary course of business and its value is not greater or the terms more favourable than those ordinarily offered by the company to persons of the same financial standing who are unconnected with the company.

(3) A statement containing the particulars of transactions, arrangements and agreements that the company is required to disclose

under this section is to be available for inspection by members for a period of fifteen days ending with the date of the annual general meeting.

(4) It is not necessary to include in the statement particulars of any transaction, arrangement or agreement if entered into in the ordinary course of the company's business and the value is not greater nor the terms more favourable than those ordinarily offered by the company or reasonably expected to have been offered to an unconnected person of the same financial standing.

(5) The auditors of the bank are required to examine and report to the members on the statement referred to in subsection (3) above.

(6) The report must give the auditors' opinion that the statement contains the details required by this section if they are reasonably able to do so.

(7) There is an exemption for a licensed bank that is a wholly owned subsidiary of a company incorporated in the state.

(8) There is provision for a penalty under section 240 for each director of the company at the time it was in default; this penalty provides only for a fine.

(9) Any person charged under subsection (6) can use as a defence that he took all reasonable action to secure compliance with subsections (1) and (2).

SECTION 45
Arrangements excluded from sections 41 and 44.

(1) Section 41 (1) and (2) and section 44 do not apply to arrangements of the kind mentioned in section 32 (2) entered into by a company or by a subsidiary of the company for a person who at any time during the relevant period was a director of the company or of its holding company or was connected with such a director, if the aggregate of the values of each arrangement so made for that director or any person connected with him, less the amount (if any) by which the liabilities of the person for whom the arrangement was made has been reduced, did not at any time during the relevant period exceed £2,500.

(2) Subsections (1) (c) and (2) (c) of section 41 do not apply, in relation to any accounts prepared by a company in respect of any relevant period, to any transaction or arrangement with a company or any of its subsidiaries in which a director of the company or of its holding company had, directly or indirectly, a material interest if—

(a) the value of each transaction or arrangement within subsection (1) (c) or (2) (c), as the case may be, in which that director had, directly or indirectly, a material interest and which was made after the commencement of that relevant period with the company or any of its subsidiaries; and
(b) the value of each such transaction or arrangement which was made before the commencement of that period less the amount (if any) by which the

liabilities of the person for whom the transaction or arrangement was made have been reduced;

did not at any time during the relevant period exceed in the aggregate £1,000 or, if more, did not exceed £5,000 or one per cent of the value of the net assets of the company preparing the accounts in question as at the end of the relevant period for those accounts, whichever is the less and for this purpose, "net assets" has the same meaning as in section 29 (9).

Definitions

'*company*': Companies Act, 1963, section 2.
'*credit transaction*': Companies Act, 1990, section 25.
'*director*': Companies Act, 1963, section 2.
'*guarantee*': Companies Act, 1990, section 25.
'*holding company*': Companies Act, 1963, section 155.
'*person connected*': Companies Act, 1990, section 26.
'*relevant period*': Companies Act, 1990, section 41.
'*subsidiary*': Companies Act, 1963, section 155.

General Note

This section sets out the exclusions from sections 41 and 44 on loans to directors or connected persons.

(1) Sections 41 and 44 do not apply to types of arrangement referred to in section 32 (2) that are entered into by a company or its subsidiary for a director of the company, its holding company or a person connected with the company if the aggregate of the arrangement less the amount of any liability relating to the arrangement during the financial period did not exceed £2,500.

(2) Section 41 (1) (*c*) and (2) (*c*) does not apply in relation to accounts prepared by a company in respect of the accounts year to any transaction or an arrangement with a company or one of its subsidiaries in which a director had directly or indirectly a material interest if (*a*) the value of each transaction or arrangement in which that director directly or indirectly had a material interest and that was made after the commencement of the relevant period and (*b*) the value of each such transaction or arrangement that was made before the commencement of the period, less any liabilities of the person relating to the transaction, did not at any time during the accounting period exceed in aggregate £1,000 or, if more, did not exceed £5,000 or 1 per cent of the value of the net assets of the company preparing the accounts.

SECTION 46
Duty of auditors of company in breach of section 41 or 43.

If in the case of any group or other accounts of a company the requirements of section 41 or 43 are not complied with, it shall be the duty of the auditors of the company by whom the accounts are examined to include in their report on the balance sheet of the company, so far as they are reasonably able to do so, a statement giving the required particulars.

Definitions

'auditor': this is not defined in the Companies Acts; but see the UK case *R.* v. *Shacter* [1960] 2 QB 252.

'company': Companies Act, 1963, section 2.

General Note

Where the particulars required by sections 41 and 43 are not supplied, the auditors are required to supply them in their report as far as possible. The purpose of this provision is to ensure that there is at least some disclosure even if the directors and the company have failed to supply them. This is a similar provision to section 192 (3) of the Companies Act, 1963.

SECTION 47
Disclosure by directors of interests in contracts, etc.

(1) Any reference in section 194 of the Principal Act to a contract shall be construed as including a reference to any transaction or arrangement (whether or not constituting a contract) made or entered into on or after the commencement of this section.

(2) For the purposes of the said section 194, a transaction or arrangement of a kind described in section 31 made by a company for a director of the company or a person connected with such a director shall, if it would not otherwise be so treated (and whether or not prohibited by that section), be treated as a transaction or arrangement in which that director is interested.

(3) The following shall be substituted for subsection (3) of the said section 194—

"(3) Subject to subsection (4), for the purposes of this section, a general notice given to the directors of a company by a director to the effect that—

(a) he is a member of a specified company or firm and is to be regarded as interested in any contract which may, after the date of the notice, be made with that company or firm; or
(b) he is to be regarded as interested in any contract which may after the date of the notice be made with a specified person who is connected with him (within the meaning of section 26 of the Companies Act, 1990),

shall be deemed to be a sufficient declaration of interest in relation to any such contract.".

Definitions

'company': Companies Act, 1963, section 2.

'director': Companies Act, 1963, section 2.
'person connected': Companies Act, 1990, section 26.
'Principal Act': Companies Act, 1990, section 3.

General Note

This section widens the scope under section 194 of the Companies Act, 1963, covering disclosure to the board by a director of his interest in contracts to which the company is a party. The section also extends the possibility in section 194 for a director to give a general notice to the other directors that he is to be taken to be interested in any contract that may come in relation to any other company in which he has an interest.

(1) Any reference in section 194 of the Companies Act, 1963, to a contract is also construed to include any transaction or arrangement made after the commencement of this section.

(2) A transaction or arrangement of the type described in section 31 made by the company for a director or a person connected with him will be treated as one in which that director is interested.

(3) Section 194 (3) of the Companies Act, 1963, is amended to provide that a general notice given to directors of a company to the effect that a director is a member of a specified company or is interested in any contract that may be made with a specified person who is connected with him will be deemed to be a sufficient declaration of interest in a contract.

SECTION 48
Power to alter financial limits under Part III.

(1) The Minister may, by order, alter any of the financial limits specified in this Part.

(2) Every order made under this section shall be laid before each House of the Oireachtas as soon as may be after it is made and if a resolution annulling the order is passed by either House within the next 21 days on which that House has sat after the order is laid before it, the order shall be annulled accordingly but without prejudice to the validity of anything previously done thereunder.

Definitions

'Minister': Companies Act, 1990, section 3.

General Note

This section empowers the Minister for Industry and Commerce to alter, by order, the financial limits set out in this part of the Act, and allows the limits to be adjusted to keep in line with any change in money values.

SECTION 49

Cessation of section 192 of Principal Act.

Section 192 of the Principal Act shall cease to have effect except—

(a) in relation to accounts and directors' reports prepared in respect of any financial year ending before the commencement of this section; and

(b) in relation to accounts and directors' reports prepared in respect of the first financial year ending after the commencement of this section but only in relation to loans and contracts entered into before the commencement of this section which do not subsist on or after that day.

Definitions

'financial year': Companies Act, 1963, section 2.
'Principal Act': Companies Act, 1990, section 3.

General Note

This section has the effect of replacing the provisions relating to loans to directors in sections 192 and 193 of the Companies Act, 1963. The provisions relating to loans in this Act are more onerous, and accordingly the 1963 Act will cease to have effect except for certain transitional arrangements. Paragraph (*a*) of the section provides that the repeal of section 192 of the 1963 Act will not affect any company accounts or directors' reports prepared in respect of financial years ending before the section came into effect.

SECTION 50

Inspection of directors' service contracts.

(1) Subject to the provisions of this section every company shall keep at an appropriate place—

(a) in the case of each director whose contract of service with the company is in writing, a copy of that contract;

(b) in the case of each director whose contract of service with the company is not in writing, a written memorandum setting out the terms of that contract;

(c) in the case of each director who is employed under a contract of service with a subsidiary of the company, a copy of that contract or, if it is not in writing, a written memorandum setting out the terms of that contract;

(d) a copy or written memorandum, as the case may be, of any variation of any contract of service referred to in paragraph (a), (b) or (c);

and all copies and memoranda kept by a company in pursuance of this sub-section shall be kept at the same place.

(2) Where a contract of service is only partially in writing, paragraphs (a), (b), (c) and (d), as appropriate, of subsection (1), and subsections (4) and (5), shall also apply to such a contract.

(3) The following shall, as regards a company, be appropriate places for the purposes of subsection (1), namely—

(a) its registered office;
(b) the place where its register of members is kept if other than its registered office;
(c) its principal place of business.

(4) Every company shall send notice in the prescribed form to the registrar of companies of the place where copies and memoranda required by subsection (1) to be kept by it are kept and of any change in that place, save in a case in which they have at all times been kept at its registered office.

(5) Subsection (1) shall not apply in relation to a director's contract of service with the company or with a subsidiary of the company if that contract required him to work wholly or mainly outside the State, but the company shall keep a memorandum—

(a) in the case of a contract of service with the company, setting out the name of the director and the provisions of the contract relating to its duration;
(b) in the case of a contract of service with a subsidiary of the company setting out the name of the director, the name and place of incorporation of the subsidiary and the provisions of the contract relating to its duration,

at the same place as copies and the memoranda are kept by the company in pursuance of subsection (1).

(6) Every copy and memorandum required to be kept by subsections (1) and (5) shall, during business hours (subject to such reasonable restrictions as the company may in general meeting impose, so that not less than two hours in each day be allowed for inspection), be open to the inspection of any member of the company without charge.

(7) If default is made in complying with subsection (1) or (5) or if an inspection required under subsection (6) is refused, the company and every officer of the company who is in default shall be liable on summary conviction to a fine not exceeding £1,000, and, for continued contravention, to a daily default fine not exceeding £50 and, if default is made for 14 days in complying with subsection (4), the company and every officer of the company who is in default shall be liable to a fine not exceeding £1,000 and, for continued contravention, to a daily default fine not exceeding £50.

(8) In the case of a refusal of an inspection required under subsection (6) of a copy or memorandum the court may by order compel an immediate inspection thereof.

(9) This section shall not require to be kept a copy of, or memorandum setting out the terms of, a contract or a copy of, or memorandum setting out the terms of a variation of, a contract at a time at which the unexpired portion of the term for which the contract is to be in force is less than three years or at a time at which the contract can, within the next ensuing three years, be terminated by the company without payment of compensation.

Definitions

'*company*': Companies Act, 1963, section 2.

'*director*': Companies Act, 1963, section 2.

'*officer*': Companies Act, 1963, section 2.

'*subsidiary*': Companies Act, 1963, section 155.

General Note

This section provides for inspection by members of a company of copies of the directors' service contracts and, if these are not in writing, of memorandums of the terms of the contract. This is to give the members a true and complete indication of the obligations of the company to the directors. The documents must be kept either at the company's registered office or its principal place of business.

(1) Every company must keep at an appropriate place (see subsection (2)) copies of contracts of service or variation of any contract of service with directors or, if the contract is not in writing, a memorandum setting out the terms of that contract.

(2) Where a contract is only partly in writing, paragraphs (*a*), (*b*), (*c*) and (*d*) of subsection (1), and subsections (4) and (5), would also apply to the contract.

(3) The appropriate place for keeping copies of contracts of service will be either its registered office, the place where the register of members is normally kept, or the company's principal place of business.

(4) Every company must send a notice to the Registrar of Companies stating where copies of contracts are kept, except where they have always been kept at the company's registered office.

(5) Subsection (1) does not apply where the director is required by his contract to work wholly or mainly outside the state; but the company must keep a memorandum setting out the main provisions of the contract.

(6) Any member of the company may inspect the contracts of service and memorandums during normal business hours, free of charge. The company must have this information available for inspection for at least two hours each day.

(7) The penalties for being in default of this section are set out. The company and every officer who is in default is liable to a fine on summary conviction of not more than £1,000 and for continued contravention to a daily default fine of not more than £50.

(8) Where there is a refusal to permit inspection, the High Court may order immediate inspection.

(9) The section will not apply where less than three years of the service contract is unexpired or where at any time within the

following three years the contract can be terminated by the company without payment of compensation.

SECTION 51
Register of directors and secretaries.

The Principal Act is hereby amended by the substitution for section 195 of the following section—

"195.—(1) Every company shall keep at its registered office a register of its directors and secretaries.

(2) Subject to subsection (3), the said register shall contain the following particulars relating to each director—

(a) his present forename and surname and any former forename and surname; and

(b) his date of birth; and

(c) his usual residential address; and

(d) his nationality; and

(e) his business occupation, if any; and

(f) particulars of any other directorships of bodies corporate, whether incorporated in the State or elsewhere, held by him or which have been held by him.

(3) It shall not be necessary for the said register to contain on any day particulars of any directorship—

(a) which has not been held by a director at any time during the ten years preceding that day;

(b) which is held or was held by a director in bodies corporate of which the company is or was the wholly owned subsidiary or which are or were the wholly owned subsidiaries either of the company or of another body corporate of which the company is or was the wholly owned subsidiary;

and for the purposes of this subsection a body corporate shall be deemed to be the wholly owned subsidiary of another if it has no members except that other and that other's wholly owned subsidiaries and its or their nominees.

(4) Subject to subsection (5), the said register shall contain the following particulars relating to the secretary or, where there are joint secretaries, in relation to each of them—

(a) in the case of an individual, his present forename and surname, any former forename and surname and his usual residential address; and

(b) in the case of a body corporate, the corporate name and registered office.

(5) Where all the partners in a firm are joint secretaries of a company, the name and principal office of the firm may be stated instead of the said particulars.

(6) The company shall, within the period of 14 days from the happening of—

(a) any change among its directors or in its secretary, or

(b) any change in any of the particulars contained in the register,

send to the registrar of companies a notification in the prescribed form of the change and of the date on which it occurred.

(7) A notification sent to the registrar of companies pursuant to subsection (6) of the appointment of a person as a director, secretary or joint secretary of a company shall be accompanied by a consent signed by that person to act as director, secretary or joint secretary, as the case may be.

(8) Without prejudice to subsection (6), a person who has ceased to be a director or secretary of a company may send to the registrar of companies a notification in the prescribed form of such cessation, and of the date on which it occurred.

(9) Subsection (6) shall not apply to any change in the particulars contained in a company's register of directors and secretaries made solely by reason of the coming into force of section 51 of the Companies Act, 1990 but if after any such change has occurred and before the company makes its next annual return, any other change in those particulars occurs, the company shall send to the registrar of companies a notification in the prescribed form of any such earlier changes and the date on which they occurred at the same time as it notifies the registrar of the later changes in accordance with this section.

(10) The register to be kept under this section shall, during business hours (subject to such reasonable restrictions as the company may by its articles or in general meeting impose, so that not less than 2 hours in each day be allowed for inspection) be open to the inspection of any member of the company without charge, and of any other person, on payment of one pound or such less sum as the company may prescribe, for each inspection.

(11) It shall be the duty of each director and secretary of a company to give information in writing to the company as soon as may be of such matters as may be necessary to enable the company to comply with this section.

(12) If any inspection required under this section is refused or if default is made in complying with subsection (1), (2), (4), (6) or (7), the company and every officer of the company who is in default shall be liable to a fine not exceeding £1,000 and, for continued contravention, to a daily default fine not exceeding £50.

(13) In the case of any such refusal, the court may by order compel an immediate inspection of the register.

(14) A person who fails to comply with subsection (11) shall be guilty of an offence and liable to a fine.

(15) For the purposes of this section—

(*a*) in the case of a person usually known by a title different from his surname, the expression 'surname' means that title;

(*b*) references to a 'former forename' or 'surname' do not include—
(i) in the case of a person usually known by a title different from his surname, the name by which he was known previous to the adoption of or succession to the title; or
(ii) in the case of any person, a former forename or surname where that name or surname was changed or disused before the person bearing the name attained the age of 18 years or has been changed or disused for a period of not less than 20 years; or
(iii) in the case of a married woman, the name or surname by which she was known previous to the marriage.".

Definitions

'*body corporate*': Companies Act, 1963, section 2 (3).

'*company*': Companies Act, 1963, section 2.

'*director*': Companies Act, 1963, section 2.

'*Principal Act*': Companies Act, 1990, section 3.

'*subsidiary*': Companies Act, 1963, section 155.

General Note

This section re-enacts section 195 of the Companies Act, 1963, with amendments. The primary object of the amendment is to make it possible for interested parties to identify and to ascertain the record of other companies with which a director has been associated in the past. As a result, a company's register of directors and secretaries will be required to include details of directorships held in the previous ten years.

(1) The register of directors and secretaries is to be kept at the registered office.

(2) This subsection specifies the details to be included in the register of directors and secretaries. 'Forenames' rather than 'Christian names' are now specified. In addition, the nationality of the person must be specified, even if the person is Irish.

(3) This subsection specifies the exceptions to details to be included in the register; for example, subsidiaries of the company need not be included in the list of directorships.

(4) This subsection sets out the details to be included in the register regarding company secretaries.

(5) Where the partners in a firm are joint secretaries, the name and principal office of the firm are to be stated.

(6) Any changes of directors or secretary are to be lodged with the Registrar of Companies within fourteen days of the change.

(7) The notification to the Companies Registration Office is to be signed by a director or secretary of the company.

(8) A director or secretary who has resigned may notify the Registrar of the cessation and the date on which it occurred.

(9) Subsection (6) does not apply to any change solely by reason of the coming into force of this section.

(10) The register is to be available for inspection by members free of charge, and by anyone else for a charge of not more than £1, for not less than two hours each day.

(11) It will be the duty of each director and secretary of a company to give information to the company as soon as possible so as to comply with the section.

(12) The company and every officer who is in default of this section will be liable to a fine not exceeding £1,000 and for continued contravention to a daily default fine not exceeding £50.

(13) If a company refuses to allow inspection, the High Court may order immediate inspection of the register.

(14) A person who fails to comply with the section will be guilty of an offence and liable to a fine under section 240.

(15) Technical definitions and terms are set out in this subsection.

SECTION 52
Directors to have regard to interests of employees.

(1) The matters to which the directors of a company are to have regard in the performance of their functions shall include the interests of the company's employees in general, as well as the interests of its members.

(2) Accordingly, the duty imposed by this section on the directors shall be owed by them to the company (and the company alone) and shall be enforceable in the same way as any other fiduciary duty owed to a company by its directors.

Definitions

'company': Companies Act, 1963, section 2.
'director': Companies Act, 1963, section 2.

General Note

It has been well established in law that a director owes the duties arising out of his office to the company itself and to no-one else. This section now expands the duty owed by a director, in that he has to take into account the interests of the employees in general as well as the members in the performance of his duties for the company.

(1) The directors of the company will be required to take into account the interests of the company's employees and members in general.

(2) The duty imposed by this section on directors will be owed by them to the company alone and enforceable in the same way as a fiduciary duty is owed by the directors of the company.

4
DISCLOSURE OF INTERESTS IN SHARES

This part of the Act is of relevance only to public limited companies. The main aim of part IV is that the beneficial owner of a given percentage of the issued share capital of a public limited company should be required to declare that fact to the company, and that such information should be available to directors, shareholders, employees and creditors of the company. This information could be regarded as being important to persons who wish to establish a relationship with the company, and should lead to a better-informed environment in which to do business.

SECTION 53
Obligation of director or secretary to notify interests in shares or debentures of company.

(1) Subject to the provisions of this section a person who, at the commencement of this section is a director or secretary of a company and is then interested in shares in, or debentures of, the company or any other body corporate, being the company's subsidiary or holding company or a subsidiary of the company's holding company or thereafter becomes a director or secretary of a company and, at the time when he becomes a director or secretary of a company, is so interested, shall notify the company in writing—

(*a*) of the subsistence of his interests at that time, and
(*b*) of the number of shares of each class in, and the amount of debentures of each class of, the company or any such other body corporate as aforesaid in which each interest of his subsists at that time.

(2) A director or secretary of a company shall notify the company in writing of the occurrence, while he is a director or secretary, of any of the following events and the date on which it occurred—

(*a*) any event in consequence of whose occurrence he becomes, or ceases to be, interested in shares in, or debentures of, the company or any other body corporate, being the company's subsidiary or holding company or a subsidiary of the company's holding company;
(*b*) the entering into by him of a contract to sell any such shares or debentures;
(*c*) the assignment by him of a right granted to him by the company to subscribe for shares in, or debentures of, the company; and
(*d*) the grant to him by another body corporate, being the company's subsidiary or holding company or a subsidiary of the company's holding company, of a right to subscribe for shares in, or debentures of, that other body corporate, the exercise of such a right granted to him and the assignment by him of such a right so granted;

stating the number or amount, and class, of shares or debentures involved.

(3) The provisions of section 54 shall have effect for the interpretation of, and otherwise in relation to, subsections (1) and (2).

(4) Section 56 shall have effect with respect to the periods within which obligations imposed by subsections (1) and (2) on persons must be fulfilled by them.

(5) Section 57 shall have effect with respect to certain circumstances in which obligations imposed by subsections (1) and (2) are to be treated as not discharged.

(6) In the case of a person who is a director or secretary of a company at the time when this section comes into operation subsection (2) shall not require the notification by him of the occurrence of an event before that time; and that subsection shall not require the notification by a person of the occurrence of an event whose occurrence comes to his knowledge after he has ceased to be a director or secretary.

(7) A person who fails to fulfil, within the proper period, an obligation to which he is subject by virtue of subsection (1) or (2) shall be guilty of an offence.

(8) An obligation imposed by this section shall be treated as not being fulfilled unless the notice by means of which it purports to be fulfilled is expressed to be given in fulfilment of that obligation.

(9) This section applies to shadow directors as to directors, but the making of a notification by a person under this section shall not, in itself, be proof that the person making the notification is a shadow director.

(10) Nothing in this section shall operate so as to impose an obligation with respect to shares in a body corporate which is the wholly owned subsidiary of another body corporate; and for this purpose a body corporate shall be deemed to be the wholly owned subsidiary of another if it has no members but that other and that other's wholly owned subsidiaries and its or their nominees.

(11) This section and sections 54, 56, 57 and 59 shall have effect in place of section 190 of the Principal Act and of so much of section 193 of that Act as relates to section 190, and that section and so much of section 193 as relates thereto shall, accordingly, cease to have effect.

Definitions

'*body corporate*': Companies Act, 1963, section 2 (3).

'*company*': Companies Act, 1963, section 2.

'*debentures*': Companies Act, 1963, section 2.

'*director*': Companies Act, 1963, section 2.

'*holding company*': Companies Act, 1963, section 155.

'*Principal Act*': Companies Act, 1990, section 3.

'*shadow directors*': Companies Act, 1990, section 3.

'*subsidiary*': Companies Act, 1963, section 155.

General Note

This section requires a director or secretary of a company to notify the company within five days of the coming into operation of this provision of the extent of his interest in shares or debentures of the company or any related company. Such a person must keep the company advised of the extent of his interest.

(1) The directors and secretary of any company (including private and unlimited companies) who have an interest in shares or debentures of the company or any other related company are required to notify their interest, and when a person becomes a director or secretary of such a company they must notify the company in writing of the subsistence of the interest, together with the number of shares and the class and/or amount of debentures. Section 54 below defines the nature of 'an interest' as one of any kind whatsoever, regardless of whether there are any restrictions or restraints attaching to it.

(2) A director or secretary of a company is required to make a notification to the company of certain events and the date on which they occur, namely:

(*a*) any event the consequence of which is that the person becomes or ceases to be interested in shares or debentures of the company or a related company;

(*b*) the entering into a contract to sell any such shares or debentures;

(*c*) the assignment of a right granted to him by the company to subscribe for shares or debentures;

(*d*) the grant to him by a related company of a right to subscribe for shares or debentures or the assignment of right or exercise of right in such related company.

Therefore, if a director or secretary receives an interest in shares or debentures in the company or related company under a will, for example, he would be obliged to notify the company.

(3) This subsection provides that the definition of an interest in section 54 will apply to this section.

(4) The notice period in section 55 applies·to this section. In section 54 it is provided that notice must be given within five days of the occurrence of the event.

(5) The provisions of section 57 apply to this section: that is, that the obligation to notify will not be regarded as being discharged in the absence of inclusion of the price paid or received for the shares or debentures, assignment of shares, right to subscribe for shares or debentures etc. in the notice to the company.

(6) When the section comes into operation a person who is a director or secretary is not required to give notice of an event that occurred before the date on which the section came into operation. Furthermore, a person is not required to give notification of an event if its occurrence came into his knowledge after he ceased to be a director or secretary.

(7) If a person does not comply with the provisions of subsection (1) or (2) he will be guilty of an offence. The penalties that can be imposed on conviction are set out in section 240.

(8) Notice is not regarded as being fulfilled unless the notice by means of which it purports to be fulfilled is expressed as the fulfilment of the obligation.

(9) This section applies to shadow directors, except that the making of a notification will not be itself proof that a person is a shadow director.

(10) The provisions do not apply to wholly owned subsidiaries of parent companies.

(11) This section, together with sections 54, 56, 57, and 59, has effect in place of section 190 of the Companies Act, 1963, concerning the register of directors' shareholdings as well as the obligations to make such disclosure under section 193 of that Act.

SECTION 54
Nature of an interest within section 53.

(1) The provisions of this section shall apply in determining for the purposes of section 53 whether a person has an interest in shares or debentures.

(2) Any reference to an interest in shares or debentures shall be read as including a reference to any interest of any kind whatsoever in shares or debentures; and accordingly there shall be disregarded any restraints or restrictions to which the exercise of any right attached to the interest is or may be subject.

(3) Where any property is held on trust and any interest in shares or debentures is comprised in that property, any beneficiary of that trust who, apart from this subsection, does not have an interest in the shares or debentures shall be taken to have such an interest; but this subsection is without prejudice to the following provisions of this section.

(4) A person shall be taken to have an interest in shares or debentures if—

(a) he enters into a contract for their purchase by him (whether for cash or other consideration); or

(b) not being the registered holder, he is entitled to exercise any right conferred by the holding of those shares or debentures or is entitled to control the exercise of any such right.

(5) A person shall be taken to be interested in shares or debentures if a body corporate is interested in them and—

(*a*) that body corporate or its directors are accustomed·to act in accordance with his directions or instructions; or

(*b*) he is entitled to exercise or control the exercise of one-third or more of the voting power at general meetings of that body corporate.

(6) Where a person is entitled to exercise or control the exercise of one-third or more of the voting power at general meetings of a body corporate and that body corporate is entitled to exercise or control the exercise of any of the voting power at general meetings of another body corporate (the "relevant voting power"), then, for the purposes of subsection (5) (*b*), the relevant voting power shall be taken to be exercisable by that person.

(7) A person shall be taken to have an interest in shares or debentures if, otherwise than by virtue of having an interest under a trust—

(*a*) he has a right to call for delivery of the shares or debentures to himself or to his order; or

(*b*) he has a right to acquire an interest in shares or debentures or is under an obligation to take an interest in shares or debentures;

whether in any case the right or obligation is conditional or absolute.

(8) For the purposes of subsection (4) (*b*) a person shall be taken to be entitled to exercise or control the exercise of any right conferred by the holding of shares or debentures if he has a right (whether subject to conditions or not) the exercise of which would make him so entitled or is under an obligation (whether so subject or not) the fulfilment of which would make him so entitled.

(9) A person shall not by virtue of subsection (4) (*b*) be taken to be interested in any shares or debentures by reason only that he has been appointed a proxy to vote at a specified meeting of a company or of any class of its members and at any adjournment of that meeting or has been appointed by a body corporate to act as its representative at any meeting of a company or of any class of its members.

(10) Without prejudice to subsection (2), rights or obligations to subscribe for any shares or debentures shall not be taken for the purposes of subsection (7) to be rights to acquire, or obligations to take, any interest in shares or debentures.

(11) Where persons have a joint interest each of them shall be deemed to have that interest.

(12) It is immaterial that shares or debentures in which a person has an interest are unidentifiable.

(13) Delivery to a person's order of shares or debentures in fulfilment of a contract for the purchase thereof by him or in satisfaction of a right of his to call for delivery thereof, or failure to deliver shares or debentures in accordance with the terms of such a contract or on which such a right falls to be satisfied, shall be deemed to constitute an event in consequence of the occurrence of which he ceases to be interested in them, and so shall the lapse of a person's right to call for delivery of shares or debentures.

Definitions

'body corporate': Companies Act, 1963, section 2 (3).

'debentures': Companies Act, 1963, section 2.
'director': Companies Act, 1963, section 2.
'relevant voting power': Companies Act, 1990, section 54 (6).
'share': Companies Act, 1963, section 2.

General Note

This section sets out the circumstances in which a person is regarded as having an interest in shares for the purposes of section 54 of the Act.

(1) The provisions of this section will apply in determining whether in section 53 a person has an interest in shares or debentures.

(2) Any reference to an interest in shares or debentures will include a reference to any interest of any kind whatsoever, disregarding any restraints or restrictions to which the exercise of any right attached to the interest is or may be subject.

(3) Where any of the property is held on trust and any interest in shares or debentures is comprised in that property, any beneficiary who apart from this subsection has not got an interest in such shares or debentures will be regarded as having an interest and be subject to the provisions of the section. This basically re-establishes the principle that where shares in a company are held in some kind of trust and a director or secretary is the beneficiary of the trust concerned, he will in general be deemed to have an interest for the purposes of this chapter of the Act.

(4) A person is regarded as having an interest in shares or debentures if he enters into a contract for their purchase or, not being the registered holder, is entitled to exercise any right conferred by the holding or is entitled to control the exercise of any such right. This would apply to a person who has a beneficial interest but not a legal interest in the shares or debentures.

(5) A person is regarded as having an interest in shares or debentures if a body corporate is interested in them and that body corporate or its directors or secretary are accustomed to taking that person's instructions or directions, or if that person is entitled to exercise or control the exercise of one-third or more of the voting power at general meetings of that body corporate.

(6) Where a person controls or exercises control over one-third or more of the voting power in a body corporate and that body

corporate controls or exercises control over another company, that person is deemed to control that latter company.

(7) A person will be regarded as having an interest in shares or debentures if he has a right to call for the delivery of the shares or debentures to himself or his order or where he has the right to acquire an interest in shares or debentures or is under an obligation to take such an interest. Subsection (7) (*a*) would apply in a case where a person has a beneficial interest in shares or debentures and the legal interest is vested in some other person.

(8) A person is regarded as being entitled to exercise control of any right conferred by the holding of shares or debentures if he has a right which if exercised would make him entitled or is under an obligation which if fulfilled would make him entitled.

(9) The fact that a person is appointed a proxy to vote or be a representative at a specified meeting does not mean that he has an interest in shares or debentures.

(10) The right or obligation to subscribe for shares or debentures does not necessarily mean that they are rights or obligations within the meaning of subsection (7) above.

(11) Each person having a joint interest is regarded as having an interest for the purposes of the section.

(12) It is immaterial whether the shares or debentures in which the person has an interest are identifiable.

(13) A person is regarded as ceasing to have an interest in shares on the delivery of shares in fulfilment of a contract or failure to deliver shares on the terms of the contract or on which such a right falls to be satisfied.

SECTION 55
Interests to be disregarded.

(1) The following interests shall be disregarded for the purposes of section 54 and sections 56 to 58—

(*a*) where property is held on trust and an interest in shares or debentures is comprised in that property, an interest in reversion or remainder or of a bare trustee and any discretionary interest;

(*b*) an interest of a person subsisting by virtue of—
(i) his holding units in—
(I) a registered unit trust scheme within the meaning of section 3 of the Unit Trusts Act, 1972;
(II) a unit trust to which section 31 of the Capital Gains Tax Act, 1975, as amended by section 34 of the Finance Act, 1977 relates;

       (III) an undertaking for collective investment in transferable securities, within the meaning of the European Communities (Undertakings for Collective Investment in Transferable Securities) Regulations, 1989 (S.I. No. 78 of 1989);

      (ii) a scheme made under section 46 of the Charities Act, 1961;

(c) an interest for the life of himself or another of a person under a settlement in the case of which the property comprised in the settlement consists of or includes shares or debentures, and the conditions mentioned in subsection (3) are satisfied;

(d) an interest in shares or debentures held by a member of a recognised stock exchange carrying on business as a stockbroker which is held by way of security only for the purposes of a transaction entered into by the person or body concerned in the ordinary course of business of such person or body;

(e) such interests, or interests of such a class, as may be prescribed for the purposes of this paragraph by regulations made by the Minister.

(2) A person shall not by virtue of section 54 (4) (b) be taken to be interested in shares or debentures by reason only that he has been appointed a proxy to vote at a specified meeting of a company or of any class of its members and at any adjournment of that meeting, or has been appointed by a body corporate to act as its representative at any meeting of a company or of any class of its members.

(3) The conditions referred to in subsection (1) (c) are, in relation to a settlement—

(a) that it is irrevocable, and

(b) that the settlor (within the meaning of section 96 of the Income Tax Act, 1967) has no interest in any income arising under, or property comprised in, the settlement.

Definitions

'body corporate': Companies Act, 1963, section 2 (3).

'debenture': Companies Act, 1963, section 2.

'Minister': Companies Act, 1990, section 3.

'prescribe': Companies Act, 1990, section 3.

'recognised stock exchange': Companies Act, 1990, section 3.

'share': Companies Act, 1963, section 2.

General Note

This section lists the interests that are to be disregarded for the purposes of disclosure.

(1) Certain interests can be disregarded for the purposes of disclosure, including:

- property held on trust;
- units held in a unit trust;
- an interest for life under a settlement;

- an interest in shares or debentures held by a member of a recognised stock exchange such as a stockbroker and that is held by way of security for the purpose of the transaction.

(2) If a person is appointed a proxy only to attend and vote at meetings he will not be deemed to have an interest.

(3) An interest for life in a settlement must contain certain conditions, such as that it must be irrevocable and that the settlor has no interest in any income arising under the settlement.

SECTION 56
Periods within which obligations under section 53 must be discharged.

(1) An obligation imposed on a person by section 53 (1) to notify an interest must, if he knows of the existence of the interest on the relevant day (that is to say, in a case in which he is a director or secretary at the beginning of the day on which that section comes into operation, the last previous day, and, in a case in which he thereafter becomes a director or secretary, the day on which he becomes it), be fulfilled before the expiration of the period of five days beginning with the day next following the relevant day; otherwise it must be fulfilled before the expiration of the period of five days beginning with the day next following that on which the existence of the interest comes to his knowledge.

(2) An obligation imposed on a person by section 53 (2) to notify the occurrence of an event must, if at the time at which the event occurs he knows of its occurrence, be fulfilled before the expiration of the period of five days beginning with the day next following that on which it occurs; otherwise, it must be fulfilled before the expiration of the period of five days beginning with the day next following that on which the occurrence of the event comes to his knowledge.

Definitions
'director': Companies Act, 1963, section 2.
'relevant day': Companies Act, 1990, section 56.

General Note
This section sets out the periods within which interests must be notified.

(1) If a person knows of the existence of an interest on the relevant day, i.e. the day before the date on which the section comes into operation, he is obliged to notify his interest within five days of the relevant day.

(2) Notification must be made within five days following the relevant day of the occurrence of an event, if at the time of the event the person knows of its occurrence and the fact that it gives rise to an obligation.

SECTION 57
Circumstances in which obligation under section 53 is not discharged.

(1) Where an event of whose occurrence a director or secretary is, by virtue of section 53 (2) (*a*), under obligation to notify a company consists of his entering into a contract for the purchase by him of shares or debentures, the obligation shall be taken not to be discharged in the absence of inclusion in the notice of a statement of the price to be paid by him under the contract, and an obligation imposed on a director or secretary by virtue of section 53 (2) (*b*) shall be taken not to be discharged in the absence of inclusion in the notice of the price to be received by him under the contract.

(2) An obligation imposed on a director or secretary by virtue of section 53 (2) (*c*) to notify a company shall be taken not to be discharged in the absence of inclusion in the notice of a statement of the consideration for the assignment (or, if it be the case that there is no consideration, that fact), and where an event of whose occurrence a director is, by virtue of section 53 (2) (*d*), under obligation to notify a company consists in his assigning a right, the obligation shall be taken not to be discharged in the absence of inclusion in the notice of a similar statement.

(3) Where an event of whose occurrence a director or secretary is, by virtue of section 53 (2) (*d*), under obligation to notify a company consists in the grant to him of a right to subscribe for shares or debentures, the obligation shall not be taken to be discharged in the absence of inclusion in the notice of a statement of—

(*a*) the date on which the right was granted,
(*b*) the period during which or time at which the right is exercisable,
(*c*) the consideration for the grant (or, if it be the case that there is no consideration, that fact), and
(*d*) the price to be paid for the shares or debentures.

(4) Where an event of whose occurrence a director or secretary is, by virtue of section 53 (2) (*d*), under obligation to notify a company consists in the exercise of a right granted to him to subscribe for shares or debentures, the obligation shall be taken not to be discharged in the absence of inclusion in the notice of a statement of—

(*a*) the number of shares or amount of debentures in respect of which the right was exercised, and
(*b*) if it be the case that they were registered in his name, that fact, and, if not, the name or names of the person or persons in whose name or names they were registered,

together (if they were registered in the names of two persons or more) with the number or amount thereof registered in the name of each of them.

(5) For the purposes of this section any reference, however expressed, to any price paid, given or received in respect of any interest in shares or debentures shall be construed as including a reference to any consideration other than money given or received in respect of any such interest.

Definitions

'*company*': Companies Act, 1963, section 2.
'*debenture*': Companies Act, 1963, section 2.
'*director*': Companies Act, 1963, section 2.
'*share*': Companies Act, 1963, section 2.

General Note

Section 57 provides that the notification of a director's or secretary's interest must include details of the price paid or received for shares or debentures or assignment of shares or a right to subscribe for shares or debentures.

(1) The obligation to notify an interest will not be discharged unless the price paid or received is disclosed on the purchase or sale of shares or debentures.

(2) The obligation to notify an interest will not be discharged unless the notice includes the consideration or otherwise for the assignment of the right.

(3) The obligation to notify an interest will not be discharged unless the notice of the grant of the right to subscribe for shares or debentures includes certain information, namely:
(*a*) the date on which the right was granted;
(*b*) the period during which the right may be exercised;
(*c*) the consideration for the grant, if any;
(*d*) the price to be paid for the shares or debentures.

(4) The obligation to notify an interest exercising a right to subscribe for shares or debentures will not be discharged unless the notice includes the number of shares or amount of debentures in respect of which the right was exercised, together with details of the name of the person in whose name they were registered.

(5) Any reference to price paid includes any consideration other than money given or received in connection with any such interest.

SECTION 58
Other provisions relating to notification.

(1) Where a person authorises any other person ("the agent") to acquire or dispose of, on his behalf, interests in shares in, or debentures of, a company, he shall secure that the agent notifies him immediately of acquisitions or disposals of interests in such shares or debentures effected by the agent which will or may give rise to any obligation on his part to make a notification under this Chapter with respect to his interest in those shares or debentures.

(2) An obligation to make any notification imposed on any person by this Chapter shall be treated as not being fulfilled unless the notice by means of which it purports to be fulfilled identifies him and gives his address.

(3) Where a person fails to fulfil, within the proper period, an obligation to which he is subject by virtue of section 53, no right or interest of any kind whatsoever in respect of the shares or debentures concerned shall be enforceable by him, whether directly or indirectly, by action or legal proceeding.

(4) Where any right or interest is restricted under subsection (3), any person in default under that subsection or any other person affected by such restriction may apply to the court for relief against a disability imposed by or arising out of subsection (3) and the court on being satisfied that the default was accidental, or due to inadvertence, or some other sufficient cause, or that on other grounds it is just and equitable to grant relief, may grant such relief either generally, or as respects any particular right or interest on such terms and conditions as it sees fit.

(5) Where an applicant for relief under subsection (4) is a person referred to in subsection (3), the court may not grant such relief if it appears that the default has arisen as a result of any deliberate act or omission on the part of the applicant.

(6) Subsection (3) shall not apply to an obligation relating to a person ceasing to be interested in shares in, or debentures of, a company.

(7) A person who fails without reasonable excuse to comply with subsection (1) shall be guilty of an offence.

Definitions
'agent': Companies Act, 1990, section 57.
'company': Companies Act, 1963, section 2.
'court': Companies Act, 1990, section 235.
'debentures': Companies Act, 1963, section 2.
'shares': Companies Act, 1963, section 2.

General Note
The purpose of this section is to cover the position on notification of interests when some other authorised person acquires or disposes of the shares or debentures.

(1) Where an agent (an authorised person) acquires or disposes on behalf of a director or secretary, that person must ensure that he is notified by the agent immediately the transaction occurs.

(2) The obligation to make a notification will not be fulfilled unless the notice identifies the person and gives the full address.

(3) If the obligation to notify is not fulfilled, no right or interest is enforceable directly or indirectly in any legal action or proceeding.

(4) Any person in default and any other person who may be affected by the default may apply to the court for relief, which may be granted on such terms and conditions as the court thinks fit. The grounds for seeking relief include accidental default, due to inadvertence or some other sufficient cause, where it is considered just and equitable.

(5) If the court is of the view that the omission was the result of a deliberate act or omission, it may not grant the relief.

(6) Where a person ceases to have an interest in shares or debentures, as in the non-enforceability of an interest as a result of legal proceedings, subsection (3) will not apply.

(7) A person who fails without reasonable excuse to comply with subsection (1) will be guilty of an offence. The penalties that can be imposed on conviction are set out in section 240.

SECTION 59

Register of interests.

(1) Every company shall keep a register for the purposes of section 53.

(2) Whenever the company receives information from a director or secretary in consequence of the fulfilment of an obligation imposed on him by that section, the company shall enter in the register, against the name of that person, that information and the date of the entry.

(3) Every company shall, whenever it grants to a director or secretary a right to subscribe for shares in, or debentures of, the company, enter in the register against his name—

(*a*) the date on which the right is granted,
(*b*) the period during which or time at which it is exercisable,
(*c*) the consideration for the grant (or, if it be the case that there is no consideration, that fact), and
(*d*) the description of shares or debentures involved and the number or amount thereof, and the price to be paid therefor.

(4) Whenever such a right as is mentioned in subsection (3) is exercised by a director or secretary, the company shall enter in the said register against his name that fact (identifying the right), the number or amount of shares or debentures in respect of which it is exercised and, if it be the case that they were registered in his name, that fact, and, if not, the name or names of the person or persons in whose name or names they were registered, together (if they were registered in the names of two persons or more) with the number or amount thereof registered in the name of each of them.

(5) This section applies to shadow directors as to directors.

Definitions

'*company*': Companies Act, 1963, section 2.
'*debentures*': Companies Act, 1963, section 2.
'*director*': Companies Act, 1963, section 2.
'*shadow directors*': Companies Act, 1990, section 3.
'*shares*': Companies Act, 1963, section 2.

General Note

This section provides that interests notified to the company by directors or secretaries must be recorded by the company in a register kept for this purpose, called a register of interests.

(1) Every company is required to keep a register of interests.

(2) When the company receives a notification of an interest from a director or secretary it must enter the name of that person, the information and the date of entry in the register of interests.

(3) When a company grants a right to subscribe for shares or debentures it must enter in the register of interests against that person's name
(*a*) the date the right is granted,
(*b*) the period or time during which it is exercisable,
(*c*) the consideration for the grant, if any, and
(*d*) the description and number of shares or debentures involved and the price to be paid for the shares or debentures.

(4) Whenever a right is exercised for the subscription of shares or debentures the company must enter this fact in the register together with the number of shares or amount of debentures involved.

(5) The reference to directors includes shadow directors.

SECTION 60

Provisions relating to register.

(1) The register to be kept under section 59 shall be so made up that the entries therein against the several names inscribed therein appear in chronological order.

(2) An obligation imposed by section 59 (2) to (4) shall be fulfilled before the expiration of the period of 3 days beginning with the day next following that on which it arises.

(3) The nature and extent of an interest recorded in the said register of a director or secretary in any shares or debentures shall, if he so requires, be recorded in the said register.

(4) The company shall not, by virtue of anything done for the purposes of this section, be affected with notice of, or put upon inquiry as to, the rights of any person in relation to any shares or debentures.

(5) The said register shall—

(*a*) if the company's register of members is kept at its registered office, be kept there;
(*b*) if the company's register of members is not so kept, be kept at the company's registered office or at the place where its register of members is kept;

and shall during business hours (subject to such reasonable restrictions as the company in general meeting may impose, so that not less than two hours in each day be allowed for inspection) be open to the inspection of any member of the company without charge and of any other person on payment of 30p or such less sum as the company may prescribe for each inspection.

(6) The company shall send notice to the registrar of companies of the place where the said register is kept and of any change in that place, save in a case in which it has at all times been kept at its registered office.

(7) Unless the said register is in such a form as to constitute in itself an index, the company shall keep an index of the names entered therein which shall—

(*a*) in respect of each name, contain a sufficient indication to enable the information inscribed against it to be readily found; and

(*b*) be kept at the same place as the said register;

and the company shall, within 14 days after the date on which a name is entered in the said register, make any necessary alteration in the index.

(8) Any member of the company or other person may require a copy of the said register, or of any part thereof, on payment of 15p or such less sum as the company may prescribe, for every hundred words or fractional part thereof required to be copied.

The company shall cause any copy so required by any person to be sent to that person within the period of 10 days beginning with the day next following that on which the requirement is received by the company.

(9) The said register shall also be and remain open and accessible to any person attending the company's annual general meeting at least one quarter hour before the appointed time for the commencement of the meeting and during the continuance of the meeting.

(10) If default is made in compliance with subsection (9), the company and every officer of the company who is in default shall be guilty of an offence and shall be liable to a fine not exceeding £1,000; and if default is made for 14 days in complying with subsection (6) the company and every officer of the company who is in default shall be liable to a fine not exceeding £1,000; and if default is made in complying with section 59 or with subsection (1), (2) or (7) of this section or if an inspection required under this section is refused or any copy required thereunder is not sent within the proper period the company and every officer of the company who is in default shall be liable to a fine not exceeding £1,000.

(11) In the case of a refusal of an inspection required under this section of the said register, the court may by order compel an immediate inspection thereof; and in the case of a failure to send within the proper period a copy required under this section, the court may by order direct that the copy required shall be sent to the person requiring it.

Definitions

'*company*': Companies Act, 1963, section 2.

'*court*': Companies Act, 1990, section 235.

'*debentures*': Companies Act, 1963, section 2.

'*director*': Companies Act, 1963, section 2.

'*officer*': Companies Act, 1963, section 2.

'*register*': Companies Act, 1990, section 55.

'*registrar of companies*': Companies Act, 1963, section 2.
'*shares*': Companies Act, 1963, section 2.

General Note

This section sets out the detailed rules concerning the keeping of the register of interests and of its opening to inspection by any person.

(1) The entries must be made in chronological order.

(2) The obligation to make an entry in the register of interests is to be fulfilled within a period of three days from the date on which the obligation to register arises.

(3) The nature and extent of the interest is to be recorded if so required.

(4) The company will not be regarded as being put on notice or put upon enquiry as to the rights of any person concerning the shares or debentures.

(5) The register must be kept at the company's registered office or such place as the register of members is kept and must be made available for inspection during normal business hours. There is no charge for inspection by a member, but a charge not exceeding 30p may be levied on anyone else seeking to inspect the register.

(6) The Registrar of Companies is to be notified as to where the register of interests is kept and of any change in that place, except when it is kept at all times at the company's registered office.

(7) A separate index is to be maintained of the names entered in the register, unless the register itself is in a form that constitutes an index. The company must update the index within fourteen days of any change being made to the register.

(8) Any person, including shareholders and members of the public, may obtain a copy of the register on the payment of not more than 15p per hundred words or part thereof, and the copy is to be provided to the person within ten days following the date of receipt of the request.

(9) The register of interests must remain open for inspection by any person attending the company's annual general meeting for fifteen minutes before the commencement of the meeting and for the duration of the meeting.

(10) If there is default in compliance with subsection (9) the company and every officer in the company who is in default will be guilty of an offence and liable to a fine not exceeding £1,000.

(11) If the company refuses a person permission to inspect a register, the High Court may make an order compelling the company to grant immediate inspection or provision of a copy of the register, as the case may be.

SECTION 61
Removal of entries from register.

(1) A company may remove an entry against a person's name from the register of interests in shares and debentures kept under section 59 if more than 6 years has elapsed since the date of the entry being made, and either—

(a) that entry recorded the fact that the person in question has ceased to have an interest notifiable under this Chapter in shares in, or debentures of, the company, or

(b) it has been superseded by a later entry made under the said section 59 against the same person's name;

and in a case within paragraph (a) the company may also remove that person's name from the register.

(2) Where a name is removed from a company's register of interests in shares or debentures in pursuance of subsection (1), the company shall within 14 days of the date of that removal make any necessary alterations in any associated index.

(3) If default is made in complying with subsection (2), the company and every officer of it who is in default shall be guilty of an offence and liable to a fine.

Definitions

'company': Companies Act, 1963, section 2.

'debenture': Companies Act, 1963, section 2.

'officer': Companies Act, 1963, section 2.

'register of interests': Companies Act, 1990, section 58.

'share': Companies Act, 1963, section 2.

General Note

This section concerns the removal of entries from the register of interests, and sets out when such entries may be removed.

(1) A company may remove an entry from the register of interests if more than six years has elapsed from the date of the entry in the register and either the company has recorded the fact that the person ceased to have a notifiable interest in the company or it has been superseded by a later entry.

(2) Where a name has been removed from the register of interests the necessary alterations must be made to the index.

(3) For failing to comply with this section a company and every officer will be guilty of an offence and liable to a fine not exceeding £1,000 under section 240.

SECTION 62
Entries, when not to be removed.

(1) Entries in a company's register of interests in shares and debentures under this Chapter shall not be deleted except in accordance with section 61.

(2) If an entry is deleted from a company's register of interests in shares in contravention of subsection (1), the company shall restore that entry to the register as soon as is reasonable and practicable.

(3) If default is made in complying with subsection (1) or (2), the company and every officer of it who is in default shall be guilty of an offence and liable to a fine.

Definitions

'company': Companies Act, 1963, section 2.
'debenture': Companies Act, 1963, section 2.
'officer': Companies Act, 1963, section 2.
'register of interests': Companies Act, 1990, section 59.
'share': Companies Act, 1963, section 2.

General Note

This section stipulates that no entry may be deleted from the register of interests except in accordance with the provisions of section 61.

(1) No entry may be deleted from the register of interests except in accordance with the provisions of section 61.

(2) If an entry is removed in contravention of subsection (1) the company must restore the entry as soon as is reasonable and practicable.

(3) In the event of a default in complying with this section the company and every officer who is in default will be guilty of an offence and liable to a fine under section 240.

SECTION 63
Disclosure of interests in directors' report

(1) Subject to subsection (2), the directors' report or the notes to the company's accounts in respect of a financial year shall, as respects each person who, at the end of that year, was a director of the company, state—

(a) whether or not he was, at the end of that year, interested in shares in, or debentures of, the company or any other body corporate being the company's subsidiary or holding company or a subsidiary of the company's holding company;

(*b*) if he was so interested—

(i) the number and amount of shares in, and debentures of, each body (specifying it) in which he was then interested,

(ii) whether or not he was, at the beginning of that year (or, if he was not then a director, when he became a director), interested in shares in, or debentures of, the company or any other such body corporate, and,

(iii) if he was, the number and amount of shares in, and debentures of, each body (specifying it) in which he was interested at the beginning of that year or, as the case may be, when he became a director.

(2) The reference in subsection (1) to the directors' report and the notes to the company's accounts are references to the report and notes respectively which are required by virtue of the Companies (Amendment) Act, 1986 to be annexed to the Annual Return and where a company does not annex the report of the directors, as permitted by section 10 (2) of the aforementioned Act, the information required in subsection (1) shall be contained in the notes to the company's accounts.

(3) The references in subsection (1) to the time when a person became a director shall, in the case of a person who became a director on more than one occasion, be construed as referring to the time when he first became a director.

(4) For the purposes of this section "the directors' report" means the report by the directors of a company which, by section 158 (1) of the Principal Act, is required to be attached to every balance sheet of the company.

(5) The information required by subsection (1) to be given in respect of the directors of the company shall also be given in respect of the person who was the secretary of the company at the end of the financial year concerned.

Definitions

'body corporate': Companies Act, 1963, section 2 (3).

'company': Companies Act, 1963, section 2.

'debentures': Companies Act, 1963, section 2.

'director': Companies Act, 1963, section 2.

'directors' report': Companies Act, 1963, section 158.

'financial year': Companies Act, 1963, section 2.

'holding company': Companies Act, 1963, section 155.

'Principal Act': Companies Act, 1990, section 3.

'register of interests': Companies Act, 1990, section 59.

'shares': Companies Act, 1963, section 2.

'subsidiary': Companies Act, 1963, section 155.

General Note

This section requires a company to disclose in its annual accounts the extent of the interests of each director and secretary in the shares and debentures of the company.

A small company under section 10 of the Companies (Amendment) Act, 1986, is not required to publish a directors' report. A small company could thus avoid disclosure, and accordingly this section provides that the disclosure be included in the notes to the accounts.

(1) The directors' report or note to the accounts must state the number of shares or debentures held by each director and the secretary in the company or in its holding company or any of its subsidiary companies at the end of the financial year. If a person was interested, that person's holding at the beginning of the financial year, or at the time the person was appointed a director or secretary, must also be disclosed.

(2) Where a company does not annex its directors' report to the annual return under the Companies (Amendment) Act, 1986, it must include a note to the accounts of the interests of the directors. The purpose of this provision is to ensure that this section will apply equally to small companies as to medium and large companies.

(3) Where a person was a director of a company on more than one occasion, any reference made will be to the time when the person was first appointed a director of the company.

(4) The reference in this section to the 'directors' report' is to the report required to be prepared under section 158 of the Companies Act, 1963.

(5) For the purpose of this section the reference to a 'director' is to be construed as including the secretary.

SECTION 64

Extension of section 53 to spouses and children.

(1) For the purposes of section 53—

(a) an interest of the spouse of a director or secretary of a company (not being himself or herself a director or secretary thereof) in shares or debentures shall be treated as being the director's or secretary's interest, and

(b) the same applies to an interest of a minor child of a director or secretary of a company (not being himself or herself a director or secretary thereof) in shares or debentures.

(2) For those purposes—

(a) a contract, assignment or right of subscription entered into, exercised or made by, or grant made to, the spouse of a director or secretary of a company (not being himself or herself a director or secretary thereof) shall be treated as having been entered into, exercised or made by, or, as the case may be, as having been made to, the director or secretary, and (*b*) the same applies to a contract, assignment or right of subscription entered into, exercised or made by, or grant made to, a minor child of a director or secretary of a company (not being himself or herself a director or secretary thereof).

(3) A director or secretary of a company shall be under obligation to notify the company in writing of the occurrence, while he or she is director or secretary, of either of the following events, namely—

(*a*) the grant to his or her spouse or minor child by the company, of a right to subscribe for shares in, or debentures of, the company; and
(*b*) the exercise by the spouse or minor child of such a right as aforesaid granted by the company to the spouse or child.

(4) In a notice given to the company under subsection (3) there shall be stated—

(*a*) in the case of the grant of a right, the like information as is required by section 53 to be stated by the director or secretary on the grant to him by another body corporate of a right to subscribe for shares in, or debentures of, that other body corporate, and
(*b*) in the case of the exercise of a right, the like information as is required by that section to be stated by the director or secretary on the exercise of a right granted to him by another body corporate to subscribe for shares in, or debentures of, that other body corporate.

(5) An obligation imposed by subsection (3) on a director or secretary must be fulfilled by him before the expiration of the period of 5 days beginning with the day next folowing that on which the occurrence of the event that gives rise to it comes to his knowledge.

(6) A person who fails to fulfil, within the proper period, an obligation to which he is subject under subsection (3) shall be guilty of an offence.

(7) The provisions set out in sections 54 and 55 shall have effect for the interpretation of, and otherwise in relation to, subsections (1) and (2), and subsections (8) and (9) of section 53 shall, with any requisite modification, have effect for the purposes of this section as they have effect for the purposes of that section.

(8) For the purposes of section 59 an obligation imposed on a director or secretary by this section shall be treated as if imposed by section 53.

Definitions

'*body corporate*': Companies Act, 1963, section 2 (3).

'*company*': Companies Act, 1963, section 2.

'*debenture*': Companies Act, 1963, section 2.

'*director*': Companies Act, 1963, section 2.

'*minor child*': Age of Minority Act, 1963, section 2.

'*share*': Companies Act, 1963, section 2.

General Note

This section extends the application of the notification provisions by providing that any interest of the spouse or minor child of a director or secretary will be treated as being that director's or secretary's interest. Where the company grants such a person rights to subscribe for shares or debentures or if the rights are exercised, the director or secretary concerned must notify the company within five days of such event.

(1) The interest of a spouse or minor child (i.e. a person of not more than eighteen years of age) will be deemed to be an interest of the director or secretary.

(2) A contract, assignment or right of subscription entered into or exercised by a spouse or minor child of a director or secretary will be deemed to be an interest of the director or secretary.

(3) A director or secretary is obliged to notify the company in writing on the occurrence of a grant or exercise of a right to subscribe for shares or debentures by a spouse or minor child.

(4) There is a requirement to provide similar information as required by section 53 of this Act (Obligation by director or secretary to notify their interest in shares or debentures).

(5) The obligation to notify the interests of a spouse or minor child of a director or secretary must be fulfilled within five days from the date on which the occurrence came to his knowledge.

(6) A person who fails to fulfil the notification obligation or recklessly makes a false statement to the company will be guilty of an offence. The penalty on conviction of an offence is set out in section 240.

(7) The provisions in section 54 and 55 of this Act as to the nature of an interest apply to this section.

(8) The obligations imposed on a director or secretary will be treated as if they were imposed by section 59 of this Act (Obligation of director or secretary to notify interests in shares or debentures of a company).

SECTION 65
Duty of company to notify stock exchange.

(1) Whenever a company in the case of whose shares or debentures dealing facilities are provided by a recognised stock exchange is notified of any matter by a director or secretary in consequence of the fulfilment of an obligation imposed on him by section 53 or 64, and that matter relates to shares or debentures for which such dealing facilities are provided, the company shall be under an obligation to notify that stock exchange of that matter; and the stock exchange may publish, in such manner as it may determine, any information received by it under this subsection.

(2) An obligation imposed by subsection (1) must be fulfilled before the end of the day next following that on which it arises.

(3) If default is made in complying with this section, the company and every officer of the company who is in default shall be guilty of an offence.

Definitions

'*company*': Companies Act, 1963, section 2.
'*debenture*': Companies Act, 1963, section 2.
'*officer*': Companies Act, 1963, section 2.
'*publish*': Companies (Amendment) Act, 1986, section 19.
'*recognised stock exchange*': Companies Act, 1990, section 3.
'*share*': Companies Act, 1963, section 2.

General Note

(1) This section provides that where a company listed on a stock exchange is notified by a director or secretary of any matter relating to listed shares or debentures, the stock exchange must be notified and may publish the information received.

(2) Any obligation imposed by this section must be fulfilled before the end of the day following that on which the obligation arose.

(3) If there is a default in complying with this section the company and every officer who is in default will be guilty of an offence. The penalty on conviction of an offence is set out in section 240. The phrase 'in the case of whose shares or debentures dealing facilities are provided by a recognised stock exchange' is used so as to include companies whose shares are quoted not only on the main stock exchange but also on the USM and Smaller Companies Market.

SECTION 66
Investigation of share dealing.

(1) If it appears to the Minister that there are circumstances suggesting that contraventions may have occurred, in relation to shares in, or debentures of, a company, of section 30, 53 or 64 (3) to (5) he may appoint one or more competent inspectors to carry out such investigations as are requisite to establish whether or not contraventions have occurred as aforesaid and to report the result of their investigations to the Minister.

(2) The appointment under this section of an inspector may limit the period to which his investigation is to extend or confine it to shares or debentures of a particular class or both.

(3) For the purposes of any investigation under this section, section 10 shall apply—

(a) with the substitution, for references to any other body corporate whose affairs are investigated by virtue of section 9, of a reference to any other body corporate which is, or has at any relevant time been, the company's subsidiary or holding company, and (*b*) with the necessary modification of the reference, in section 10 (5), to the affairs of the company or other body corporate, so, however, that it shall apply to members of a recognised stock exchange who are individuals and to officers (past as well as present) of members of such an exchange who are bodies corporate as it applies to officers of the company or of the other body corporate.

(4) The inspectors may, and, if so directed by the Minister, shall, make interim reports to the Minister, and, on the conclusion of the investigation, shall make a final report to the Minister.

(5) Any such report shall be written or printed, as the Minister may direct, and the Minister may cause it to be published.

(6) Sections 9, 16 to 18, 22, 23 (1) and 23 (3) shall, with any necessary modifications, apply for the purposes of this section.

(7) The expenses of an investigation under this section shall be defrayed by the Minister.

(8) Where a person is convicted of an offence on a prosecution instituted as a result of the investigation the High Court may, on the application of the Minister, order that person to pay the said expenses to such extent as the court may direct.

Definitions

'*body corporate*': Companies Act, 1963, section 2 (3).

'*company*': Companies Act, 1963, section 2.

'*debenture*': Companies Act, 1963, section 2.

'*holding company*': Companies Act, 1963, section 155.

'*Minister*': Companies Act, 1990, section 3.

'*officer*': Companies Act, 1963, section 2.

'*recognised stock exchange*': Companies Act, 1990, section 3.

'*share*': Companies Act, 1963, section 2.

'*subsidiary*': Companies Act, 1963, section 155.

General Note

This section empowers the Minister for Industry and Commerce to appoint inspectors to investigate alleged contraventions in dealing in shares or debentures.

(1) Where it appears to the Minister that there may have been a contravention of some of the provisions he may appoint inspectors to investigate whether contraventions have occurred. The contraventions may be in regard to substantial property transactions under section 30 of this Act or to the disclosure obligations of interests in shares or debentures under sections 53 and 64 of this Act.

(2) The time for which an inspector is appointed may be limited to a set period, and the investigation may be confined to a particular class of shares and/or debentures.

(3) In an investigation, the provisions of section 10 of this Act relating to the production of documents as evidence will apply. However, the production of documents will be limited to those relating to any holding company or subsidiary of the company and can apply to members of a recognised stock exchange who are shareholders and past and present officers of the company.

(4) The inspectors may, if directed, make interim reports to the Minister and on the conclusion of the investigation submit a final report to the Minister.

(5) The Minister may, at his option, publish the report. He is under no obligation in the legislation to do so. In practice it has not been the policy to publish any reports of investigations carried out by inspectors.

(6) Section 9 (giving the inspectors power to extend investigations), sections 16–18 (giving power to impose restrictions on shares or debentures and admissibility of certain evidence) and sections 22–23 (regarding the use of inspectors' reports as evidence) apply to this section. The provisions relating to the use of privileged information as set out in section 23 do not apply to this investigation.

(7–8) The cost of the investigation will be borne by the Minister. However, under subsection (8) if a person is convicted by the High Court on proceedings resulting from this investigation the Minister has the right to apply to the court to order that person to pay the expenses to such extent as may be directed by the court.

SECTION 67

Obligation of disclosure and the cases in which it may arise.

(1) Where a person either—

(a) to his knowledge acquires an interest in shares comprised in a public limited company's relevant share capital, or ceases to be interested in shares so comprised (whether or not retaining an interest in other shares so comprised), or

(b) becomes aware that he has acquired an interest in shares so comprised or that he has ceased to be interested in shares so comprised in which he was previously interested,

then, subject to the provisions of sections 68 to 79, he shall be under an obligation ("the obligation of disclosure") to make notification to the company of the interests which he has, or had, in its shares.

(2) In relation to a public limited company, "relevant share capital" means the company's issued share capital of a class carrying rights to vote in all circumstances at general meetings of the company and it is hereby declared for the avoidance of doubt that—

(a) where a company's relevant share capital is divided into different classes of shares, references in this Chapter to a percentage of the nominal value of its relevant share capital are to a percentage of the nominal value of the issued shares comprised in each of the classes taken separately, and

(b) the temporary suspension of voting rights in respect of shares comprised in issued share capital of a company of any such class does not affect the application of this Chapter in relation to interests in those or any other shares comprised in that class.

(3) Where, otherwise than in circumstances within subsection (1), a person—

(a) is aware at the time when it occurs of any change of circumstances affecting facts relevant to the application of the next following section to an existing interest of his in shares comprised in a company's share capital of any description, or

(b) otherwise becomes aware of any such facts (whether or not arising from any such change of circumstances),

then, subject to the provisions of sections 68 to 79, he shall be under the obligation of disclosure.

(4) The acquisition by any person of an interest in shares or debentures of a company registered in the State shall be deemed to be a consent by that person to the disclosure by him, his agents or intermediaries of any information required to be disclosed in relation to shares or debentures by the Companies Acts.

Definitions

'*company*': Companies Act, 1963, section 2.

'*debenture*': Companies Act, 1963, section 2.

'*obligation of disclosure*': Companies Act, 1990, section 67.

'*public limited company*': Companies (Amendment) Act, 1983, section 2.

'*relevant share capital*': Companies Act, 1990, section 67.

'*share*': Companies Act, 1963, section 2.

General Note

In general this section applies only to public limited companies. It sets out the basic notification requirements, and provides that the obligation to notify arises where a person is aware or becomes aware of any change of circumstances affecting any fact that is relevant to the application of the notification requirement.

(1) Where a person becomes aware that he has acquired an interest in shares or to his knowledge has acquired an interest in shares or for that matter has ceased to have an interest in shares (by way of disposal or otherwise) then he has an obligation to notify the

company of the interest he has or had in the shares. This will only apply to voting share capital (see subsection (2) below).

(2) The term 'relevant share capital' is defined, to provide that this is applicable only to a class of shares carrying voting rights in all circumstances in general meetings. Therefore it would be applicable to ordinary and preferred or deferred shares provided they confer the right to vote in all circumstances: hence shares with restricted or limited voting rights are not covered by this obligation. If a class of share is temporarily suspended it will apply as if the suspension had not taken place.

(3) A person is obliged to notify the company of a change in circumstances that alters the situation whereby shares do come within subsection (1) above or when he becomes aware of any such facts.

(4) The acquisition by any person of an interest in shares or debentures in a company will be regarded as a consent to disclosure by him, his agents or intermediaries of any information required to be disclosed under the Companies Acts.

SECTION 68
Interests to be disclosed.

(1) For the purposes of the obligation of disclosure, the interests to be taken into account are those in relevant share capital of the company concerned.

(2) A person has a notifiable interest at any time when he is interested in shares comprised in that share capital of an aggregate nominal value equal to or more than the percentage of the nominal value of that share capital which is for the time being the notifiable percentage.

(3) All facts relevant to determining whether a person has a notifiable interest at any time (or the percentage level of his interest) are taken to be what he knows the facts to be at that time.

(4) The obligation of disclosure arises under section 67 (1) or (3) where the person has a notifiable interest immediately after the relevant time, but did not have such an interest immediately before that time.

(5) The obligation also arises under section 67 (1) where—

(*a*) the person had a notifiable interest immediately before the relevant time, but does not have such an interest immediately after it, or
(*b*) he had a notifiable interest immediately before that time, and has such an interest immediately after it, but the percentage levels of his interest immediately before and immediately after that time are not the same.

(6) For the purposes of this section, "the relevant time" means—

(*a*) in a case within section 67 (1) (*a*) or (3) (*a*), the time of the event or change of circumstances there mentioned, and
(*b*) in a case within section 67 (1) (*b*) or (3) (*b*), the time at which the person became aware of the facts in question.

Definitions

'notifiable percentage': Companies Act, 1990, section 69.
'obligation of disclosure': Companies Act, 1990, section 67.
'percentage level': Companies Act, 1990, section 69.
'relevant share capital': Companies Act, 1990, section 67.
'relevant time': Companies Act, 1990, section 68.
'share': Companies Act, 1963, section 2.

General Note

This section sets out when the obligation to notify arises. This occurs when a person holds more than the notifiable percentage set out in section 69 (i.e. 5 per cent of the nominal share capital) and at any subsequent time when the extent of the shareholding varies.

(1) The obligation to disclose arises only when the interest in the issued share capital that has the capability of voting on all matters in general meetings is concerned.

(2) A person has a notifiable interest when he is interested in shares the aggregate nominal value of which equals or exceeds the percentage that is regarded as the notifiable percentage.

(3) All facts that a person knows at the time are to be considered in determining whether or not he has a notifiable percentage.

(4) The obligation of disclosure arises where a person has a notifiable interest immediately after he is aware of the facts but had not got the necessary level until the change of circumstances or the time he became aware of the extent of the interest in shares.

(5) This obligation also arises in section 67, where a person has the necessary shareholding immediately before the relevant time but not afterwards, or had the holding immediately before that time and has an interest after it but, because of the change in circumstances, the percentage level of the interest is not the same.

(6) The term 'relevant time' is defined as that when there is a change in circumstances or the time when a person became aware of the facts in question.

SECTION 69
"Percentage level" in relation to notifiable interests.

(1) Subject to the qualification mentioned below, "percentage level", in section 68 (5) (*b*), means the percentage figure found by expressing the aggregate nominal value of all the shares comprised in the share capital concerned in which the person is interested immediately before or (as the case may be)

immediately after the relevant time as a percentage of the nominal value of that share capital and rounding that figure down, if it is not a whole number, to the next whole number.

(2) Where the nominal value of the share capital is greater immediately after the relevant time than it was immediately before, the percentage level of the person's interest immediately before (as well as immediately after) that time is determined by reference to the larger amount.

Definitions

'notifiable percentage': Companies Act, 1990, section 70.

'percentage level': Companies Act, 1990, section 69.

'relevant time': Companies Act, 1990, section 68.

'share': Companies Act, 1963, section 2.

General Note

This section sets out how a person's shareholding percentage interest is to be determined.

(1) The term 'percentage level' is defined as the aggregate of the nominal value of all the shares in the share capital in which the person is interested as a percentage of the nominal value of the share capital, rounding down to the next whole number.

(2) Where the nominal value of the share capital is greater after the 'relevant time' than before it, the percentage level is determined by reference to the larger percentage.

SECTION 70
The notifiable percentage.

(1) The reference in section 68 (2) to the notifiable percentage is to 5 per cent, or such other percentage as may be prescribed by the Minister under this section.

(2) The Minister may prescribe the percentage to apply in determining whether a person's interest in a company's shares is notifiable under section 67; and different percentages may be prescribed in relation to companies of different classes or descriptions.

(3) Where in consequence of a reduction prescribed under this section in the percentage made by such order a person's interest in a company's shares becomes notifiable, he shall then come under the obligation of disclosure in respect of it; and the obligation must be performed within the period of 10 days next following the day on which it arises.

Definitions

'company': Companies Act, 1963, section 2.

'Minister': Companies Act, 1990, section 3.

'notifiable percentage': Companies Act, 1990, section 70.

'share': Companies Act, 1963, section 2.

General Note

The notifiable percentage is set at 5 per cent, but this can be amended by statutory instrument.

(1) The notifiable percentage is set at 5 per cent or other percentage as prescribed by the Minister.

(2) The Minister may prescribe different percentages for different classes or descriptions of shares.

(3) If there is a reduction in the percentage level at which notification takes place the reduced percentage will apply, and the obligation must be performed within ten days following the date on which the reduced notifiable percentage takes effect.

SECTION 71
Particulars to be contained in notification.

(1) Subject to section 70 (3) a person's obligation to make a notification under section 67 must be performed within the period of 5 days next following the day on which the obligation arises; and the notification must be in writing to the company.

(2) The notification must specify the share capital to which it relates, and must also—

(*a*) state the number of shares comprised in that share capital in which the person making the notification knows he was interested immediately after the time when the obligation arose, or

(*b*) in a case where the person no longer has a notifiable interest in shares comprised in that share capital, state that he no longer has that interest.

(3) A notification with respect to a person's interest in a company's relevant share capital (other than one stating that he no longer has a notifiable interest in shares comprised in that share capital) shall include particulars of—

(*a*) the identity of each registered holder of shares to which the notification relates, and

(*b*) the number of those shares held by each such registered holder,

so far as known to the person making the notification at the date when the notification is made.

(4) A person who has an interest in shares comprised in a company's relevant share capital, that interest being notifiable, is under obligation to notify the company in writing—

(*a*) of any particulars in relation to those shares which are specified in subsection (3), and

(*b*) of any change in those particulars,

of which in either case he becomes aware at any time after any interest notification date and before the first occasion following that date on which he comes under any further obligation of disclosure with respect to his interest in shares comprised in that share capital.

An obligation arising under this section must be performed within the period of 5 days next following the day on which it arises.

(5) The reference in subsection (4) to an interest notification date, in relation to a person's interest in shares comprised in a public limited company's relevant share capital, is to either of the following—

(*a*) the date of any notification made by him with respect to his interest under this Part, and

(*b*) where he has failed to make a notification, the date on which the period allowed for making it came to an end.

(6) A person who at any time has an interest in shares which is notifiable is to be regarded under subsection (4) as continuing to have a notifiable interest in them unless and until he comes under obligation to make a notification stating that he no longer has such an interest in those shares.

Definitions

'*company*': Companies Act, 1963, section 2.

'*interest notification date*': Companies Act, 1990, section 72 (5).

'*notifiable interest*': Companies Act, 1990, section 71.

'*public limited company*': Companies (Amendment) Act, 1983, section 2.

'*relevant share capital*': Companies Act, 1990, section 67.

'*share*': Companies Act, 1963, section 2.

General Note

This section sets out the details that must be specified in a notification of an interest in shares, and provides that such notification be made within a five-day period.

(1) A person is obliged to notify an interest to the company in writing within a period of five days after the day on which the obligation arose.

(2) The notification must specify the share capital to which it relates, together with the number of shares in which the person is interested. In the case where the person no longer has a notifiable interest, a statement to that effect must be made.

(3) A notification of a person's interest must include details of the identity of each registered holder and the number of shares held by each registered holder to which the shares relate that are known at the notification date.

(4) Any person who has an interest in shares and who is obliged to make a notification in writing is obliged to do so within five days following the date on which he became aware of his interest.

(5) An interest notification date is either the date of notification made by him with respect to his interest or, in the case where he has failed to make a notification, the date on which notification became due.

(6) A person should be regarded as continuing to have a notifiable interest until such time as he comes under an obligation to state that he no longer has an interest in those shares.

SECTION 72
Notification of family and corporate interests.

(1) For the purposes of sections 67 to 71 a person is taken to be interested in any shares in which his spouse or any minor child of his is interested.

(2) For those purposes, a person is taken to be interested in shares if a body corporate is interested in them and—

(*a*) that body or its directors are accustomed to act in accordance with his directions or instructions, or
(*b*) he is entitled to exercise or control the exercise of one-third or more of the voting power at general meetings of that body corporate.

(3) Where a person is entitled to exercise or control the exercise of one-third or more of the voting power at general meetings of a body corporate and that body corporate is entitled to exercise or control the exercise of any of the voting power at general meetings of another body corporate ("the effective voting power") then, for the purposes of subsection (2) (*b*), the effective voting power is taken as exercisable by that person.

(4) For the purposes of subsections (2) and (3) a person is entitled to exercise or control the exercise of voting power if—

(*a*) he has a right (whether subject to conditions or not) the exercise of which would make him so entitled, or
(*b*) he is under an obligation (whether or not so subject) the fulfilment of which would make him so entitled.

Definitions

'*body corporate*': Companies Act, 1963, section 2 (3).
'*director*': Companies Act, 1963, section 2.
'*effective voting power*': Companies Act, 1990, section 72.
'*minor child*': Age of Majority Act, 1985, section 2.

General Note

This section provides that a person is regarded as being interested in shares in which his spouse or minor child has an interest. In addition it covers situations where an interest is held by shadow directors or through a chain of companies.

(1) A person is regarded as having an interest in shares if his spouse or minor child has an interest in them.

(2) A person is regarded as having an interest in shares if a body corporate is interested in them and such body corporate is accustomed to acting on his instructions or directions or he is entitled to exercise or control at least one-third of the voting power of the company in general meetings.

(3) Where a person controls more than one-third of the voting power of a body corporate that in turn is able to exercise its voting power at the general meeting of another body corporate then he is regarded as controlling that other body corporate.

(4) A person is entitled to exercise or control the exercise of voting power if he has a right which if exercised would so entitle him or is under an obligation the fulfilment of which would make him so entitled.

SECTION 73
Agreement to acquire interests in a public limited compnay.

(1) Subject to the following provisions of this section an agreement between two or more persons which includes provision for the acquisition by any one or more of the parties to the agreement of interests in shares comprised in relevant share capital of a particular public limited company ("the target company") is an agreement to which this section applies if—

(a) it also includes provisions imposing obligations or restrictions on any one or more of the parties to the agreement with respect to their use, retention or disposal of interests in that company's shares acquired in pursuance of the agreement (whether or not together with any other interests of theirs in that company's shares to which the agreement relates); and

(b) any interest in the company's shares is in fact acquired by any of the parties in pursuance of the agreement;

and in relation to such an agreement references in this section, and in sections 74 and 75, to the target company are to the company which is the target company for that agreement in accordance with this section.

(2) The reference in subsection (1) (a) to the use of interests in shares in the target company is to the exercise of any rights or of any control or influence arising from those interests (including the right to enter into any agreement for the exercise, or for control of the exercise, of any of those rights by another person).

(3) Once any interest in shares in the target company has been acquired in pursuance of such an agreement as is mentioned above, this section continues to apply to that agreement irrespective of—

(a) whether or not any further acquisitions of interests in the company's shares take place in pursuance of the agreement, and

(b) any change in the persons who are for the time being parties to it, and

(c) any variation of the agreement,

so long as the agreement continues to include provisions of any description mentioned in subsection (1) (a).

References in this subsection to the agreement include any agreement having effect (whether directly or indirectly) in substitution for the original agreement.

(4) In this section, and also in references elsewhere in this Part to an agreement to which this section applies, "agreement" includes any agreement or arrangement; and references in this section to provisions of an agreement—

(*a*) accordingly include undertakings, expectations or understandings operative under any arrangement, and

(*b*) (without prejudice to the above) also include any provisions, whether express or implied and whether absolute or not.

(5) This section does not apply to an agreement which is not legally binding unless it involves mutuality in the undertakings, expectations or understandings of the parties to it; nor does the section apply to an agreement to underwrite or sub-underwrite any offer of shares in a company, provided the agreement is confined to that purpose and any matters incidental to it.

Definitions

'*agreement*': Companies Act, 1990, section 73.

'*company*': Companies Act, 1963, section 2.

'*public limited company*': Companies (Amendment) Act, 1983, section 2.

'*target company*': Companies Act, 1990, section 73.

General Note

This section deals with interests held by concert parties and defines a concert party agreement as one that can be regarded as some type of an arrangement (even an informal one if it is capable of being legally binding) by which at least one party to an agreement embracing two or more persons will acquire an interest in a company's shares or retain an interest in a company's shares or retain an interest on behalf of all the parties to the agreement. There must be an actual acquisition before a concert party agreement can come into effect.

(1) This subsection sets out what is regarded as a concert party agreement. In ascertaining whether a person is bound to notify his interest under sections 74–75 of this Act, the interests of other members of a concert party attributed to him must be taken into account.

(2) It should be noted that not every agreement concerning shares will be a notifiable concert party. There must be an agreement by which at least one party either will retain an interest in the company's shares acquired by agreement or will acquire an interest in shares, as distinct from an agreement as to how rights attached to interests in shares already held might be exercised. The section

does not refer to the latter, so that agreement between existing members to bring concerted pressure would not necessarily be notifiable.

(3) This section will continue to apply to a concert party so long as the agreement continues, irrespective of any further acquisitions, changes in the parties, or attempts to vary or discharge it.

(4) 'Agreement' is defined to include any meeting of minds, mutual undertakings, expectations or undertakings expressed or implied and whether absolute or not. It is sufficient of each party that it relies on the other or if the acquirer of shares is relied upon by the other party to the agreement.

(5) This subsection excludes arrangements involving a meeting of minds but no mutual reliance (e.g. as between a broker and a client), and provides special exemptions for underwriting and sub-underwriting agreements. It should be noted that such agreements are not exempt and must be restricted specifically to underwriting and to anything incidental to it.

SECTION 74
Obligation of disclosure arising under section 73.

(1) In the case of an agreement to which section 73 applies, each party to the agreement shall be taken (for purposes of the obligation of disclosure) to be interested in all shares in the target company in which any other party to it is interested apart from the agreement (whether or not the interest of the other party in question was acquired, or includes any interest which was acquired, in pursuance of the agreement).

(2) For those purposes, and also for those of section 75, an interest of a party to such an agreement in shares in the target company is an interest apart from the agreement if he is interested in those shares otherwise than by virtue of the application of section 73 and this section in relation to the agreement.

(3) Accordingly, any such interest of the person (apart from the agreement) includes for those purposes any interest treated as his under section 72 or by the application of section 73 and this section in relation to any other agreement with respect to shares in the target company to which he is a party.

(4) A notification with respect to his interest in shares in the target company made to that company under this Part by a person who is for the time being a party to an agreement to which section 73 applies shall—

(a) state that the person making the notification is a party to such an agreement,
(b) include the names and (so far as known to him) the addresses of the other parties to the agreement, identifying them as such, and
(c) state whether or not any of the shares to which the notification relates are shares in which he is interested by virtue of section 73 and this section and, if so, the number of those shares.

(5) Where a person makes a notification to a company under this Part in consequence of ceasing to be interested in any shares of that company by virtue

of the fact that he or any other person has ceased to be a party to an agreement to which section 73 applies, the notification shall include a statement that he or that other person has ceased to be a party to the agreement (as the case may require) and also (in the latter case) the name and (if known to him) the address of that other.

Definitions

'*company*': Companies Act, 1963, section 2.
'*target company*': Companies Act, 1990, section 73.

General Note

This section provides that it is not simply interests obtained under the concert party agreement that are attributed to each party but also any other interests that any party to the agreement has in shares of the company concerned. The effect of this section is that if the parties to the agreement have an interest that is in aggregate equal to or exceeds 5 per cent of the voting shares and is therefore notifiable in the normal way, they are each obliged to make the notification required under section 67. It also provides for the notification by a person who is party to a concert party agreement of any information concerning the agreement as well as the details of the interests he would be notifying under section 67 of the Act.

(1) All the persons involved in a concert party are attributed with all of the interest of the others in the share capital of the company under the obligations to disclose. This is to be added to their own interest so as to ascertain whether each, or any, has an obligation to notify their interests. The company will thus be able to see the amount of the relevant share capital that the parties are in a position to control in concert.

(2–3) Where a party to an agreement is also a party to other separate agreements, all these separate interests will be attributed to him. It should be noted that the obligation to notify the company concerned falls upon each party, although this obligation may be met by one member acting as agent on behalf of all the members.

(4) This subsection requires clear notification and recording of the fact that a concert party is involved and that such notifications include the names and addresses of the other parties to the agreement.

(5) Where a person makes a notification as a result of his ceasing to have an interest in shares, or a notification that some other party has

ceased to have an interest in shares, the notification must include a statement that he or the other person has ceased to be a party to the agreement, and include his name and address or that of the other party.

SECTION 75

Obligation of persons acting together to keep each other informed.

(1) A person who is a party to an agreement to which section 73 applies shall be subject to the requirements of this section at any time when—

(a) the target company is a public limited company, and he knows it to be so, and

(b) the shares in that company to which the agreement relates consist of or include shares comprised in relevant share capital of the company, and he knows that to be the case, and

(c) he knows the facts which make the agreement one to which section 73 applies.

(2) Such a person shall be under obligation to notify every other party to the agreement, in writing, of the relevant particulars of his interest (if any) apart from the agreement in shares comprised in relevant share capital of the target company—

(a) on his first becoming subject to the requirements of this section, and

(b) on each occurrence after that time while he is still subject to those requirements of any event or circumstances within section 67 (1) (as it applies to his case otherwise than by reference to interests treated as his under section 74 as applying to that agreement).

(3) The relevant particulars to be notified under subsection (2) are—

(a) the number of shares (if any) comprised in the target company's relevant share capital in which the person giving the notice would be required to state his interest if he were under the obligation of disclosure with respect to that interest (apart from the agreement) immediately after the time when the obligation to give notice under subsection (2) arose, and

(b) the relevant particulars with respect to the registered ownership of those shares, so far as known to him at the date of the notice.

(4) A person who is for the time being subject to the requirements of this section shall be under obligation to notify every other party to the agreement, in writing—

(a) of any relevant particulars with respect to the registered ownership of any shares comprised in relevant share capital of the target company in which he is interested apart from the agreement, and

(b) of any change in those particulars, of which in either case he becomes aware at any time after any interest notification date and before the first occasion following that date on which he becomes subject to any further obligation to give notice under subsection (2) with respect to his interest in shares comprised in that share capital.

(5) The reference in subsection (4) to an interest notification date, in relation to a person's interest in shares comprised in the target company's relevant share capital, is to either of the following—

(a) the date of any notice given by him with respect to his interest under subsection (2), and

(b) where he has failed to give that notice, the date on which the period allowed by this section for giving the notice came to an end.

(6) A person who is a party to an agreement to which section 73 applies shall be under an obligation to notify each other party to the agreement, in writing, of his current address—

(a) on his first becoming subject to the requirements of this section, and
(b) on any change in his address occurring after that time and while he is still subject to those requirements.

(7) A reference to the relevant particulars with respect to the registered ownership of shares is to such particulars in relation to those shares as mentioned in section 71 (3) (a) or (b).

(8) A person's obligation to give any notice required by this section to any other person must be performed within the period of 5 days next following the day on which that obligation arose.

Definitions

'company': Companies Act, 1963, section 2.
'notification date': Companies Act, 1990, section 71.
'public limited company': Companies (Amendment) Act, 1983, section 2.
'relevant share capital': Companies Act, 1990, section 67.
'share': Companies Act, 1963, section 2.
'target company': Companies Act, 1990, section 73.

General Note

This section provides that each of the parties to a concert party agreement must keep the other parties supplied with information necessary to enable them to fulfil their own notification requirements. A person's obligation to report will depend on his knowledge of the relevant facts. The incidence of the reporting obligation will depend on the agreement being activated, and it is essential that once the agreement is activated the parties should inform every other party to the agreement of their existing interests and acquisitions.

(1) The circumstances are set out as to when a person who is a party to a concert party agreement will be subject to this section.

(2) A person will be obliged to notify in writing every other party to the agreement of the details of his interest when he first became subject to the requirements and on each occurrence while he is still subject to the requirements on the happening of an event.

(3) The particulars required to be notified are:
- the number of shares comprised in the target company's share capital in which the person would be required to state his interest immediately after the time he was obliged to give notice;

- the details relating to the registered ownership of those shares, so far as they are known to him.

(4) Where a person is obliged to give notice he must notify in writing every other party to the agreement of the particulars of the registered ownership of the shares in the share capital of the target company in which he has an interest and of any change in the particulars of which he has become aware.

(5) The term 'interest notification date' is defined as the date on which the person was obliged to give notice, irrespective of whether the notice was given.

(6) A person who is subject to a concert party agreement must give his current address and notify any change of address as long as he is the subject of an agreement.

(7) The registered ownership of shares is clarified.

(8) The obligation to notify must be fulfilled within five days following the date on which the obligation to notify arose.

SECTION 76
Interests in shares by attribution.

(1) Where section 67 or 68 refers to a person acquiring an interest in shares or ceasing to be interested in shares, that reference in certain cases includes his becoming or ceasing to be interested in those shares by virtue of another person's interest.

(2) This section applies where he becomes or ceases to be interested by virtue of section 72 or (as the case may be) section 74 whether—

(a) by virtue of the fact that the person who is interested in the shares becomes or ceases to be a person whose interests (if any) fall by virtue of either section to be treated as his, or
(b) in consequence of the fact that such a person has become or ceased to be interested in the shares, or
(c) in consequence of the fact that he himself becomes or ceases to be a party to an agreement to which section 73 applies to which the person interested in the shares is for the time being a party, or
(d) in consequence of the fact that an agreement to which both he and that person are parties becomes or ceases to be one to which the said section 73 applies.

(3) The person shall be treated under section 67 as knowing he has acquired an interest in the shares or (as the case may be) that he has ceased to be interested in them, if and when he knows both—

(a) the relevant facts with respect to the other person's interest in the shares, and
(b) the relevant facts by virtue of which he himself has become or ceased to be interested in them in accordance with section 72 or 74.

(4) He shall be deemed to know the relevant facts referred to in subsection (3) (a) if he knows (whether contemporaneously or not) either of the subsistence of the

other person's interest at any material time or of the fact that the other has become or ceased to be interested in the shares at any such time; and "material time" is any time at which the other's interests (if any) fall or fell to be treated as his under section 72 or 74.

(5) A person is to be regarded as knowing of the subsistence of another's interest in shares or (as the case may be) that another has become or ceased to be interested in shares if he has been notified under section 75 of facts with respect to the other's interest which indicate that he is or has become or ceased to be interested in the shares (whether on his own account or by virtue of a third party's interest in them).

Definitions
'*material time*': Companies Act, 1990, section 75.
'*share*': Companies Act, 1963, section 2.

General Note
This section deals with the circumstances where a person is deemed to have taken an interest in shares in which he is not personally directly interested by virtue of some relationship with another person who is directly interested in them, either because that other person is his spouse or minor child or is party to a concert party agreement.

(1) The purpose of the section is to provide that a reference to an interest in shares includes the becoming or ceasing to be interested in shares because of the other person's interest.

(2) This subsection explains when the acquisition or disposal of interests arises, including the becoming or ceasing to be interested by virtue of another person's interest.

(3) A person is deemed to have knowledge if he knows that the related person has or had the interest and the facts that make that attributable are no longer attributable to him.

(4) This subsection defines 'material time', and provides that a person is regarded as having knowledge if he knows of the substance of another's interest in shares.

(5) This subsection clarifies the position that in relation to concert parties a person is deemed to have knowledge of facts that he is informed of by another party under section 75 (which obliges persons acting together to keep each other informed of relevant facts).

SECTION 77
Interests in
shares which are
to be notified.

(1) This section applies, subject to section 78, in determining for purposes of sections 67 to 71 whether a person has a notifiable interest in shares.

(2) A reference to an interest in shares is to be read as including an interest of any kind whatsoever in the shares. Accordingly there are to be disregarded any restraints or restrictions to which the exercise of any right attached to the interest is or may be subject.

(3) Where property is held on trust and an interest in shares is comprised in the property, a beneficiary of the trust who apart from this subsection does not have an interest in the shares is to be taken as having such an interest; but this subsection is without prejudice to the following provisions of this section.

(4) A person is taken to have an interest in shares if—

(*a*) he enters into a contract for their purchase by him (whether for cash or other consideration), or
(*b*) not being the registered holder, he is entitled to exercise any right conferred by the holding of the shares or is entitled to control the exercise of any such right.

(5) For the purposes of subsection (4) (*b*), a person is entitled to exercise or control the exercise of any right conferred by the holding of shares if he—

(*a*) has a right (whether subject to conditions or not) the exercise of which would make him so entitled, or
(*b*) is under an obligation (whether so subject or not) the fulfilment of which would make him so entitled.

(6) A person is taken to have an interest in shares if, otherwise than by virtue of having an interest under a trust—

(*a*) he has a right to call for delivery of the shares to himself or to his order, or
(*b*) he has a right to acquire an interest in shares or is under an obligation to take an interest in shares,

whether in any case the right or obligation is conditional or absolute.

(7) Without prejudice to subsection (2), rights or obligations to subscribe for any shares shall not be taken for the purposes of subsection (6) to be rights to acquire, or obligations to take, any interest in shares.

(8) Where persons have a joint interest each of them shall be taken to have that interest.

(9) It is immaterial that shares in which a person has an interest are unidentifiable.

(10) Delivery to a person's order of shares in fulfilment of a contract for the purchase thereof by him or in satisfaction of a right of his to call for delivery thereof, or failure to deliver shares in accordance with the terms of such a contract or on which such a right falls to be satisfied, shall be deemed to constitute an event in consequence of the occurrence of which he ceases to be interested in them, and so shall the lapse of a person's right to call for delivery of shares.

Definitions

'share': Companies Act, 1963, section 2.

General Note

This section sets down the specific rules for determining precisely if a person has a notifiable interest in shares or is substantially interested in them.

(1) The section applies in the determination as to whether a person has a notifiable interest in shares for the purposes of sections 67–71.

(2) This subsection elaborates the idea of an interest of any kind whatsoever, irrespective of the fact that the exercise of any right attaching to the interest may be subject to any restraint or restriction and where it is assumed that an 'interest in shares' refers to an interest recognised by law or existing in the shares themselves. This includes the interest of a holder of shares who is both the legal and beneficial owner, and also the interest of other holders, such as nominees and trustees. A trustee may be exempt under section 78, but if a trustee has a discretion as to the exercise of the rights arising by virtue of interests in shares held under trust he should be obliged to notify a substantial interest.

(3) This subsection includes in the definition of interest any interest a beneficiary has under a trust that is not already included under other provisions.

(4–5) These subsections include all forms of contract and options to acquire an interest in shares exercisable at present or some time in the future and any form of agreement that may confer a present or future right to exercise or control the exercise of voting power or any other right conferred by the holder of shares.

(6) A person is deemed to be entitled to exercise or control the rights conferred by shares if he has a right or obligation that would make him so entitled. This subsection also provides that any contingent agreement that might otherwise have been used to hide an interest requiring disclosure until it suited the holder of such a right to make disclosure must be disclosed under this section.

(7) The rights and obligations to subscribe for shares are not for the purposes of subsection (6) rights to acquire an interest in shares.

(8) Where there is a joint interest in shares it will be regarded as having an interest.

(9) It is immaterial that the shares in which a person has an interest cannot be identified, e.g. if serial numbers are not allocated to each share.

(10) The delivery of shares in fulfilment of a contract to purchase shares or the satisfaction of a right to call for delivery in accordance with the terms of an agreement will constitute an event.

SECTION 78
Interests to be
disregarded.

(1) The following interests in shares shall be disregarded for the purposes of sections 67 to 71—

(*a*) where property is held on trust and an interest in shares is comprised in that property, an interest in reversion or remainder or of a bare trustee and any discretionary interest;

(*b*) an interest of a person subsisting by virtue of—
　(i) his holding units in—
　　(I) a registered unit trust scheme within the meaning of section 3 of the Unit Trusts Act, 1972;
　　(II) a unit trust to which section 31 of the Capital Gains Tax Act, 1975, as amended by section 34 of the Finance Act, 1977, relates;
　　(III) an undertaking for collective investment in transferable securities, within the meaning of the European Communities (Undertakings for Collective Investment in Transferable Securities) Regulations, 1989 (S.I. No. 78 of 1989); or
　(ii) a scheme made under section 46 of the Charities Act, 1961;

(*c*) an interest for the life of himself or another of a person under a settlement in the case of which the property comprised in the settlement consists of or includes shares, and the conditions mentioned in subsection (3) are satisfied;

(*d*) an exempt security interest;

(*e*) an interest of the President of the High Court subsisting by virtue of section 13 of the Succession Act, 1965;

(*f*) an interest of the Accountant of the High Court in shares held by him in accordance with rules of court;

(*g*) such interests, or interests of such a class, as may be prescribed for purposes of this paragraph by regulations made by the Minister.

(2) A person shall not by virtue of section 77 (4) (*b*) be taken to be interested in shares by reason only that he has been appointed a proxy to vote at a specified meeting of a company or of any class of its members and at any adjournment of that meeting, or has been appointed by a body corporate to act as its representative at any meeting of a company or of any class of its members.

(3) The conditions referred to in subsection (1) (*c*) are, in relation to a settlement—

(*a*) that it is irrevocable, and

(*b*) that the settlor (within the meaning of section 96 of the Income Tax Act, 1967) has no interest in any income arising under, or property comprised in, the settlement.

(4) An interest in shares is an exempt security interest for purposes of subsection (1) (*d*) if—

(*a*) it is held by—
　(i) the holder of a licence under section 9 of the Central Bank Act, 1971, or an insurance company within the meaning of the Insurance Acts, 1909 to 1990,
　(ii) a trustee savings bank (within the meaning of the Trustee Savings Banks Acts, 1863 to 1979) or a Post Office Savings Bank within the meaning of the Post Office Savings Bank Acts, 1861 to 1958,

(iii) Agricultural Credit Corporation plc or Industrial Credit Corporation plc,
(iv) a member of a recognised stock exchange carrying on business as a stockbroker, and
(*b*) it is held by way of security only for the purposes of a transaction entered into by the person or body concerned in the ordinary course of business of such person or body.

Definitions

'*body corporate*': Companies Act, 1963, section 2 (3).

'*company*': Companies Act, 1963, section 2.

'*exempt security interest*': Companies Act, 1990, section 78.

'*Minister*': Companies Act, 1990, section 3.

'*recognised stock exchange*': Companies Act, 1990, section 3.

General Note

This section sets out the interests that are to be disregarded when ascertaining whether or not a person has a notifiable interest under section 60.

(1) A list of the interests that are disregarded for purposes of notification is set out, and includes undertakings for collective investment in transferable securities (UCITS), which is a new form of instrument introduced by the European Community.

(2) A person is not taken to be interested in shares only because he was appointed a proxy or representative to vote at a specified meeting or any adjournment of such meeting.

(3) This subsection refers to the conditions to be regarded as a settlement for the purposes of section 78 (1) (c).

(4) This subsection elaborates on what are exempt security interests for the purposes of the Act, including shares held by

(*a*) holders of licences under section 9 of the Central Bank Act, 1971,

(*b*) insurance companies, within the meaning of the Insurance Acts,

(*c*) trustee savings banks,

(*d*) the Post Office Savings Bank,

(*e*) the Agricultural Credit Corporation or the Industrial Credit Corporation,

(*f*) a stockbroker who is a member of a recognised stock exchange, or

(*g*) a person in the ordinary course of business as a security.

SECTION 79
Other provisions
relating to
notification.

(1) Where a person authorises any other person ("the agent") to acquire or dispose of, on his behalf, interests in shares comprised in relevant share capital of a public limited company, he shall secure that the agent notifies him immediately of acquisitions or disposals of interests in shares so comprised effected by the agent which will or may give rise to any obligation on his part to make a notification under this Chapter with respect to his interest in that share capital.

(2) An obligation to make any notification imposed on any person by this Chapter shall be treated as not being fulfilled unless the notice by means of which it purports to be fulfilled identifies him and gives his address, and in a case where he is a director or secretary of the company, is expressed to be given in fulfilment of that obligation.

(3) Where a person—

(*a*) fails to fulfil, within the proper period, an obligation to make any notification required by this Chapter; or

(*b*) in purported fulfilment of any such obligation makes to a company a statement which he knows to be false or recklessly makes to a company a statement which is false; or

(*c*) fails to fulfil, within the proper period, an obligation to give any other person any notice required by section 75,

no right or interest of any kind whatsoever in respect of any shares in the company concerned, held by him, shall be enforceable by him, whether directly or indirectly, by action or legal proceeding.

(4) Where any right or interest is restricted under subsection (3), any person in default under that subsection or any other person affected by such restriction may apply to the court for relief against a disability imposed by or arising out of subsection (3) and the court on being satisfied that the default was accidental, or due to inadvertence, or some other sufficient cause, or that on other grounds it is just and equitable to grant relief, may grant such relief either generally, or as respects any particular right or interest on such terms and conditions as it sees fit.

(5) Where an applicant for relief under subsection (4) is a person referred to in subsection (3), the court may not grant such relief if it appears that the default has arisen as a result of any deliberate act or omission on the part of the applicant.

(6) Subsection (3) shall not apply to an obligation relating to a person ceasing to be interested in shares in any company.

(7) A person who—

(*a*) fails to fulfil, within the proper period, an obligation of disclosure imposed on him by this Chapter, or

(*b*) fails to fulfil, within the proper period, an obligation to give any other person a notice required by section 75, or

(*c*) fails without reasonable excuse to comply with subsection (1),

shall be guilty of an offence.

(8) It shall be a defence for a person charged with an offence under subsection (7) (*b*) to prove that it was not possible for him to give the notice to that other person required by section 75 within the proper period, and either—

(*a*) that it has not since become possible for him to give the notice so required; or

123

(*b*) that he gave that notice as soon after the end of that period as it became possible for him to do so.

Definitions

'*company*': Companies Act, 1963, section 2.

'*court*': Companies Act, 1990, section 235.

'*director*': Companies Act, 1963, section 2.

'*public limited company*': Companies (Amendment) Act, 1983, section 2.

'*relevant share capital*': Companies Act, 1990, section 67.

General Note

This section aims to prevent the avoidance of notification of being an agent of a person to acquire interests in shares, and to prevent the influencing of that person in the decision to make the relevant acquisition.

(1) A person who authorises an agent to acquire or dispose of interests in shares for him must ensure that he is notified by the agent immediately of any transaction that might give rise to an obligation to notify a company under the Act. If this section was not put in place it would be relatively simple to avoid disclosure of interests.

(2) The obligation to notify is not fulfilled unless the name and address is given.

(3) It is an offence for a person to fail to make a notification under this chapter or to make a statement that he knows to be false or to recklessly make a statement that is false.

(4) It is possible for the person in default or any other person affected by the restriction to apply to the High Court for relief on the basis that the default in subsection (3) above was accidental or due to inadvertence or some other course or that it is just and equitable to grant relief.

(5) The High Court may not grant relief where there is evidence that the failure to notify an interest in shares was due to some deliberate act or omission on the part of the applicant.

(6) Subsection (3) does not apply where a person is ceasing to have an interest in shares.

(7) A person will be guilty of an offence and liable to the penalties imposed by section 240 if he does not fulfil his obligation with regard to the disclosure period and has no reasonable excuse for the failure to comply with the notification.

(8) The applicant may use as a defence the excuse that it was not possible to give notice and that he did so as soon as he was in a position to do so.

SECTION 80
Register of interests in shares.

(1) Every public limited company shall keep a register for purposes of sections 67 to 71 and whenever the company receives information from a person in consequence of the fulfilment of an obligation imposed on him by any of those sections, it is under obligation to inscribe in the register, against that person's name, that information and the date of the inscription.

(2) Without prejudice to subsection (1), where a company receives a notification under this Part which includes a statement that the person making the notification, or any other person, has ceased to be a party to an agreement to which section 73 applies, the company shall be under obligation to record that information against the name of that person in every place where his name appears in the register as a party to that agreement (including any entry relating to him made against another person's name).

(3) An obligation imposed by subsection (1) or (2) must be fulfilled within the period of 3 days next following the day on which it arises.

(4) The nature and extent of an interest recorded in the said register of a person in any shares shall, if he so requires, be recorded in the said register.

(5) The company shall not, by virtue of anything done for the purposes of this section, be affected with notice of, or put upon enquiry as to, the rights of any person in relation to any shares.

(6) The register must be so made up that the entries against the several names entered in it appear in chronological order.

(7) Unless the register is in such form as to constitute in itself an index, the company shall keep an index of the names entered in the register which shall in respect of each name contain a sufficient indication to enable the information entered against it to be readily found; and the company shall, within 10 days after the date on which a name is entered in the register, make any necessary alteration in the index.

(8) If the company ceases to be a public limited company it shall continue to keep the register and any associated index until the end of the period of 6 years beginning with the day next following that on which it ceases to be such a company.

(9) The register and any associated index—

(*a*) shall be kept at the place at which the register required to be kept by the company by section 59 (register of directors' and secretaries' interests) is kept, and

(*b*) shall be available for inspection in accordance with section 88.

(10) If default is made in complying with any of the provisions of this section, the company and every officer of it who is in default shall be liable to a fine not exceeding £1,000, and for continued contravention, to a daily default fine not exceeding £50.

Definitions

'*company*': Companies Act, 1963, section 2.
'*daily default fine*': Companies Act, 1990, section 3.
'*officer*': Companies Act, 1963, section 2.
'*public limited company*': Companies (Amendment) Act, 1983, section 2.

General Note

This section requires every public limited company to maintain a register of interests in shares and to record information received in notifications in this register. The register must also have an index attached, and the documents must be kept at the company's registered office or its principal place of business.

(1) Every public limited company is required to keep a register of interests in shares, and when a company receives notification of an interest such information must be inscribed in the register.

(2) The company must record notifications in the register, including information that a party has ceased to be a member of a concert party agreement.

(3) The obligation to register must be fulfilled within three days following the day on which it arises.

(4) The nature and interest in shares must be noted in the register if so required by the holder of the shares.

(5) The company will not be put on notice or enquiry by reason of anything done to comply with this section.

(6) The register must be maintained in chronological order.

(7) The register must contain an index if the register does not itself constitute an index.

(8) The company must continue to keep the index and register for a period of six years from the time it ceases to be a public limited company.

(9) The register and index must be kept at the company's registered office or principal place of business.

(10) A company and every officer of a company that is in default will be guilty of an offence and liable to a fine not exceeding £1,000 and, for continued contravention, to a daily default fine not exceeding £50 for each day thereafter.

SECTION 81
Company investigations.

(1) A public limited company may by notice in writing require a person whom the company knows or has reasonable cause to believe to be or, at any time during the 3 years immediately preceding the date on which the notice is issued (but excluding any time before the commencement of this section), to have been interested in shares comprised in the company's relevant share capital—

(a) to confirm that fact or (as the case may be) to indicate whether or not it is the case, and
(b) where he holds or has during that time held an interest in shares so comprised, to give such further information as may be required in accordance with the following subsection.

(2) A notice under this section may require the person to whom it is addressed—

(a) to give particulars of his own past or present interest in shares comprised in relevant share capital of the company (held by him at any time during the 3 year period mentioned in subsection (1)),
(b) where the interest is a present interest and any other interest in shares subsists or, in any case, where another interest in the shares subsisted during that 3 year period at any time when his own interest subsisted, to give (so far as lies within his knowledge) such particulars with respect to that other interest as may be required by the notice,
(c) where his interest is a past interest, to give (so far as lies within his knowledge) particulars of the identity of the person who held that interest immediately upon his ceasing to hold it.

(3) The particulars referred to in subsection (2) (a) and (2) (b) include particulars of the identity of persons interested in the shares in question and of whether persons interested in the same shares are or were parties to any agreement to which section 73 applies or to any agreement or arrangement relating to the exercise of any rights conferred by the holding of the shares.

(4) A notice under this section shall require any information given in response to the notice to be given in writing within such reasonable time as may be specified in the notice.

(5) Sections 72 to 74 and 77 apply for the purpose of construing references in this section to persons interested in shares and to interests in shares respectively, as they apply in relation to sections 67 to 70 (but with the omission of any reference to section 78).

(6) This section applies in relation to a person who has or previously had, or is or was entitled to acquire, a right to subscribe for shares in a public limited company which would on issue be comprised in relevant share capital of that company as it applies in relation to a person who is or was interested in shares so comprised; and references in this section to an interest in shares so comprised and to shares so comprised are to be read accordingly in any such

case as including respectively any such right and shares which would on issue be so comprised.

Definitions

'company': Companies Act, 1963, section 2.

'public limited company': Companies (Amendment) Act, 1983, section 2.

'relevant share capital': Companies Act, 1990, section 67.

'share': Companies Act, 1963, section 2.

General Note

This section enables a public limited company to investigate past and present holdings of its vote-carrying shares and enables such a company to require anyone who it knows or believes to have or have had an interest at any time during the previous three years to confirm that fact and, where it is confirmed, to give particulars of that interest. Under the section a company can require information from existing members about the capacity in which they hold shares. If they are not the beneficial owners it can enquire who is interested in the shares and in what manner. Similarly it may make enquiries about any person who it has been informed is or who in subsequent enquiry is revealed to be interested in shares. It may also enquire whether any voting rights or shares of a member are controlled by another under any agreement and, if so, request the particulars of the agreement and the parties to it in so far as they are known to the member. It may also request the information from anyone who is named as a party to such an agreement.

(1) An enquiry can start where the company is believed to be or have been interested in shares within the previous three years.

(2) The person who is the subject of the enquiry must provide information including particulars of his present interest or any past interest in shares held within the previous three years, together with particulars of any other known past or present interests in the shares in addition to the interest about which notice has been issued under the provisions of this section.

(3) The company is enabled by this subsection to identify interested persons and to cross-check any links between them.

(4) The information must be provided within a reasonable time, which time must be specified in the notice.

Disclosure of interests in shares

(5) Sections 72–74 and 77 apply in construing interests in shares.

(6) A company is enabled to make enquiries of persons who have or had a right to subscribe for the relevant share capital.

SECTION 82
Registration of interests disclosed under section 81.

(1) Whenever in pursuance of a requirement imposed on a person under section 81 a company receives information to which this section applies relating to shares comprised in its relevant share capital, it is under obligation to enter against the name of the registered holder of those shares, in a separate part of its register of interests in shares—

(*a*) the fact that the requirement was imposed and the date on which it was imposed, and

(*b*) any information to which this section applies received in pursuance of the requirement.

(2) This section applies to any information received in pursuance of a requirement imposed by section 81 which relates to the present interests held by any persons in shares comprised in relevant share capital of the company in question.

(3) Subsections (3) to (10) of section 80 apply in relation to any part of the register maintained in accordance with subsection (1) of this section, reading references to subsection (1) of that section to include subsection (1) of this section.

Definitions
'*company*': Companies Act, 1963, section 2.
'*relevant share capital*': Companies Act, 1990, section 67.

General Note
This section obliges public limited companies to register information received in response to enquiries made under section 81 against the name of the registered holder in the register of interests in shares.

(1) A public limited company is required to record against the name of the shareholder in a separate part of the register the fact and date of the requirement imposed by the company.

(2) The information that is subject to section 81 is defined as all that relating to present interests held by any person.

(3) The provisions for maintenance of the register set out in section 80 apply to this section.

SECTION 83
Company investigations on requisition by members.

(1) A company may be required to exercise its powers under section 81 on the requisition of members of the company holding at the date of the deposit of the requisition not less than one-tenth of such of the paid-up capital of the company as carries at that date the right of voting at general meetings of the company.

129

(2) The requisition must—

(*a*) state that the requisitionists are requiring the company to exercise its powers under section 81,
(*b*) specify the manner in which they require those powers to be exercised, and
(*c*) give reasonable grounds for requiring the company to exercise those powers in the manner specified,

and must be signed by the requisitionists and deposited at the company's registered office.

(3) The requisition may consist of several documents in like form each signed by one or more requisitionists.

(4) On the deposit of a requisition complying with this section the company shall exercise its powers under section 81 in the manner specified in the requisition.

(5) If default is made in complying with subsection (4), the court may, on the application of the requisitionists, or any of them, and on being satisfied that it is reasonable to do so, require the company to exercise its powers under section 81 in a manner specified in the order.

Definitions

'*company*': Companies Act, 1963, section 2.
'*court*': Companies Act, 1990, section 235.

General Note

This section empowers a minority representing not less than 10 per cent of the voting shares to require a public limited company to investigate and report under the authority given by section 81 on those persons who hold substantial interests in the company.

(1) A minority representing not less than 10 per cent of the paid-up share capital carrying voting rights is empowered to require a public limited company to exercise its powers.

(2) The requisitionists must specify the manner in which the company is to exercise its powers and they must provide reasonable grounds for their request. When a proper requisition has been received the company is obliged to exercise its investigating powers. The requisition must be signed by the requisitionists and deposited at the company's registered office.

(3) The requisition can consist of one or several documents.

(4) When a requisition is deposited complying with this section the company must exercise its powers under section 81.

(5) The High Court may compel the company to exercise its powers if it is considered reasonable to do so in the event of default under subsection (4).

SECTION 84
Company report to members.

(1) On the conclusion of an investigation carried out by a company in pursuance of a requisition under section 83 it is the company's duty to cause a report of the information received in pursuance of that investigation to be prepared, and the report shall be made available at the company's registered office within a reasonable period after the conclusion of that investigation.

(2) Where—

(*a*) a company undertakes an investigation in pursuance of a requisition under section 83, and

(*b*) the investigation is not concluded before the end of 3 months beginning with the date immediately following the date of the deposit of the requisition,

the company shall cause to be prepared, in respect of that period and each successive period of 3 months ending before the conclusion of the investigation, an interim report of the information received during that period in pursuance of the investigation. Each such report shall be made available at the company's registered office within a reasonable period after the end of the period to which it relates.

(3) The period for making any report prepared under this section available as required by subsection (1) or (2) shall not exceed 15 days.

(4) The company shall, within 3 days of making any report prepared under this section available at its registered office, notify the requisitionists that the report is so available.

(5) An investigation carried out by a company in pursuance of a requisition under section 83 shall be regarded for the purposes of this section as concluded when the company has made all such inquiries as are necessary or expedient for the purposes of the requisition and in the case of each such inquiry, either a response has been received by the company or the time allowed for a response has elapsed.

(6) A report prepared under this section—

(*a*) shall be kept at the company's registered office from the day on which it is first available there in accordance with subsection (1) or (2) until the expiration of 6 years beginning with the day next following that day, and

(*b*) shall be available for inspection in accordance with section 88 so long as it is so kept.

(7) If default is made in complying with subsection (1), (2), (3), (4) or (6) (*a*), the company and every officer of the company who is in default shall be guilty of an offence and be liable to a fine.

Definitions

'*company*': Companies Act, 1963, section 2.
'*officer*': Companies Act, 1963, section 2.

General Note

This section obliges the company on conclusion of an investigation carried out in pursuance of section 83 to make a report on such investigation available at its registered office within fifteen days.

(1) The company must make a copy of the report available for inspection at the company's registered office within a reasonable period after the conclusion of the investigation.

(2) Where an investigation is undertaken under section 83 and is not completed within a period of three months from the date of requisition there must be made available at the registered office an interim report of the information received during the investigation and a similar report for each successive three-month period within a reasonable period of such three-month period.

(3) A report must be made available within fifteen days.

(4) The company must notify the requisitionists that the report is available at the company's registered office within three days of making the report available at the registered office.

(5) An investigation made under section 83 will be regarded as concluded when the company has made all the enquiries necessary or expedient for the purposes of the requisition, and the enquiry together with a response has been received, or the time allowed for a response has lapsed.

(6) A copy of the report must be kept at the company's registered office for a period of six years from the day following the date on which the report is made available and shall remain available for inspection during such period.

(7) If the company is in default the company and every officer who is in default will be guilty of an offence and liable to a fine under the provisions of section 240.

SECTION 85 Penalty for failure to provide information.	(1) Where notice is served by a company under section 81 on a person who is or was interested in shares of the company and that person fails to give the company any information required by the notice within the time specified in it, the company may apply to the court for an order directing that the shares in question be subject to restrictions under section 16.

(2) Such an order may be made by the court notwithstanding any power contained in the applicant company's memorandum or articles enabling the company itself to impose similar restrictions on the shares in question.

(3) Subject to the following subsections, a person who fails to comply with a notice under section 81 shall be guilty of an offence.

(4) A person shall not be guilty of an offence by virtue of failing to comply with a notice under section 81 if he proves that the requirement to give the information was frivolous or vexatious.

(5) Where an order is made under this section directing that shares shall be subject to restrictions under section 16, the company or any person aggrieved by the order may apply to the court for an order directing that the shares shall cease to be subject thereto.

(6) Subsections (6) to (16) of section 16 shall apply in relation to any shares subject to the restrictions imposed by that section by virtue of an order under this section but with the omission in subsections (6) to (15) of any reference to the Minister.

Definitions
'company': Companies Act, 1963, section 2.
'court': Companies Act, 1990, section 235.
'Minister': Companies Act, 1990, section 3.
'share': Companies Act, 1963, section 2.

General Note
This section provides for penalties for failure by any person who is or was interested in the voting shares of a public limited company to provide information about his interests in the company required by section 81. In addition to criminal sanctions there may be restrictions on the transfer or voting on the relevant shares.

(1) Where a notice was served on a person in respect of information on an interest in shares under section 81 and he fails to provide the information, the company may apply to the High Court for an order imposing restrictions on the shares in accordance with section 16 of the Act, for example transfer of shares or exercise of voting rights.

(2) An order may be made by the High Court restricting the relevant shares, irrespective of the provisions of the memorandum and articles of association.

(3) If a person fails to comply with a notice under section 81 he will be guilty of an offence and be subject to the penalties imposed by section 240.

(4) A person would not be guilty of an offence for failing to provide the information under a notice if he proves that the requirement to give the information was frivolous or vexatious.

(5) Where an order is made by the High Court an aggrieved person can apply for an order directing that the shares cease to be subject to restrictions.

(6) Subsections 6–16 of section 16 apply in relation to any shares subject to the restrictions imposed under that section by the court order.

SECTION 86
Removal of entries from register.

(1) A company may remove an entry against a person's name from its register of interests in shares if more than 6 years have elapsed since the date of the entry being made, and either—

(a) that entry recorded the fact that the person in question had ceased to have an interest notifiable under this Chapter in relevant share capital of the company, or

(b) it has been superseded by a later entry made under section 80 against the same person's name;

and in a case within paragraph (a) the company may also remove that person's name from the register.

(2) If a person in pursuance of an obligation imposed on him by any provision of this Chapter gives to a company the name and address of another person as being interested in shares in the company, the company shall, within 15 days of the date on which it was given that information, notify the other person that he has been so named and shall include in that notification—

(a) particulars of any entry relating to him made, in consequence of its being given that information, by the company in its register of interests in shares, and

(b) a statement informing him of his right to apply to have the entry removed in accordance with the following provisions of this section.

(3) A person who has been notified by a company in pursuance of subsection (2) that an entry relating to him has been made in the company's register of interests in shares may apply in writing to the company for the removal of that entry from the register; and the company shall remove the entry if satisfied that the information in pursuance of which the entry was made was incorrect.

(4) If a person who is identified in a company's register of interests in shares as being a party to an agreement to which section 73 applies (whether by an entry against his own name or by an entry relating to him made against another person's name as mentioned in subsection (2) (a)) ceases to be a party to that agreement, he may apply in writing to the company for the inclusion of that information in the register; and if the company is satisfied that he has ceased to be a party to the agreement, it shall record that information (if not already recorded) in every place where his name appears as a party to that agreement in the register.

(5) If an application under subsection (3) or (4) is refused (in a case within subsection (4), otherwise than on the ground that the information has already been recorded) the applicant may apply to the court for an order directing the company to remove the entry in question from the register or (as the case may be) to include the information in question in the register; and the court may, if it thinks fit, make such an order.

(6) Where a name is removed from a company's register of interests in shares in pursuance of subsection (1) or (3) or an order under subsection (5), the company shall within 14 days of the date of that removal make any necessary alteration in any associated index.

(7) If default is made in complying with subsection (2) or (6), the company and every officer of it who is in default shall be guilty of an offence and liable to a fine.

Definitions
'company': Companies Act, 1963, section 2.
'court': Companies Act, 1990, section 235.
'officer': Companies Act, 1963, section 2.
'relevant share capital': Companies Act, 1990, section 67.
'share': Companies Act, 1963, section 2.

General Note
This section sets out the detailed circumstances in which an entry against a person's name in a register of interests may be removed.

(1) Companies are empowered to remove out-of-date entries from the register of interests in shares. It is permissible to remove records if they are six years old and record that a person has ceased to be a member or they have been superseded by later entries against the same name.

(2) A company that has been notified that a person, other than the person giving notice, is a member of a concert party or has an interest in shares is required to notify that person within fifteen days that he has been notified to the company as being a member of such company.

(3) A person who is wrongly named as a member or as having an interest can have his name removed, and if on receipt of an application the company is notified that he is not a member it is obliged to remove his name. Failure to do so can result in a High Court order compelling it to do so.

(4) Where a company has not been notified by any other means, a person who has ceased to be a member may notify it in writing, and the company is then compelled to record the information if the company is satisfied that the information is correct.

(5) It is permissible to apply to the High Court for an order compelling the company to record the correct information.

(6) Where a name is removed from the register of interests the company must within fourteen days make the necessary alterations to the associated index.

(7) If the company or any officer is in default it will be guilty of an offence and liable to the penalties provided for in section 240.

SECTION 87
Entries, when not to be removed.

(1) Entries in a company's register of interests in shares under this Chapter shall not be deleted except in accordance with section 86.

(2) If an entry is deleted from a company's register of interests in shares in contravention of subsection (1), the company shall restore that entry to the register as soon as is reasonably practicable.

(3) If default is made in complying with subsection (1) or (2), the company and every officer of it who is in default shall be guilty of an offence and liable to a fine.

Definitions

'*company*': Companies Act, 1963, section 2.
'*officer*': Companies Act, 1963, section 2.
'*share*': Companies Act, 1963, section 2.

General Note

This section prohibits the deletion of entries from a company's register of interests in shares except in accordance with section 86. If an entry has been unlawfully deleted it must be restored.

(1) Entries must not be deleted except in accordance with section 86.

(2) If an entry has been unlawfully deleted it must be restored as soon as reasonably practicable.

(3) If the company or any officer is in default he will be guilty of an offence and liable to the penalties provided in section 240.

SECTION 88
Inspection of register and reports.

(1) Any register of interests in shares and any report which is required by section 84 (6) to be available for inspection in accordance with this section shall, during business hours (subject to such reasonable restrictions as the company may in general meeting impose, but so that not less than 2 hours in each day are allowed for inspection) be open to the inspection of any member of the company or of any other person without charge.

(2) The register referred to in subsection (1) shall also be and remain open and accessible to any person attending the company's annual general meeting at least one quarter hour before the appointed time for the commencement of the meeting and during the continuance of the meeting.

(3) Any such member or other person may require a copy of any such register or report, or any part of it, on payment of 15 pence or such less sum as the company may prescribe, for every 100 words or fractional part of 100 words

required to be copied; and the company shall cause any copy so required by a person to be sent to him before the expiration of the period of 10 days beginning with the day next following that on which the requirement is received by the company.

(4) If an inspection required under this section is refused or a copy so required is not sent within the proper period, the company and every officer of it who is in default shall be guilty of an offence and liable to a fine.

(5) In the case of a refusal of an inspection required under this section of any register or report, the court may by order compel an immediate inspection of it; and in the case of failure to send a copy required under this section, the court may by order direct that the copy required shall be sent to the person requiring it.

Definitions

'company': Companies Act, 1963, section 2.
'court': Companies Act, 1990, section 235.
'Minister': Companies Act, 1990, section 3.
'officer': Companies Act, 1963, section 2.
'prescribe': Companies Act, 1990, section 3.
'share': Companies Act, 1963, section 2.

General Note

This section provides for the inspection of the register of interests in shares and reports on any investigation of its share ownership.

(1) The register and any report that is required under section 84 is to be available for inspection for at least two hours each day during normal business hours to members of the company and the general public without charge.

(2) The register must remain open to any person attending the company's annual general meeting for at least fifteen minutes before the meeting and for the duration of the meeting.

(3) The maximum fee that the company may charge members of the company or other members of the public for a copy of all or part of the register or report is 15p per hundred words. The copy is to be made available within ten days following the date on which the request is received.

(4) The company and every officer who is in default and refuses to give the required information will be guilty of an offence and liable to a fine under the penalties set out in section 240.

(5) The High Court may order immediate inspection where the company has refused inspection of the register. Similarly, where a

company has refused to provide a copy of the register it can be ordered to do so.

SECTION 89
The 1988 Directive.

Sections 90 to 96 are for the purpose of giving effect to Council Directive 88/ 627/ EEC of 12th December, 1988 ("the 1988 Directive") on the information to be published when a major holding in a listed company is acquired or disposed of.

Definitions
'company': Companies Act, 1963, section 2.

General Note
This section is intended to give effect to the EC directive of 12 December 1988 on the information to be published when a major holding in a listed company is acquired or disposed of. In general, the directive requires disclosure when a shareholder passes a certain percentage level in a listed company.

Whereas the Act specifies a minimum threshold of 5 per cent, beyond which single percentage point disclosures must be made, the directive only requires disclosures where certain specified thresholds are passed.

SECTION 90

Provisions as to interpretation.

(1) In sections 91 to 96—

"the Exchange" means the Committee of the Irish Unit of the International Stock Exchange of the United Kingdom and the Republic of Ireland Limited;

"functions" includes powers and duties and references to the exercise of functions include, as respects powers and duties, references to the exercise of powers and the carrying out of duties.

(2) For the purposes of sections 91 to 96, each of the following shall be a "relevant authority" in relation to the Exchange—

   (i) its committee of management,
   (ii) its manager, however described.

Definitions
'Exchange': Companies Act, 1990, section 90.
'functions': Companies Act, 1990, section 90.
'relevant authority': Companies Act, 1990, section 90.

General Note
This section defines the terms 'Exchange', 'functions' and 'relevant authority' for the purposes of section 91.

SECTION 91

Obligation to notify certain interests to the Exchange.

(1) This section applies to interests in shares which—

(*a*) are comprised in relevant share capital of a public limited company, and

(*b*) are officially listed on the Exchange.

(2) Where a person becomes aware that he has acquired or ceased to have an interest in shares to which this section applies and, following that acquisition or disposal, the percentage level (within the meaning of section 69) of his interest in that share capital exceeds or falls below the percentage levels referred to in subsection (3), he shall, in addition to the obligation of disclosure to which he is subject under section 67, be under an obligation to notify the Exchange of his interest in the shares following the acquisition or cessation, as the case may be.

(3) The percentage levels referred to in subsection (2) are 10 per cent, 25 per cent, 50 per cent and 75 per cent.

(4) The provisions of this Chapter shall apply as regards the interests which are to be notified to the Exchange, and the manner in which they are to be so notified, as they apply to the interests to be notified to a company under this Chapter.

(5) Where the Exchange receives a declaration under this section it shall, subject to subsection (6), publish, in such manner as it shall determine, and within three days of its receipt, the information contained in that declaration.

(6) The Exchange may decide not to publish the information contained in the declaration if, but only if, it is satisfied—

(*a*) that the disclosure of such information would be contrary to the public interest, or

(*b*) that such disclosure would be seriously detrimental to the company or companies concerned:

Provided that—

(i) the Exchange shall not decide not to publish the information under paragraph (*b*) unless it is satisfied that a decision to do so would be unlikely to mislead the public with regard to the facts and circumstances knowledge of which is necessary for the assessment of the interests in question, and

(ii) notwithstanding any decision taken under this subsection, the Exchange may publish the information later than three days after its receipt where it is satisfied that the considerations in paragraph (*a*) or (*b*) no longer apply.

Definitions

'Exchange': Companies Act, 1990, section 90.

'public limited company': Companies (Amendment) Act, 1983, section 2.

'relevant share capital': Companies Act, 1990, section 67.

'share': Companies Act, 1963, section 2.

General Note

This section requires the disclosure of interests in shares of a publicly quoted company. It includes the obligation to notify the stock exchange when an interest in shares exceeds or falls below the percentage levels set out in subsection (3).

(1) This section applies to an interest in shares of companies that are public limited companies and are listed on a recognised stock exchange.

(2) Where a person becomes aware that he has acquired or disposed of an interest in shares where the transaction results in the interest exceeding or falling below the percentage level, there is an obligation to notify the stock exchange of the interest in the shares.

(3) The percentage levels at which disclosure is required are set out in this subsection.

(4) The manner in which interests are to be notified will be the same as that required for disclosure to the company under this Act.

(5) The stock exchange must publish a declaration received by it not later than three days after its receipt of such information.

(6) The stock exchange may decide not to publish such information if it is satisfied that it would not be in the public interest to do so or that such disclosure would be 'seriously detrimental' to the company. The stock exchange may not publish the information if it would be likely to mislead the public as to the facts and circumstances knowledge of which would be necessary for the assessment of the interest in the shares in question. It can also publish information previously withheld where the reasons for the original decision not to publish the information no longer apply.

SECTION 92
Duty of relevant authority to report to Director of Public Prosecutions.

(1) If it appears to a relevant authority of the Exchange that any person has contravened section 91, such authority shall forthwith report the matter to the Director of Public Prosecutions and shall furnish to the Director of Public Prosecutions such information and give to him such access to and facilities for inspecting and taking copies of any documents, being information or documents in the possession or under the control of such authority and relating to the matter in question, as the Director of Public Prosecutions may require.

(2) Where it appears to a member of the Exchange that any person has contravened section 91, he shall report the matter forthwith to a relevant authority of the Exchange, who shall thereupon come under the duty referred to in subsection (1).

(3) If it appears to a court in any proceedings that any person has committed a contravention as aforesaid, and that no report relating to the matter has been made to the Director of Public Prosecutions under subsection (1), that court may, on the application of any person interested in the proceedings concerned

or of its own motion, direct a relevant authority of the Exchange to make such a report, and on a report being made accordingly, this section shall have effect as though the report had been made in pursuance of subsection (1).

(4) If, where any matter is reported or referred to the Director of Public Prosecutions under this section, he considers that the case is one in which a prosecution ought to be instituted and institutes proceedings accordingly, it shall be the duty of a relevant authority of the Exchange, and of every officer of the company whose securities are concerned, and of any other person who appears to the Director of Public Prosecutions to have relevant information (other than any defendant in the proceedings) to give all assistance in connection with the prosecution which he or they are reasonably able to give.

(5) A relevant authority shall have the same powers and duties for the purposes of this section as it has under section 117.

(6) Where the Minister considers it necessary or expedient to do so for the proper and effective administration of this section, he may make such regulations as he thinks appropriate in relation to—

(*a*) the powers of authorised persons, or

(*b*) the matters in respect of which, or the persons from whom, authorised persons may require information under section 117, as applied by subsection (5).

Definitions

'*company*': Companies Act, 1963, section 2.

'*Exchange*': Companies Act, 1990, section 90.

'*officer*': Companies Act, 1963, section 2.

'*relevant authority*': Companies Act, 1990, section 90.

General Note

This section provides that there is a duty on the management of the stock exchange in the event of a contravention under section 91 to report the matter to the Director of Public Prosecutions.

(1) If it appears to the management of the stock exchange that a contravention under section 91 has occurred, the matter will be referred to the Director of Public Prosecutions together with such information as the Director of Public Prosecutions may require.

(2) Where it appears to a member of the stock exchange that there has been a contravention under section 91 it is his duty to report the matter to the management of the stock exchange.

(3) If it appears to a court that any person has committed a contravention and no report has been made to the Director of Public Prosecutions, the High Court may on the application of anyone interested in the proceedings direct a 'relevant authority' of the stock exchange to make a report on the matter.

(4) Where the Director of Public Prosecutions considers that a matter that has been reported to him should be the subject of a prosecution it is the duty of the stock exchange management and every officer of the company whose securities are concerned to give all assistance in connection with the prosecution that they may reasonably give.

(5) The relevant authority of the stock exchange has the same powers as it has under section 117, which include the power to obtain information relating to the securities.

(6) If he considers it necessary or expedient the Minister may make regulations relating to the powers of authorised persons or relating to the obtaining of information by authorised persons.

SECTION 93
Application and amendment of the 1984 Regulations.

(1) The annual report required by Regulation 11 of the European Communities (Stock Exchange) Regulations, 1984 (S.I. No. 282 of 1984) ("the 1984 Regulations") shall include—

(a) the number of written complaints received suggesting possible contraventions of section 91,

(b) the number of reports made under section 92,

(c) the number of instances in which, following the exercise of powers by authorised persons under section 117, as applied by section 92, reports were not so made, and

(d) such other information as may be prescribed.

(2) The First Schedule to the 1984 Regulations is hereby amended by the substitution, for paragraph 5 (c) of Schedule C of the Annex to Council Directive 79/279/EEC of 5 March 1979 set out in that Schedule, of the following:

"(c) The company must inform the public of any changes in the structure (shareholders and breakdown of holdings) of the major holdings in its capital as compared with information previously published on that subject as soon as such changes come to its notice.

In particular, a company which is not subject to Council Directive 88/627/EEC on the information to be published when a major holding in a listed company is acquired or disposed of must inform the public within nine calendar days whenever it comes to its notice that a person or entity has acquired or disposed of a number of shares such that his or its holding exceeds or falls below one of the thresholds laid down in Article 4 of that Directive.".

Definitions

'*company*': Companies Act, 1963, section 2.

General Note

This section stipulates that the annual report required under the 1984 stock exchange regulations contain certain information.

(1) The annual report required under the 1984 stock exchange regulations must include:

(*a*) the number of written complaints suggesting possible contraventions of notification of interests;

(*b*) the number of reports made to the Director of Public Prosecutions;

(*c*) the number of instances in which reports were not made.

(2) This subsection amends paragraph 5 (*c*) of schedule C of the annex to EC directive 79/279/EEC and provides that the company must inform the public of any changes in the structure of a major holding in its capital as compared to the previously published information.

SECTION 94
Obligation of professional secrecy.

(1) Information obtained by any of the following persons by virtue of the exercise by the Exchange of its functions under this Part shall not be disclosed except in accordance with law, namely—

(*a*) a relevant authority of the Exchange,
(*b*) an authorised person, or
(*c*) any person employed or formerly employed by the Exchange.

(2) Subsection (1) shall not prevent a relevant authority of the Exchange from disclosing any information to the Minister under this Part or to a similar authority in another Member State of the European Communities pursuant to section 96.

(3) Any person who contravenes subsection (1) shall be guilty of an offence.

Definitions

'*Exchange*': Companies Act, 1990, section 90.
'*relevant authority*': Companies 1990, section 90.

General Note

This section stipulates that the management of the stock exchange or an authorised person or employee or former employee of the stock exchange may not disclose any information except in accordance with the law; but this does not prevent the disclosure of information to the Minister under the Act or a similar authority in another member-state of the EC. Anyone who contravenes this provision will be guilty of an offence under section 240 of the Act.

SECTION 95
Immunity from suit.

A relevant authority of the Exchange shall not be liable in damages in respect of anything done or omitted to be done by the authority in connection with the exercise by it of its functions under sections 91 to 96 unless the act or omission complained of was done or omitted to be done in bad faith.

Definitions

'*relevant authority*': Companies Act, 1990, section 90.

General Note

The committee of management of the stock exchange or its manager as the case may be will not be liable for damages for anything done in connection with the execution of its functions under sections 91–96 of the Act unless the act or omission complained of was omitted or done in bad faith.

SECTION 96
Co-operation between authorities in Member States.

A relevant authority of the Exchange in exercising its functions under sections 91 to 94 shall comply with Article 12 (co-operation between competent authorities in Member States) of the 1988 Directive.

Definitions

'*Exchange*': Companies Act, 1990, section 90.

'*relevant authority*': Companies Act, 1990, section 90.

General Note

This section stipulates that the committee of management or manager as the case may be of the stock exchange must comply with article 12 of the 1988 directive, which provides for co-operation between competent authorities in the member-states of the EC.

SECTION 97
Application of Chapter 3.

(1) The provisions of this Chapter shall apply to all bodies corporate incorporated in the State other than—

(*a*) a public limited company;

(*b*) a society registered under the Industrial and Provident Societies Acts, 1893 to 1978;

(*c*) a society registered under the Building Societies Act, 1989; and

(*d*) any body corporate which is prohibited by statute or otherwise from making any distribution of its income or property among its members while it is a going concern or when it is in liquidation.

(2) Any reference in this Chapter to a company shall be deemed to be a reference to any body corporate to which, by virtue of subsection (1), this Chapter applies.

(3) Any reference in this Chapter to share capital or relevant share capital shall, in relation to a company, be deemed to be a reference to the issued share capital of a class carrying rights to vote in all circumstances at general meetings of the company, and references to shares shall be construed accordingly.

Definitions

'body corporate': Companies Act, 1963, section 2 (3).

'company': Companies Act, 1963, section 2.

'public limited company': Companies (Amendment) Act, 1983, section 2.

General Note

This section defines the scope of application of chapter 3, which deals with the disclosure of share ownership in certain cases of companies other than public limited companies.

(1) The provisions of this chapter apply to all companies incorporated in the state other than

- public limited companies,
- industrial and provident societies,
- building societies, and
- bodies corporate that are prohibited by statute or otherwise from making any distribution of income or property.

In other words, the provisions of the chapter apply to all private companies.

(2) Any reference to a company will be a reference to any body corporate.

(3) The reference to share capital is elaborated, and is confined to relevant shares, i.e. shares carrying full, unrestricted voting rights.

SECTION 98
Disclosure order.

(1) For the purposes of this Chapter, "disclosure order" means an order of the court which obliges—

(*a*) any person whom the court believes to have or to be able to obtain any information as to—
(i) persons interested at present, or at any time during a period specified in the order, in the shares or debentures of a company,
(ii) the names and addresses of any of those persons,
(iii) the name and address of any person who acts or has acted on behalf of any of those persons in relation to the shares or debentures,
to give such information to the court; or

(*b*) any person whom the court believes to be, or at any time during a period specified in the order to have been, interested in shares or debentures of a company to confirm that fact or (as the case may be) to indicate whether or not it is the case and, where he holds or has during that period held any interest in such shares or debentures, to give such further information as the court may require; or

(c) any person interested in shares or debentures of a company specified in the order to disclose to the court the information required under subparagraphs (i) and (ii) and (iii) of paragraph (a) and such further information as the court may require.

(2) Any person who has a financial interest in a company may apply to the court for a disclosure order in respect of all or any of the shares of or debentures in the company.

(3) An application under subsection (2) shall be supported by such evidence as the court may require.

(4) The court may, before hearing an application under subsection (2), require the applicant to give security for payment of the costs of hearing the application or any consequential proceedings.

(5) The court may make a disclosure order only if—

(a) it deems it just and equitable to do so; and
(b) it is of the opinion that the financial interest of the applicant is or will be prejudiced by the non-disclosure of any interest in the shares or debentures of the company.

(6) For the purposes of subsection (2) "financial interest" includes any interest as member, contributory, creditor, employee, co-adventurer, examiner, lessor, lessee, licensor, licensee, liquidator or receiver either in relation to the company in respect of whose shares or debentures a disclosure order is sought or a related company.

(7) Where a person authorises any other person ("the agent") to acquire or dispose of, on his behalf, interests in shares comprised in relevant share capital of a company or in debentures of the company in respect of which a disclosure order is made, he shall, for the duration of that order, ensure that the agent notifies him immediately of acquisitions or disposals of interests in shares or debentures so comprised effected by the agent which will or may give rise to any obligation on his part to provide information in accordance with the terms of the order with respect to his interest in that share capital or those debentures.

Definitions

'company': Companies Act, 1963, section 2.

'court': Companies Act, 1990, section 235.

'debenture': Companies Act, 1963, section 2.

'disclosure order': Companies Act, 1990, section 98.

'financial interest': Companies Act, 1990, section 98.

'relevant share capital': Companies Act, 1990, section 67.

General Note

This section enables a person with a defined financial interest to apply to the High Court for a disclosure order in respect of some or all of the shares or debentures of a company. The High Court may require supporting evidence and security for costs to be given by the applicant. The court may make a disclosure order only if it deems it just and equitable to do so and is satisfied that the financial interest of the applicant is or will be prejudiced by the non-disclosure of any interest in the shares or debentures of the company.

(1) A disclosure order is defined as one where a person is obliged to give information to the court regarding persons interested in shares or debentures of the company that is the subject of the disclosure order.

(2) Anyone who has a financial interest in a company may apply to the court for a disclosure order on some or all of the shares or debentures of the company. The definition of a person who has a financial interest is elaborated in subsection (6).

(3) The application may be supported by such evidence as the court may require.

(4) The High Court has power to require the applicant to give security for payment of the costs before hearing the applicant.

(5) The court will only grant a disclosure order if
• it is just and equitable to do so, and
• it is of the opinion that the applicant's financial interest will be prejudiced by the non-disclosure of the interest.

(6) Financial interest is defined for the purposes of subsection (2).

(7) Where a person appoints an agent to acquire or dispose of shares or debentures or interests in them in respect of which a disclosure order has been made, the agent must notify him immediately of any acquisitions or disposals of shares.

SECTION 99
Procedure on application for disclosure order.

(1) A person intending to apply for the making of a disclosure order shall give not less than 10 days' notice of his intention to the company in respect of whose shares or debentures the order is sought and to the person to whom the order is intended to be directed.

(2) The applicant shall also serve on any person specified by the court such notice of the application as the court may direct.

(3) On the hearing of the application every person notified under subsection (1) or (2) may appear and adduce evidence.

Definitions

'*company*': the Companies Act, 1963, section 2.
'*court*': Companies Act, 1990, section 235.
'*debenture*': Companies Act, 1963, section 2.
'*disclosure order*': Companies Act, 1990, section 98.

General Note

This section provides that the application for a disclosure order be subject to ten days' notice of the intention to apply. The court may direct that the applicant serve notice on anyone so specified by the court order.

SECTION 100

Scope of disclosure order.

(1) A disclosure order may require the person to whom it is addressed—

(a) to give particulars of his own past or present interest in shares comprised in relevant share capital of the company or in debentures of the company held by him at any time during the period mentioned in the order;

(b) where the interest is a present interest and any other interest in the shares or debentures subsists or, in any case, where another interest in the shares or debentures subsisted during that period at any time when his own interest subsisted, to give so far as lies within his knowledge such particulars with respect to that other interest as may be required by the order;

(c) where his interest is a past interest, to give so far as lies within his knowledge particulars of the identity of the person who held that interest immediately upon his ceasing to hold it.

(2) A disclosure order shall specify the information to be supplied to the court under the order in respect of any person, shares or debentures to which it refers and any such information shall be given in writing.

(3) Sections 68 to 79 shall apply as appropriate for the purposes of construing references in this Chapter to persons interested in shares and debentures and to interests in shares and debentures respectively as they apply in relation to section 67 (disregarding section 78) and any reference in those sections to a "percentage level" shall be disregarded.

(4) For the purposes of this section any reference in sections 67 to 79 to "shares" shall, where appropriate and unless the contrary is stated, be deemed to include a reference to debentures.

(5) This section shall apply in relation to a person who has or previously had or is or was entitled to acquire a right to subscribe for shares in or debentures of a company which would on issue be comprised in relevant share capital of that company as it applies in relation to a person who is or was interested in shares so comprised or in debentures of the company; and references in the preceding provisions of this section to an interest in shares so comprised or an interest in debentures and to shares so comprised or debentures shall be read accordingly in any such case as including references respectively to any such right and to shares which would on issue be so comprised.

Definitions

'company': Companies Act, 1963, section 2.
'court': Companies Act, 1990, section 235.
'debenture': Companies Act, 1963, section 2.
'disclosure order': Companies Act, 1990, section 98.
'relevant share capital': Companies Act, 1990, section 67.

General Note

This section sets out the scope of the disclosure order, which must specify the information required and require the person to whom it is addressed to give particulars of his own past or present interest in the company or, in the case where he has ceased to have an interest, to give whatever information he has on the identity of the person who subsequently held it.

(1) The information that a person may be required to give under a disclosure order is specified in this subsection. The information includes particulars of present or past interests in shares or debentures. Where a person has ceased to have an interest in the shares or debentures he should provide the full identity of the person who subsequently held it.

(2) The information required to be provided under the disclosure order must be in writing.

(3–4) The construction of references for the purposes of this chapter are explained.

(5) This section will also apply to a person who had a right to subscribe for shares or debentures in the company.

SECTION 101

Powers of court.

(1) The court may, on cause shown, rescind or vary a disclosure order.

(2) A disclosure order may specify a person, group or class of persons to which the order applies.

(3) The court may, if it considers—

(a) that it would be just and equitable to do so, and
(b) that the financial interest of the applicant would not be prejudiced thereby, exempt in whole or in part from the requirements of a disclosure order—
    (i) any person or class of persons,
    (ii) any interest or class of interest in shares or debentures,
    (iii) any share, group or class of shares,
    (iv) any debenture, group or class of debentures.

(4) When the court makes a disclosure order it may impose, for a specific period of time, such conditions or restrictions on the rights or obligations attaching to the shares or debentures in respect of which the order is made as it deems fit.

(5) Any person whose interests are affected by any conditions or restrictions imposed on shares or debentures under subsection (4) may apply to the court for relief from all or any of those conditions and the court may, if it considers it just and equitable to do so, grant such relief in whole or in part and on such terms and conditions as it sees fit.

Definitions

'*court*': Companies Act, 1990, section 235.

'*debenture*': Companies Act, 1963, section 2.

'*disclosure order*': Companies Act, 1990, section 98.

'*share*': Companies Act, 1963, section 2.

General Note

This section outlines the general powers of the court in relation to a disclosure order.

(1) The High Court has the power to rescind or vary any disclosure order.

(2) The disclosure order may specify the person, group or class of persons to which the disclosure order applies.

(3) The High Court may, if it considers it just and equitable and that the financial interest of the applicant would not be prejudiced, exempt in whole or in part any person, class of persons, interest or class of interest in shares or debentures or any share, group or class of shares or debentures from the disclosure order.

(4) The High Court may specify the period of time to which the disclosure order will apply.

(5) Any person who is affected by a disclosure order may apply to the court for relief from some or all of the conditions if it is considered by the court to be just and equitable to do so.

SECTION 102
Notice of disclosure order.

(1) The applicant shall cause notice in the prescribed form of the making of a disclosure order together with a copy of the order to be sent by registered post within 7 days of the making of the order to—

(*a*) the company (at its registered office) in respect of whose shares or debentures the order has been made,

(*b*) the registrar of companies,

(*c*) the registered holder of any shares or debentures in respect of which the disclosure order has been made where it appears to the court that—

(i) such holder is not at the date of the making of the order resident in the State, and

(ii) such holder should be notified,

(*d*) such other person as the court sees fit.

(2) The applicant shall cause notice of the making of a disclosure order to be published, within 7 days of the making of the order, in at least 2 daily newspapers which circulate in the district in which the registered office of the company, in respect of whose shares or debentures the order has been made, is situate.

(3) For the purposes of subsection (1) (*a*)—

(*a*) the address of the registered office of the company at the date of the making of the disclosure order shall be deemed to be the address of that office which was last delivered to the registrar of companies or otherwise published, as such case may be (in accordance with and in the manner required by the law relating to the company) prior to the date of making the order; and

(*b*) if no address of the registered office has ever been duly delivered to the registrar of companies or if the location of the last delivered address has been destroyed, the requirements of subsection (1) (*a*) shall be deemed to have been complied with by sending the required notice of the order together with a copy thereof to the registrar of companies.

(4) For the purposes of subsection (1) (*c*)—

(*a*) the address of a non-resident registered holder of shares or debentures shall be deemed to be the address of that holder which was last delivered to the registrar of companies or otherwise published, as the case may be (in accordance with and in the manner required by the law relating to the company) prior to the date of making of the order; and

(*b*) if no address of the non-resident registered holder has ever been duly delivered to the registrar of companies the requirements of subsection (1) (*c*) shall be deemed to have been complied with by sending the required notice of the order together with a copy thereof to the registrar of companies.

(5) Any reference in this section to the registered office of a company shall, in the case of a company not registered under the Companies Acts, be construed as a reference to the principal office of the company.

Definitions

'*company*': the Companies Act, 1963, section 2.

'*court*': Companies Act, 1990, section 235.

'*debenture*': Companies Act, 1963, section 2.

'*disclosure order*': Companies Act, 1990, section 98.

'*prescribe*': Companies Act, 1990, section 3.

'*registrar of companies*': Companies Act, 1963, section 2.

General Note

This section provides that where a disclosure order has been made the applicant must notify the company, the Registrar of Companies and foreign shareholders etc. of the making of the order. The applicant must also publish in certain newspapers a notice of the making of the order.

(1) The applicant must notify the following persons of the disclosure order within seven days of the making of the order:
- the Registrar of Companies;
- overseas shareholders and debenture holders;
- any other person the court sees fit.

(2) The applicant must publish a notice of the disclosure order within seven days of the making of the order in two newspapers circulating in the district where the registered office of the company is located.

(3) The address of the registered office is the one last notified to the Registrar of Companies, or if no registered office address was ever notified, the notice of the order with a copy thereof to the Registrar of Companies will suffice.

(4) This subsection imposes similar provisions to those of subsection (3) for non-resident shareholders or debenture holders.

(5) The reference to the registered office is explained.

SECTION 103
Information disclosed under order.

(1) An obligation to provide any information imposed on any person by a disclosure order shall be treated as not being fulfilled unless the notice by means of which it purports to be fulfilled identifies him and gives his current address.

(2) Where information is given to the court in compliance with the terms of a disclosure order, a prescribed officer of the court shall, unless the court otherwise directs, cause such information to be furnished (in whole or in part as the court may direct) to the applicant and to the company in respect of whose shares or debentures the order was made.

(3) In reaching its decision under subsection (2), the court shall have regard to whether the requirements of section 102 have been complied with.

(4) Where any information is furnished to the applicant or the company in pursuance of subsection (2), the court may impose such restrictions as it sees fit as to the publication of the information by the person to whom it has been furnished.

Definitions

'*company*': Companies Act, 1963, section 2.
'*court*': Companies Act, 1990, section 235.
'*debenture*': Companies Act, 1963, section 2.

'disclosure order': Companies Act, 1990, section 98.
'share': Companies Act, 1963, section 2.

General Note

This section elaborates on information to be disclosed under disclosure orders.

(1) An obligation to provide information under a disclosure order is not fulfilled unless it identifies the person and gives his current address.

(2) Where information is given to the court in compliance with the disclosure order an officer of the court will ensure that the information is furnished to the company and the applicant concerned.

(3) The court will have regard to whether section 101 (2) above has been complied with. For example, if the applicant has not complied with section 101 the court could withhold the information from that person.

(4) The court has the power to impose such restrictions as it considers fit concerning the publication of the information by the applicant or the company.

SECTION 104

Civil consequences of contravention of disclosure order.

(1) Where a person—

(a) fails to fulfil, within the proper period, an obligation to provide information required by a disclosure order, or
(b) in purported fulfilment of any such obligation makes to the court a statement which he knows to be false or recklessly makes to the court a statement which is false,

no right or interest of any kind whatsoever in respect of any shares in or debentures of the company concerned held by him shall be enforceable by him whether directly or indirectly, by action or legal proceeding.

(2) Where any right or interest is restricted under subsection (1), any person in default under that subsection or any other person affected by such restriction may apply to the court for relief against a disability imposed by or arising out of subsection (1) and the court on being satisfied that the default was accidental, or due to inadvertence, or some other sufficient cause, or that on other grounds it is just and equitable to grant relief, may grant such relief either generally, or as respects any particular right or interest on such terms and conditions as it sees fit.

(3) Where an applicant for relief under subsection (2) is a person referred to in subsection (1), the court may not grant such relief if it appears that the default has arisen as a result of any deliberate act or omission on the part of the applicant.

(4) The acquisition by any person of an interest in shares or debentures of a company registered in the State shall be deemed to be a consent by that person to the disclosure by him, his agents or intermediaries of any information required to be disclosed in relation to shares or debentures by the Companies Acts.

Definitions

'*company*': Companies Act, 1963, section 2.
'*court*': Companies Act, 1990, section 235.
'*debenture*': Companies Act, 1963, section 2.
'*disclosure order*': Companies Act, 1990, section 98.
'*share*': Companies Act, 1963, section 2.

General Note

This section provides that where a person does not comply with a disclosure order or gives false information about his interest he cannot enforce his interest in the shares, by legal proceedings or otherwise.

(1) Where a person fails to fulfil an obligation under a disclosure order within the specified period he will not be able to enforce any interest or right in the shares or debentures directly or indirectly by legal action.

(2) Any person in default under subsection (1) or any other person affected by the restriction may apply to the court for relief against any disability imposed, and the court may grant relief if it is satisfied that the default was due to an accident or inadvertence or some other ground and that it is just and equitable to grant relief on such conditions as it sees fit.

(3) If it appears that the default was due to a deliberate act or omission the court may not grant relief.

(4) The acquisition of an interest in shares or debentures is deemed to be consent by that person to disclosure by him, his agents or intermediaries.

SECTION 105

Power to alter maximum inspection etc. charges.

(1) The Minister may, by order, alter any of the charges referred to in—

(a) section 60 (5) of this Act or section 92 (1), 119 (1) or 195 (10) (inserted by section 51 of this Act) of the Principal Act, or
(b) section 60 (8) or 88 (3) of this Act, or section 92 (2), 92 (3), 119 (2) or 146 (2) of the Principal Act.

(2) The Minister may also, by order, alter the basis of any of the charges referred to in the provisions specified in subsection (1) (b) from the basis referred to in those provisions to some other basis.

(3) In making any order under this section, the Minister shall take into account the general costs incurred by a company in facilitating the inspection, or providing copies, of the registers or other documents referred to in subsection (1).

(4) Every order made under this section shall be laid before each House of the Oireachtas as soon as may be after it is made and if a resolution annulling the order is passed by either House within the next 21 days on which that House has sat after the order is laid before it, the order shall be annulled accordingly but without prejudice to the validity of anything previously done thereunder.

Definitions

'*company*': Companies Act, 1963, section 2.

'*Minister*': Companies Act, 1990, section 3.

'*Principal Act*': Companies Act, 1990, section 3.

General Note

This section gives the Minister the power by Ministerial order to alter any charges in connection with obtaining copies of the register of directors and secretaries or register of interests or the periods of time during which the registers are open for inspection. Every Ministerial order made under this section will be laid before each house of the Oireachtas as soon as possible thereafter. The order will become effective unless an order is passed by either house within twenty-one days of the sitting of the house after the order has been laid before it.

SECTION 106
Transitional
provisions.

(1) Where on the commencement of this section a person has an interest which, if it was acquired after such commencement, would be subject to a notification requirement under Chapter 1 or 2 he shall be under an obligation to make to the company the notification with respect to his interest required by the Chapter concerned.

(2) For the purposes of subsection (1), sections 56 and 71 (1) shall apply as if, for the period of 5 days mentioned in each of those provisions, there were substituted a period of 14 days.

(3) Section 73 shall apply in relation to an agreement notwithstanding that it was made before the commencement of this section or that any such acquisition of shares as is mentioned in subsection (1) (*b*) of that section took place before such commencement.

Definitions

'*share*': Companies Act, 1963, section 2.

General Note

This section sets out the transitional arrangements for the implementation and operation of the chapter concerning the disclosure of interests in shares.

(1) Where on the commencement of the Act a person has an interest which if it was acquired after the commencement would be subject to notification, there is an obligation to make such notification to the company with respect to his interest.

(2) The period of notice within which disclosure of the interests referred to in subsection (1) must be made is fourteen days instead of the usual five days.

(3) The provision of section 73 (Agreement to acquire interest in a public limited company) will apply even though made before the commencement of the Act.

5
INSIDER DEALING

Part V of the Act makes it unlawful for a person in possession of inside information to deal in securities on a recognised stock exchange, and provides penalties for those found guilty of an offence.

The provisions concerning insider dealing, which refer only to publicly quoted companies, are extremely complex. It must be questioned whether they can be effectively enforced, especially when consideration is given to the small number of prosecutions that have occurred in the UK since the enactment of similar legislation.

The definitions in section 107 are very broad; for example, the term 'dealing' extends to making or offering to make an agreement relating to acquiring, disposing of, subscribing for or underwriting securities. It also includes inducing or attempting to induce any other person to do likewise. Similarly the term 'officer' includes not only the accepted persons covered by this term but also 'secretaries and employees'.

Section 108, which sets out the prohibitions, extends the legislation to those who are not 'connected with' the company but who are in possession of relevant information received, whether directly or indirectly, from someone who is prohibited from dealing in the securities if they are aware or ought reasonably to be aware that the person is prohibited from dealing.

Furthermore the Act does not contain any provision to help explain what is meant by 'not generally available'. Information could be in the public domain but not available generally to shareholders: would the passing on of such information be construed as insider dealing? Similarly there is no guidance as to what constitutes materiality as it affects a share price.

The provisions of this part will give rise to many problems in the future; and whereas they will provide a deterrent by being on the statute book, they are unlikely to be frequently applied.

SECTION 107

Interpretation.

In this Part, except where the context otherwise requires—

"dealing", in relation to securities, means (whether as principal or agent) acquiring, disposing of, subscribing for or underwriting the securities, or making or offering to make, or inducing or attempting to induce a person to make or to offer to make, an agreement—

(a) for or relating to acquiring, disposing of, subscribing for or underwriting the securities; or

(b) the purpose or purported purpose of which is to secure a profit or gain to a person who acquires, disposes of, subscribes for or underwrites the securities or to any of the parties to the agreement in relation to the securities;

"director" includes a shadow director within the meaning of section 27;

"officer", in relation to a company, includes—

(a) a director, secretary or employee;

(b) a liquidator;

(c) any person administering a compromise or arrangement made between the company and its creditors;

(d) an examiner;

(e) an auditor; and

(f) a receiver;

"public office" means an office or employment which is remunerated out of the Central Fund or out of moneys provided by the Oireachtas or money raised by local taxation or charges, or an appointment to or employment under any commission, committee, tribunal, board or body established by the Government or any Minister of the Government or by or under any statutory authority;

"recognised stock exchange" includes, in particular, any exchange prescribed by the Minister which provides facilities for the buying and selling of rights or obligations to acquire stock;

"related company", in relation to a company, means any body corporate which is the company's subsidiary or holding company, or a subsidiary of the company's holding company;

"relevant authority", in relation to a recognised stock exchange, means—

(i) its board of directors, committee of management or other management body, or

(ii) its manager, however described;

"securities" means—

(a) shares, debentures or other debt securities issued or proposed to be issued, whether in the State or otherwise, and for which dealing facilities are, or are to be, provided by a recognised stock exchange;

(b) any right, option or obligation in respect of any such shares, debentures or other debt securities referred to in paragraph (a);

(c) any right, option or obligation in respect of any index relating to any such shares, debentures or other debt securities referred to in paragraph (a); or

(d) such interests as may be prescribed;

"underwrite" includes sub-underwrite.

Definitions

'auditor': this is not defined in the Companies Acts; but see the UK case *R.* v. *Shacter* [1960] 2 QB 252.

'body corporate': Companies Act, 1963, section 2 (3).

'company': Companies Act, 1963, section 2.

'dealing': Companies Act, 1990, section 107.

'debenture': Companies Act, 1963, section 2.

'director': Companies Act, 1990, section 107.

'holding company': Companies Act, 1963, section 155.

'Minister': Companies Act, 1990, section 3.

'officer': Companies Act, 1990, section 107.

'prescribe': Companies Act, 1990, section 3.

'public office': Companies Act, 1990, section 107.

'recognised stock exchange': Companies Act, 1990, section 107.

'related company': Companies Act, 1990, section 107.

'relevant authority': Companies Act, 1990, section 107.

'securities': Companies Act, 1990, section 107.

'shadow director': Companies Act, 1990, section 3.

'share': Companies Act, 1963, section 2.

'subsidiary': Companies Act, 1963, section 155.

'underwrite': Companies Act, 1990, section 107.

General Note

This section provides a number of definitions for the purposes of part V of the Act concerning insider dealing. The provisions will only apply to public limited companies with shares listed on a recognised stock exchange.

It is noteworthy that the definition for this part of the Act of 'officer' has been expanded to include not only a director, secretary or employee but also a liquidator, examiner, auditor, or receiver.

SECTION 108
Unlawful dealings in securities by insiders.

(1) It shall not be lawful for a person who is, or at any time in the preceding 6 months has been, connected with a company to deal in any securities of that company if by reason of his so being, or having been, connected with that company he is in possession of information that is not generally available, but, if it were, would be likely materially to affect the price of those securities.

(2) It shall not be lawful for a person who is, or at any time in the preceding 6 months has been, connected with a company to deal in any securities of any other company if by reason of his so being, or having been, connected with the first-mentioned company he is in possession of information that—

(*a*) is not generally available but, if it were, would be likely materially to affect the price of those securities, and

(*b*) relates to any transaction (actual or contemplated) involving both those companies or involving one of them and securities of the other, or to the fact that any such transaction is no longer contemplated.

(3) Where a person is in possession of any such information as is mentioned in subsection (1) or (2) that if generally available would be likely materially to affect

the price of securities but is not precluded by either of those subsections from dealing in those securities, it shall not be lawful for him to deal in those securities if he has received the information, directly or indirectly, from another person and is aware, or ought reasonably to be aware, of facts or circumstances by virtue of which that other person is then himself precluded by subsection (1) or (2) from dealing in those securities.

(4) It shall not be lawful for a person at any time when he is precluded by subsection (1), (2) or (3) from dealing in any securities, to cause or procure any other person to deal in those securities.

(5) It shall not be lawful for a person, at any time when he is precluded by subsection (1), (2) or (3) from dealing in any securities by reason of his being in possession of any information, to communicate that information to any other person if he knows, or ought reasonably to know, that the other person will make use of the information for the purpose of dealing, or causing or procuring another person to deal, in those securities.

(6) Without prejudice to subsection (3), but subject to subsections (7) and (8), it shall not be lawful for a company to deal in any securities at a time when any officer of that company is precluded by subsection (1), (2) or (3) from dealing in those securities.

(7) Subsection (6) does not preclude a company from entering into a transaction at any time by reason only of information in the possession of an officer of that company if—

(*a*) the decision to enter into the transaction was taken on its behalf by a person other than the officer;
(*b*) it had in operation at that time written arrangements to ensure that the information was not communicated to that person and that no- advice relating to the transaction was given to him by a person in possession of the information; and
(*c*) the information was not so communicated and such advice was not so given.

(8) Subsection (6) does not preclude a company from dealing in securities of another company at any time by reason only of information in the possession of an officer of the first-mentioned company, being information that was received by the officer in the course of the performance of his duties as an officer of the first-mentioned company and that consists only of the fact that the first-mentioned company proposes to deal in securities of that other company.

(9) This section does not preclude a person from dealing in securities, or rights or interests in securities, of a company if—

(*a*) he enters into the transaction concerned as agent for another person pursuant to a specified instruction of that other person to effect that transaction; and
(*b*) he has not given any advice to the other person in relation to dealing in securities, or rights or interests in securities, of that company that are included in the same class as the first-mentioned securities.

(10) This section does not preclude a person from dealing in securities if, while not otherwise taking advantage of his possession of information referred to in subsection (1)—

(*a*) he gives at least 21 days' notice to a relevant authority of the relevant stock exchange of his intention to deal, within the period referred to in paragraph (*b*), in the securities of the company concerned, and (*b*) the dealing takes place within a period beginning 7 days after the publication of the company's interim or final results, as the case may be and ending 14 days after such publication, and

(*c*) the notice referred to in paragraph (*a*) is published by the exchange concerned immediately on its receipt.

(11) For the purposes of this section, a person is connected with a company if, being a natural person—

(*a*) he is an officer of that company or of a related company;

(*b*) he is a shareholder in that company or in a related company; or

(*c*) he occupies a position (including a public office) that may reasonably be expected to give him access to information of a kind to which subsections (1) and (2) apply by virtue of—

(i) any professional, business or other relationship existing between himself (or his employer or a company of which he is an officer) and that company or a related company; or

(ii) his being an officer of a substantial shareholder in that company or in a related company.

(12) For the purposes of subsection (11) "substantial shareholder" means a person who holds shares in a company, the number of which is above the notifiable percentage for the time being in force under section 70.

(13) The prohibitions in subsections (1), (3), (4) and (5) shall extend to dealings in securities issued by the State as if the references in subsections (1), (9) and (11) (other than paragraphs (*a*) and (*b*) of the last mentioned subsection) to a company were references to the State.

Definitions

'*company*': Companies Act, 1963, section 2.

'*dealing*': Companies Act, 1990, section 107.

'*notifiable percentage*': Companies Act, 1990, section 70.

'*officer*': Companies Act, 1990, section 107.

'*public office*': Companies Act, 1990, section 107.

'*recognised stock exchange*': Companies Act, 1990, section 3.

'*related company*': Companies Act, 1990, section 3.

'*securities*': Companies Act, 1990, section 107.

'*substantial shareholder*': Companies Act, 1990, section 107.

General Note

This section makes it unlawful for a person connected with a company to deal in securities if he has any inside information relating to it. Such a person is also precluded from dealing in the securities of any other company if he has inside information relating to his employment in the first company. A person who receives inside information is precluded from dealing, and it is unlawful to engage in tipping on the basis of such inside information.

(1) It is not lawful for anyone who in the preceding six months has been connected with a company (see subsection 11 for a definition of 'connected person') to deal in securities if he is in possession of information that is not generally available and which if it were available would materially affect the price of the particular securities.

(2) It is not lawful for a person who in the preceding six months has been connected with a company to deal in securities of any other company if by reason of being connected with the first company he is in possession of information which if generally made available would materially affect the price of the particular securities relating to a transaction involving at least one of them or of the fact that the transaction contemplated is no longer going to occur.

(3) Where a person is in possession of information as set out in subsection (1) or (2) above that would materially affect the price and is not precluded by either subsection from dealing in the securities, it is not lawful for him to deal in the securities if he has received the information directly or indirectly from a person who would be precluded by the subsection from dealing in the shares. This subsection was amended in the Seanad by the substitution of 'received' for 'obtained'. This was because of the decision in Southwood Crown Court, London, where it was held that to 'obtain information' meant 'not simply to get or have the information but to actively seek or acquire it.' This decision was overturned subsequently in the Court of Appeal; however, the Government preferred to be cautious, and in the debate (*Seanad Debates*, 4 May 1988, at 731) Mr Séamus Brennan TD, Minister for Trade and Marketing, stated: 'What we want to provide is that no matter how the insider got his information, in other words, whether he went looking for it or not, he should still be prohibited from dealing under the section. Therefore, "received" seems a better word than "obtained".'

(4) It is not lawful for a person who is prohibited from dealing in any securities to arrange for someone else to procure such securities.

(5) It is not lawful for a person who is precluded from dealing in securities by reason of being in possession of information obtained to communicate it to another person if he knows or ought reasonably to have known that the other person would make use of

the information for the purpose of dealing in securities or causing someone else to deal in the securities.

(6) It is unlawful for a company to deal in securities if an officer of that company is precluded at that time from dealing in such securities.

(7) A company is not precluded from dealing in securities in subsection (6) above if the officer who was in possession of the information was not involved in any way with the decision to deal in the securities and there was no communication of information with the officer, and the company had a written arrangement in operation to ensure that the information was not communicated or advice given to another person.

(8) A company is not precluded from dealing in securities by the fact that the officer of the first company is in possession of information obtained in the course of his ordinary duties. What is being exempted in this subsection is the very possession among the personnel of institution A of the single piece of information that the institution proposes to buy or sell the other company's stock.

(9) A person is not precluded from dealing in securities where he carries out a transaction as agent carrying out a specified instruction to effect a transaction and he has not given any advice to the other person in relation to securities.

(10) The general prohibition will not apply where certain conditions are fulfilled, namely:
- the person concerned must not take advantage of insider information to deal;
- he must give the stock exchange at least twenty-one days' notice of his intention to deal;
- the dealing must take place within a limited period after the publication of the company's interim or final financial results.

This provision is designed to give a means whereby directors and senior executives can deal in shares in their company.

(11) This subsection defines who is 'connected' for the purposes of subsection (1) above.

(12) 'Substantial shareholder' is defined for the purposes of subsection (10) above.

(13) The prohibitions in subsections (1), (3), (4) and (5) are extended to include dealings in securities issued by the state.

SECTION 109
Civil liability for
unlawful dealing.

(1) Where a person deals in or causes or procures another person to deal in securities in a manner declared unlawful by section 108 or communicates information in any such manner, that person shall, without prejudice to any other cause of action which may lie against him, be liable—

(*a*) to compensate any other party to the transaction who was not in possession of the relevant information for any loss sustained by that party by reason of any difference between the price at which the securities were dealt in in that transaction and the price at which they would have been likely to have been dealt in in such a transaction at the time when the first-mentioned transaction took place if that information had been generally available; and

(*b*) to account to the company that issued or made available those securities for any profit accruing to the first-mentioned person from dealing in those securities.

(2) The amount of compensation for which a person is liable under subsection (1) or the amount of the profit for which a person is liable to account under that subsection is—

(*a*) subject to paragraph (*b*), the amount of the loss sustained by the person claiming the compensation or the amount of the profit referred to in subsection (1) (*b*), as the case may be; or

(*b*) if the person so liable has been found by a court to be liable to pay an amount or amounts to any other person or persons by reason of the same act or transaction, the amount of that loss or profit less the amount or the sum of the amounts for which that person has been found to be liable.

(3) For the purposes of subsection (2), the onus of proving that the liability of a person to pay an amount to another person arose from the same act or transaction from which another liability arose lies on the person liable to pay the amount.

(4) An action under this section for recovery of a loss or profit shall not be commenced after the expiration of 2 years after the date of completion of the transaction in which the loss or profit occurred.

Definitions

'*company*': Companies Act, 1963, section 2.
'*court*': Companies Act, 1990, section 235.
'*dealing*': Companies Act, 1990, section 107.
'*securities*': Companies Act, 1990, section 107.

General Note

This section sets out the consequences of insider dealing. There is a twofold liability: firstly, a person who engages in insider dealing will be liable to compensate any other party to the transaction who was not in possession of the relevant information; in addition, he may be liable to account to the company that issued the securities for any profit on the transaction.

Insider dealing

(1) Where a person deals in securities as an 'insider' he may be liable to compensate any other party to the transaction who was not in possession of the relevant information for the difference between the price at which the securities were dealt in and the price at which they would have been dealt in had the person been in possession of the relevant information at the time of the transaction, and to account to the company that issued the securities for any profit accruing to the first-mentioned person.

(2) The amount of profit the person will be liable to account for is the amount of loss sustained by the person claiming compensation or the profit accrued, as the case may be, or, if the person has been found by the court to be liable, the amount of the loss or profit less the amount for which that person has been found to be liable by reason of the transaction.

(3) The onus of proving that the liability of a person to pay an amount lies with the person who is liable to pay the amount.

(4) Any action for recovery of loss of profits must be made within two years from the date of completion of the transaction in which the profit or loss occurred.

SECTION 110

Exempt transactions.

(1) Nothing in section 108 shall prevent a person from—

(a) acquiring securities under a will or on the intestacy of another person; or

(b) acquiring securities in a company pursuant to an employee profit sharing scheme—
(i) approved by the Revenue Commissioners for the purposes of the Finance Acts, and
(ii) the terms of which were approved by the company in general meeting, and
(iii) under which all permanent employees of the company are offered the opportunity to participate on equal terms relative to specified objective criteria;

(c) entering in good faith into a transaction to which subsection (2) applies.

(2) This subsection applies to the following kinds of transactions—

(a) the obtaining by a director of a share qualification under section 180 of the Principal Act;

(b) a transaction entered into by a person in accordance with his obligations under an underwriting agreement;

(c) a transaction entered into by a personal representative of a deceased person, a trustee, or liquidator, receiver or examiner in the performance of the functions of his office; or

(d) a transaction by way of, or arising out of, a mortgage of or charge on securities or a mortgage, charge, pledge or lien on documents of title to securities.

(3) This Part shall not apply to transactions entered into in pursuit of monetary, exchange rate, national debt management or foreign exchange reserve policies by any Minister of the Government or the Central Bank, or by any person on their behalf.

Definitions

'director': Companies Act, 1963, section 2.
'examiner': Companies (Amendment) Act, 1990, section 1.
'Principal Act': Companies Act, 1990, section 3.
'securities': Companies Act, 1990, section 107.
'underwrite': Companies Act, 1990, section 107.

General Note

This section sets out the various exceptions to the rules concerning insider dealing prescribed in part V of the Act.

(1) The provisions of section 108 do not prevent a person from—

(*a*) acquiring securities under a will,

(*b*) acquiring shares under an employee profit-sharing scheme approved by the Revenue Commissioners, or

(*c*) entering into a transaction in good faith subject to subsection (2) below.

(2) Exempt transactions will include:

(*a*) obtaining a share qualification under section 180 of the Companies Act, 1963;

(*b*) a transaction entered into under the obligations of an underwriting agreement;

(*c*) a transaction entered into by a personal representative of a deceased person, or a trustee, liquidator, examiner or receiver in the performance of the functions of the office;

(*d*) a transaction in connection with or arising out of a mortgage, charge, pledge, or lien on securities.

(3) Transactions undertaken in pursuit of monetary, exchange or national credit management by the Government or the Central Bank or anyone acting on their behalf will be exempted.

SECTION 111
Criminal liability for unlawful dealing.

A person who deals in securities in a manner declared unlawful by section 108 shall be guilty of an offence.

Definitions

'*securities*': Companies Act, 1990, section 107.

General Note

This section provides for the criminalisation of insider dealing and the introduction of an enforcement role for the stock exchange.

SECTION 112

Restriction on dealing.

(1) Subject to subsection (2), a person convicted of an offence under section 111 or this section shall not deal within the period of 12 months from the date of the conviction.

(2) Where a person convicted of an offence under subsection (1) has, before the date of his conviction, initiated a transaction under which some element of performance remains to be rendered, subsection (1) shall not prohibit him from completing the transaction where a relevant authority of a recognised stock exchange has indicated in writing, to the parties to the transaction, its satisfaction that—

(*a*) the transaction was initiated but not completed before the date of the conviction, and

(*b*) if the transaction were not concluded, the rights of an innocent third party would be prejudiced, and

(*c*) the transaction would not be unlawful under any other provision of this Part.

(3) A person who contravenes this section shall be guilty of an offence.

Definitions

'*recognised stock exchange*': Companies Act, 1990, section 107.
'*relevant authority*': Companies Act, 1990, section 107.

General Note

This section restricts a person who has been convicted of an offence relating to insider dealing from dealing in securities.

(1) A person who has been convicted of an offence relating to insider dealing is prohibited from dealing in securities within a twelve-month period from the date of his conviction. If despite such a prohibition a person does deal and is convicted of an offence under this section he is automatically prohibited from dealing for a further twelve months from the date of his second conviction.

(2) Where a person has initiated a transaction before the date of conviction and such transaction remains uncompleted at the date of conviction he will be permitted to complete such transaction where the relevant authority of the stock exchange has indicated to the parties in writing that it was satisfied the transaction was incomplete and provided it was not an unlawful transaction.

(3) If a person contravenes this section he will be guilty of an offence.

SECTION 113
Duty of agents in relation to unlawful dealing.

(1) A person shall not deal on behalf of another person if he has reasonable cause to believe or ought to conclude that the deal would be unlawful, within the meaning of section 108.

(2) A person who contravenes this section shall be guilty of an offence.

General Note

The purpose of this section is to provide that a person will be guilty of insider dealing if he has reasonable cause to conclude that the dealing in securities on behalf of the other person would be in contravention of section 108.

SECTION 114
Penalties for offences under this Part.

A person who commits an offence under this Part shall be liable—

(*a*) on summary conviction to imprisonment for a term not exceeding 12 months or to a fine not exceeding £1,000 or to both, or

(*b*) on conviction on indictment, to imprisonment for a term not exceeding 10 years or to a fine not exceeding £200,000 or to both.

General Note

This section sets out the penalties on conviction of insider dealings.

SECTION 115
Duty of recognised stock exchange in relation to unlawful dealing.

(1) If it appears to a relevant authority of a recognised stock exchange that any person has committed an offence under this Part, such authority shall forthwith report the matter to the Director of Public Prosecutions and shall furnish to the Director of Public Prosecutions such information and give to him such access to and facilities for inspecting and taking copies of any documents, being information or documents in the possession or under the control of such authority and relating to the matter in question, as the Director of Public Prosecutions may require.

(2) Where it appears to a member of a recognised stock exchange that any person has committed an offence under this Part, he shall report the matter forthwith to a relevant authority of the recognised stock exchange concerned, who shall thereupon come under the duty referred to in subsection (1).

(3) If it appears to a court in any proceedings that any person has committed an offence as aforesaid, and that no report relating to the matter has been made to the Director of Public Prosecutions under subsection (1), that court may, on the application of any person interested in the proceedings concerned or of its own motion, direct a relevant authority of the recognised stock exchange concerned to make such a report, and on a report being made accordingly, this section shall have effect as though the report had been made in pursuance of subsection (1).

(4) If, where any matter is reported or referred to the Director of Public Prosecutions under this section, he considers that the case is one in which a prosecution ought to be instituted and institutes proceedings accordingly, it shall be the duty of a relevant authority of the recognised stock exchange concerned, and of every officer of the company whose securities are concerned, and of any other person who appears to the Director of Public Prosecutions to have relevant information (other than any defendant in the proceedings) to give all assistance in connection with the prosecution which he or they are reasonably able to give.

(5) If it appears to the Minister, arising from a complaint to a relevant authority of a recognised stock exchange concerning an alleged offence under this Part, that there are circumstances suggesting that—

(a) the relevant authority ought to use its powers under this Part but has not done so, or

(b) that a report ought to be made to the Director of Public Prosecutions under subsection (1), but that the relevant authority concerned has not so reported,

he may direct the relevant authority to use such powers or make such a report, and on a report being made accordingly, this section shall have effect as though the report had been made in pursuance of subsection (1).

(6) Where the Minister gives a direction under subsection (5), the relevant authority concerned shall communicate the results of its investigations, or a copy of its report under subsection (1), as the case may be, to the Minister.

(7) A relevant authority of a recognised stock exchange shall not be liable in damages in respect of anything done or omitted to be done by the authority in connection with the exercise by it of its functions under this Part unless the act or omission complained of was done or omitted to be done in bad faith.

Definitions

'*company*': Companies Act, 1963, section 2.

'*court*': Companies Act, 1990, section 235.

'*officer*': Companies Act, 1990, section 107.

'*recognised stock exchange*': Companies Act, 1990, section 107.

'*relevant authority*': Companies Act, 1990, section 107.

'*securities*': Companies Act, 1990, section 107.

General Note

This section sets out the duties of a recognised stock exchange in relation to insider dealing and gives an enforcement role to the stock exchange.

(1) Where it appears to the relevant authority of a recognised stock exchange, i.e. its manager or board, that a person has committed an insider dealing offence it must report the matter to the Director of Public Prosecutions and provide all relevant information and documents as the Director of Public Prosecutions may require.

(2) A member of a recognised stock exchange must report to the relevant authority where it appears to him that a person has committed an insider dealing offence.

(3) Where in court proceedings for insider dealing no report has been made to the Director of Public Prosecutions by a relevant authority of a recognised stock exchange, any person interested in the proceedings may direct that a report be made by the relevant authority of the stock exchange.

(4) Where any matter has been referred to the Director of Public Prosecutions and he considers it one in which proceedings should be instituted, the relevant authority of a recognised stock exchange and every officer of the company whose securities are concerned and any other person involved is obliged to give to the Director of Public Prosecutions all relevant information and assistance that they are reasonably able to give.

(5) The Minister for Industry and Commerce can direct a relevant authority of the stock exchange to use its powers to investigate and to produce a report where it has not done so.

(6) Where the Minister has made a direction to a relevant authority of the stock exchange for a report he must receive a copy of such report when completed by the relevant authority.

(7) A relevant authority of a recognised stock exchange will not be liable for damages for anything done or omitted to be done unless the act or omission complained of was done in bad faith.

SECTION 116 Co-operation with other authorities outside the State.	(1) This section applies where a relevant authority of a recognised stock exchange receives a request for information from a similar authority in another Member State of the European Communities in relation to the exercise by the second-named authority of its functions under any enactment of the European Communities relating to unlawful dealing within the meaning of this Part, whether in the State or elsewhere.

(2) The relevant authority concerned shall, in so far as it is reasonably able to do so, and making use of its powers under this Part where appropriate, obtain the information requested and shall, subject to the following provisions of this section, provide such information accordingly.

(3) Where a relevant authority of a recognised stock exchange receives a request under subsection (1), it shall advise the Minister who, on being satisfied as to any of the matters referred to in subsection (4), may direct the authority to refuse to provide all or part of the information requested.

(4) The matters referred to in subsection (3) are that—

(a) communication of the information requested might adversely affect the sovereignty, security or public policy of the State;

(b) civil or criminal proceedings in the State have already been commenced against a person in respect of any acts in relation to which a request for information has been received under subsection (1);

(c) any person has been convicted in the State of a criminal offence in respect of any such acts.

Definitions

'dealing': Companies Act, 1990, section 107.

'Minister': Companies Act, 1990, section 3.

'recognised stock exchange': Companies Act, 1990, section 107.

'relevant authority ': Companies Act, 1990, section 107.

General Note

This section arises as a result of article 10 of the EC directive on insider dealing adopted by the Council on 13 November 1989, which requires a framework to be set up within which the competent authorities in the various member-states can co-operate with each other by exchanging information.

(1) The section applies in a case where a relevant authority of a recognised stock exchange receives a request for information from a similar authority in another member-state of the EC in the exercise of its function on insider dealing.

(2) The relevant authority will use its powers to obtain the information required by the other EC authority and provide such information to that authority.

(3) The relevant authority of a recognised stock exchange will advise the Minister of the request, and he may direct the authority to refuse to furnish some or all of the information requested.

(4) The circumstances are set out whereby information may not be passed on, and include cases where matters of public policy, security or sovereignty are involved as well as matters that are the subject of criminal proceedings in the state or where a person has been convicted of a criminal offence in the state in respect of such acts.

SECTION 117
Authorised persons.

(1) In this section and sections 118 and 121, "authorised person" means a person approved by the Minister to be an authorised person for the purposes of this Part being—

(a) the manager, however described, of a recognised stock exchange, or

(b) a person nominated by a relevant authority of a recognised stock exchange.

(2) Where an alleged offence under this Part is investigated by an authorised person, the relevant authorities of the recognised stock exchange concerned shall be under a general duty to ensure that potential conflicts of interest are avoided, as far as possible, on the part of any such authorised person.

(3) For the purpose of obtaining any information necessary for the exercise by a relevant authority of such exchange of the function referred to in section 115, an authorised person may, on production of his authorisation if so required, require any person whom he or such relevant authority has reasonable cause to believe to have dealt in securities, or to have any information about such dealings, to give the authorised person any information which he may reasonably require in regard to—

(*a*) the securities concerned,
(*b*) the company which issued the securities,
(*c*) his dealings in such securities, or
(*d*) any other information the authorised person reasonably requires in relation to such securities or such dealings,

and give him such access to and facilities for inspecting and taking copies of any documents relating to the matter as he reasonably requires.

(4) Every document purporting to be a warrant or authorisation and to be signed or authenticated by or on behalf of a relevant authority shall be received in evidence and shall be deemed to be such warrant or authorisation without further proof until the contrary is shown.

(5) An authorised person, or any person on whom he has made a requirement under this section, may apply to the court for a declaration under this section.

(6) The court, having heard such evidence as may be adduced and any representations that may be made by the authorised person and a person referred to in subsection (5), may at its discretion declare—

(*a*) that the exigencies of the common good do not warrant the exercise by the authorised person of the powers conferred on him by this section, or
(*b*) that the exigencies of the common good do so warrant.

(7) Where the court makes a declaration under subsection (6) (*a*), the authorised person shall, as soon as may be, withdraw the relevant requirement under this section.

(8) Where the court makes a declaration under subsection (6) (*b*), the person on whom the requirement was imposed shall, as soon as may be, furnish the required information to the authorised person.

(9) Where, in contravention of subsection (8), a person refuses, or fails within a reasonable time, to comply with a requirement of an authorised person, the authorised person may certify the refusal under his hand to the court, and the court may, after hearing any statement which may be offered in defence, punish the offender in like manner as if he had been guilty of contempt of court.

Definitions

'*authorised person*': Companies Act, 1990, section 117.

'*company*': Companies Act, 1963, section 2.

'*court*': Companies Act, 1990, section 235.

'*dealing*': Companies Act, 1990, section 107.

'*Minister*': Companies Act, 1990, section 3.
'*recognised stock exchange*': Companies Act, 1990, section 107.
'*relevant authority*': Companies Act, 1990, section 107.
'*securities*': Companies Act, 1990, section 107.

General Note

With the introduction of an enforcement role for a recognised stock exchange, it is necessary to give the stock exchange the statutory authority to establish the information on which to base its referral of suspicious cases to the Director of Public Prosecutions. This section enables the stock exchange, with the agreement of the Minister, to appoint authorised persons to investigate suspicious cases and to give such people the necessary powers to establish the required information.

(1) 'Authorised person' is defined as being the manager of the stock exchange or some person nominated by the relevant authority of the stock exchange.

(2) Where an alleged offence is being investigated by an authorised person the stock exchange authorities must ensure that potential conflicts of interest are avoided as far as possible; for instance, it may be inappropriate to have one stockbroker investigating another.

(3) The authorised person has the authority to require persons to provide information relating to dealings in securities and to give access and facilities for the inspection of and taking copies of any necessary documents that he may reasonably require.

(4) Every document purporting to be a warrant will be accepted as such.

(5) Either the authorised officer or the person who is the subject of the investigation is permitted to apply to the court for a decision as to whether the exigencies of the common good require that the information be given.

(6) The court, having heard the evidence, may decide that for the purposes of the common good the information need not be given.

(7) Where the court decides that the information need not be given, the authorised person must withdraw the relevant requirement as soon as possible.

(8) Where the court upholds the request as being in the public interest, the person concerned must give the information.

(9) Failure to give the information will be a contempt of court.

SECTION 118
Obligation of professional secrecy.

(1) Information obtained by any of the following persons by virtue of the exercise by a recognised stock exchange of its functions under this Part shall not be disclosed except in accordance with law, namely—

(*a*) a relevant authority of the exchange,
(*b*) an authorised person, or
(*c*) any person employed or formerly employed by the exchange.

(2) Subsection (1) shall not prevent a relevant authority of a recognised stock exchange from disclosing any information to the Minister, whether pursuant to a request under section 115 (5) or otherwise, or to a similar authority in another Member State of the European Communities.

(3) Any person who contravenes subsection (1) shall be guilty of an offence.

Definitions

'authorised person': Companies Act, 1990, section 117.
'Minister': Companies Act, 1990, section 3.
'recognised stock exchange': Companies Act, 1990, section 107.
'relevant authority': Companies Act, 1990, section 107.

General Note

The purpose of this section is to ensure that any information coming from the stock exchange authorities as a result of the functions imposed on them by this Act will not be disclosed except where required by law.

(1) Information obtained by the stock exchange or any of its officers or former employees in the execution of their functions under the Act will be disclosed only in accordance with law.

(2) Subsection (1) does not prevent the disclosure of information to the Minister in connection with a request made under section 114 of the Act.

(3) Anyone who contravenes subsection (1) will be guilty of an offence.

SECTION 119
Extension of Council Directive 79/279/EEC.

The provisions of Schedule C.5 (*a*) of Council Directive 79/279/EEC of 5 March 1979 coordinating the conditions for the admission of securities to official stock exchange listing, as given effect by the European Communities (Stock Exchange) Regulations, 1984 (S.I. No. 282 of 1984), shall also apply to securities within the meaning of section 107.

General Note

This section is a technical provision. Paragraph 5 of schedule C of the EC directive on insider dealing requires a listed company to make public announcements as soon as possible regarding any new developments in its sphere of activity that may have the effect of moving the share price, and places this requirement within the scope of this part of the Act.

SECTION 120 **Annual report of** **recognised stock** **exchange.**	(1) An annual report shall be presented to the Minister on behalf of every recognised stock exchange on the exercise of the functions of the relevant authorities of the exchange concerned under this Part and, in particular, the report shall include—

    (*a*) the number of written complaints received concerning possible contraventions of this Part,

    (*b*) the number of reports made to the Director of Public Prosecutions under this Part,

    (*c*) the number of instances in which, following the exercise of powers by authorised persons under this Part, reports were not made to the Director of Public Prosecutions, and

    (*d*) such other information as may be prescribed.

(2) A copy of the report referred to in subsection (1) shall, subject to subsection (3), be laid before each House of the Oireachtas.

(3) If the Minister, after consultation with a relevant authority of the recognised stock exchange concerned, is of the opinion that the disclosure of any information contained in the report referred to in subsection (1) would materially injure or unfairly prejudice the legitimate interests of any person, or that otherwise there is good reason for not divulging any part of such a report, he may lay the report under subsection (2) with that information or that part omitted.

Definitions

'*authorised person*': Companies Act, 1990, section 117.

'*Minister*': Companies Act, 1990, section 3.

'*prescribe*': Companies Act, 1990, section 3.

'*recognised stock exchange*': Companies Act, 1990, section 107.

'*relevant authority*': Companies Act, 1990, section 107.

General Note

This section provides that, as certain powers are being devolved to the stock exchange, to counterbalance this the stock exchange will be required to submit an annual report to the Minister containing certain information in regard to the discharge by the stock exchange of its functions under this part of the Act.

(1) This subsection sets out what the annual report to the Minister shall contain.

(2) A copy of the report is to be laid before each house of the Oireachtas.

(3) The Minister may permit certain information contained in the report to be omitted if, after consultation with the stock exchange authority, he is of the opinion that disclosure of information would materially injure or unfairly prejudice the interests of any person.

SECTION 121
Power of Minister to make supplementary regulations.

(1) If, in any respect, any difficulty arises in bringing any provision of this Part into operation or in relation to the operation of any such provision, the Minister may by regulations do anything which appears to him to be necessary or expedient for removing that difficulty, for bringing the provision into operation, or for securing or facilitating its operation, and any such regulations may modify any provision of this Part so far as may be necessary or expedient for carrying such provision into effect for the purposes aforesaid.

(2) Without prejudice to the generality of subsection (1), where the Minister considers it necessary or expedient to do so for the proper and effective administration of sections 115 and 117, he may make such regulations as he thinks appropriate in relation to—

(*a*) the powers of authorised persons, or
(*b*) the matters in respect of which, or the persons from whom, authorised persons may require information under this Part.

(3) Every regulation made by the Minister under this section shall be laid before each House of the Oireachtas as soon as may be after it is made and, if a resolution annulling the regulation is passed by either House within the next 21 days on which that House has sat after the regulation is laid before it, the regulation shall be annulled accordingly, but without prejudice to the validity of anything previously done thereunder.

Definitions

'*authorised person*': Companies Act, 1990, section 117.
'*Minister*': Companies Act, 1990, section 3.

General Note

This section enables the Minister to make regulations regarding the effective administration of sections 115–117 in relation to the powers of authorised persons.

6
WINDING UP AND RELATED MATTERS

The provisions of part VI of the Act are designed to strengthen existing provisions of the Companies Act, 1963. There is a common theme throughout this part, in the form of increased accountability of company officers who, when the company is liquidated, are shown to have engaged in malpractice.

Furthermore, there are increased powers for the company creditors in a winding up. Specific measures in this part include:

Declarations of solvency: The declaration will in future have to be certified by an independent person, and there will be the prospect of personal liability for company debts attaching to directors who make unfounded declarations.

Civil actions against fraudulent trading: The legislation now separates the criminal law offence from the civil sanction. The civil process does not require the same technical legal reasons required for a criminal action.

Reckless trading: This provides for situations that do not amount to fraud, which is difficult to prove, but would constitute an unreasonable level of recklessness with regard to the company's affairs.

SECTION 122

Amendment of section 99 of the Principal Act.

Section 99 of the Principal Act is hereby amended—

(a) in subsection (2), by the substitution for paragraph (h) of the following paragraph—

"(h) a charge on a ship or aircraft or any share in a ship or aircraft;", and

(b) by the insertion of the following subsections—

"(2A) The Minister may by regulations amend subsection (2) so as to add any description of charge to, or remove any description of charge from, the charges requiring registration under this section.

(2B) The power of the Minister under subsection (2A) shall include a power to amend by regulations the description of any charge referred to in subsection (2).

(2C) Every regulation made by the Minister under this section shall be laid before each House of the Oireachtas as soon as may be after it is made and, if a resolution annulling the regulation is passed by either House within the next 21 days on which that House has sat after the regulation is laid before it, the regulation shall be annulled accordingly, but without prejudice to the validity of anything previously done thereunder.".

Definitions

'Principal Act': Companies Act, 1990, section 3.

General Note

This section amends section 99 (2) of the Companies Act, 1963, by requiring charges not only on ships to be registered but also charges on aircraft. It also requires charges on a share of an aircraft to be registered.

Furthermore, the Minister for Industry and Commerce has been given powers to enable him to make regulations to add to, or subtract from, the list of charges in section 99 of the Companies Act, 1963, that require registration.

SECTION 123
Amendment of sections 214 and 345 of Principal Act.

Section 214 (*a*) (which relates to the circumstances in which a company is unable to pay its debts) and section 345 (5) (*a*) (which relates to unregistered companies) of the Principal Act are hereby amended by the substitution in each case for "£50" of "£1,000".

Definitions

'company': Companies Act, 1963, section 2.
'Principal Act': Companies Act, 1990, section 3.

General Note

This section increases the amount by which a company is deemed to be unable to pay its debts from £50 to £1,000.

SECTION 124
Amendment of section 231 of the Principal Act.

Section 231 of the Principal Act is hereby amended by the insertion after subsection (1) of the following subsection—

"(1A) (*a*) The liquidator of a company shall not sell by private contract a non-cash asset of the requisite value to a person who is, or who, within three years prior to the date of commencement of the winding-up, has been, an officer of the company unless the liquidator has given at least 14 days' notice of his intention to do so to all creditors of the company who are known to him or who have been intimated to him.

(*b*) In this subsection—
(i) 'non-cash asset' and 'requisite value' have the meanings assigned to them by section 29 of the Companies Act, 1990, and
(ii) 'officer' includes a person connected, within the meaning of section 26 of the Companies Act, 1990, with a director, and a shadow director.".

Definitions

'company': Companies Act, 1963, section 2.
'director': Companies Act, 1963, section 2.

'*non-cash asset*': Companies Act, 1990, section 124.
'*officer*': Companies Act, 1963, section 2.
'*Principal Act*': Companies Act, 1990, section 3.
'*shadow director*': Companies Act, 1990, section 3.

General Note

Where a liquidator proposes to sell assets to a former officer he must give the creditors fourteen days' notice of his intention to do so. In this case anyone who was an officer within three years before the liquidation would be regarded as a person who would be the subject of the notification.

SECTION 125
No lien over company's books, records, etc.

The Principal Act is hereby amended by the insertion after section 244 of the following section—

"244A.—Where the court has appointed a provisional liquidator or a company is being wound up by the court or by means of a creditors' voluntary winding up, no person shall be entitled as against the liquidator or provisional liquidator to withhold possession of any deed, instrument, or other document belonging to the company, or the books of account, receipts, bills, invoices, or other papers of a like nature relating to the accounts or trade, dealings or business of the company, or to claim any lien thereon provided that—

(*a*) where a mortgage, charge or pledge has been created by the deposit of any such document or paper with a person, the production of the document or paper to the liquidator or provisional liquidator by the person shall be without prejudice to the person's rights under the mortgage, charge or pledge (other than any right to possession of the document or paper),

(*b*) where by virtue of this section a liquidator or provisional liquidator has possession of any document or papers of a receiver or that a receiver is entitled to examine, the liquidator or provisional liquidator shall, unless the court otherwise orders, make the document or papers available for inspection by the receiver at all reasonable times.".

Definitions

'*company*': Companies Act, 1963, section 2.
'*court*': Companies Act, 1990, section 235.
'*Principal Act*': Companies Act, 1990, section 3.

General Note

This section provides that no person will be entitled to withhold any documents or records of a company from the liquidator or provisional liquidator or to claim any lien on them. The section does not, however, protect the rights of any person who has had a charge, mortgage or pledge created in his favour by the deposit with him of a document of the company (other than rights to possession of the document).

SECTION 126
Power of court to summon persons for examination.

The Principal Act is hereby amended by the substitution for section 245 of the following section—

"245.—(1) The court may, at any time after the appointment of a provisional liquidator or the making of a winding-up order, summon before it any officer of the company or person known or suspected to have in his possession any property of the company or supposed to be indebted to the company, or any person whom the court deems capable of giving information relating to the promotion, formation, trade, dealings, affairs or property of the company.

(2) The court may examine such person on oath concerning the matters aforesaid, either by word of mouth or on written interrogatories, and may reduce his answers to writing and require him to sign them.

(3) The court may require such person to produce any accounting records, deed, instrument, or other document or paper relating to the company that are in his custody or power.

(4) The court may, before the examination takes place, require such person to place before it a statement, in such form as the court may direct, of any transactions between him and the company of a type or class which the court may specify.

(5) If, in the opinion of the court, it is just and equitable to do so, it may direct that the costs of the examination be paid by the person examined.

(6) A person who is examined under this section shall not be entitled to refuse to answer any question put to him on the ground that his answer might incriminate him but none of the answers of such person shall be admissible in evidence against him in any other proceedings, civil or criminal, except in the case of any criminal proceedings for perjury in respect of any such answer.

(7) If a person without reasonable excuse fails at any time to attend his examination under this section, he shall be guilty of contempt of court and liable to be punished accordingly.

(8) In a case where a person without reasonable excuse fails at any time to attend his examination under this section or there are reasonable grounds for believing that a person has absconded, or is about to abscond, with a view to avoiding or delaying his examination under this section, the court may cause that person to be arrested and his books and documents and moveable personal property to be seized and him and them to be detained until such time as the court may order.".

Definitions

'*books and documents*': Companies Act, 1990, section 3.

'*company*': Companies Act, 1963, section 2.

'*court*': Companies Act, 1990, section 235.

'*officer*': Companies Act, 1963, section 2.

'*Principal Act*': Companies Act, 1990, section 3.

General Note

This section replaces section 245 of the Companies Act, 1963, dealing with the powers of the court to summon persons for examination. It has the effect of strengthening the powers of the court to examine such persons.

(1) The court may at any time after the appointment of a liquidator summon any officer of the company or other person suspected of having relevant books or documents in their possession.

(2) The court is empowered to examine such person on oath or in writing and to reduce such answers to writing, requiring the person to sign them.

(3) The court is empowered to require the person to produce any records or documents in his custody or power.

(4) The court may require any person before examination to place in a statement details of any transactions between him and the company.

(5) The court may direct that the costs of examination be paid by the person being examined.

(6) A person who is being examined will not be entitled to refuse to answer a question on the grounds that it may incriminate him; but ‚none of the answers can be used against him in any civil or criminal proceedings except in the case of criminal proceedings for perjury.

(7) A person will be guilty of contempt if he fails to attend for examination without reasonable excuse.

(8) If a person has failed to attend for examination without reasonable excuse and there are grounds for believing that he has absconded or is about to abscond with a view to avoiding or delaying his examination, the court is empowered to direct the arrest of such person and the books, documents and personal property of the person seized.

SECTION 127
Order for payment or delivery of property against person examined under section 245 of Principal Act.

The Principal Act is hereby amended by the insertion before section 246 of the following section—

"245A.—If in the course of an examination under section 245 it appears to the court that any person being examined—

(a) is indebted to the company, or
(b) has in his possession or control any money, property or books and papers of the company,

the court may order such person—

(i) to pay to the liquidator the amount of the debt or any part thereof, or

(ii) to pay, deliver, convey, surrender or transfer to the liquidator such money, property or books and papers or any part thereof,

as the case may be, at such time and in such manner and on such terms as the court may direct.".

Definitions

'*company*': Companies Act, 1963, section 2.

'*court*': Companies Act, 1990, section 235.

'*Principal Act*': Companies Act, 1990, section 3.

General Note

Where any person is examined under section 124 he may be directed to hand back company property and pay any debts he owes to the company. This will strengthen the position of the liquidator in order to improve the efficiency of the liquidator.

SECTION 128
Statutory declaration of solvency in case of proposal to wind up voluntarily.

The Principal Act is hereby amended by the substitution for section 256 of the following section—

"256.—(1) Where it is proposed to wind up a company voluntarily, the directors of the company or, in the case of a company having more than two directors, the majority of the directors may, at a meeting of the directors, make a statutory declaration to the effect that they have made a full inquiry into the affairs of the company, and that having done so, they have formed the opinion that the company will be able to pay its debts in full within such period not exceeding 12 months from the commencement of the winding up as may be specified in the declaration.

(2) A declaration made as aforesaid shall have no effect for the purposes of this Act unless—

(a) it is made within the 28 days immediately preceding the date of the passing of the resolution for winding up the company and delivered to the registrar of companies not later than the date of the delivery to the registrar, in accordance with the provisions of section 143, of a copy of the resolution for winding up the company;

(b) it embodies a statement of the company's assets and liabilities as at the latest practicable date before the making of the declaration and in any event at a date not more than three months before the making of the declaration;

(c) a report made by an independent person in accordance with the provisions of this section is attached thereto;

(d) it embodies a statement by the independent person referred to in paragraph (c) that he has given and has not withdrawn his written consent to the issue of the declaration with the report attached thereto; and

(e) a copy of the declaration is attached to the notice issued by the company of the general meeting at which it is intended to propose a resolution for voluntary winding up under paragraph (a) or (b) of section 251 (1).

(3) The report referred to in paragraph (c) of subsection (2) shall be made by an independent person, that is to say, a person qualified at the time of the report to be appointed, or to continue to be, auditor of the company.

(4) The report shall state whether, in his opinion and to the best of his information and according to the explanations given to him—

(*a*) the opinion of the directors referred to in subsection (1), and

(*b*) the statement of the company's assets and liabilities embodied in the said declaration,

are reasonable.

(5) If within 28 days after the resolution for voluntary winding up has been advertised under subsection (1) of section 252, a creditor applies to the court for an order under this subsection, and the court is satisfied that such creditor together with any creditors supporting him in his application represents one-fifth at least in number or value of the creditors of the company, and the court is of opinion that it is unlikely that the company will be able to pay its debts within the period specified in the declaration, the court may order that all the provisions of this Act relating to a creditors' voluntary winding up shall apply to the winding up.

(6) If the court orders that all the provisions of this Act in relation to a creditors' voluntary winding up shall apply to the winding up, the person who held the office of liquidator immediately prior to the making of the order or, if no liquidator is acting, the company shall within 21 days after the making of the order, deliver an office copy of such order to the registrar of companies.

(7) If default is made in complying with subsection (6), any person who is in default shall be liable to a fine not exceeding £1,000.

(8) Where a statutory declaration is made under this section and it is subsequently proved to the satisfaction of the court that the company is unable to pay its debts, the court on the application of the liquidator or any creditor or contributory of the company may, if it thinks it proper to do so, declare that any director who was a party to the declaration without having reasonable grounds for the opinion that the company would be able to pay its debts in full within the period specified in the declaration shall be personally responsible, without any limitation of liability, for all or any of the debts or other liabilities of the company as the court may direct.

(9) Where a company's debts are not paid or provided for in full within the period stated in the declaration of solvency, it shall for the purposes of subsection (8) be presumed, until the contrary is shown, that the director did not have reasonable grounds for his opinion.

(10) Where the court makes a declaration under subsection (8), it may give such further directions as it thinks proper for the purpose of giving effect to that declaration.

(11) A winding up in the case of which a declaration has been made and delivered in accordance with this section is in this Act referred to as 'a members' voluntary winding up' and a voluntary winding up in the case of which a declaration has not been made and delivered as aforesaid or in the case of which an order is made under subsection (5) or in the case to which section 261 (3) applies is in this Act referred to as 'a creditors' voluntary winding up'.".

Definitions

'*company*': Companies Act, 1963, section 2.

'*court*': Companies Act, 1990, section 235.

'*director*': Companies Act, 1963, section 2.

'*Principal Act*': Companies Act, 1990, section 3.

General Note

This section substitutes a new section for section 256 of the Companies Act, 1963, and deals with the declaration of solvency made by the directors of a company in a members' voluntary winding up. The main change in this section is the introduction of a requirement that the declaration of solvency be accompanied by the report of an independent person (this is a person who is qualified to be the company's auditor). This report must give a view as to whether the opinion of the directors in the declaration of solvency is reasonable and whether the statement of the company's assets and liabilities embodied in the declaration gives a true and fair view of the company's assets and liabilities.

(1) The directors or a majority of them having made a full enquiry into the affairs of the company and having formed the opinion that the company will be able to pay the debts in full within the next twelve months from the date of the commencement of the winding up must make a statutory declaration to this effect.

(2) The declaration will have no effect unless it is made within the 28-day period immediately preceding the date of passing the winding up resolution and delivered to the Registrar of Companies. The declaration must embody a statement of the company's assets and liabilities at the latest practicable date before the making of the declaration and not more than three months before the making of the declaration, together with the report of an independent person and a statement that he has not withdrawn his consent to the declaration.

(3) An independent person is defined for the purpose of this section as one who is qualified to be the company's auditor.

(4) The independent person in his report must comment on the opinion of the directors and the statement of assets and liabilities, having checked on them but not having undertaken a full audit.

(5) If within twenty-eight days after the passing of the voluntary winding up resolution a creditor or group of creditors representing one-fifth or more in number or value of the company's creditors may apply to the court, and if the court is of the opinion that the company is unlikely to repay its debts within twelve months the court may order that the company be wound up under the provisions of a creditors' winding up.

(6) If it is ordered to be a creditors' voluntary winding up by the court, the liquidator or if there is no liquidator the company must deliver a copy of the statement to the Registrar of Companies within twenty-one days after the making of the order.

(7) The penalty for default is a fine not exceeding £1,000 for any person in default.

(8) The court on the application of the liquidator or any creditor or contributory may declare that any director who was a party to the declaration without having reasonable ground for the opinion that the company will be able to pay its debts in full within the period may be personally responsible, without any limitation on liability, for the debts and liabilities as the court may direct.

(9) If the debts are not paid within the specified period it will be presumed that the director had not got reasonable grounds for his opinion.

(10) The court may make such declarations as it considers proper to give effect to the declaration.

(11) . This subsection explains the terms 'members' voluntary winding up' and 'creditors' voluntary winding up'.

SECTION 129
Duty of liquidator to call creditors' meeting if he is of opinion that company is unable to pay its debts.

The Principal Act is hereby amended by the substitution for section 261 of the following section—

"261.—(1) If the liquidator is at any time of the opinion that the company will not be able to pay its debts in full within the period stated in the declaration under section 256 he shall—

(a) summon a meeting of creditors for a day not later than the fourteenth day after the day on which he formed that opinion;

(b) send notices of the creditors' meeting to the creditors by post not less than seven days before the day on which that meeting is to be held;

(c) cause notice of the creditors' meeting to be advertised, at least ten days before the date of the meeting, once in *Iris Oifigiúil* and once at least in two daily newspapers circulating in the locality in which the company's principal place of business in the State was situated during the relevant period; and

(d) during the period before the day on which the creditors' meeting is to be held, furnish creditors free of charge with such information concerning the affairs of the company as they may reasonably require;

and the notice of the creditors' meeting shall state the duty imposed by paragraph (d).

(2) The liquidator shall also—

(a) make out a statement in the prescribed form as to the affairs of the company, including a statement of the company's assets and liabilities, a list of the outstanding creditors and the estimated amount of their claims;

(b) lay that statement before the creditors' meeting; and

(c) attend and preside at that meeting.

(3) As from the day on which the creditors' meeting is held under this section, the Companies Acts shall have effect as if—

(a) without prejudice to the powers of the court under section 256, the directors' declaration under that section had not been made; and

(b) the creditors' meeting and the company meetings at which it was resolved that the company be wound up voluntarily were the meetings mentioned in section 266;

and, accordingly, the winding up shall become a creditors' voluntary winding up and any appointment made or committee established by the creditors' meeting shall be deemed to have been made or established by the creditors' meeting so mentioned.

(4) The appointment of a liquidator at a meeting called under this section shall not, subject to subsection (5), affect the validity of any action previously taken by the liquidator appointed by the members of the company.

(5) Where the creditors appoint a liquidator at a meeting called under this section and there is a dispute as to any or all of the costs, charges or expenses incurred by, including the remuneration of, the liquidator appointed by the members of the company, the liquidator appointed by the creditors, or any creditor, may apply to the court to determine the dispute and the court may, on such application, make such order as it deems fit.

(6) Nothing in this section shall be deemed to take away any right in this Act of any person to present a petition to the court for the winding up of a company.

(7) If the liquidator fails to comply with subsection (1) he shall be liable to a fine.".

Definitions

'company': Companies Act, 1963, section 2.

'court': Companies Act, 1990, section 235.

'Principal Act': Companies Act, 1990, section 3.

General Note

This section substitutes a new section for section 261 of the Companies Act, 1963, and provides that where the liquidator in the members' voluntary winding up forms the opinion that the company will not be able to pay its debts, the creditors can substitute their own liquidator for the liquidator already appointed by the members. It also provides for greater disclosure by the liquidator to the creditors in such circumstances and that where the creditors take this action the winding up will become a creditors' winding up.

(1) If a liquidator is at any time of the opinion that the company will be unable to pay its debts in full during the period stated in a declaration made under section 256 of the Companies Act, 1963, he

must call a creditors' meeting within fourteen days after the day he formed that opinion. He must send notices to the creditors and publish such notices in two newspapers. He must also furnish free of charge to the creditors before the creditors' meeting such information concerning the company's affairs as they may reasonably require.

(2) The liquidator must prepare a statement of the company's affairs, together with a list of outstanding creditors. He must, further, lay such statement before the meeting and attend and preside at such meeting.

(3) From the day the creditors' meeting is held the Companies Acts will apply as if the directors' declaration under section 256 of the Companies Act, 1963, had not been made and as if the creditors' and company meetings resolving that the company be wound up were the meetings referred to in section 266, and the winding up will become a creditors' voluntary winding up.

(4) The appointment of the liquidator under this section will not affect the validity of any action previously taken by the liquidator who was appointed by the members of the company.

(5) Where a liquidator is appointed by the creditors in place of the one appointed by the company and there is a dispute as to fees and expenses, the creditors' liquidator or any creditor may apply to the court to determine the dispute, and the court may make such order as it deems fit.

(6) There is nothing in this section to prevent a person from petitioning the court for the winding up of the company.

(7) If a liquidator fails to comply with this section he will be liable to a fine.

SECTION 130
Amendment of
section 266 of the
Principal Act.

Section 266 of the Principal Act is hereby amended by the insertion in subsection (2) after "advertised" of the following:

", at least ten days before the date of the meeting,".

Definitions
'Principal Act': Companies Act, 1990, section 3.

General Note
The purpose of this amendment is to ensure that the advertisement of creditors' meetings be published in two newspapers at least ten

days before the meeting, so as to give adequate notice of meetings to creditors.

SECTION 131

Creditors' voluntary winding up.

(1) This section applies where, in the case of a creditors' voluntary winding up, a liquidator has been nominated by the company.

(2) The powers conferred on the liquidator by section 276 of the Principal Act shall not be exercised, except with sanction of the court, during the period before the holding of the creditors' meeting under section 266 of that Act.

(3) Subsection (2) does not apply in relation to the power of the liquidator—

(*a*) to take into his custody or under his control all the property to which the company is or appears to be entitled;

(*b*) to dispose of perishable goods and other goods the value of which is likely to diminish if they are not immediately disposed of;

(*c*) to do all such other things as may be necessary for the protection of the company's assets.

(4) The liquidator shall attend the creditors' meeting held under section 266 of the Principal Act and shall report to the meeting on any exercise by him of his powers (whether or not under this section or under section 276 or 280 of that Act).

(5) If default is made—

(*a*) by the company in complying with subsection (1) or (2) of section 266 of the Principal Act, or

(*b*) by the directors in complying with subsection (3) of the said section,

the liquidator shall, within 7 days of the relevant day, apply to the court for directions as to the manner in which that default is to be remedied.

(6) "The relevant day" means the day on which the liquidator was nominated by the company or the day on which he first became aware of the default, whichever is the later.

(7) If a liquidator without reasonable excuse fails to comply with this section, he shall be guilty of an offence.

Definitions

'company': Companies Act, 1963, section 2.

'court': Companies Act, 1990, section 235.

'Principal Act': Companies Act, 1990, section 3.

'relevant day': Companies Act, 1990, section 131.

General Note

This section sets out the procedure to be followed where a liquidator is nominated by the company in a creditors' winding up.

(1) The section applies where the liquidator is nominated by the company in a creditors' winding up.

(2) The powers conferred by section 276 of the Companies Act, 1963 (Powers and duties of liquidator in a voluntary winding up), may not be exercised except with court approval before the holding of the meeting of creditors under the provisions of section 266 of the Companies Act, 1963.

(3) Subsection (2) above will not prevent the liquidator from taking control of or taking into his custody all the property to which the company is entitled, to dispose of any perishable goods or other property that would diminish in value if not disposed of, or to take whatever steps are necessary to protect the company's assets.

(4) The liquidator must attend the meeting of creditors held under section 266 of the Companies Act, 1963, and report to the meeting on what powers have been exercised by him.

(5) If the company or the directors are in default in complying with subsections (1), (2) or (3) of section 266 of the Companies Act, 1963, the liquidator must apply to the court within seven days for directions as to how to remedy the default.

(6) 'Relevant day' is defined for the purpose of this section.

(7) The liquidator will be guilty of an offence if he fails to comply with this section.

SECTION 132
Amendment of section 275 of the Principal Act.

The Principal Act is hereby amended by the substitution for section 275 of the following section—

"275.—(1) Subject to the provisions of this Act as to preferential payments, the property of a company on its winding up—

(a) shall, subject to subsection (2), be applied in satisfaction of its liabilities *pari passu*, and
(b) shall, subject to such application, and unless the articles otherwise provide, be distributed among the members according to their rights and interests in the company.

(2) Nothing in paragraph (a) of subsection (1) shall in any way affect any rights or obligations of the company or any other person arising as a result of any agreement entered into (whether before or after the commencement of section 132 of the Companies Act, 1990) by any person under which any particular liability of the company to any general creditor is postponed in favour of or subordinated to the rights or claims of any other person to whom the company may be in any way liable.

(3) In subsection (2)—

'liability' includes a contingent liability; and

'person' includes a class of persons.".

Definitions

'*company*': Companies Act, 1963, section 2.
'*liability*': Companies Act, 1990, section 132.
'*person*': Companies Act, 1990, section 132.
'*Principal Act*': Companies Act, 1990, section 3.

General Note

Section 275 of the Companies Act, 1963, provides that the property of a company on its winding up be applied in satisfaction of its liabilities *pari passu*, but subject to the rights of the preferential creditors.

Banks tend to issue Eurobonds in the form of unsecured floating rate notes, and this has given rise to questions as to the subordination of the claims of one class of unsecured creditors even with their consent or agreement. The amendment provided in this section is designed to introduce certainty into this area.

SECTION 133
Consent to appointment as liquidator and notification of appointment.

The Principal Act is hereby amended by the insertion after section 276 of the following section—

"276A.—(1) The appointment of a liquidator shall be of no effect unless the person nominated has, prior to his appointment, signified his written consent to the appointment.

(2) The chairman of any meeting at which a liquidator is appointed shall, within 7 days of the meeting, notify the liquidator in writing of his appointment, unless the liquidator or his duly authorised representative is present at the meeting where the appointment is made.

(3) A person who fails to comply with subsection (2) shall be liable to a fine not exceeding £1,000.".

Definitions

'*Principal Act*': Companies Act, 1990, section 3.

General Note

This section amends the Companies Act, 1963, by the insertion of a new section 276A. This provides that the appointment of a liquidator will be of no effect until such time as the person nominated for the position of liquidator has consented in writing to the appointment.

Furthermore, the chairman of the meeting at which the liquidator is appointed must notify the liquidator of his appointment in writing within seven days unless the liquidator or his authorised representative were present at the meeting. Failure to comply with this section will result in a fine not exceeding £1,000.

SECTION 134
Preferential payments in a winding up.

Section 285 of the Principal Act is hereby amended by the insertion of the following subsection—

"(14) The priority conferred by subsection (2) shall apply only to those debts which, within the period of six months after advertisement by the liquidator for claims in at least two daily newspapers circulating in the district where the registered office of the company is situated, either—

(*a*) have been notified to him; or
(*b*) have become known to him.".

Definitions

'*Principal Act*': Companies Act, 1990, section 3.

General Note

This section amends section 285 of the Companies Act, 1963, dealing with preferential payments in a winding up. The amendment provides that in order to speed up liquidations generally the liquidator can advertise for creditors to lodge their claims within a period of six months from the date of the advertisement and can exclude any claims lodged after the specified time.

SECTION 135
Fraudulent preference.

The Principal Act is hereby amended by the substitution for section 286 of the following section—

"286.—(1) Subject to the provisions of this section, any conveyance, mortgage, delivery of goods, payment, execution or other act relating to property made or done by or against a company which is unable to pay its debts as they become due in favour of any creditor, or of any person on trust for any creditor, with a view to giving such creditor, or any surety or guarantor for the debt due to such creditor, a preference over the other creditors, shall, if a winding-up of the company commences within 6 months of the making or doing the same and the company is at the time of the commencement of the winding-up unable to pay its debts (taking into account the contingent and prospective liabilities), be deemed a fraudulent preference of its creditors and be invalid accordingly.

(2) Any conveyance or assignment by a company of all its property to trustees for the benefit of all its creditors shall be void to all intents.

(3) A transaction to which subsection (1) applies in favour of a connected person which was made within two years before the commencement of the winding up of the company shall, unless the contrary is shown, be deemed in the event of the company being wound up—

(*a*) to have been made with a view to giving such person a preference over the other creditors, and
(*b*) to be a fraudulent preference,

and be invalid accordingly.

(4) Subsections (1) and (3) shall not affect the rights of any person making title in good faith and for valuable consideration through or under a creditor of the company.

(5) In this section, 'a connected person' means a person who, at the time the transaction was made, was—

(*a*) a director of the company;

(*b*) a shadow director of the company;

(*c*) a person connected, within the meaning of section 26 (1) (*a*) of the Companies Act, 1990, with a director;

(*d*) a related company, within the meaning of section 140 of the said Act, or

(*e*) any trustee of, or surety or guarantor for the debt due to, any person described in paragraph (*a*), (*b*), (*c*) or (*d*).".

Definitions

'*company*': Companies Act, 1963, section 2.

'*connected person*': Companies Act, 1990, section 135.

'*director*': Companies Act, 1963, section 2.

'*Principal Act*': Companies Act, 1990, section 3.

'*related company*': Companies Act, 1990, section 140.

'*shadow director*': Companies Act, 1990, section 3.

General Note

This section substitutes a new section for section 286 of the Companies Act, 1963, dealing with fraudulent preference. The object of the section is to prevent an insolvent company when a winding up is imminent from giving preference to certain creditors, such as directors and their friends, to the detriment of its other creditors. The amendment has the effect of extending the period from six months to two years in the case of transactions undertaken between 'connected persons'.

(1) Where a company is unable to pay its debts as they become due and where a preference is given to payment to a creditor or group of creditors within a period of six months of the commencement of the winding up, this will be deemed to be fraudulent preference of its creditors, and any such payment made will be invalid.

(2) The assignment or conveyance of all its property to trustees for the benefit of all its creditors will be void.

(3) Where a transaction was made in favour of a 'connected person', any payment or transfer made within the two-year period before the commencement of the winding up will be invalid and deemed to be a fraudulent preference.

(4) Subsections (1) and (3) do not affect the rights of any person making title in good faith and for consideration as a creditor of the company.

(5) 'Connected person' is defined for the purposes of this section.

SECTION 136
Circumstances in
which floating
charge is invalid.

The Principal Act is hereby amended by the substitution for section 288 of the following section—

"288.—(1) Where a company is being wound up, a floating charge on the undertaking or property of the company created within 12 months before the commencement of the winding up shall, unless it is proved that the company immediately after the creation of the charge was solvent, be invalid, except as to money actually advanced or paid, or the actual price or value of goods or services sold or supplied, to the company at the time of or subsequently to the creation of, and in consideration for, the charge, together with interest on that amount at the rate of 5 per cent per annum.

(2) For the purposes of subsection (1) the value of any goods or services sold or supplied by way of consideration for a floating charge is the amount in money which at the time they were sold or supplied could reasonably have been expected to be obtained for the goods or services in the ordinary course of business and on the same terms (apart from the consideration) as those on which they were sold or supplied to the company.

(3) Where a floating charge on the undertaking or property of a company is created in favour of a connected person, subsection (1) shall apply to such a charge as if the period of 12 months mentioned in that subsection were a period of 2 years.

(4) In this section 'a connected person' means a person who, at the time the transaction was made, was—

(a) a director of the company;
(b) a shadow director of the company;
(c) a person connected, within the meaning of section 26 (1) (a) of the Companies Act, 1990, with a director;
(d) a related company, within the meaning of section 140 of the said Act; or
(e) any trustee of, or any surety or guarantor for the debt due to, any person described in paragraph (a), (b), (c) or (d).".

Definitions

'*company*': Companies Act, 1963, section 2.

'*connected person*': Companies Act, 1990, section 136.

'*director*': Companies Act, 1963, section 2.

'*Principal Act*': Companies Act, 1990, section 3.

'*related company*': Companies Act, 1990, section 140.

'*shadow director*': Companies Act, 1990, section 3.

General Note

This section substitutes a new section for section 288 of the Companies Act, 1963 (Circumstances in which a floating charge is invalid). There are three main amendments to the 1963 Act, in that the reference to 'cash paid' in subsection (1) has been expanded to include goods or services sold or supplied to the company. In addition it is provided that a floating charge given to a person connected with the company within two years of the date on which the company goes into liquidation will be invalid unless it can be shown that the company was solvent after the creation of the charge.

(1) A floating charge created within twelve months of a company going into liquidation will be invalid unless it is proved that the company was solvent immediately after the creation of the charge.

(2) This subsection is based on section 245 (6) of the UK Insolvency Act, 1986, and provides that where a floating charge is created within twelve months before a company goes into insolvent liquidation, the charge will be invalid except as to the money actually advanced or paid, or the actual price or value of goods, or the actual price or value of goods or services sold or supplied to the company in consideration for the charge. This amendment makes it clear that when the section speaks of the value of the goods or services sold or supplied what it means is the real or true value.

(3) Where a floating charge is made in favour of a 'connected person' the period of invalidation of the charge is extended from six months to two years should the company go into liquidation.

(4) A definition of 'connected person' is given for the purpose of the section, similar to that in section 135 (5).

SECTION 137 **Criminal liability of persons concerned for fraudulent trading of company.**	The Principal Act is hereby amended by the substitution for section 297 of the following section—

"297.—(1) If any person is knowingly a party to the carrying on of the business of a company with intent to defraud creditors of the company or creditors of any other person or for any fraudulent purpose, that person shall be guilty of an offence.

(2) Any person who is convicted of an offence under this section shall be liable—

(a) on summary conviction to imprisonment for a term not exceeding 12 months or to a fine not exceeding £1,000 or to both, or

(b) on conviction on indictment, to imprisonment for a term not exceeding 7 years or to a fine not exceeding £50,000 or to both.".

Definitions

'*company*': Companies Act, 1963, section 2.

'*Principal Act*': Companies Act, 1990, section 3.

General Note

This section has the effect of strengthening the provisions concerning the criminal liability of persons concerned with fraudulent trading under section 297 of the Companies Act, 1963.

(1) If a person is knowingly a party to the carrying on of the business of a company with the intent to defraud creditors of the company or creditors of anyone else or for any fraudulent purpose that person will be guilty of an offence.

(2) A person who is convicted of an offence under subsection (1) above will be liable to a fine not exceeding £1,000 and/or up to one year's imprisonment on summary conviction; on conviction on indictment he will be liable to a fine not exceeding £10,000 and/or up to seven years' imprisonment.

SECTION 138
Civil liability of persons concerned for fraudulent or reckless trading of company.

The Principal Act is hereby amended by the insertion after section 297 of the following section—

"297A.—(1) If in the course of winding up of a company or in the course of proceedings under the Companies (Amendment) Act, 1990, it appears that—

(a) any person was, while an officer of the company, knowingly a party to the carrying on of any business of the company in a reckless manner; or

(b) any person was knowingly a party to the carrying on of any business of the company with intent to defraud creditors of the company, or creditors of any other person or for any fraudulent purpose;

the court, on the application of the receiver, examiner, liquidator or any creditor or contributory of the company, may, if it thinks it proper to do so, declare that such person shall be personally responsible, without any limitation of liability, for all or any part of the debts or other liabilities of the company as the court may direct.

(2) Without prejudice to the generality of subsection (1) (a), an officer of a company shall be deemed to have been knowingly a party to the carrying on of any business of the company in a reckless manner if—

(a) he was a party to the carrying on of such business and, having regard to the general knowledge, skill and experience that may reasonably be expected of a person in his position, he ought to have known that his actions or those of the company would cause loss to the creditors of the company, or any of them, or

(b) he was a party to the contracting of a debt by the company and did not honestly believe on reasonable grounds that the company would be able to pay the debt when it fell due for payment as well as all its other debts (taking into account the contingent and prospective liabilities).

(3) Notwithstanding anything contained in subsection (1) the court may grant a declaration on the grounds set out in paragraph (a) of that subsection only if—

(a) paragraph (a), (b) or (c) of section 214 applies to the company concerned, and (*b*) an applicant for such a declaration, being a creditor or contributory of the company, or any person on whose behalf such application is made, suffered loss or damage as a consequence of any behaviour mentioned in subsection (1).

(4) In deciding whether it is proper to make an order on the ground set out in subsection (2) (*b*), the court shall have regard to whether the creditor in question was, at the time the debt was incurred, aware of the company's financial state of affairs and, notwithstanding such awareness, nevertheless assented to the incurring of the debt.

(5) On the hearing of an application under this section, the applicant may himself give evidence or call witnesses.

(6) Where it appears to the court that any person in respect of whom a declaration has been sought under subsection (1) (*a*), has acted honestly and responsibly in relation to the conduct of the affairs of the company or any matter or matters on the ground of which such declaration is sought to be made, the court may, having regard to all the circumstances of the case, relieve him either wholly or in part, from personal liability on such terms as it may think fit.

(7) Where the court makes any such declaration, it may—

(*a*) give such further directions as it thinks proper for the purpose of giving effect to that declaration and in particular may make provision for making the liability of any such person under the declaration a charge on any debt or obligation due from the company to him, or on any mortgage or charge or any interest in any mortgage or charge on any assets of the company held by or vested in him or any company or person on his behalf, or any person claiming as assignee from or through the person liable or any company or person acting on his behalf, and may from time to time make such further order as may be necessary for the purpose of enforcing any charge imposed under this subsection;

(*b*) provide that sums recovered under this section shall be paid to such person or classes of persons, for such purposes, in such amounts or proportions at such time or times and in such respective priorities among themselves as such declaration may specify.

(8) Subsection (1) (*a*) shall not apply in relation to the carrying on of the business of a company during a period when the company is under the protection of the court.

(9) This section shall have effect notwithstanding that—

(*a*) the person in respect of whom the declaration has been sought under subsection (1) may be criminally liable in respect of the matters on the ground of which such declaration is to be made; or

(*b*) any matter or matters on the ground of which the declaration under subsection (1) is to be made have occurred outside the State.

(10) For the purposes of this section—

'assignee' includes any person to whom or in whose favour, by the directions of the person liable, the debt, obligation, mortgage or charge was created, issued or transferred or the interest created, but does not include an assignee for valuable consideration (not including consideration by way of marriage) given in good faith and without notice of any of the matters on the ground of which the declaration is made;

'company' includes any body which may be wound up under the Companies Acts; and

'officer' includes any auditor, liquidator, receiver, or shadow director.".

Definitions

'assignee': Companies Act, 1990, section 138.

'company': Companies Act, 1990, section 138.

'contributory': Companies Act, 1963, section 2.

'court': Companies Act, 1990, section 235.

'examiner': Companies (Amendment) Act, 1990, section 1.

'officer': Companies Act, 1990, section 138.

'Principal Act': Companies Act, 1990, section 3.

General Note

This section has a twofold objective, in that the question of civil liability for fraudulent trading has been separated from criminal liability, and the civil liability provision has been expanded to include reckless trading.

The concept of reckless trading will apply to any person who has, while he was an officer of the company, knowingly been a party to the contracting of a debt by the company that he did not honestly believe on reasonable grounds the company would be able to pay when it fell due for payment as well as its other debts, or was knowingly a party to the carrying on of any business of the company in a reckless manner. If a company is wound up and unable to pay its debts, a person in such a situation may be made personally liable for all or any part of its debts or other liabilities. If the High Court considers that the person acted honestly and responsibly it may relieve him wholly or partly from personal liability on whatever terms it thinks fit.

(1) The court on an application from a receiver, liquidator, examiner, creditor or contributory of the company may declare that a person shall be personally liable with unlimited liability for some or all of the debts of the company as it may direct where

(*a*) the person while an officer of the company was knowingly a party to the carrying on of any business in a reckless manner, or

(*b*) the person was knowingly a party to the carrying on of a business with the intention of defrauding creditors of the company or creditors of some other person or for any fraudulent purpose.

An officer for the purposes of this section is defined in subsection (10), and would include directors, secretary, auditor, liquidator, examiner, receiver, or shadow director.

(2) An officer will be deemed to have been knowingly a party to the carrying on of the business of the company in a reckless manner if he was

(*a*) a party to the carrying on of the business and, having regard to the general knowledge, skill and experience that he ought reasonably be expected to have in his position, ought to have known that the actions would cause loss to the creditors, or

(*b*) a party to the contracting of a debt by the company and did not honestly believe on reasonable grounds that the company would be able to pay the debt when it fell due, taking into account contingent and prospective liabilities.

(3) The court may grant a declaration under subsection (1) only if

(*a*) paragraph (*a*), (*b*) or (*c*) of section 214 of the Companies Act, 1963, applies (relating to the circumstances in which a company is unable to pay its debts), and

(*b*) an applicant for such a declaration has suffered loss or damage as a consequence of any behaviour mentioned in subsection (1).

(4) In deciding to make an order the court will take into consideration whether the creditor was aware of the company's financial position and, having such knowledge, assented to the incurring of the debt.

(5) The applicant may give evidence or call witnesses during the hearing for an application under this section.

(6) Where the court is of the opinion that a person against whom a declaration is sought has acted honestly and responsibly in relation to the conduct of the company's affairs it may relieve him wholly or partly of personal liability, having regard to all the circumstances of the case.

(7) Where the court makes a declaration it may

(*a*) give such directions as it thinks proper to give effect to the declaration and make provision for making the liability of any person under the declaration a charge on any debt or obligation due from the company to him or any mortgage or chattel or interest in one (the court may make such further order as is necessary for enforcing the charge imposed under this subsection), or (*b*) provide that any sum recovered shall be paid to the persons in proportion to their respective priorities as the declaration may specify.

(8) Subsection (1) (*a*) will not apply to the carrying on of the business of a company while it is under court protection.

(9) The person in respect of whom the declaration is made may also be criminally liable on the grounds for which the declaration is made or any matter that may have occurred outside the state.

(10) 'Assignee', 'company' and 'officer' are defined for the purposes of this section.

SECTION 139
Power of the court to order the return of assets which have been improperly transferred.

(1) Where, on the application of a liquidator, creditor or contributory of a company which is being wound up, it can be shown to the satisfaction of the court that—

(*a*) any property of the company of any kind whatsoever was disposed of either by way of conveyance, transfer, mortgage, security, loan, or in any way whatsoever whether by act or omission, direct or indirect, and

(*b*) the effect of such disposal was to perpetrate a fraud on the company, its creditors or members,

the court may, if it deems it just and equitable to do so, order any person who appears to have the use, control or possession of such property or the proceeds of the sale or development thereof to deliver it or pay a sum in respect of it to the liquidator on such terms or conditions as the court sees fit.

(2) Subsection (1) shall not apply to any conveyance, mortgage, delivery of goods, payment, execution or other act relating to property made or done by or against a company to which section 286 (1) of the Principal Act applies.

(3) In deciding whether it is just and equitable to make an order under this section, the court shall have regard to the rights of persons who have *bona fide* and for value acquired an interest in the property the subject of the application.

Definitions
'*company*': Companies Act, 1963, section 2.
'*contributory*': Companies Act, 1963, section 2.
'*court*': Companies Act, 1990, section 235.
'*Principal Act*': Companies Act, 1990, section 3.

General Note
This section provides that where a liquidator can show that any property of a company was fraudulently disposed of, the court may order the return of such property or the proceeds of its sale or development. These provisions do not apply to a case of fraudulent preference.

(1) If it can be shown to the satisfaction of the court that any property of the company was disposed of and the effect of such disposal was to perpetrate a fraud on the company or its creditors or members, the court may if it considers it to be just and equitable order any person who appears to have the use, control or possession of such property or the proceeds of sale or development to deliver it or pay the sum to the liquidator on the terms or conditions as may be set by the court.

(2) Subsection (1) does not apply to any conveyance, mortgage, delivery of goods or other act relating to property to which section 286 (1) of the Companies Act, 1963, applies.

(3) In deciding whether it is just and equitable the court will have regard to the rights of persons who have in good faith and for value acquired an interest in the property that is the subject of the application.

SECTION 140

Company may be required to contribute to debts of related companies.

(1) On the application of the liquidator or any creditor or contributory of any company that is being wound up, the court, if it is satisfied that it is just and equitable to do so, may order that any company that is or has been related to the company being wound up shall pay to the liquidator of that company an amount equivalent to the whole or part of all or any of the debts provable in that winding up. Any order under this section may be made on such terms and conditions as the court thinks fit.

(2) In deciding whether it is just and equitable to make an order under subsection (1) the court shall have regard to the following matters—

(*a*) the extent to which the related company took part in the management of the company being wound up;

(*b*) the conduct of the related company towards the creditors of the company being wound up;

(*c*) the effect which such order would be likely to have on the creditors of the related company concerned.

(3) No order shall be made under subsection (1) unless the court is satisfied that the circumstances that gave rise to the winding up of the company are attributable to the actions or omissions of the related company.

(4) Notwithstanding any other provision, it shall not be just and equitable to make an order under subsection (1) if the only ground for making the order is—

(*a*) the fact that a company is related to another company, or

(*b*) that creditors of the company being wound up have relied on the fact that another company is or has been related to the first mentioned company.

(5) For the purposes of this Act, a company is related to another company if—

(*a*) that other company is its holding company or subsidiary; or

(*b*) more than half in nominal value of its equity share capital (as defined in section 155 (5) of the Principal Act) is held by the other company and companies related to that other company (whether directly or indirectly, but other than in a fiduciary capacity); or

(c) more than half in nominal value of the equity share capital (as defined in section 155 (5) of the Principal Act) of each of them is held by members of the other (whether directly or indirectly, but other than in a fiduciary capacity); or

(d) that other company or a company or companies related to that other company or that other company together with a company or companies related to it are entitled to exercise or control the exercise of more than one half of the voting power at any general meeting of the company; or

(e) the businesses of the companies have been so carried on that the separate business of each company, or a substantial part thereof, is not readily identifiable; or

(f) there is another company to which both companies are related;

and "related company" has a corresponding meaning.

(6) For the purposes of this section "company" includes any body which is liable to be wound up under the Companies Acts and "creditor" means one or more creditors to whom the company being wound up is indebted by more, in aggregate, than £10,000.

(7) Where an application for an order under subsection (1) seeks to require a licensed bank, within the meaning of section 25, to contribute to the debts of a related company, a copy of every such application shall be sent by the applicant to the Central Bank who shall be entitled to be heard by the court before an order is made.

Definitions

'*company*': Companies Act, 1990, section 140.

'*contributory*': Companies Act, 1963, section 2.

'*court*': Companies Act, 1990, section 235.

'*creditor*': Companies Act, 1990, section 140.

'*equity share capital*': Companies Act, 1963, section 155.

'*holding company*': Companies Act, 1963, section 155.

'*Principal Act*': Companies Act, 1990, section 3.

'*related company*': Companies Act, 1990, section 140.

'*subsidiary*': Companies Act, 1963, section 155.

General Note

This section provides that a court may order a company that is related to another company in liquidation to pay all or part of the debts of that other company, if it is considered just and equitable by the court. The mere fact that companies are related will not be a ground for making an order, and the section contains guidelines for the court in deciding whether it is just and equitable in making an order.

(1) The court may, on the application of a liquidator, creditor or contributory of any company being wound up, if it is considered just and equitable, order that any related company of the company being wound up pay an amount equivalent to some or all of the debts provable in the winding up, on such terms and conditions as it thinks fit.

(2) The court in deciding whether it is just and equitable to make an order will take into account such things as the extent to which the management of the related company participated in the management of the company being wound up, the conduct of the related company towards the creditors of the company being wound up, and the effect an order would have on the creditors of the related company.

(3) The court will not make an order unless it is satisfied that the circumstances that gave rise to the winding up were attributable to the actions or omissions of the related company.

(4) It would not be just and equitable to make an order making the company responsible for the debts if the only ground was the fact that it was a related company or that the creditors relied on the fact that it was a company related to the company being wound up.

(5) The circumstances when companies are deemed to be related companies are set out.

(6) 'Company' and 'creditor' are defined for the purposes of this section.

(7) Where a licensed bank is the subject of an order to contribute to the debts of a related company, a copy of the application must be given to the Central Bank by the applicant, who would be entitled to be heard at a court hearing before an order is made.

SECTION 141
Pooling of assets of related companies.

(1) Where two or more related companies are being wound up and the court, on the application of the liquidator of any of the companies, is satisfied that it is just and equitable to make an order under this section, the court may order that, subject to such terms and conditions as the court may impose and to the extent that the court orders, the companies shall be wound up together as if they were one company, and, subject to the provisions of this section, the order shall have effect and all the provisions of this Part and Part VI of the Principal Act shall apply accordingly.

(2) In deciding the terms and conditions of an order under this section the court shall have particular regard to the interests of those persons who are members of some, but not all, of the companies.

(3) Where the court makes an order under subsection (1)—

(a) the court may remove any liquidator of any of the companies, and appoint any person to act as liquidator of any one or more of the companies;

(b) the court may give such directions as it thinks fit for the purpose of giving effect to the order;

(c) nothing in this section or the order shall affect the rights of any secured creditor of any of the companies;

(d) debts of a company that are to be paid in priority to all other debts of the company pursuant to section 285 of the Principal Act shall, to the extent that they are not paid out of the assets of that company, be subject to the claims of holders of debentures under any floating charge (as defined in that section) created by any of the other companies;

(e) unless the court otherwise orders, the claims of all unsecured creditors of the companies shall rank equally among themselves.

(4) In deciding whether it is just and equitable to make an order under subsection (1) the court shall have regard to the following matters—

(a) the extent to which any of the companies took part in the management of any of the other companies;

(b) the conduct of any of the companies towards the creditors of any of the other companies;

(c) the extent to which the circumstances that gave rise to the winding up of any of the companies are attributable to the actions or omissions of any of the other companies;

(d) the extent to which the businesses of the companies have been intermingled.

(5) Notwithstanding any other provision, it shall not be just and equitable to make an order under subsection (1) if the only ground for making the order is—

(a) the fact that a company is related to another company, or

(b) that creditors of a company being wound up have relied on the fact that another company is or has been related to the first mentioned company.

(6) Notice of an application to the court for the purposes of this section shall be served on every company specified in the application, and on such other persons as the court may direct, not later than the end of the eighth day before the day the application is heard.

Definitions

'company': Companies Act, 1963, section 2.

'court': Companies Act, 1990, section 235.

'Principal Act': Companies Act, 1990, section 3.

'related company': Companies Act, 1990, section 140.

General Note

This section provides that the court, if it considers that it is just and equitable to do so, may order that in cases where two or more related companies are being wound up they shall be wound up together as one company, and it sets out guidelines for deciding whether it is just and equitable to make such an order.

(1) Where two or more related companies are being wound up, the court may on application by the liquidator of any of the companies, if it is satisfied that it is just and equitable, make an order that they be wound up together as if they were one company.

(2) In deciding the terms and conditions relating to the order, the court will have regard to the interests of the persons who are members of some but not all of the companies.

(3) Where the court makes an order it may remove any liquidator of any of the companies and appoint a person to act as liquidator of one or more of the companies and give such directions as it thinks fit. However, the making of the order will not have any effect on the rights of the secured creditors, and the claims of all unsecured creditors will rank equally among themselves.

(4) In considering whether it is just and equitable to make an order, the court will take into consideration such things as the extent to which any of the companies took part in the management of any of the other companies, the conduct of any of the companies towards the creditors of any of the other companies, the extent to which the companies are intermingled, and the extent to which the circumstances of the winding up of the companies were attributable to the actions or omissions of any of the other companies.

(5) It is not just and equitable for the court to make an order merely because the companies are related or because the creditors of the company being wound up have relied on the fact that the companies were related.

(6) The notice of application to the court must be served on every company specified in the application and such other persons as directed by the court not later than eight days before the hearing of the application.

SECTION 142
Amendment of section 298 of the Principal Act.

The Principal Act is hereby amended by the substitution for section 298 of the following section—

"298.—(1) Subsection (2) applies if in the course of winding up a company it appears that any person who has taken part in the formation or promotion of the company, or any past or present officer, liquidator, receiver or examiner of the company, has misapplied or retained or become liable or accountable for any money or property of the company, or has been guilty of any misfeasance or other breach of duty or trust in relation to the company.

(2) The court may, on the application of the liquidator, or any creditor or contributory, examine into the conduct of the promoter, officer, liquidator, receiver or examiner, and compel him—

(*a*) to repay or restore the money or property or any part thereof respectively with interest at such rate as the court thinks just, or

(*b*) to contribute such sum to the assets of the company by way of compensation in respect of the misapplication, retainer, misfeasance or other breach of duty or trust as the court thinks just.

(3) This section has effect notwithstanding that the offence is one for which the offender may be criminally liable.".

Definitions

'*company*': Companies Act, 1963, section 2.

'*contributory*': Companies Act, 1963, section 2.

'*director*': Companies Act, 1963, section 2.

'*examiner*': Companies (Amendment) Act, 1990, section 1.

'*officer*': Companies Act, 1963, section 2.

'*Principal Act*': Companies Act, 1990, section 3.

General Note

This section substitutes a new section for section 298 of the Companies Act, 1963 (Power of court to assess damages against directors). It is a procedural section, in that it provides a swifter and simpler method for the court to assess damages against any promoter, director, liquidator or officer of the company who has been guilty of misfeasance or a breach of trust in relation to the company.

(1) Subsection (2) will apply if in the winding up of a company any person who has taken part in the promotion or formation of the company or has been an officer, liquidator, receiver or examiner has misapplied or retained any company property or has been in breach of trust in relation to the company.

(2) The court may on an application from a liquidator, contributory or creditor examine into the conduct of such person mentioned in subsection (1) and can compel him to repay or return such property together with interest or contribute such sum to the assets of the company by way of compensation as the court thinks fit.

(3) A person found guilty under this section may be subject to a criminal liability.

SECTION 143
Amendment of section 299 of the Principal Act.

Section 299 of the Principal Act is hereby amended by the substitution of the following subsection for subsection (1)—

"(1) If it appears to the court in the course of a winding-up by the court that any past or present officer, or any member, of the company has been guilty of an offence in relation to the company for which he is criminally liable, the court may either on the application of any person interested in the winding-up or of its own motion direct the liquidator to refer the matter to the Director of Public Prosecutions and in such a case the liquidator shall furnish to the Director of Public Prosecutions such information and give to him such access to and facilities for inspecting and taking any copies of any documents, being information or documents in the possession or under the control of the liquidator and relating to the matter in question, as the Director of Public Prosecutions may require.".

Definitions

'*court*': Companies Act, 1990, section 235.
'*officer*': Companies Act, 1963, section 2.
'*Principal Act*': Companies Act, 1990, section 3.

General Note

This section amends section 299 (1) of the Companies Act, 1963 (Prosecution of criminal offences committed by officers and members of a company), and provides that if during the course of the winding up it appears to the court that any present or past officer or member of the company has been guilty of a criminal offence it may on the application of anyone interested in the winding up or on its own motion direct the liquidator to refer the matter to the Director of Public Prosecutions. In such case the liquidator must furnish such information relating to the matter as the Director of Public Prosecutions may require.

SECTION 144
Duty of liquidators and receivers to include certain information in returns etc.

(1) Where a receiver or liquidator of a company is obliged by the Companies Acts to make a periodic account, abstract, statement or return in relation to his activities as receiver or liquidator he shall incorporate in such account, abstract, statement or return a report as to whether, at the date of such account, abstract, statement or return any past or present director or other officer, or any member, of the company is a person—

(a) in respect of whom a declaration has been made under any provision of the Companies Acts that he should be personally liable for all or any part of the debts of a company,
(b) who is, or is deemed to be, subject to a disqualification order under Part VII.

(2) A receiver or liquidator who contravenes subsection (1) shall be guilty of an offence and liable to a fine.

Definitions

'*company*': Companies Act, 1963, section 2.

'*director*': Companies Act, 1963, section 2.
'*officer*': Companies Act, 1963, section 2.

General Note

This section sets out information that liquidators and receivers are obliged to include in returns, etc.

(1) The receiver or liquidator is obliged to make certain returns, and he must include in the report a statement as to whether any past or present director, member or officer should be made personally liable for all or part of the debts of a company and whether that person should be subject to a disqualification order under part VII of this Act.

(2) A receiver or liquidator who contravenes this section will be guilty of an offence and liable to a fine.

SECTION 145
Penalty for default of receiver or liquidator in making certain accounts and returns.

(1) Where a receiver or liquidator is in default in relation to the making or filing of a periodic account, abstract, statement or return in pursuance of any provision of the Companies Acts he shall be guilty of an offence and liable—

(a) on summary conviction to a fine not exceeding £1,000 and, for continued contravention, to a daily default fine not exceeding £50;

(b) on conviction on indictment to a fine not exceeding £1,000 and, for continued contravention, to a daily default fine not exceeding £250.

(2) A person convicted of an offence under any of the following provisions, namely section 262, 272, 306, 319 (2) or 321 of the Principal Act, shall, in lieu of the penalty provided in any such section (as increased by section 15 of the Companies (Amendment) Act, 1982), be liable to the penalties specified in subsection (1).

Definitions

'*daily default fine*': Companies Act, 1990, section 3.
'*Principal Act*': Companies Act, 1990, section 3.

General Note

This section sets out the penalties that can be imposed on a receiver or liquidator for failure to make certain accounts and returns as required by the Companies Acts.

SECTION 146
Disqualification for appointment as liquidator.

The Principal Act is hereby amended by the insertion after section 300 of the following section—

"300A.—(1) None of the following persons shall be qualified for appointment as liquidator of a company—

(*a*) a person who is, or who has within 12 months of the commencement of the winding up been, an officer or servant of the company;

(*b*) except with the leave of the court, a parent, spouse, brother, sister or child of an officer of the company;

(*c*) a person who is a partner or in the employment of an officer or servant of the company;

(*d*) a person who is not qualified by virtue of this subsection for appointment as liquidator of any other body corporate which is that company's subsidiary or holding company or a subsidiary of that company's holding company, or would be so disqualified if the body corporate were a company.

References in this subsection to an officer or servant of the company include references to an auditor.

(2) An application for leave under subsection (1) (*b*) shall be supported by such evidence as the court may require.

(3) If a liquidator becomes disqualified by virtue of this section he shall thereupon vacate his office and give notice in writing within 14 days to—

(*a*) the court in a court winding up,

(*b*) the company in a members' voluntary winding up,

(*c*) the company and the creditors in a creditors' voluntary winding up,

that he has vacated it by reason of such disqualification.

(4) Any person who acts as a liquidator when disqualified by this section from so doing or who fails to comply with subsection (3), if that subsection applies to him, shall be guilty of an offence and shall be liable—

(*a*) on summary conviction, to a fine not exceeding £1,000 and, for continued contravention, a daily default fine not exceeding £50;

(*b*) on conviction on indictment, to a fine of £10,000 and, for continued contravention, a daily default fine not exceeding £250.

(5) This section shall not apply to a winding-up commenced before the commencement of section 146 of the Companies Act, 1990.".

Definitions

'*auditor*': this is not defined in the Companies Acts; but see the UK case *R. v. Shacter* [1960] 2 QB 252.

'*company*': Companies Act, 1963, section 2.

'*court*': Companies Act, 1990, section 235.

'*daily default fine*': Companies Act, 1990, section 3.

'*holding company*': Companies Act, 1963, section 155.

'*officer*': Companies Act, 1963, section 2.

'*Principal Act*': Companies Act, 1990, section 3.

'*subsidiary*': Companies Act, 1963, section 155.

General Note

This section sets out the categories of person who will be disqualified from acting as a liquidator of the company.

(1) The categories of person not qualified to act as an auditor of the company are listed.

(2) The court may give leave to certain persons under subsection (1) (*b*), supported by such evidence as it may require.

(3) In the event that a liquidator becomes disqualified he must vacate his office and give written notice within fourteen days that he has vacated his position as a result of disqualification

- in the case of a court winding up, to the court;
- in the case of a members' voluntary winding up, to the company;
- in the case of a creditors' voluntary winding up, to the company and creditors.

(4) If a person acts as a liquidator when disqualified he will be guilty of an offence and liable to a fine.

(5) This section will not apply to a winding up begun before the commencement of this section.

SECTION 147
Disclosure of interest by creditors etc. at creditors' meetings.

The Principal Act is hereby amended by the insertion after section 301 of the following section—

"301A.—(1) Where, at a meeting of creditors, a resolution is proposed for the appointment of a liquidator, any creditor who has a connection with the proposed liquidator shall, before the resolution is put, make such connection known to the chairman of the meeting who shall disclose that fact to the meeting, together with details thereof.

(2) Subsection (1) shall also apply to any person at the meeting, being a representative of a creditor and entitled to vote on the resolution on his behalf.

(3) Where the chairman of a meeting of creditors has any such connection as is mentioned in subsection (1), he shall disclose that fact to the meeting, together with details thereof.

(4) For the purposes of this section, a person has a connection with a proposed liquidator if he is—

(*a*) a parent, spouse, brother, sister or child of, or
(*b*) employed by, or a partner of,

the proposed liquidator.

(5) A person who fails to comply with this section shall be liable to a fine not exceeding £1,000.

(6) In exercising its jurisdiction under section 267 (2) or 272 (2) (which relate to the appointment or removal of a liquidator) the court may have regard to any failure to comply with this section.".

Definitions

'child': Companies Act, 1990, section 3.

'court': Companies Act, 1990, section 235.

'Principal Act': Companies Act, 1990, section 3.

General Note

This section provides that at a meeting of creditors to appoint a liquidator, if a creditor has a connection with the person nominated as liquidator he is required to declare his interest.

(1) Where at a meeting of creditors a person is proposed as liquidator with whom a creditor present has a connection, the creditor must make this connection known to the chairman of the meeting together with details before the resolution is put to the meeting.

(2) Subsection (1) will apply to any person at the meeting who is a representative of a creditor and is entitled to vote on the resolution on his behalf.

(3) Where the chairman of the meeting has any connection as mentioned in subsection (1) he must disclose that fact together with details to the meeting.

(4) The circumstances in which a person is deemed to be connected are set out for the purposes of this section.

(5) A fine not exceeding £1,000 may be imposed for failure to comply with this section.

(6) The court may take into account failure to comply with this section in any matter concerning section 267 or 272 of the Companies Act, 1963.

SECTION 148
Extension of power of court to assess damages against directors.

(1) Subsection (2) applies if in the course of winding up a company which is a subsidiary of another company, it appears that any director of the subsidiary's holding company has misapplied or retained or become liable or accountable for any money or property of the subsidiary, or has been guilty of any misfeasance or other breach of duty or trust in relation to the subsidiary.

(2) The court may, on the application of the liquidator, any creditor or contributory of the subsidiary, examine into the conduct of the director concerned and compel him—

(a) to repay or restore the money or property or any part thereof respectively with interest at such rate as the court thinks just, or (*b*) to contribute such sum to the assets of the subsidiary by way of compensation in respect of the misapplication, retainer, misfeasance or other breach of duty or trust as the court thinks just.

Definitions

'*company*': Companies Act, 1963, section 2.

'*contributory*': Companies Act, 1963, section 2.

'*court*': Companies Act, 1990, section 235.

'*director*': Companies Act, 1963, section 2.

'*holding company*': Companies Act, 1963, section 155.

'*subsidiary*': Companies Act, 1963, section 155.

General Note

This section extends the powers of the court to assess damages against directors.

(1) Subsection (2) will apply if in the course of a winding up a company is unable to pay its debts and it appears that any director of the holding company misapplied any of the property or is guilty of misfeasance or breach of duty or trust.

(2) The court on the application of the liquidator, creditor or contributory of the subsidiary will examine into the conduct of the director concerned and compel him to repay or restore the property with such interest as the court thinks fit or to compensate for the misfeasance, breach of duty or trust as the court thinks just.

7

DISQUALIFICATIONS AND RESTRICTIONS: DIRECTORS AND OTHER OFFICERS

Part VII of the Act is a new provision, and deals with disqualification and other restrictions on company directors and other officers.

Section 184 of the Companies Act, 1963, already permitted the High Court to disqualify a person from being a company director where he is guilty of fraud or breach of duty in relation to a company. This part of the Act imposes additional restrictions. Where a company is insolvent on its winding up, any person who is or within the previous twelve months has been a director, shadow director or secretary of that company may not become involved in the direction of another company for a period of five years, at the direction of the court, unless that company had a minimum allotted share capital fully paid up in cash.

This part has the effect of making directors, particularly non-executive directors, aware of their potential responsibilities and liabilities should a company be wound up. It will have a significant positive effect on persons willing to act as directors of companies, and should result in directors taking a greater interest in the affairs of a company. If a director is dissatisfied with the way a company is being run and its business is being carried on he will be more likely to raise his reservations and to resign to avoid being implicated with the company should it become insolvent.

SECTION 149

Application of Chapter I.

(1) This Chapter applies to any company if—

(a) at the date of the commencement of its winding-up it is proved to the court, or
(b) at any time during the course of its winding-up the liquidator of the company certifies, or it is otherwise proved, to the court,

that it is unable to pay its debts (within the meaning of section 214 of the Principal Act).

(2) This Chapter applies to any person who was a director of a company to which this section applies at the date of, or within 12 months prior to, the commencement of its winding-up.

(3) This Chapter shall not apply to a company which commences to be wound up before the commencement of this section.

(4) In this Chapter "company" includes a company to which section 351 of the Principal Act applies.

(5) This Chapter applies to shadow directors as it applies to directors.

Definitions

'company': Companies Act, 1990, section 149.
'court': Companies Act, 1990, section 235.
'director': Companies Act, 1963, section 2.
'Principal Act': Companies Act, 1990, section 3.
'relevant date': Companies Act, 1990, section 149.
'shadow director': Companies Act, 1990, section 3.

General Note

This section sets out the scope of the chapter concerning restrictions on directors of insolvent companies. It applies where a company is insolvent and unable to pay its debts and to any person who was a director at the date of the commencement of the winding up or at any time within the previous twelve months.

(1) The chapter applies to any company if at the date of the commencement of winding up it is proved to the court, or if at any time during the course of the winding up the liquidator certifies, that the company is unable to pay its debts.

(2) The chapter will apply to any person who was a director of a company to which subsection (1) applies at the date of the commencement of the winding up or was a director within twelve months before the commencement of the winding up.

(3) This chapter does not apply to companies that commenced to be wound up before the commencement of this section.

(4) 'Company' is defined for the purpose of this chapter.

(5) The section applies not only to directors but equally to shadow directors.

SECTION 150
Restriction.

(1) The court shall, unless it is satisfied as to any of the matters specified in subsection (2), declare that a person to whom this Chapter applies shall not, for a period of five years, be appointed or act in any way, whether directly or indirectly, as a director or secretary or be concerned or take part in the promotion or formation of any company unless it meets the requirements set out in subsection (3); and, in subsequent provisions of this Part, the expression "a person to whom section 150 applies" shall be construed as a reference to a person in respect of whom such a declaration has been made.

(2) The matters referred to in subsection (1) are—

(a) that the person concerned has acted honestly and responsibly in relation to the conduct of the affairs of the company and that there is no other reason why it would be just and equitable that he should be subject to the restrictions imposed by this section, or

(b) subject to paragraph (a), that the person concerned was a director of the company solely by reason of his nomination as such by a financial institution in connection with the giving of credit facilities to the company by such institution, provided that the institution in question has not obtained from any director of the company a personal or individual guarantee of repayment to it of the loans or other forms of credit advanced to the company, or

(c) subject to paragraph (a), that the person concerned was a director of the company solely by reason of his nomination as such by a venture capital company in connection with the purchase of, or subscription for, shares by it in the first-mentioned company.

(3) The requirements specified in subsection (1) are that—

(a) the nominal value of the allotted share capital of the company shall—
  (i) in the case of a public limited company, be at least £100,000,
  (ii) in the case of any other company, be at least £20,000,

(b) each allotted share to an aggregate amount not less than the amount referred to in subparagraph (i) or (ii) of paragraph (a), as the case may be, shall be fully paid up, including the whole of any premium thereon, and

(c) each such allotted share and the whole of any premium thereon shall be paid for in cash.

(4) Where a court makes a declaration under subsection (1), a prescribed officer of the court shall cause the registrar of companies to be furnished with prescribed particulars of the declaration in such form and manner as may be prescribed.

(5) In this section—

"financial institution" means—

(a) a licensed bank, within the meaning of section 25, or

(b) a company the ordinary business of which includes the making of loans or the giving of guarantees in connection with loans, and

"venture capital company" means a company prescribed by the Minister the principal ordinary business of which is the making of share investments.

Definitions

'company': Companies Act, 1990, section 149.

'court': Companies Act, 1990, section 235.

'director': Companies Act, 1963, section 2.

'financial institution': Companies Act, 1990, section 150.

'prescribe': Companies Act, 1990, section 3.

'public limited company': Companies (Amendment) Act, 1983, section 2.

'venture capital company': Companies Act, 1990, section 150.

General Note

This section sets out the restrictions imposed by this chapter. In general it provides that unless a person has acted honestly and responsibly in connection with the conduct of the company's affairs the court may prevent him from acting as a director or secretary or from being involved in the promotion or formation of a company for a period of five years, unless certain conditions as set out in subsection (3) are complied with. The conditions include in relation to a public limited company an allotted share capital of at least £100,000 or in the case of any other company £20,000, which must be paid up in cash. A person who has acted as a director solely as a result of his nomination by a venture capital company will not be affected by this section.

(1) Unless the court is satisfied of the matters in subsection (2) below it will declare that a director or shadow director to which the chapter applies shall not for a period of five years act directly or indirectly as director or secretary or be involved in the promotion or formation of a company unless the requirements specified in subsection (3) have been complied with.

(2) The restrictions set out in subsection (1) will not apply if the court is satisfied that

(*a*) the person concerned acted honestly and responsibly in relation to the conduct of the company's affairs and that there is no reason why it is just and equitable that the restrictions be imposed,

(*b*) the person concerned was a director or secretary solely because of his nomination by a financial institution in connection with the giving of credit facilities or purchase of shares, provided the institution in question has not obtained from any director of the company a personal indemnity or guarantee in respect of the repayment of the loans or other forms of credit, or

(*c*) the person concerned was a director of the company solely by reason of his nomination by a venture capital company in connection with the purchase of or subscription for shares in the company.

(3) The requirements a disqualified person must comply with are:

(*a*) in a public limited company, the nominal value of the shares allotted must be at least £100,000;

(*b*) in any other case, the nominal value of the shares allotted must be at least £20,000.

All shares and the whole of the premium (if any) must be fully paid up in cash.

(4) Where the court makes a declaration under subsection (1) a prescribed officer of the court will ensure that the Registrar of Companies is furnished with the relevant particulars of the declaration.

(5) 'Financial institution' and 'venture capital company' are defined for the purposes of this section.

SECTION 151
Duty of liquidator under this Chapter.

(1) Where it appears to the liquidator of a company to which this Chapter applies that the interests of any other company or its creditors may be placed in jeopardy by the relevant matters referred to in subsection (2) the liquidator shall inform the court of his opinion forthwith and the court may, on receipt of such report, make whatever order it sees fit.

(2) The relevant matters are that a person to whom section 150 applies is appointed or is acting in any way, whether directly or indirectly, as a director or is concerned or is taking part in the promotion or formation of such other company as is referred to in subsection (1).

(3) Any liquidator who contravenes subsection (1) shall be guilty of an offence and shall be liable—

(*a*) on summary conviction, to a fine not exceeding £1,000 and, for continued contravention, to a daily default fine not exceeding £50, or
(*b*) on conviction on indictment, to a fine not exceeding £10,000 and, for continued contravention, to a daily default fine not exceeding £250.

Definitions

'*company*': Companies Act, 1990, section 149.
'*daily default fine*': Companies Act, 1990, section 3.
'*director*': Companies Act, 1963, section 2.

General Note

This section sets out the duty of the liquidator of a company to which the chapter applies.

(1) Where the liquidator considers that the interests of any other company or its creditors may be in jeopardy by the matters referred to in subsection (2) below, he must inform the court of his opinion, and on receipt of his report the court may make such order as it sees fit.

(2) The relevant matters are that a person to whom section 150 applies is acting in any way directly or indirectly as director taking part in the formation or promotion of another company.

(3) Any liquidator who contravenes this section will be guilty of an offence and liable to a fine.

SECTION 152
Relief.

(1) A person to whom section 150 applies may, within not more than one year after a declaration has been made in respect of him under that section, apply to the court for relief, either in whole or in part, from the restrictions referred to in that section or from any order made in relation to him under section 151 and the court may, if it deems it just and equitable to do so, grant such relief on whatever terms and conditions it sees fit.

(2) Where it is intended to make an application for relief under subsection (1) the applicant shall give not less than 14 days' notice of his intention to the liquidator (if any) of the company the insolvency of which caused him to be subject to this Chapter.

(3) On receipt of a notice under subsection (2), the liquidator shall forthwith notify such creditors and contributories of the company as have been notified to him or become known to him, that he has received such notice.

(4) On the hearing of an application under this section the liquidator or any creditor or contributory of the company, the insolvency of which caused the applicant to be subject to this Chapter may appear and give evidence.

(5) Any liquidator who contravenes subsection (3) shall be guilty of an offence and liable to a fine.

Definitions

'*company*': Companies Act, 1990, section 149.
'*contributory*': Companies Act, 1963, section 2.
'*court*': Companies Act, 1990, section 235.

General Note

This section provides relief in that a person to whom section 150 applies may apply for relief to the court.

(1) Within one year after a notice under the Act has been furnished, a person may apply to the High Court for relief in whole or part from the restrictions. The court may grant relief on the terms and conditions it thinks fit if it considers it just and equitable.

(2) An applicant for relief must give not less than fourteen days' notice of his intention to the liquidator of the company.

(3) The liquidator must notify any creditors or contributories of the company as have been notified to him that he has received a notice.

(4) The liquidator or any creditor or contributory of the company may appear in court and give evidence.

(5) Any liquidator who contravenes subsection (3) will be guilty of an offence.

SECTION 153
Register of restricted persons.

(1) The registrar shall, subject to the provisions of this section, keep a register of the particulars which have been notified to him under section 150, and the following provisions of this section shall apply to the keeping of such a register.

(2) Where the court grants partial relief to a person under section 152 a prescribed officer of the court shall cause the registrar to be furnished with prescribed particulars of the relief, and the registrar shall, as soon as may be, enter the particulars on the register referred to in subsection (1).

(3) Where the court grants full relief to a person under section 152 a prescribed officer of the court shall cause the registrar to be so notified, and the registrar shall, as soon as may be, remove the particulars of any such person from the register referred to in subsection (1).

(4) The registrar shall also remove from the register any particulars in relation to a person on the expiry of five years from the date of the declaration to which the original notification under section 150 relates.

(5) Nothing in this section shall prevent the registrar from keeping the register required by this section as part of any other system of classification, whether pursuant to section 247 or otherwise.

Definitions

'court': Companies Act, 1990, section 235.
'registrar of companies': Companies Act, 1963, section 2.

General Note

The Registrar of Companies will keep a register of persons who have been notified to him under section 150.

(1) The Registrar is obliged to maintain a register of persons notified to him under section 150.

(2) Where a person is granted partial relief under section 152 the court will notify the Registrar, who will ensure that the particulars are entered in the register.

(3) Where the court grants full relief under section 152 the court will notify the Registrar, who will ensure that the particulars are entered in the register.

(4) The Registrar will remove particulars relating to a person five years from the date on which the original notification under section 150 relates.

(5) The Registrar may keep the register as part of any other system of classification.

SECTION 154
Application of this Chapter to receivers.

Where a receiver of the property of a company is appointed, the provisions of this Chapter shall, with the necessary modifications, apply as if the references therein to the liquidator and to winding up were construed as references to the receiver and to receivership.

Definitions
'company': Companies Act, 1990, section 149.

General Note
The provisions of this chapter of the Act apply to receivers in the same way as they apply to liquidators.

SECTION 155
Restrictions on company to which section 150 (3) applies.

(1) This section applies to any company in relation to which a person who is the subject of a declaration under section 150 is appointed or acts in any way, whether directly or indirectly, as a director or secretary or is concerned in or takes part in the promotion or formation of that company.

(2) Subsections (2) to (11) of section 60 of the Principal Act shall not apply to any company to which this section applies.

(3) Sections 32 to 36 of the Companies (Amendment) Act, 1983, shall, with the necessary modifications, apply to any company to which this section applies as if the company were a public limited company so, however, that for the purposes of this subsection those sections shall apply as if—

(a) in subsection (1) of section 32 the words "during the initial period" were deleted;
(b) any other reference in any of those sections to "initial period" were deleted; and
(c) in subsection (2) of section 32 the words "relevant person" were defined to mean "any subscriber to the memorandum, any director or any person involved in the promotion or formation of the company".

(4) Without prejudice to section 39, sections 32 and 37 shall not apply to any company to which subsection (1) applies.

(5) From the date of a declaration under section 150 a person in respect of whom the declaration was made shall not accept appointment to a position or act in any manner mentioned in subsection (1) of this section in relation to a company unless he has, within the 14 days immediately preceeding such appointment or so acting, sent to the registered office of the company a notification that he is a person to whom section 150 applies.

Definitions

'company': Companies Act, 1990, section 149.
'director': Companies Act, 1963, section 2.
'Principal Act': Companies Act, 1990, section 3.
'public limited company': Companies (Amendment) Act, 1983, section 2.

General Note

This section imposes further restrictions on a company when a director to whom section 149 applies becomes involved with it. These additional restrictions generally concern the giving of financial assistance for the purchase of the company's own shares, as well as the acquisition of non-cash assets from subscribers. In addition, such a company may not make any loans or quasi-loans or engage in any credit transactions on behalf of its directors.

(1) This section applies to any company that appoints a person to whom section 150 applies, whether directly or indirectly, to act as a director or secretary or in the formation or promotion of which company such a person takes part.

(2) A company will in general be prohibited from giving financial assistance for the purchase of its own shares. Financial assistance will only be given in the circumstances set out in section 60 (12) and (13) of the Companies Act, 1963.

(3) This subsection imposes restrictions relating to sections 32–36 of the Companies (Amendment) Act, 1983, which impose restrictions in relation to the acquisition of non-cash assets by public limited companies. This restriction for the purposes of this section is extended to all companies.

(4) A company is prohibited from making loans to directors under sections 32 and 36 of the Act.

(5) From the date of the declaration under section 150, a person who is the subject of a declaration must not accept an appointment to a position or act in any manner referred to in subsection (1) unless he has within fourteen days immediately before his appointment sent to the registered office of the company a notification that he is a person to whom section 150 applies.

SECTION 156

Requirements as
to shares allotted
by a company to
which section
155 applies.

(1) Where a company to which section 155 applies allots a share which is not fully paid up as required by section 150 (3) (*b*) the share shall be treated as if its nominal value together with the whole of any premium had been received, but the allottee shall be liable to pay the company in cash the full amount which should have been received in respect of the share under that subsection less the value of any consideration actually applied in payment up (to any extent) of the share and any premium on it, and interest at the appropriate rate on the amount payable under this subsection.

(2) Where a company to which section 155 applies allots a share which is not fully paid for in cash as required by section 150 (3) (*c*) the allottee of the share shall be liable to pay the company in cash an amount equal to its nominal value, together with the whole of any premium, and shall be liable to pay interest at the appropriate rate on the amount payable under this subsection.

(3) Subsection (1) shall not apply in relation to the allotment of a bonus share which is not fully paid up as required by section 150 (3) (*b*) unless the allottee knew or ought to have known that the share was so allotted.

(4) Subsection (1) does not apply to shares allotted in pursuance of an employees' share scheme within the meaning of section 2 of the Companies (Amendment) Act, 1983.

(5) In this section, "appropriate rate" has the meaning assigned to it by section 2 of the Companies (Amendment) Act, 1983.

(6) Section 26 (4) of the Companies (Amendment) Act, 1983, shall apply for the purposes of this section as it applies for the purposes of that section.

Definitions

'*appropriate rate*': Companies (Amendment) Act, 1983, section 2, and Companies Act, 1990, section 156.
'*company*': Companies Act, 1990, section 149.
'*share*': Companies Act, 1963, section 2.

General Note

This section sets out ancillary provisions of section 149 providing that shares allotted must be paid for in cash.

(1) Where a share has been allotted and is not fully paid up in cash as required by section 150 (3) (*b*) it will be treated as if its nominal value together with the whole of the premium had been received, but the allottee will be liable in cash for the full amount that should have been received.

(2) Where a share has been issued that is not fully paid up in cash the allottee is liable to pay the balance together with any premium and accrued interest on any outstanding amount.

(3) Subsection (1) does not apply to a bonus share unless the allottee knew or ought to have known of the requirements.

(4) The provisions of subsection (1) do not apply to shares issued under an employees' share scheme.

(5) 'Appropriate rate' is defined for the purposes of the section.

(6) Section 26 (4) of the Companies (Amendment) Act, 1983, also applies to this section.

SECTION 157
Relief for a company in respect of prohibited transactions.

(1) The court may, if it deems it just and equitable to do so, grant relief to a company to which section 155 applies in respect of any act or omission which, by virtue of that section, contravened a provision of the Companies Acts or to any person adversely affected thereby, on whatever terms and conditions the court sees fit, including exemption from any such provision.

(2) Relief shall not be granted to the company where the person referred to in section 155 (1) complied with subsection (5) of that section.

Definitions
'company': Companies Act, 1990, section 149.
'court': Companies Act, 1990, section 235.

General Note
The court may grant relief to a company to which section 155 applies or to any person adversely affected if it is considered just and equitable in respect of any act or omission that contravened the Companies Act.

SECTION 158
Power to vary amounts mentioned in section 150 (3).

The Minister may, by order, vary the amounts mentioned in section 150 (3) (*a*) and the order may—

(*a*) require any company to which that section applies having an allotted share capital of which the nominal value is less than the amount specified in the order to increase the value to not less than that amount;

(*b*) make, in connection with any such requirement provision for any of the matters for which provision is made in the Companies Acts in relation to a company's registration, re-registration, change of name, winding-up or dissolution, payment for any share comprised in a company's capital and offers of shares in or debentures of a company to the public, including provision as to the consequences (whether in criminal law or otherwise) of a failure to comply with any requirement of the order, and

(*c*) contain such supplemental and transitional provisions as the Minister thinks appropriate, specify different amounts in relation to companies of different classes or descriptions and, in particular, provide for any provision of the order to come into operation on different days for different purposes.

Definitions

'company': Companies Act, 1990, section 149.
'debenture': Companies Act, 1963, section 2.
'Minister': Companies Act, 1990, section 3.
'share': Companies Act, 1963, section 2.

General Note

This section enables the Minister for Industry and Commerce to vary the amounts set out in section 148, which relates to the amount of the paid-up capital that must be paid up if a company is to take on a person who was a director of an insolvent company. It also provides that the Minister may make supplemental or transitional provisions as he considers appropriate.

SECTION 159

Interpretation of Chapters 2 and 3.

In this Chapter and Chapter 3, except where the context otherwise requires—

"company" includes every company and every body, whether corporate or unincorporated, which may be wound up under Part X of the Principal Act and, without prejudice to the generality of the foregoing, includes a friendly society within the meaning of the Friendly Societies Acts, 1896 to 1977;

"the court" means the High Court except in relation to a disqualification order made by a court of its own motion under section 160 (2), paragraph (*a*), (*b*), (*c*), (*d*) or (*f*), in which case it includes any court;

"default order" means an order made against any person under section 371 of the Principal Act by virtue of any contravention of or failure to comply with any relevant requirement (whether on his own part or on the part of any company);

"disqualification order" means—

(*a*) an order under this Part that the person against whom the order is made shall not be appointed or act as an auditor, director or other officer, receiver, liquidator or examiner or be in any way, whether directly or indirectly, concerned or take part in the promotion, formation or management of any company, or any society registered under the Industrial and Provident Societies Acts, 1893 to 1978, or
(*b*) an order under section 184 of the Principal Act;

"officer" in relation to any company, includes any director, shadow director or secretary of the company;

"relevant requirement" means any provision of the Companies Acts (including a provision repealed by this Act) which requires or required any return, account or other document to be filed with, delivered or sent to, or notice of any matter to be given to, the registrar of companies.

Definitions

'auditor': this is not defined in the Companies Acts; but see the UK case *R. v. Shacter* [1960] 2 QB 252.

'*company*': Companies Act, 1990, section 159.

'*court*': Companies Act, 1990, section 159.

'*default order*': Companies Act, 1990, section 159.

'*director*': Companies Act, 1963, section 2.

'*disqualification order*': Companies Act, 1990, section 159.

'*officer*': Companies Act, 1990, section 159.

'*Principal Act*': Companies Act, 1990, section 3.

'*relevant requirement*': Companies Act, 1990, section 159.

'*shadow director*': Companies Act, 1990, section 3.

General Note

This section sets out the definitions of terms for the purposes of chapter 2 (Disqualification generally) and chapter 3 (Enforcement) of part VII of the Act.

SECTION 160

Disqualification of certain persons from acting as directors or auditors of or managing companies.

(1) Where a person is convicted on indictment of any indictable offence in relation to a company, or involving fraud or dishonesty, then during the period of five years from the date of conviction or such other period as the court, on the application of the prosecutor and having regard to all the circumstances of the case, may order—

(*a*) he shall not be appointed or act as an auditor, director or other officer, receiver, liquidator or examiner or be in any way, whether directly or indirectly, concerned or take part in the promotion, formation or management of any company or any society registered under the Industrial and Provident Societies Acts, 1893 to 1978;

(*b*) he shall be deemed, for the purposes of this Act, to be subject to a disqualification order for that period.

(2) Where the court is satisfied in any proceedings or as a result of an application under this section that—

(*a*) a person has been guilty, while a promoter, officer, auditor, receiver, liquidator or examiner of a company, of any fraud in relation to the company, its members or creditors; or

(*b*) a person has been guilty, while a promoter, officer, auditor, receiver, liquidator or examiner of a company, of any breach of his duty as such promoter, officer, auditor, receiver, liquidator or examiner; or

(*c*) a declaration has been granted under section 297A of the Principal Act (inserted by section 138 of this Act) in respect of a person; or

(*d*) the conduct of any person as promoter, officer, auditor, receiver, liquidator or examiner of a company, makes him unfit to be concerned in the management of a company; or

(*e*) in consequence of a report of inspectors appointed by the court or the Minister under the Companies Acts, the conduct of any person makes him unfit to be concerned in the management of a company; or

(*f*) a person has been persistently in default in relation to the relevant requirements;

the court may, of its own motion, or as a result of the application, make a disqualification order against such a person for such period as it sees fit.

(3) (*a*) For the purposes of subsection (2) (*f*) the fact that a person has been persistently in default in relation to the relevant requirements may (without prejudice to its proof in any other manner) be conclusively proved by showing that in the five years ending with the date of the application he has been adjudged guilty (whether or not on the same occasion) of three or more defaults in relation to those requirements.

(*b*) A person shall be treated as being adjudged guilty of a default in relation to a relevant requirement for the purposes of this subsection if he is convicted of any offence consisting of a contravention of a relevant requirement or a default order is made against him.

(4) An application under paragraph (*a*), (*b*), (*c*) or (*d*) of subsection (2) may be made by—

(*a*) the Director of Public Prosecutions; or

(*b*) any member, contributory, officer, employee, receiver, liquidator, examiner or creditor of any company in relation to which the person who is the subject of the application—

(i) has been or is acting or is proposing to or being proposed to act as officer, auditor, receiver, liquidator or examiner, or

(ii) has been or is concerned or taking part, or is proposing to be concerned or take part, in the promotion, formation or management of any company,

and where the application is made by a member, contributory, employee or creditor of the company, the court may require security for all or some of the costs of the application.

(5) An application under paragraph (*e*) of subsection (2) may be made by the Director of Public Prosecutions.

(6) An application under paragraph (*f*) of subsection (2) may be made by—

(*a*) the Director of Public Prosecutions; or

(*b*) the registrar of companies.

(7) Where it is intended to make an application under subsection (2) in respect of any person, the applicant shall give not less than ten days' notice of his intention to that person.

(8) Any person who is subject or deemed subject to a disqualification order by virtue of this Part may apply to the court for relief, either in whole or in part, from that disqualification and the court may, if it deems it just and equitable to do so, grant such relief on whatever terms and conditions it sees fit.

(9) A disqualification order may be made on grounds which are or include matters other than criminal convictions notwithstanding that the person in respect of whom the order is to be made may be criminally liable in respect of those matters.

(10) A reference in any other enactment to section 184 of the Principal Act shall be construed as including a reference to this section.

Definitions

'*auditor*': this is not defined in the Companies Acts; but see the UK case *R.* v. *Shacter* [1960] 2 QB 252.

'*company*': Companies Act, 1990, section 159.

'contributory': Companies Act, 1963, section 2.

'court': Companies Act, 1990, section 159.

'default order': Companies Act, 1990, section 159.

'director': Companies Act, 1963, section 2.

'disqualification order': Companies Act, 1990, section 159.

'examiner': Companies (Amendment) Act, 1990, section 1.

'Minister': Companies Act, 1990, section 3.

'officer': Companies Act, 1990, section 159.

'Principal Act': Companies Act, 1990, section 3.

'relevant requirement': Companies Act, 1990, section 159.

General Note

This section replaces section 184 of the Companies Act, 1963, with a much stronger provision dealing with the disqualification of directors by the court. Where a person is convicted on indictment of an indictable offence in relation to a company or involving fraud or dishonesty he will be deemed to be disqualified for a period of five years or such other period as considered fit by the court. In addition the court may disqualify a person for such period as it sees fit where it is satisfied that a person has been guilty of any fraud or breach of duty in relation to the company or if he has been made personally liable for the company's debts, etc.

A person who is the subject of a disqualification order cannot be appointed or act as an auditor, director or other officer, receiver, liquidator or examiner of a company or be in any way directly or indirectly concerned or take part in the promotion, formation or management of any company.

(1) Where a person is convicted on indictment of an indictable offence in relation to a company or involving fraud or dishonesty the court may as it considers fit direct that during a period of up to five years he shall not act or be appointed as an auditor, director or other officer, receiver, liquidator, or examiner, or be involved in any way with the formation, promotion or management of any company or friendly society, and shall be deemed to be subject to a disqualification order for the period.

(2) If the court is satisfied that a person has been guilty of any fraud in relation to a company or has been in breach of his duty or has conducted himself in a manner that makes him unfit to be concerned in the management of a company, or if a declaration has been granted under section 297A of the Companies Act, 1963, or if

as a consequence of a report of inspectors his conduct makes him unfit to be concerned in the management of a company, or if he has been persistently in default in relation to the relevant requirement, it may make a disqualification order against such a person for such period as it considers fit.

(3) A person will be regarded as being persistently in default in relation to relevant requirements if it is shown that in the five years ending with the date of application he has been adjudged guilty of three or more defaults in relation to the requirements.

(4) An application under subsection (2) may be made by the Director of Public Prosecutions or by any member, contributory, officer, employee, receiver, liquidator, examiner or creditor of any company in relation to which the person who is the subject of the application has been involved in the promotion, formation or management of the company or is involved as officer, auditor, receiver, liquidator, or examiner. The court may require security for some or all of the costs of the application by the applicant.

(5) An application may be made by the Director of Public Prosecutions under subsection (2) (*e*).

(6) An application may be made by the Director of Public Prosecutions or the Registrar of Companies under subsection (2) (*f*).

(7) Where it is intended to make an application against a person that person will be given not less than ten days' notice by the applicant.

(8) A person who is the subject of a disqualification order may apply to the court for relief, and the court if it considers it equitable and fit may grant relief on such terms and conditions as it considers fit.

(9) A disqualification order may be granted on grounds that are or include matters other than criminal convictions, even though it is made on matters to which a person may be criminally liable.

(10) Any reference to section 184 of the Companies Act, 1963, will include a reference to this section.

SECTION 161
Penalty for acting contrary to the provisions of Chapter 1 or 2.

(1) Any person who, in relation to any company, acts in a manner or capacity which, by virtue of being a person to whom section 150 applies or being subject or deemed to be subject to a disqualification order, he is prohibited from doing shall be guilty of an offence.

(2) Where a person is convicted of an offence under subsection (1) he shall be deemed to be subject to a disqualification order from the date of such conviction if he was not, or was not deemed to be, subject to such an order on that date.

(3) Where a person convicted of an offence under subsection (1) was subject, or deemed to be subject, to a disqualification order immediately prior to the date of such conviction, the period for which he was disqualified shall be extended for a further period of ten years from such date, or such other further period as the court, on the application of the prosecutor and having regard to all the circumstances of the case, may order.

(4) Section 160 (8) shall not apply to a person convicted of an offence under subsection (1) of this section.

(5) Where—

(a) a person who is a person to whom section 150 applies is or becomes a director of a company which commences to be wound up within the period of 5 years after the date of commencement of the winding-up of the company whose insolvency caused that section to apply to him; and

(b) it appears to the liquidator of the first-mentioned company that that company is, at the date of commencement of its winding-up or at any time during the course of its winding-up, unable to pay its debts;

the liquidator shall report those matters to the court and the court, on receiving the report and if it considers it proper to do so, may make a disqualification order against that person for such period as it thinks fit.

(6) If the liquidator fails to comply with subsection (5) he shall be liable to a fine not exceeding £1,000.

Definitions

'company': Companies Act, 1990, section 159.

'court': Companies Act, 1990, section 159.

'director': Companies Act, 1963, section 2.

'disqualification order': Companies Act, 1990, section 159.

General Note

This section sets out the criminal and civil consequences of contravening a disqualification order or of being a person to whom section 150 applies with regard to acting in a manner in which he is prohibited from acting.

(1) Anyone who is a person to whom section 150 applies or who is subject to a disqualification order will be guilty of an offence if he acts in a capacity in which he is prohibited from acting.

(2) Where a person is convicted of an offence under subsection (1) he will be deemed to be subject to a disqualification order on the date of such conviction if he had not already been subject to a disqualification order.

(3) If a person had already been subject to a disqualification order immediately before a conviction under subsection (1) the disqualification will be extended for a further period of ten years or such period as the court thinks fit having regard to all the circumstances of the case.

(4) Section 160 (8) will not apply to a person convicted under subsection (1).

(5) Where a person is one to whom section 150 applies or becomes a director of a company that commences to be wound up within the five-year period after the date of the commencement of the winding up of the company that made him subject to section 150 and it appears to the liquidator of the company that it is unable to pay its debts, the liquidator must make a report to the court, which may make a disqualification order if it considers it appropriate.

(6) If a liquidator fails to comply with subsection (5) he will be liable to a fine not exceeding £1,000.

SECTION 162
Period of disqualification order to which person is deemed to be subject.

Where a person is, as a consequence of his conviction of an offence under this Chapter, deemed to be subject to a disqualification order, he shall be deemed to be so subject for a period of five years from the date of such conviction or such other period as the court, on the application of the prosecutor and having regard to all the circumstances of the case, may order.

Definitions

'*court*': Companies Act, 1990, section 159.
'*disqualification order*': Companies Act, 1990, section 159.

General Note

This section stipulates that a person who is the subject of a disqualification order shall be deemed to be so disqualified for a period of five years from the date of conviction or such other period as the court may order.

SECTION 163
Civil consequences of acting contrary to the provisions of Chapter 1 or 2.

(1) Subsections (2) and (3) apply to any person who acts, in relation to a company, in a manner or capacity which, by virtue of being a person to whom section 150 applies or being subject or deemed to be subject to a disqualification order, he is prohibited from doing.

(2) Where any consideration is given by or on behalf of a company for an act done or service performed by a person referred to in subsection (1) while he was acting in a manner or capacity described in that subsection, the company shall be entitled to recover from him, as a simple contract debt in any court of competent jurisdiction, the consideration or an amount representing its value.

(3) Where—

(a) a person referred to in subsection (1) acts, in relation to a company, in a manner or capacity described in that subsection, and

(b) the company concerned commences to be wound up—
   (i) while he is acting in such a manner or capacity, or
   (ii) within 12 months of his so acting, and

(c) the company is unable to pay its debts, within the meaning of section 214 of the Principal Act,

the court may, on the application of the liquidator or any creditor of the company, declare that such person shall be personally liable, without any limitation of liability, for all or any part of the debts or other liabilities of the company incurred in the period during which he was acting in such a manner or capacity.

(4) Where a company which has received a notification under section 155 (5) and which carries on business following such notification without the requirements of section 150 (3) being fulfilled within a reasonable period—

(a) is subsequently wound up, and

(b) is at the time of the commencement of the winding-up unable to pay its debts (taking into account the contingent and prospective liabilities),

the court may, on the application of the liquidator or any creditor or contributory of the company, declare that any person who was an officer of the company while the company so carried on business and who knew or ought to have known that the company had been so notified shall be personally responsible, without any limitation of liability, for all or any part of the debts or other liabilities of the company as the court may direct.

(5) In any proceedings brought against a person by virtue of this section the court may if, having regard to the circumstances of the case, it considers it just and equitable to do so, grant relief in whole or in part from the liability to which he would otherwise be subject thereunder and the court may attach to its order such conditions as it sees fit.

Definitions

'company': Companies Act, 1990, section 159.

'contributory': Companies Act, 1963, section 2.

'court': Companies Act, 1990, section 159.

'disqualification order': Companies Act, 1990, section 159.

'Principal Act': Companies Act, 1990, section 3.

General Note

This section sets out further civil consequences of contravening section 150. A person may also be personally liable for any debts of the company that were incurred while he was acting in relation to the company.

(1) Subsections (2) and (3) will apply to any person who is subject to a disqualification order or to section 150 of this Act.

(2) When consideration is given on behalf of a company for any act done or service given by a person to whom subsection (1) applies, it shall be entitled to recover from him as a simple debt in any court the consideration or an amount representing its value.

(3) On the application of a creditor or liquidator of any company that is being wound up the court may declare that a person who was subject to subsection (1) while he was acting in that capacity, or within twelve months of his so acting, or if the company is unable to pay its debts within the meaning of section 214 of the Companies Act, 1963, may be personally liable with unlimited liability for all the debts or liabilities incurred during the period in which he was acting in such a manner or capacity.

(4) Where a company that has received a notification under section 155 (5) continues to carry on business following such notification and within a reasonable period is subsequently wound up and is at the time of commencement of winding up found to be unable to pay its debts, the court may, on the application of the liquidator or any creditor or contributory of the company, declare that any person who was an officer of the company while the company carried on its business and who knew or ought to have known that the company had been so notified will be personally liable without any limitation of liability for all or part of the debts of the company as may be decided by the court.

(5) The court has power to grant relief to any person who is the subject of proceedings under this section if it considers it just and equitable to do so.

SECTION 164
Penalty for acting under directions of disqualified person.

(1) If any person while a director or other officer or a member of a committee of management or trustee of any company acts in accordance with the directions or instructions of another person knowing that such other person is disqualified or that, in giving the directions or instructions, he is acting in contravention of any provision of this Part he shall be guilty of an offence.

(2) Where a person is convicted of an offence under subsection (1) he shall be deemed to be subject to a disqualification order from the date of such conviction if he was not, or was not deemed to be, subject to such an order on that date.

Definitions

'*company*': Companies Act, 1990, section 159.
'*director*': Companies Act, 1963, section 2.
'*disqualification order*': Companies Act, 1990, section 159.
'*officer*': Companies Act, 1990, section 159.

General Note

A person who acts in accordance with the directions or instructions of another person knowing that that person is a disqualified person is guilty of an offence.

(1) If any director, officer, member of a committee of management or trustee of a company acts under instruction or direction of a person whom he knows to be a disqualified person, he shall be guilty of an offence.

(2) If a person is convicted of an offence under subsection (1) he will be deemed to be subject to a disqualification order from the date of such conviction if he was not already subject to a disqualification order.

SECTION 165
Civil consequences of acting under directions of disqualified person.

(1) A person who is convicted of an offence under section 164 for acting in accordance with the directions or instructions of a disqualified person shall, subject to subsection (2), be personally liable for the debts of the company concerned incurred in the period during which he was so acting.

(2) In any proceedings brought against a person for the recovery of any such debt the court may if, having regard to the circumstances of the case, it considers it just and equitable to do so, grant relief in whole or in part from the liability to which he would otherwise be subject under subsection (1) and the court may attach to its order such conditions as it sees fit.

Definitions

'company': Companies Act, 1990, section 159.
'court': Companies Act, 1990, section 159.

General Note

This section provides that if a person is convicted of an offence under section 164 he may also be personally liable for the debts of the company concerned that were incurred during the period when he was so acting.

(1) If a person is convicted of an offence under section 164 he may also be personally liable for the debts of the company concerned during the period when he was so acting.

(2) In any action to recover a debt against such a person the court may grant relief in whole or part of the liability under such conditions as it sees fit if it considers it just and equitable to do so.

SECTION 166

Information to be given by directors to the court.

(1) Where—

(a) a director of a company is charged with an offence or civil proceedings are instituted against such a director, and

(b) the charge or proceedings relate to the company or involve alleged fraud or dishonesty,

the director shall, by notice in writing to the court lodged before the hearing of the case—

(i) give the names of all companies of which he is a director at the date of the notice,

(ii) give the names of all companies of which he was a director within a period commencing not earlier than 12 months prior to the commencement of proceedings and ending at the date of the notice,

(iii) state whether he is at the date of the notice or ever was subject or deemed to be subject to a disqualification order, and

(iv) give the dates and duration of each period in respect of which he is or was disqualified.

(2) This section applies to shadow directors as it applies to directors.

(3) Any person who contravenes subsection (1) shall be guilty of an offence.

Definitions

'*company*': Companies Act, 1990, section 159.

'*court*': Companies Act, 1990, section 159.

'*director*': Companies Act, 1963, section 2.

'*shadow director*': Companies Act, 1990, section 3.

General Note

Where a director is involved in certain proceedings related to fraud or dishonesty, he must notify the court of present and recent directorships and also any past or present disqualification to which he is or was subject.

This section applies to shadow directors in the same way as to directors, and anyone in contravention of subsection (1) will be guilty of an offence.

SECTION 167

Information to be supplied to registrar of companies.

Where a court—

(a) makes a disqualification order;

(b) grants or varies relief under section 160 (8); or

(c) convicts a person of an offence—

(i) which has the effect of his being deemed to be subject to a disqualification order, or

(ii) under section 161 (1) or 164,

a prescribed officer of the court shall cause the registrar of companies to be furnished with prescribed particulars of the order, relief or conviction at such time and in such form and manner as may be prescribed.

Definitions

'disqualification order': Companies Act, 1990, section 159.

'officer': Companies Act, 1990, section 159.

'registrar of companies': Companies Act, 1963, section 2.

General Note

A prescribed officer of the court will supply the Registrar of Companies with information about disqualification orders and offences that have the effect of making a person subject to disqualification orders. The information supplied will also provide details of any relief granted to such person.

SECTION 168
Register of persons subject to disqualification orders.

(1) The registrar shall, subject to the provisions of this section, keep a register of the particulars which have been notified to him under section 167, and the following provisions of this section shall apply to the keeping of such a register.

(2) Where the particulars referred to in section 167 (*b*) comprise the grant of full relief under section 160 (8), the registrar shall not enter such particulars on the register referred to in subsection (1), but shall, as soon as may be, remove any existing particulars in respect of the person concerned from the register.

(3) The registrar shall also remove from the register any particulars in relation to a person on the expiry of five years from the date of the original notification under section 167, or such other period in respect of which the person concerned is deemed to be subject to a disqualification order, unless the registrar has received a further notification in respect of that person under this section.

(4) Nothing in this section shall prevent the registrar from keeping the register required by this section as part of any other system of classification, whether pursuant to section 247 or otherwise.

Definitions

'disqualification order': Companies Act, 1990, section 159.

'registrar of companies': Companies Act, 1963, section 2.

General Note

This section enables a register to be kept of persons who are disqualified and notified under section 167.

(1) The Registrar of Companies will maintain a register of persons who have been notified to him under section 167 (Persons subject to disqualification orders).

(2) Where a person has been granted full relief under section 160 (8) The Registrar will not enter the particulars but will remove any existing entry concerning the person from the register.

(3) The Registrar will also remove particulars concerning any person five years after the date of the original entry under section 167 or such other period during which the person is subject to the disqualification order.

(4) The Registrar is entitled to maintain the register as part of any other classification system as he may consider pursuant to section 247 of the Act.

SECTION 169
Prohibition of undischarged bankrupts acting as directors or other officers of companies.

The Principal Act is hereby amended by the substitution for section 183 of the following section—

"183.—(1) Subject to subsection (2), if any person being an undischarged bankrupt acts as officer, auditor, liquidator or examiner of, or directly or indirectly takes part or is concerned in the promotion, formation or management of, any company except with the leave of the court, he shall be guilty of an offence.

(2) Where a person is convicted of an offence under subsection (1) he shall be deemed to be subject to a disqualification order from the date of such conviction if he was not, or was not deemed to be, subject to such an order on that date.

(3) In this section 'company' includes a company incorporated outside the State which has an established place of business within the State.".

Definitions

'auditor': this is not defined in the Companies Acts; but see the UK case *R.* v. *Shacter* [1960] 2 QB 252.

'company': Companies Act, 1990, section 169.

'court': Companies Act, 1990, section 159.

'disqualification order': Companies Act, 1990, section 159.

'officer': Companies Act, 1990, section 159.

'Principal Act': Companies Act, 1990, section 3.

General Note

This section amends section 183 of the Companies Act, 1963, by providing that an undischarged bankrupt may not act as an auditor, liquidator or examiner of a company, except with the leave of the court. Such a person is already prohibited from acting as a director under section 183 of the 1963 Act.

8
RECEIVERS

In part VIII of the Act there are additional provisions dealing with the role and duties of receivers. These include the imposition of a new duty on a receiver in selling property to ensure that he gets the best price reasonably obtainable.

There are also amended provisions concerning the removal or resignation of a receiver and the determination or limitation of a receivership by the court.

SECTION 170
Disqualification for appointment as receiver.

The Principal Act is hereby amended by the substitution for section 315 of the following section—

"315.—(1) None of the following persons shall be qualified for appointment as receiver of the property of a company—

(a) an undischarged bankrupt;

(b) a person who is, or who has within 12 months of the commencement of the receivership been, an officer or servant of the company;

(c) a parent, spouse, brother, sister or child of an officer of the company;

(d) a person who is a partner of or in the employment of an officer or servant of the company;

(e) a person who is not qualified by virtue of this subsection for appointment as receiver of the property of any other body corporate which is that company's subsidiary or holding company or a subsidiary of that company's holding company, or would be so disqualified if the body corporate were a company.

References in this subsection to an officer or servant of the company include references to an auditor.

(2) If a receiver of the property of a company becomes disqualified by virtue of this section, he shall thereupon vacate his office and give notice in writing within 14 days to—

(a) the company;

(b) the registrar of companies;

(c) (i) the debenture-holder, if the receiver was appointed by a debenture-holder, or
(ii) the court, if the receiver was appointed by the court,

that he has vacated it by reason of such disqualification.

(3) Subsection (2) is without prejudice to sections 107, 319 (2) and 321.

(4) Nothing in this section shall require a receiver appointed before the commencement of section 170 of the Companies Act, 1990, to vacate the office to which he was so appointed.

(5) Any person who acts as a receiver when disqualified by this section from so doing or who fails to comply with subsection (2), if that subsection applies to him, shall be guilty of an offence and shall be liable—

(*a*) on summary conviction, to a fine not exceeding £1,000 and, for continued contravention, to a daily default fine not exceeding £50;

(*b*) on conviction on indictment, to a fine not exceeding £5,000 and, for continued contravention, to a daily default fine not exceeding £250.".

Definitions

'auditor': this is not defined in the Companies Acts; but see the UK case *R.* v. *Shacter* [1960] 2 QB 252.

'body corporate': Companies Act, 1963, section 2 (3).

'child': Companies Act, 1990, section 3.

'company': Companies Act, 1963, section 2.

'court': Companies Act, 1990, section 235.

'daily default fine': Companies Act, 1990, section 3.

'holding company': Companies Act, 1963, section 155.

'officer': Companies Act, 1963, section 2.

'Principal Act': Companies Act, 1990, section 3.

'registrar of companies': Companies Act, 1963, section 2.

'subsidiary': Companies Act, 1963, section 155.

General Note

This section substitutes a new section for section 315 of the Companies Act, 1963, which prohibits an undischarged bankrupt from acting as a receiver of the property of a company. The section extends the disqualification to persons connected professionally or through close family relationship with the company and to the company's auditors.

(1) Certain persons are prohibited from acting as a receiver of a company, including:

(*a*) an undischarged bankrupt;

(*b*) a person who within twelve months of the commencement of the receivership was an officer or servant of the company;

(*c*) a parent, spouse, brother, sister or child of an officer of the company;

(*d*) a person who is a partner or is employed by an officer or servant of the company;

(*e*) a person who is disqualified from acting as a receiver of the property of any other body corporate that is the company's subsidiary or holding company.

(2) If a person becomes disqualified by virtue of this section he must vacate his office and give notice in writing within fourteen

days to the company, to the Registrar of Companies, to the debenture holder if appointed by him, or to the court if appointed by the court.

(3) Subsection (2) is without prejudice to sections 107 (Notice to registrar of appointment of receiver and of receiver ceasing to act), 319 (2) (Information to be given when a receiver is appointed) and 321 (Delivery to registrar of accounts of receivers) of the Companies Act, 1963.

(4) Any receiver who was appointed before the commencement of this section will not be required to vacate the office.

(5) Anyone who acts as a receiver when disqualified or who fails to comply with subsection (2) will be guilty of an offence and liable to a fine.

SECTION 171

Amendment of section 316 of the Principal Act.

Section 316 of the Principal Act is hereby amended by the substitution for subsection (1) of the following subsections—

"(1) Where a receiver of the property of a company is appointed under the powers contained in any instrument, any of the following persons may apply to the court for directions in relation to any matter in connection with the performance or otherwise by the receiver of his functions, that is to say—

(*a*) (i) the receiver;
(ii) an officer of the company;
(iii) a member of the company;
(iv) employees of the company comprising at least half in number of the persons employed in a full-time capacity by the company;
(v) a creditor of the company; and
(*b*) (i) a liquidator;
(ii) a contributory;

and on any such application, the court may give such directions, or make such order declaring the rights of persons before the court or otherwise, as the court thinks just.

(1A) An application to the court under subsection (1), except an application under paragraph (*a*) (i) of that subsection, shall be supported by such evidence that the applicant is being unfairly prejudiced by any actual or proposed action or omission of the receiver as the court may require.

(1B) For the purposes of subsection (1), 'creditor' means one or more creditors to whom the company is indebted by more, in aggregate, than £10,000.".

Definitions

'*company*': Companies Act, 1963, section 2.
'*contributory*': Companies Act, 1963, section 2.
'*court*': Companies Act, 1990, section 235.
'*creditor*': Companies Act, 1990, section 171.

'*officer*': Companies Act, 1963, section 2.
'*Principal Act*': Companies Act, 1990, section 3.

General Note

This section enables an officer, member, creditor, liquidator, contributory or employee of a company to apply to the court for directions in relation to any matter arising in connection with the performance by a receiver of his functions.

SECTION 172
Duty of receiver selling property to get best price reasonably obtainable.

The Principal Act is hereby amended by the insertion after section 316 of the following section—

"316A.—(1) A receiver, in selling property of a company, shall exercise all reasonable care to obtain the best price reasonably obtainable for the property as at the time of sale.

(2) Notwithstanding the provisions of any instrument—

(*a*) it shall not be a defence to any action or proceeding brought against a receiver in respect of a breach of his duty under subsection (1) that the receiver was acting as the agent of the company or under a power of attorney given by the company; and

(*b*) notwithstanding anything in section 316 (2), a receiver shall not be entitled to be compensated or indemnified by the company for any liability he may incur as a result of a breach of his duty under this section.

(3) (*a*) A receiver shall not sell by private contract a non-cash asset of the requisite value to a person who is, or who, within three years prior to the date of appointment of the receiver, has been, an officer of the company unless he has given at least 14 days' notice of his intention to do so to all creditors of the company who are known to him or who have been intimated to him.

(*b*) In this subsection—
(i) 'non-cash asset' and 'requisite value' have the meanings assigned to them by section 29 of the Companies Act, 1990, and
(ii) 'officer' includes a person connected, within the meaning of section 26 of the Companies Act, 1990, with a director, and a shadow director.".

Definitions

'*company*': Companies Act, 1963, section 2.
'*non-cash asset*': Companies Act, 1990, section 172.
'*officer*': Companies Act, 1990, section 172.
'*Principal Act*': Companies Act, 1963, section 2.
'*requisite value*': Companies Act, 1990, section 172.
'*shadow director*': Companies Act, 1990, section 3.

General Note

This section, which amends section 316A of the Companies Act, 1963, provides that a receiver who sells any of a company's property owes a duty to the company to exercise all reasonable care in obtaining the best price reasonably obtainable for the property. Furthermore, it will not be a defence to any action brought against a receiver for breach of duty that the receiver was acting as an agent or a power of attorney of the company.

A receiver must not sell a non-cash asset by private contract to a person who within three years before the appointment of that receiver was an officer of the company, unless at least fourteen days' notice has been given to all the creditors of the company of his intention to do so.

SECTION 173
Amendment of section 320 of the Principal Act.

Section 320 of the Principal Act is hereby amended by the substitution for subsection (5) of the following subsection—

"(5) If any person to whom subsection (2) applies makes default in complying with the requirements of this section, he shall, unless he can prove to the satisfaction of the court that it was not possible for him to comply with the requirements of the section, be liable—

(a) on summary conviction, to imprisonment for a term not exceeding six months or to a fine not exceeding £1,000 or to both; or

(b) on conviction on indictment, to imprisonment for a term not exceeding three years or to a fine not exceeding £5,000 or to both.".

Definitions

'court': Companies Act, 1990, section 235.

'Principal Act': Companies Act, 1990, section 3.

General Note

This section amends section 320 (5) of the Companies Act, 1963, which deals with the contents of statements to be submitted to a receiver by the officers etc. of the company on his appointment. It provides for more stringent penalties for failure to make the necessary submissions.

SECTION 174
Consequences of contravention of section 319 or 320 of the Principal Act.

The Principal Act is hereby amended by the insertion after section 320 of the following section—

"320A.—Where, in contravention of section 319 (1) (b) and section 320, a statement of affairs is not submitted to the receiver as required by those provisions, the court may, on the application of the receiver or any creditor of the company, and notwithstanding the provisions of section 320 (5) (inserted by section 173 of the Companies Act, 1990), make whatever order it thinks fit, including an order compelling compliance with section 319 and section 320.".

Definitions

'*company*': Companies Act, 1963, section 2.
'*Principal Act*': Companies Act, 1990, section 3.

General Note

This section provides that if no statement has been submitted to the receiver in accordance with sections 319–320 of the Companies Act, 1963, the court may on application of the receiver or any creditor of the company make such order as it thinks fit to compel the directors to prepare and submit a statement of affairs.

SECTION 175
Removal of receiver.

The Principal Act is hereby amended by the insertion after section 322 of the following section—

"322A.—(1) The court may, on cause shown, remove a receiver and appoint another receiver.

(2) Notice of such proceedings shall be served on the receiver and on the person who appointed him not less than 7 days before the hearing of such proceedings and, in any such proceedings, the receiver and the person who appointed him may appear and be heard.".

Definitions

'*court*': Companies Act, 1990, section 235.
'*Principal Act*': Companies Act, 1990, section 3.

General Note

This section amends section 322 of the Companies Act, 1963, and permits the court to remove a receiver from office on cause shown and to appoint another receiver. In such a case there is provision for the receiver and the person who appointed the receiver to be heard by the court. Notice of the proceedings will be served on the receiver and on the person who appointed him not less than seven days before the hearing.

SECTION 176
Court may determine or limit receivership on application of liquidator.

The Principal Act is hereby amended by the insertion after section 322 of the following section—

"322B.—(1) On the application of the liquidator of a company that is being wound up (other than by means of a members' voluntary winding up) and in respect of which a receiver has been appointed (whether before or after the commencement of the winding up), the court may—

(a) order that the receiver shall cease to act as such from a date specified by the court, and prohibit the appointment of any other receiver; or
(b) order that the receiver shall, from a date specified by the court, act as such only in respect of certain assets specified by the court.

An order under this subsection may be made on such terms and conditions as the court thinks fit.

(2) The court may from time to time, on an application made either by the liquidator or by the receiver, rescind or amend an order made under subsection (1).

(3) A copy of an application made under this section shall be served on the receiver and on the person who appointed him not less than 7 days before the hearing of the application, and the receiver and any such party may appear before and be heard by the court in respect of the application.

(4) Except as provided in subsection (1), no order made under this section shall affect any security or charge over the undertaking or property of the company.".

Definitions

'company': Companies Act, 1963, section 2.
'court': Companies Act, 1990, section 235.
'Principal Act': Companies Act, 1990, section 3.

General Note

This section provides that in certain circumstances a liquidator may apply to the court for an order that any existing receiver shall cease to act and that no other receiver be appointed, or else to order that the receiver may act only in respect of certain assets. Where the court makes such an order it would not in any way affect the status of the security on foot of which the receiver was appointed.

(1) The liquidator may apply to the court in respect of the company to which the receiver has been appointed, and the court may order the receiver to cease to act from a date specified by the court and prohibit the appointment of another receiver, or order that the receiver act in respect only of certain specified assets.

(2) The court may amend or rescind an order made under subsection (1) from time to time.

(3) A copy of the application to the court must be sent to the receiver and to the person who appointed him at least seven days before the court hearing, and they may appear and be heard by the court in respect of the application.

(4) Except as provided in subsection (1) no order made under this section will affect any security or charge over the property of the company.

SECTION 177
Resignation of receiver.

The Principal Act is hereby amended by the insertion after section 322 of the following section—

"322C.—(1) A receiver of the property of a company appointed under the powers contained in any instrument may resign, provided he has given one month's notice thereof to—

(*a*) the holders of floating charges over all or any part of the property of the company;

(*b*) the company or its liquidator; and

(*c*) the holders of any fixed charge over all or any part of the property of the company.

(2) A receiver appointed by the court may resign only with the authority of the court and on such terms and conditions, if any, as may be laid down by the court.

(3) If any person makes default in complying with the requirements of this section, he shall be liable to a fine not exceeding £1,000.".

Definitions

'company': Companies Act, 1963, section 2.

'court': Companies Act, 1990, section 235.

'Principal Act': Companies Act, 1990, section 3.

General Note

This section provides that a receiver appointed otherwise than by the court cannot resign unless he has given at least one month's notice to certain parties. Furthermore, a receiver appointed by the court can only resign by leave of the court.

(1) A person who is appointed receiver of a company otherwise than by the court can only resign on giving one month's notice to the holders of the floating charges over all or part of the property of the company, to the company or its liquidator, and to the holders of the fixed charge over the property of the company.

(2) A receiver who is appointed by the court can only resign with leave of the court.

(3) Any person who is in default will be liable to a fine.

SECTION 178
Application of section 139 to receivers.

The provisions of section 139 shall, with the necessary modifications, apply to a company in receivership as if the references therein to the liquidator and to winding up were construed as references to the receiver and to receivership.

Definitions

'*company*': Companies Act, 1963, section 2.

General Note

Power is given to the court to order the return of any improperly transferred assets to the company and to prevent the receivers being frustrated in their task.

SECTION 179

Application of section 299 (2), (4) and (5) of the Principal Act to receivers.

Section 299 (2), (4) and (5) of the Principal Act shall apply, with the necessary modifications, to receivers as it applies to liquidators.

Definitions

'*Principal Act*': Companies Act, 1990, section 3.

General Note

This section obliges a receiver who becomes aware of circumstances tending to show that a criminal offence has been committed in relation to a company to report this to the Director of Public Prosecutions.

9
COMPANIES UNDER COURT PROTECTION

This part of the Act introduces some minor changes to the Companies (Amendment) Act, 1990.

SECTION 180

Amendments to the Companies (Amendment) Act, 1990.

(1) The Companies (Amendment) Act, 1990, is hereby amended as follows:

(*a*) by the substitution in section 3 (6) for "14 days" of "3 days",

(*b*) by the insertion after section 5 (2) (*f*) of the following paragraph:

"(*g*) no order for relief shall be made under section 205 of the Principal Act against the company in respect of complaints as to the conduct of the affairs of the company or the exercise of the powers of the directors prior to the presentation of the petition.",

(*c*) by the deletion in section 8 (3), of ", or past director,",

(*d*) by the insertion in section 8 (3), after "Act", where it secondly occurs, of "and 'director' includes any present or past director or any person connected, within the meaning of section 26 of the Companies Act, 1990, with such director, and any present or past shadow director",

(*e*) by the insertion in section 8 of the following subsections:

"(5A) Without prejudice to its power under subsection (5), the court may, after a hearing under that subsection, make any order or direction it thinks fit, including a direction to the person concerned to attend or re-attend before the examiner or produce particular books or documents or answer particular questions put to him by the examiner, or a direction that the person concerned need not produce a particular book or document or answer a particular question put to him by the examiner.
(5B) Section 23 (1) of the Companies Act, 1990 shall apply for the purposes of this section.",

(*f*) by the substitution in section 10 (1) of "Any" for "Where an order is made under this Act for the winding-up of the company or a receiver is appointed, any",

(*g*) by the substitution, for section 16 (*i*), of the following:

"(*i*) his opinion as to whether the facts disclosed would warrant further inquiries with a view to proceedings under section 297 or 297A of the Principal Act (inserted by the Companies Act, 1990), or both,",

(*h*) by the insertion in section 23 (5) (*b*), after "Government" of ", a local authority",

(*i*) by the insertion in section 24 of the following subsection:

"(12) Notwithstanding subsection (4), or any other provision of this Act, where the examiner forms the opinion that the company will be able to survive as a going concern, nothing in this Act shall prevent the examiner from including, in a report under section 15 or 18, proposals which will not involve the impairment of the interests of members or creditors of the company, nor the court from confirming any such proposals.".

(2) Section 244A of the Principal Act (inserted by section 125 of the Companies Act, 1990) and section 139 of the Companies Act, 1990, shall apply to a company under the protection of the court as they apply to a company being wound up, and any references in those sections to a liquidator or provisional liquidator shall be construed for the purposes of this subsection as a reference to an examiner.

(3) Sections 32, 33, 34 and 35 of the Companies (Amendment) Act, 1990, are hereby repealed.

Definitions

'*books or documents*': Companies Act, 1990, section 3.

'*company*': Companies Act, 1963, section 2.

'*court*': Companies Act, 1990, section 235.

'*director*': Companies Act, 1963, section 2.

'*examiner*': Companies (Amendment) Act, 1990, section 1.

'*Principal Act*': Companies Act, 1990, section 3.

'*shadow director*': Companies Act, 1990, section 3.

General Note

This section introduces some amendments to the Companies (Amendment) Act, 1990, which enacted a new concept under Irish company law: court protection for companies for a limited period of time. The amendments have been passed to clarify some problems that arose when the legislation was implemented.

(1) The specific amendments are as follows:

(*a*) This paragraph reduces from fourteen days to three days the period after a receiver is appointed within which an application for the appointment of an examiner may be made.

(*b*) No action may be taken by shareholders under section 205 of the Companies Act, 1963 (Remedy in cases of oppression), while the company is under court protection for anything done by the directors before the appointment of the examiner.

(*c–d*) These paragraphs enable the scope of enquiry under section 8 (3) of the Companies (Amendment) Act, 1990, to be widened so as to ensure that full information can be obtained in relation to bank accounts operated not only by the directors but by people connected with them and by shadow directors.

(*e*) Where the examiner fails to obtain the information or responses to questions and he reports the matter to the court, the court may now make an order that the person be required to attend the court and answer the questions put to him or produce the books required.

(*f*) Section 10 of the Companies (Amendment) Act, 1990, allows the examiner to certify certain liabilities if he thinks the incurring of them is vital for the survival of the company. The certification of such expenses would appear to create among creditors a class of 'supercreditor'. This status would only arise where an order is made for the winding up of the company or a receiver is appointed.

(*g*) These are tidying-up provisions arising from the enactment of the Companies (Amendment) Act, 1990.

(*h*) This provision enables local authorities to agree to a compromise or scheme of arrangement.

(*i*) Where the examiner forms the opinion that the company is able to survive as a going concern he may include in his report proposals that may require management changes and may not need to affect the interests of the creditors or members.

SECTION 181

Further amendments to the Companies (Amendment) Act, 1990.

(1) The Companies (Amendment) Act, 1990, is hereby further amended as follows:

(*a*) by the substitution for section 2 (1) (*b*) of the following:

"(*b*) no resolution subsists for the winding up of the company, and",

(*b*) by the substitution in section 4 (5) (*f*), for "company", of "body corporate",

(*c*) by the insertion after section 5 (2) (*f*) of the following paragraph:

"(*h*) no set-off between separate bank accounts of the company shall be effected, except with the consent of the examiner, and in this paragraph 'bank account' includes an account with any person exempt by virtue of section 7 (4) of the Central Bank Act, 1971, from the requirement of holding a licence under section 9 of that Act,",

(*d*) by the insertion in section 11 (5), after "towards" of "discharging", and

(*e*) by the insertion of the following section after section 36:

"36A.—Proceedings in relation to an offence under section 11 (6), 12 or 30 may be brought and prosecuted by the registrar of companies.".

(2) Section 30 (3) of the Companies (Amendment) Act, 1990, is hereby repealed.

Definitions

'*body corporate*': Companies Act, 1963, section 2 (3).

'*company*': Companies Act, 1963, section 2.

'*registrar of companies*': Companies Act, 1963, section 2.

General Note

(1) The provisions of this subsection are as follows:

(*a*) An examiner should not be capable of being appointed once an actual resolution to wind up the company has been passed.

(*b*) This paragraph enables a relationship to be shown under section 4 (5) (*f*) of the Companies (Amendment) Act, 1990, between two Irish companies where the parent of both companies was registered abroad.

(*c*) This paragraph is intended to tackle means by which creditors, particularly banks, could bypass the restrictions imposed by section 5 (2) of the Companies (Amendment) Act, 1990, by using the practice of 'set-off', whereby customers who operate separate accounts agree to the bank using the funds in one account to offset on an automatic basis the shortfall in another account.

(*d*) This paragraph inserts the word 'discharging' into the section.

(*e*) This paragraph allows the Registrar of Companies to bring and prosecute summary proceedings for offences under section 11 (6) (Power to deal with property charged), section 20 (Repudiation of certain contracts), and section 30 (Publicity) of the Companies (Amendment) Act, 1990.

10
ACCOUNTS AND AUDIT

The provisions of part X of the Act are designed to strengthen the obligation of companies to keep proper books of account and to significantly extend both the criminal and civil liabilities of a company's officers where this has not been done.

There are new obligations concerning auditors, including qualifications for the appointment of auditors and persons undergoing training and of auditing standards. The obligations on auditors also include ensuring that proper books are kept, and prohibitions from acting in certain cases.

SECTION 182

Interpretation of Part X.

In this Part—

"the Council Directive" means Council Directive No. 84/253/EEC of 10 April, 1984 on the approval of persons responsible for carrying out the statutory audits of accounting documents;

"friendly society" means a society registered under the Friendly Societies Acts, 1896 to 1977;

"practising certificate" means a certificate awarded to a person by a body of accountants entitling that person to practise as auditor of a company or as a public auditor;

"public auditor" means a public auditor for the purposes of the Industrial and Provident Societies Acts, 1893 to 1978, and the Friendly Societies Acts, 1896 to 1977.

Definitions
'Council Directive': Companies Act, 1990, section 182.
'friendly society': Companies Act, 1990, section 182.
'practising certificate': Companies Act, 1990, section 182.
'public auditor': Companies Act, 1990, section 182.

General Note
This section sets out definitions used in part X of the Act.

SECTION 183

Appointment and removal of auditors.

Section 160 of the Principal Act is hereby amended—

(a) by the substitution of the following subsections for subsection (5)—

"(5) Without prejudice to any rights of the auditor in relation to his removal under this subsection, a company may, by ordinary resolution at a general meeting, remove an auditor other than an auditor who is the first auditor or one of the first auditors of the company and appoint in his place any other person who has been nominated for appointment by any member of the company, who is qualified under the Companies Acts to be an auditor of a company and of whose nomination notice has been given to its members.

(5A) (*a*) A company shall—

(i) within one week of the Minister's power under subsection (4) becoming exercisable, give the Minister notice of that fact, and
(ii) where a resolution removing an auditor is passed, give notice of that fact in the prescribed form to the registrar of companies within 14 days of the meeting at which the resolution removing the auditor was passed.

(*b*) If a company fails to give notice as required by paragraph (*a*) of this subsection, the company and every officer of the company who is in default shall be guilty of an offence and liable, on summary conviction, to a fine not exceeding £1,000.",

and

(*b*) by the substitution of the following subsection for subsection (7)—

"(7) The directors of a company or the company in general meeting may fill any casual vacancy in the office of auditor, but while any such vacancy continues, the surviving or continuing auditor or auditors, if any, may act.".

Definitions

'auditor': this is not defined in the Companies Acts; but see the UK case *R. v. Shacter* [1960] 2 QB 252.

'company': Companies Act, 1963, section 2.

'director': Companies Act, 1963, section 2.

'Minister': Companies Act, 1990, section 3.

'officer': Companies Act, 1963, section 2.

'Principal Act': Companies Act, 1990, section 3.

'registrar of companies': Companies Act, 1963, section 2.

General Note

This section amends section 160 of the Companies Act, 1963, to provide for the removal of an auditor by a company and his replacement with another auditor by way of ordinary resolution in general meeting. Where this is done, the Registrar of Companies must be notified within fourteen days of the meeting at which the resolution was passed. The section also provides that the company in general meeting may now fill any casual vacancy in the office of auditor.

SECTION 184
Resolutions
relating to
appointment and
removal of
auditors and
rights of auditors
who have been
removed.

(1) Section 161 of the Principal Act is hereby amended by the substitution of the following subsections for subsections (1) and (2)—

"(1) Extended notice within the meaning of section 142 shall be required for—

(*a*) a resolution at an annual general meeting of a company appointing as auditor a person other than a retiring auditor or providing expressly that a retiring auditor shall not be re-appointed,

(b) a resolution at a general meeting of a company removing an auditor before the expiration of his term of office, and

(c) a resolution at a general meeting of a company filling a casual vacancy in the office of auditor.

(2) On receipt of notice of such an intended resolution as is mentioned in subsection (1), the company shall forthwith—

(a) if the resolution is a resolution mentioned in paragraph (a) of the said subsection (1), send a copy thereof to the retiring auditor (if any),

(b) if the resolution is a resolution mentioned in paragraph (b) of the said sub-section (1), send a copy thereof to the auditor proposed to be removed, and

(c) if the resolution is a resolution mentioned in paragraph (c) of the said subsection (1), send a copy thereof to the person (if any) whose ceasing to hold the office of auditor of the company occasioned the casual vacancy.

(2A) An auditor of a company who has been removed shall be entitled to attend—

(a) the annual general meeting of the company at which, but for his removal, his term of office as auditor of the company would have expired, and

(b) the general meeting of the company at which it is proposed to fill the vacancy occasioned by his removal, and

to receive all notices of, and other communications relating to, any such meeting which a member of the company is entitled to receive and to be heard at any general meeting that such a member attends on any part of the business of the meeting which concerns him as former auditor of the company.".

(2) The reference in subsection (5) of the said section 161 to a resolution to remove the first auditors by virtue of subsection (6) of section 160 of the Principal Act shall be construed as including a reference to a resolution to remove an auditor other than the first auditors before the expiration of his term of office.

Definitions

'auditor': this is not defined in the Companies Acts; but see the UK case *R. v. Shacter* [1960] 2 QB 252.

'company': Companies Act, 1963, section 2.

'Principal Act': Companies Act, 1990, section 3.

General Note

This section amends section 161 of the Companies Act, 1963, which deals with the resolutions relating to the appointment and removal of auditors. It is consequential on the amendment to section 160 in section 183. Extended notice of twenty-eight days is now required for the removal of an auditor other than the first auditor, and the auditor involved must be notified. The section provides that an auditor who is removed will be entitled to attend the next annual general meeting of the company and any general meeting at which it is proposed to fill the vacancy, and that he be permitted to speak at such meeting.

(1) Extended notice is required for a resolution of a company appointing an auditor other than the retiring auditor or expressly providing that a retiring auditor not be reappointed, or a resolution of the company removing an auditor before the expiry of his term of office, or a resolution at a general meeting filling a casual vacancy in the office of auditor.

(2) On receipt of notice of such an intended resolution a company must send a copy to the retiring auditor or the auditor who is ceasing to be auditor as a result of the casual vacancy.

(2A) An auditor who has been removed from office is entitled to attend the general meeting of the company at which his term of office as auditor would have expired and the general meeting at which it is proposed to fill the vacancy caused by his removal. He is also entitled to receive notices of and other communications to shareholders concerning him as former auditor.

SECTION 185
Resignation of auditors.

(1) An auditor of a company may, by a notice in writing that complies with subsection (2) served on the company and stating his intention to do so, resign from the office of auditor to the company; and the resignation shall take effect on the date on which the notice is so served or on such later date as may be specified in the notice.

(2) A notice under subsection (1) shall contain either—

(*a*) a statement to the effect that there are no circumstances connected with the resignation to which it relates that the auditor concerned considers should be brought to the notice of the members or creditors of the company, or

(*b*) a statement of any such circumstances as aforesaid.

(3) Where a notice under subsection (1) is served on a company—

(*a*) the auditor concerned shall, within 14 days after the date of such service, send a copy of the notice to the registrar of companies, and

(*b*) subject to subsection (4), the company shall, if the notice contains a statement referred to in subsection (2) (*b*), not later than 14 days after the date of such service send a copy of the notice to every person who is entitled under section 159 (1) of the Principal Act to be sent copies of the documents referred to in the said section 159 (1).

(4) Copies of a notice served on a company under subsection (1) need not be sent to the persons specified in subsection (3) (*b*) if, on the application of the company concerned or any other person who claims to be aggrieved, the court is satisfied that the notice contains material which has been included to secure needless publicity for defamatory matter and the court may order the company's costs on an application under this section to be paid in whole or in part by the auditor concerned notwithstanding that he is not a party to the application.

(5) This section shall also apply to a notice given by an auditor under section 160 (2) (*c*) of the Principal Act, indicating his unwillingness to be re-appointed.

(6) A person who fails to comply with subsection (2) or (3) (*a*) shall be guilty of an offence.

(7) If default is made in complying with subsection (3) (*b*), the company concerned, and every officer of such company who is in default, shall be guilty of an offence.

Definitions

'auditor': this is not defined in the Companies Acts; but see the UK case *R.* v. *Shacter* [1960] 2 QB 252.

'company': Companies Act, 1963, section 2.

'court': Companies Act, 1990, section 235.

'officer': Companies Act, 1963, section 2.

'Principal Act': Companies Act, 1990, section 3.

'registrar of companies': Companies Act, 1963, section 2.

General Note

This section provides the mechanism whereby a duly appointed auditor may resign during his term of office. While there may be straightforward reasons for the resignation of an auditor—such as ill health—the section prevents an auditor from resigning without reporting to the members on any problems or irregularities of which he is aware and that are connected with his resignation. A resignation must include a statement of any circumstances connected with it that the auditor considers should be brought to the notice of the members or creditors or else a statement to the effect that there are no such circumstances. The company is obliged to send copies of this statement to the Registrar of Companies and to those entitled to attend general meetings of the company.

(1) An auditor may serve notice on the company, subject to subsection (2) below, that he intends to resign with effect from the date of the notice.

(2) A notice under subsection (1) must contain either a statement that there are no circumstances connected with the resignation to which it relates that the auditor considers should be brought to the notice of the members of the company or a statement of any such circumstances.

(3) Where a notice is served on a company, the auditor concerned must within fourteen days send a copy of the notice to the Registrar of Companies, and if the notice contains a statement giving details of circumstances relating to his resignation in subsection (2) above a copy is to be sent to every member or person entitled to receive notices under section 159 (1) of the Companies Act, 1963.

(4) Copies of a notice served on the company under subsection (1) need not be sent to the members and other persons if the court is satisfied that it contains material that has been included to secure needless publicity for defamatory matter, and the court may order the auditor to pay some or all of the company's costs in connection with the application, even though it was not a party to the application.

(5) This section also applies in the case where an auditor indicates his unwillingness to be reappointed under section 160 (2) (*c*) of the Companies Act, 1963.

(6) If a person fails to comply with subsection (2) or (3) he will be guilty of an offence.

(7) If there is a default in complying with subsection (3) (*b*) the company concerned and every officer of the company who is in default will be guilty of an offence.

SECTION 186
Requisitioning of general meeting of company by resigning auditor.

(1) A notice served on a company under section 185 which contains a statement in accordance with subsection (2) (*b*) of that section may also requisition the convening by the directors of the company of a general meeting of the company for the purpose of receiving and considering such account and explanation of the circumstances connected with his resignation from the office of auditor to the company as he may wish to give to the meeting.

(2) Where an auditor makes a requisition under subsection (1), the directors of the company shall, within 14 days of the service on the company of the said notice, proceed duly to convene a general meeting of the company for a day not more than 28 days after such service.

(3) Subject to subsection (4), where—

(*a*) a notice served on a company under section 185 contains a statement in accordance with subsection (2) (*b*) of that section, and

(*b*) the auditor concerned requests the company to circulate to its members—
(i) before the general meeting at which, apart from the notice, his term of office would expire, or
(ii) before any general meeting at which it is proposed to fill the vacancy caused by his resignation or convened pursuant to a requisition under subsection (1),

a further statement in writing prepared by the auditor of circumstances connected with the resignation that the auditor considers should be brought to the notice of the members,

the company shall—

    (I) in any notice of the meeting given to members of the company state the fact of the statement having been made, and

    (II) send a copy of the statement to the registrar of companies and to every person who is entitled under section 159 (1) of the Principal Act to be sent copies of the documents referred to in the said section 159 (1).

(4) Subsection (3) need not be complied with by the company concerned if, on the application either of the company or any other person who claims to be aggrieved, the court is satisfied that the rights conferred by this section are being abused to secure needless publicity for defamatory matter and the court may order the company's costs on an application under this section to be paid in whole or in part by the auditor concerned notwithstanding that he is not a party to the application.

(5) An auditor of a company who has resigned from the office of auditor shall be permitted by the company to attend—

    (*a*) the annual general meeting at which, but for his resignation, his term of office would have expired, and

    (*b*) any general meeting at which it is proposed to fill the vacancy caused by his resignation or convened pursuant to a requisition of his under subsection (1),

and the company shall send him all notices of, and other communications relating to, any such meeting that a member of the company is entitled to receive and the company shall permit him to be heard at any such meeting which he attends on any part of the business of the meeting which concerns him as a former auditor of the company.

(6) If default is made in complying with subsection (2), (3) or (5), the company concerned, and every officer of the company who is in default, shall be guilty of an offence.

Definitions

'auditor': this is not defined in the Companies Acts; but see the UK case *R. v. Shacter* [1960] 2 QB 252.

'company': Companies Act, 1963, section 2.

'court': Companies Act, 1990, section 235.

'director': Companies Act, 1963, section 2.

'officer': Companies Act, 1963, section 2.

'Principal Act': Companies Act, 1990, section 3.

'registrar of companies': Companies Act, 1963, section 2.

General Note

This section allows a resigning auditor to requisition a general meeting of the company. The auditor may require the company to circulate its members with a statement prepared by him of any circumstances connected with the resignation that he considers should be brought to their notice. In addition it must allow the auditor to attend and speak at the annual general meeting at which his term of office as auditor would have expired and at any general meeting at which it is proposed to fill the vacancy.

(1) An auditor who resigns under section 185 of this Act may requisition the directors to convene a general meeting for the purpose of receiving and considering the account of the auditor and explaining the circumstances connected with his resignation.

(2) Where an auditor makes a requisition under subsection (1) the company must within fourteen days of the service of the notice proceed to convene a general meeting of the company for a day not more than twenty-eight days after the serving of such notice.

(3) If the auditor prepares and submits a further statement in writing to that submitted under section 185 of this Act, the further statement of the circumstances connected with the resignation must be brought to the notice of the members, and the company must state the fact of the statement having been made in the notice of the meeting and must send a copy of it to the Registrar of Companies and to every person entitled to receive a notice of the general meeting under section 159 (1) of the Companies Act, 1963.

(4) Subsection (3) need not be complied with if the court is satisfied, on an application from the company, that the statement contains material that has been included to secure needless publicity for defamatory matter.

(5) An auditor who has resigned must be permitted by the company to attend the annual general meeting at which but for his resignation his term of office would have expired and any general meeting called for the purpose of filling the vacancy. He will be entitled to receive notices and any other communications relating to such meeting.

(6) If the company or any officer of the company is in default of subsections (2), (3) or (5) they will be guilty of an offence.

SECTION 187
Qualification for appointment as auditor.

(1) Subject to section 190, a person shall not be qualified for appointment either as auditor of a company or as a public auditor unless—

(a) (i) he is a member of a body of accountants for the time being recognised by the Minister for the purposes of this section and holds a valid practising certificate from such a body, or

(ii) he holds an accountancy qualification that is, in the opinion of the Minister, of a standard which is not less than that required for such membership as aforesaid and which would entitle him to be granted a practising certificate by that body if he were a member of it, and is for the time being authorised by the Minister to be so appointed, or

(iii) he was, on the 31st day of December, 1990, a member of a body of accountants for the time being recognised under section 162 (1) (*a*) of the Principal Act, or

(iv) he was authorised by the Minister before the 3rd day of February, 1983, and is for the time being authorised by the Minister to be so appointed, or

(v) he is a person to whom section 188 applies, or

(vi) he is a person to whom section 189 applies, and is for the time being authorised by the Minister to be so appointed, and

(*b*) the particulars required by sections 199 and 200 in respect of such a person have been forwarded to the registrar of companies.

(2) None of the following persons shall be qualified for appointment as auditor of a company—

(*a*) an officer or servant of the company,

(*b*) a person who has been an officer or servant of the company within a period in respect of which accounts would fall to be audited by him if he were appointed auditor of the company,

(*c*) a parent, spouse, brother, sister or child of an officer of the company,

(*d*) a person who is a partner of or in the employment of an officer of the company,

(*e*) a person who is disqualified under this subsection for appointment as auditor of any other body corporate that is a subsidiary or holding company of the company or a subsidiary of the company's holding company, or would be so disqualified if the body corporate were a company,

(*f*) a person who is disqualified under subsection (3) for appointment as a public auditor of a society that is a subsidiary or holding company of the company or a subsidiary of the company's holding company,

(*g*) a body corporate.

(3) None of the following persons shall be qualified for appointment as a public auditor of a society—

(*a*) an officer or servant of the society,

(*b*) a person who has been an officer or servant of the society within a period in respect of which accounts would fall to be audited by him if he were appointed auditor of the society,

(*c*) a parent, spouse, brother, sister or child of an officer of the society,

(*d*) a person who is a partner of or in the employment of an officer of the society,

(*e*) a person who is disqualified under this subsection for appointment as a public auditor of any other society that is a subsidiary or holding company of the society or a subsidiary of the society's holding company,.

(*f*) a person who is disqualified under subsection (2) for appointment as auditor of a company that is a subsidiary or holding company of the society,

(*g*) a body corporate.

(4) None of the following persons shall be qualified for appointment as a public auditor of a friendly society—

(*a*) an officer or servant of the friendly society,

(*b*) a person who has been an officer or servant of the friendly society within a period in respect of which accounts would fall to be audited by him if he were appointed auditor of the friendly society, (*c*) a parent, spouse, brother, sister or child of an officer of the friendly society,

(*d*) a person who is a partner of or in the employment of an officer of the friendly society,

(*e*) a body corporate.

(5) A person shall not, by virtue of subsection (3) or (4), be disqualified for appointment as public auditor of a society or a friendly society at any time during the period of 2 years from the commencement of this section if on such commencement he stands duly appointed as public auditor of the society or friendly society, as the case may be.

(6) Subject to subsection (5), a person shall not act as auditor of a company or as a public auditor at a time when he is disqualified under this section for appointment to that office.

(7) If, during his term of office as auditor of a company or public auditor, a person becomes disqualified under the Companies Acts for appointment to that office, he shall thereupon vacate his office and give notice in writing to the company, society or friendly society that he has vacated his office by reason of such disqualification.

(8) This section shall not apply to the Comptroller and Auditor General.

(9) A person who contravenes subsection (6) or (7) shall be guilty of an offence and liable—

(*a*) on summary conviction, to a fine not exceeding £1,000, and, for continued contravention, to a daily default fine not exceeding £50, or

(*b*) on conviction on indictment, to a fine not exceeding £5,000 and, for continued contravention, to a daily default fine not exceeding £100.

(10) (*a*) In this section "society" means a society registered under the Industrial and Provident Societies Acts, 1893 to 1978.

(*b*) References in this section to an officer or servant do not include references to an auditor or a public auditor.

(11) A recognition or authorisation by the Minister under section 162 of the Principal Act shall, notwithstanding the repeal of that section by this Act, continue in force as if given under this section—

(*a*) in the case of a recognition, until the time limit provided expires, or the Minister's decision is communicated to the body concerned, under section 191, whichever is the earlier, and

(*b*) in the case of an authorisation, until the time limit for the person to make the notification required by section 199 (3) expires.

Definitions

'*auditor*': this is not defined in the Companies Acts; but see the UK case *R.* v. *Shacter* [1960] 2 QB 252.

'*body corporate*': Companies Act, 1963, section 2 (3).

'*company*': Companies Act, 1963, section 2.

'*daily default fine*': Companies Act, 1990, section 3.

'*holding company*': Companies Act, 1963, section 155.

'*Minister*': Companies Act, 1990, section 3.

'*officer*': Companies Act, 1990, section 2.

'practising certificate': Companies Act, 1990, section 182.
'Principal Act': Companies Act, 1990, section 3.
'society': Companies Act, 1990, section 187.
'subsidiary': Companies Act, 1963, section 155.

General Note

This section implements part of the EC Eighth Company Law Directive, dealing with auditors. It replaces section 162 of the Companies Act, 1963, which deals with the qualifications for appointment as an auditor.

The main changes in the legislation are that a person is not qualified to act as an auditor of a company if he has been an officer or servant of the company within a period in respect of which accounts would fall to be audited if he were to be appointed an auditor, or if he is a close relative of an officer of the company. The section also introduces changes in relation to the qualifications of a public auditor, and a provision that the Minister for Industry and Commerce must be satisfied in relation to the standards of training etc.

(1) A person is not qualified to be an auditor of a company or a public auditor unless he falls within one of the categories in subsection (1) (*a*) of the section.

(2) Certain persons are not qualified to act as auditor, including:

- an officer or servant of the company;
- a person who was an officer or servant of the company within a period to which accounts would be prepared if he were appointed auditor;
- a close relative of an officer of the company;
- a person who is a partner of or in the employment of an officer of the company;
- a person who is disqualified under this subsection from acting as auditor of a holding company or subsidiary of the company;
- a person who is disqualified under subsection 3 from acting as auditor of a society that is a subsidiary or holding company of the company;
- a body corporate.

(3) A list of the categories of person not qualified to act as auditor of an industrial and provident society is set out.

(4) A list of the categories of person not qualified to act as a public auditor of a friendly society is set out.

(5) A person will not be disqualified from acting as auditor to a friendly society for a period of two years from the commencement of this section if he is acting as auditor at the time of commencement of the section.

(6) A person cannot act as auditor if he is disqualified under this section from appointment, subject, however, to subsection (5) above.

(7) If during the term of office a person becomes disqualified from acting as an auditor he must vacate his office and give notice in writing to the company, society or friendly society, together with the reason for disqualification.

(8) The Comptroller and Auditor General is excluded from this section.

(9) The penalties applicable in the event of default are set out.

(10) 'Society' is defined for the purposes of the section.

(11) Recognition or authorisation by the Minister under section 162 of the Companies Act, 1963, will continue until the time limit expires or a decision is communicated to the relevant body, whichever is the earlier.

SECTION 188
Persons undergoing training on 1 January, 1990.

(1) Without prejudice to section 187, a person to whom this section applies shall also be qualified for appointment as auditor of a company or a public auditor.

(2) This section applies to a person—

(a) who on the 1st day of January, 1990, was a person to whom Article 18 of the Council Directive applies, and
(b) who, following his admission, before the 1st day of January, 1996, to the membership of a body of accountants recognised under section 191, was subsequently awarded a practising certificate by that body, and
(c) in respect of whom such certificate remains valid.

Definitions

'auditor': this is not defined in the Companies Acts; but see the UK case *R. v. Shacter* [1960] 2 QB 252.

'Council Directive': Companies Act, 1990, section 182.

'practising certificate': Companies Act, 1990, section 182.

General Note

This section provides that a person is qualified to act as an auditor if on 1 January 1990 he was a person to whom article 18 of the EC Council Directive on Auditors applies and following his admission before 1 January 1996 to membership of a recognised body of accountants he was awarded a practising certificate and that such certificate remains valid.

SECTION 189
Approval of qualifications obtained outside the State.

(1) Without prejudice to section 187, the Minister may declare that, subject to subsection (2), persons who hold—

(*a*) a qualification entitling them to audit accounts under the law of a specified country outside the State, or
(*b*) a specified accountancy qualification recognised under the law of a country outside the State,

shall be regarded as qualified for appointment as auditor of a company or a public auditor.

(2) Before making a declaration under subsection (1), the Minister—

(*a*) must be satisfied that the qualification concerned is of a standard not less than is required by the Companies Acts to qualify a person for appointment as auditor of a company or a public auditor, and
(*b*) may direct that such a person

shall not be treated as qualified for the purposes of subsection (1) unless he holds such additional educational qualifications as the Minister may specify for the purpose of ensuring that such persons have an adequate knowledge of the law and practice in the State relevant to the audit of accounts, and

(*c*) may have regard to the extent to which persons qualified under the Companies Acts for appointment as auditor of a company or a public auditor are recognised by the law of the country in question as qualified to audit accounts there.

(3) Different directions may be given under subsection (2) (*b*) in relation to different qualifications.

(4) The Minister may, if he thinks fit, revoke or suspend for a specified period, in such manner and on such conditions as he may think appropriate, any declaration previously made under subsection (1).

Definitions

'auditor': this is not defined in the Companies Acts; but see the UK case *R.* v. *Shacter* [1960] 2 QB 252.

'company': Companies Act, 1963, section 2.

'Minister': Companies Act, 1990, section 3.

General Note

This section enables the Minister to declare that the holders of a qualification obtained outside the state may be qualified for appointment as auditors of a company, and implements article 11 of the EC directive.

(1) The Minister may declare that certain persons who hold qualifications outside the state may be qualified to act as auditors or public auditors.

(2) Before making a declaration under subsection (1) the Minister must be satisfied that certain standards, including educational qualifications, are no less than those required under the Companies Acts.

(3) Different directions may be given in relation to different educational qualifications.

(4) The Minister may revoke or suspend any declaration previously made in such manner as he sees fit.

SECTION 190
Consultation by Minister regarding standards and qualifications.

(1) Before granting, renewing, withdrawing, revoking, suspending or refusing a recognition of a body of accountants under the Companies Acts, the Minister may consult with any person or body of persons as to the conditions imposed or standards required by the body of accountants concerned in connection with membership of that body or the awarding to persons of practising certificates.

(2) The Minister may also consult with any person or body of persons before forming any opinion or making any declaration in relation to the qualifications held by any person or class of persons as respects qualification for appointment as auditor of a company or a public auditor.

Definitions

'auditor': this is not defined in the Companies Acts; but see the UK case *R.* v. *Shacter* [1960] 2 QB 252.

'company': Companies Act, 1963, section 2.

'Minister': Companies Act, 1990, section 3.

'practising certificate': Companies Act, 1990, section 182.

General Note

This section aims to help the Minister in deciding whether to recognise particular accountancy bodies or to authorise particular individuals. It provides that the Minister may consult any person or body of persons in regard to conditions to be imposed or standards required by a body of accountants in connection with membership of the body or the awarding of practising certificates.

SECTION 191
Recognition of bodies of accountants.

(1) Where a body of accountants recognised under section 162 of the Principal Act satisfies the Minister, within three months after the commencement of this section—

(*a*) that the standards relating to training, qualifications and repute required by that body for the awarding to a person of a practising certificate are not less than those specified in Articles 3 to 6, 8 and 19 of the Council Directive, and (*b*) as to the standards it applies to its members in the areas of ethics, codes of conduct and practice, independence, professional integrity, technical standards, disciplinary procedures,

the Minister shall renew such recognition.

(2) Where a body of accountants referred to in subsection (1) does not satisfy the Minister as to the matters specified in that paragraph, he shall withdraw the recognition of that body until he is so satisfied.

(3) Where a body of accountants which has not previously been recognised by the Minister under section 162 of the Principal Act applies for such recognition after the commencement of this section, the Minister may grant such recognition if he is satisfied as to the matters referred to in subsection (1) in relation to that body or may refuse such recognition if he is not so satisfied.

Definitions

'Council Directive': Companies Act, 1990, section 182.
'Minister': Companies Act, 1990, section 3.
'practising certificate': Companies Act, 1990, section 182.
'Principal Act': Companies Act, 1990, section 3.

General Note

This section sets out the procedures for recognition of bodies of accountants.

(1) Where a body of accountants recognised under section 162 of the Companies Act, 1963, satisfies the Minister within three months after the commencement of the section that the training, educational and qualification standards are not less than those specified in the Council Directive and satisfies the Minister as to the standards of ethics and discipline and codes of conduct and practice, he will renew the recognition.

(2) The Minister will withdraw recognition from bodies of accountants that do not satisfy the conditions specified in subsection (1) until he is so satisfied.

(3) Where a body of accountants that was not previously recognised applies for recognition, the Minister will grant recognition where he is satisfied that the conditions referred to in subsection (1) have been complied with.

SECTION 192
Provisions in relation to recognitions and authorisations by Minister under section 187.

(1) The Minister may, at the time it is granted or at any time during the currency of a recognition or authorisation under section 187 by notice in writing given to the body of accountants or individual concerned, attach to the recognition or authorisation, as the case may be, such terms and conditions as he thinks necessary or expedient and specified in the notice.

(2) The Minister may, at any time during the currency of a recognition or authorisation under section 187, by notice in writing given to the body of accountants or individual concerned, amend its terms or conditions or insert into it or delete from it other terms or conditions.

(3) The Minister may, at any time during its currency, by notice in writing given to the body of accountants or individual concerned, revoke, or suspend for a specified period, a recognition or authorisation under the said section 187.

(4) (*a*) The Minister may require a body of accountants recognised for the purposes of the said section 187 to prepare and, within such period as may be specified in the requirement, to submit to the Minister for his approval a code prescribing standards of professional conduct for its members and providing for sanctions for breaches of the code, and the body of accountants shall comply with the requirement.

(*b*) A body of accountants may, at any time, prepare and submit to the Minister a code amending or revoking a code prepared by it under this subsection.

(*c*) The Minister may approve of a code submitted to him under this subsection.

(*d*) A code approved of by the Minister under this section shall be brought into operation and enforced by the body of accountants concerned in accordance with its terms.

(*e*) Where the Minister approves a code under this subsection, he may direct that such provisions of the code as relate to the professional integrity of auditors shall apply, with any necessary modifications approved by the Minister, to persons individually authorised by him.

(*f*) The Minister may, by regulations, make provision for the function of monitoring compliance by individuals with the code in accordance with paragraph (*e*). Such regulations may in particular provide for this function to be performed on behalf of the Minister by any body or person specified in the regulations. The regulations may also contain such incidental, consequential, transitional or supplementary provision as may appear to be necessary or proper to ensure compliance with the specified provisions of the code by the individuals concerned.

(*g*) Every regulation made by the Minister under this section shall be laid before each House of the Oireachtas as soon as may be after it is made and, if a resolution annulling the regulation is passed by either House within the next 21 days on which that House has sat after the regulation is laid before it, the regulation shall be annulled accordingly, but without prejudice to the validity of anything previously done thereunder.

(5) References in this section to recognitions under section 187 include references to recognitions under section 162 (inserted by the Companies (Amendment) Act, 1982) of the Principal Act and references in this section to an authorisation under section 187 include references to authorisations under the said section 162.

Definitions

'Minister': Companies Act, 1990, section 3.

'Principal Act': Companies Act, 1990, section 3.

General Note

This section confirms the Minister's present power to revoke, suspend or attach conditions to his recognition of a body of accountants for auditing purposes under the Companies Acts and to the authorisations of individuals who may not be members of such recognised bodies.

(1) The Minister may attach to the recognition of a body of accountants such terms and conditions as he thinks necessary or expedient.

(2) During the currency of any notice the Minister may amend, vary or delete any of the terms and conditions.

(3) The Minister may at any time by notice suspend or revoke for a specified period a recognition or authorisation of a body of accountants.

(4) The Minister may require a recognised body of accountants to submit a code of practice or standards for his approval and that such code be brought into practice by the accountancy bodies.

(5) This is a technical provision concerning recognition under section 162 of the Companies Act, 1963.

SECTION 193

Auditors' report and right of access to books and of attendance and audience at general meetings.

(1) The auditors of a company shall make a report to the members on the accounts examined by them, and on every balance sheet and profit and loss account, and all group accounts, laid before the company in general meeting during their tenure of office.

(2) The auditors' report shall be read at the annual general meeting of the company and shall be open to inspection by any member.

(3) Every auditor of a company shall have a right of access at all reasonable times to the books, accounts and vouchers of the company and shall be entitled to require from the officers (within the meaning of section 197 (5)) of the company such information and explanations that are within their knowledge or can be procured by them as he thinks necessary for the performance of the duties of the auditors.

(4) The auditors' report shall state—

(a) whether they have obtained all the information and explanations which, to the best of their knowledge and belief, are necessary for the purposes of their audit,

(b) whether, in their opinion, proper books of account have been kept by the company,

(c) whether, in their opinion, proper returns adequate for their audit have been received from branches of the company not visited by them,

(d) whether the company's balance sheet and (unless it is framed as a consolidated profit and loss account) profit and loss account are in agreement with the books of account and returns,

(e) except in the case of a company that has taken advantage of any of the provisions of Part III of the Sixth Schedule to the Principal Act, whether, in their opinion, the company's balance sheet and profit and loss account and (if it is a holding company submitting group accounts) the group accounts have been properly prepared in accordance with the provisions of the Companies Acts and give a true and fair view—

(i) in the case of the balance sheet, of the state of the company's affairs as at the end of its financial year,

(ii) in the case of the profit and loss account (if it is not framed as a consolidated profit and loss account), of the company's profit and loss for its financial year,

(iii) in the case of group accounts submitted by a holding company, of the state of affairs and profit or loss of the company and its subsidiaries dealt with thereby, so far as concerns members of the company,

(*f*) in the case of a company that has taken advantage of any of the provisions of Part III of the Sixth Schedule to the Principal Act, whether, in their opinion, its balance sheet and profit and loss account and (if it is a holding company submitting group accounts) the group accounts have been properly prepared in accordance with the provisions of the Companies Acts and give a true and fair view of the matters referred to in subparagraphs (i) and (ii) and, where appropriate, subparagraph (iii) of paragraph (*e*) subject to the non-disclosure of any matters (to be indicated in the report) which by virtue of the said Part III are not required to be disclosed, and

(*g*) whether, in their opinion, there existed at the balance sheet date a financial situation which under section 40 (1) of the Companies (Amendment) Act, 1983, would require the convening of an extraordinary general meeting of the company.

(5) The auditors of a company shall be entitled to attend any general meeting of the company and to receive all notices of, and other communications relating to, any general meeting which any member of the company is entitled to receive and to be heard at any general meeting which they attend on any part of the business of the meeting which concerns them as auditors.

(6) A person who is appointed as auditor of a company or as a public auditor shall be under a general duty to carry out such audit with professional integrity.

(7) Any reference in the Principal Act to section 163 of or the Seventh Schedule to that Act shall be construed as references to this section.

Definitions

'*auditor*': this is not defined in the Companies Acts; but see the UK case *R.* v. *Shacter* [1960] 2 QB 252.

'*company*': Companies Act, 1963, section 2.

'*financial year*': Companies Act, 1963, section 2.

'*Principal Act*': Companies Act, 1990, section 3.

'*subsidiary*': Companies Act, 1963, section 155.

General Note

This section replaces section 163 and the seventh schedule to the Companies Act, 1963, which sets out what must be contained in the annual audit report on company accounts. The matters to be dealt with in the auditors' report, which up to now have been set out in the seventh schedule to the Companies Act, 1963, are now brought into the body of the Act.

(1) The auditors of a company must make a report to the members on the accounts examined by them.

(2) The auditors' report must be read at the annual general meeting of the company and be open to inspection by the members.

(3) Every auditor of the company has the right of access at all reasonable times to the books, accounts and vouchers of the company and is entitled to require from the officers of the company such information and explanations as the auditors think necessary for the performance of their duties.

(4) The auditors' report must contain the information set out in this subsection.

(5) The auditors of the company are entitled to attend any general meeting of the company and to receive notices of and other communications relating to any general meeting and to be heard at such general meeting on matters that concern them as auditors.

(6) A person appointed as auditor must carry out the audit with professional integrity.

(7) Any reference to section 163 or the seventh schedule of the Companies Act, 1963, will be construed as a reference to this section.

SECTION 194
Duty of auditors if proper books of account not being kept.

(1) If, at any time, the auditors of a company form the opinion that the company is contravening, or has contravened, section 202 by failing to cause to be kept proper books of account (within the meaning of that section) in relation to the matters specified in subsections (1) and (2) of that section, the auditors shall—

(a) serve a notice on the company as soon as may be stating their opinion, and
(b) not later than 7 days after the service of such notice on the company, notify the registrar of companies in the prescribed form of the notice.

(2) Where the auditors form the opinion that the company has contravened section 202 but that, following such contravention, the directors of the company have taken the necessary steps to ensure that proper books of account are kept as required by that section, subsection (1) (b) shall not apply.

(3) This section shall not require the auditors to make the notifications referred to in subsection (1) if they are of opinion that the contraventions concerned are minor or otherwise immaterial in nature.

(4) A person who contravenes subsection (1) shall be guilty of an offence.

Definitions

'auditor': this is not defined in the Companies Acts; but see the UK case *R. v. Shacter* [1960] 2 QB 252.

'company': Companies Act, 1963, section 2.

'registrar of companies': Companies Act, 1963, section 2.

General Note

This section places a new duty on company auditors if it appears to them that the company is not keeping proper books of account. In such a situation the auditor is required to notify the company accordingly and to request it to rectify the situation. The directors are obliged to take the necessary action in relation to the books of account or to notify the auditors that they do not agree with their opinion. The Registrar of Companies must be notified of the matter.

(1) If the auditors are of the opinion that proper books of account are not being kept they must serve notice of their opinion on the company, and notify the Registrar of Companies within seven days after service on the company.

(2) Where the directors have taken steps to rectify the matter the auditors are not obliged to notify the Registrar of Companies.

(3) The auditors are not required to make the notifications required by subsection (1) if they are of the opinion that the contraventions are minor or of an immaterial nature.

(4) A person who contravenes subsection (1) will be guilty of an offence.

SECTION 195

Prohibition on acting in relation to audit while disqualification order in force.

(1) If a person who is subject or deemed to be subject to a disqualification order—

(a) becomes, or remains after 28 days from the date of the making of the order, a partner in a firm of auditors,

(b) gives directions or instructions in relation to the conduct of any part of the audit of the accounts of a company, or

(c) works in any capacity in the conduct of an audit of the accounts of a company,

he shall be guilty of an offence.

(2) Where a person is convicted of an offence under subsection (1), the period for which he was disqualified shall be extended for a further period of ten years from such date, or such other further period as the court, on the application of the prosecutor and having regard to all the circumstances of the case, may order.

(3) In this section—

(*a*) "company" has the meaning assigned to it by section 159, and also includes any society registered under the Industrial and Provident Societies Acts, 1893 to 1978,

(*b*) "disqualification order" has the meaning assigned to it by section 159.

Definitions

'*auditor*': this is not defined in the Companies Acts; but see the UK case *R*. v. *Shacter* [1960] 2 QB 252.

'*company*': Companies Act, 1990, section 195.

'*disqualification order*': Companies Act, 1990, section 195.

General Note

This section provides that where an auditor is subject to a disqualification order under part VII of the Act he cannot remain a partner in a firm of auditors and he may not take part, directly or indirectly, in the audit of the accounts of a body corporate or friendly society.

(1) A person who is subject to a disqualification order will be guilty of an offence if he remains a partner in the firm after twenty-eight days from the making of the disqualification order or gives instructions or directions in relation to the conduct of any part of the audit of the accounts of a company or works in any capacity in connection with the audit of a company.

(2) Where a person is convicted under subsection (1) he will be disqualified for a further period of ten years or such other period as the court, on the application of the prosecutor, may order.

(3) 'Company' and 'disqualification order' are defined for the purposes of the section.

SECTION 196
Powers of auditors in relation to subsidiaries.

(1) Where a company (referred to in this section as "the holding company") has a subsidiary, then—

(*a*) in case the subsidiary is a body corporate incorporated in the State, it shall be the duty of the subsidiary and its auditors to give to the auditors of the holding company such information and explanations as those auditors may reasonably require for the purposes of their duties as auditors of the holding company,

(*b*) in any other case, it shall be the duty of the holding company, if required by its auditors to do so, to take all such steps as are reasonably open to it to obtain from the subsidiary such information and explanations as aforesaid.

(2) If a company or an auditor fails to comply with subsection (1) within five days of the making of the relevant requirement under that subsection, the company

and every officer thereof who is in default, or the auditor, as the case may be, shall be guilty of an offence.

(3) In a prosecution for an offence under this section, it shall be a defence for the defendant to show that it was not reasonably possible for him to comply with the requirement under subsection (1) to which the offence relates within the time specified in subsection (2) but that he complied therewith as soon as was reasonably possible after the expiration of such time.

(4) A person guilty of an offence under this section shall be liable to a fine.

Definitions

'auditor': this is not defined in the Companies Acts; but see the UK case *R.* v. *Shacter* [1960] 2 QB 252.
'body corporate': Companies Act, 1963, section 2 (3).
'company': Companies Act, 1963, section 2.
'holding company': Companies Act, 1963, section 155.
'officer': Companies Act, 1963, section 2.
'subsidiary': Companies Act, 1963, section 155.

General Note

This section requires a subsidiary company and its auditors to provide such information and explanations as might reasonably be required by the auditors of the holding company. This is to ensure that a situation cannot arise where the auditor of a holding company could have reservations about the accounts of that company because of inability to obtain information from or about any of its subsidiaries.

(1) Where a company has a subsidiary incorporated in the state it is the duty of the subsidiary and its auditors to provide information and explanations to the auditors of the holding company. It is the duty of the holding company, in any other case, to take such steps as are reasonably required to obtain information from the subsidiary as required by the auditors.

(2) In the event that a company or auditor fails to comply with subsection (1) within five days of the making of the relevant requirement under the subsection, the company and every officer who is in default, or the auditor, as the case may be, will be guilty of an offence.

(3) It will be a defence in any action brought under this section to show that it was not reasonably possible for the defendant to comply with the requirements under the section but that they were

complied with as soon as reasonably possible after the expiry of the relevant time.

(4) A person who is guilty of an offence under this section will be liable to a fine.

SECTION 197
Penalty for false
statements to
auditors.

(1) An officer of a company who knowingly or recklessly makes a statement to which this section applies that is misleading, false or deceptive in a material particular shall be guilty of an offence.

(2) This section applies to any statement made to the auditors of a company (whether orally or in writing) which conveys, or purports to convey, any information or explanation which they require under the Companies Acts, or are entitled so to require, as auditors of the company.

(3) An officer of a company who fails to provide to the auditors of the company or of the holding company of the company, within two days of the making of the relevant requirement, any information or explanations that the auditors require as auditors of the company or of the holding company of the company and that is within the knowledge of or can be procured by the officer shall be guilty of an offence.

(4) In a prosecution for an offence under this section, it shall be a defence for the defendant to show that it was not reasonably possible for him to comply with the requirement under subsection (3) to which the offence relates within the time specified in that subsection but that he complied therewith as soon as was reasonably possible after the expiration of such time.

(5) In this section "officer", in relation to a company, includes any employee of the company.

Definitions

'auditor': this is not defined in the Companies Acts; but see the UK case *R. v. Shacter* [1960] 2 QB 252.

'company': Companies Act, 1963, section 2.

'holding company': Companies Act, 1963, section 155.

'officer': Companies Act, 1990, section 197.

General Note

This section makes it an offence for an officer or employee of a company to deliberately give false or misleading information to the company's auditors or to fail to give any information they require or are entitled to require.

(1) An officer of a company who knowingly or recklessly makes a statement to which this section applies that is misleading, false or deceptive will be guilty of an offence.

(2) The section applies to any statement made to the auditors of a company that conveys any information or explanation that is required by the auditors or under the Companies Acts.

(3) An officer who fails within two days of the making of the relevant requirement to provide the auditors with any information or explanations that they require as auditors will be guilty of an offence.

(4) It will be a defence in any prosecution to show that it was not reasonably possible for the defendant to comply but that he complied as soon as possible thereafter.

(5) 'Officer' is defined for the purpose of the section.

SECTION 198
Register of auditors.

(1) The registrar of companies shall maintain a register containing the names and addresses of persons who have been notified to him as qualified for appointment as auditor of a company or as a public auditor.

(2) In this section and in section 199, "address", in relation to a person, means his usual residential or business address.

Definitions

'*address*': Companies Act, 1990, section 198.
'*auditor*': this is not defined in the Companies Acts; but see the UK case *R.* v. *Shacter* [1960] 2 QB 252.
'*company*': Companies Act, 1963, section 2.
'*registrar of companies*': Companies Act, 1963, section 2.

General Note

This section provides that the Registrar of Companies will maintain a register of the names and addresses of persons who have been notified by him as qualified for appointment as auditor or public auditor.

SECTION 199
Transitional provisions concerning register.

(1) Subject to subsection (2), a body of accountants whose recognition has been renewed by the Minister under section 191 (1) or which has been recognised under section 191 (3) shall, within one month after such renewal or recognition, deliver to the registrar of companies the name and address of each of its members who is qualified for appointment under the Companies Acts as auditor of a company or as a public auditor.

(2) Without prejudice to the generality of subsection (1), a body of accountants based outside the State, whose recognition is renewed or granted as aforesaid, shall notify details of those of its members who wish to practise in the State.

(3) Every person who, immediately before the commencement of this section, holds an authorisation from the Minister under the Companies Acts to act as auditor of a company or as a public auditor (otherwise than by virtue of membership of a recognised body of accountants) shall, within one month after such commencement, deliver his name and address to the registrar of companies.

(4) If default is made in complying with subsection (1), the body of accountants concerned shall be guilty of an offence.

Definitions

'auditor': this is not defined in the Companies Acts; but see the UK case *R. v. Shacter* [1960] 2 QB 252.

'company': Companies Act, 1963, section 2.

'Minister': Companies Act, 1990, section 2.

'registrar of companies': Companies Act, 1963, section 2.

General Note

This section sets out the transitional matters in relation to the setting up of the register of auditors.

(1) A recognised body of accountants must within one month of renewal or recognition by the Minister forward to the Registrar of Companies a list of the names and addresses of those members who are qualified to act as auditors.

(2) A body of accountants based outside the state whose recognition is renewed or granted must supply a list of those of its members who wish to practise in the state.

(3) Every person who immediately before the commencement of this section held an authorisation under the Companies Acts must within one month deliver his name and address to the Registrar of Companies.

(4) Anyone who fails to comply with this section will be guilty of an offence.

SECTION 200

Duty to keep registrar informed.

(1) Subject to subsection (2), where, by virtue of his becoming a member of a body of accountants, a person (other than a person referred to in section 199 (1)) becomes qualified for appointment as auditor of a company or as a public auditor, the body concerned shall, within one month of his becoming so qualified, deliver his name and address to the registrar of companies for inclusion in the register referred to in section 198.

(2) Without prejudice to the generality of subsection (1), a recognised body of accountants based outside the State shall notify details of those of its members who wish to practise in the State.

(3) Every person who, after the commencement of this section, is granted an authorisation by the Minister under the Companies Acts to act as auditor of a company or as a public auditor (otherwise than by virtue of membership of a recognised body of accountants) shall, within one month after such grant, deliver his name and address to the registrar of companies.

(4) If default is made in complying with subsection (1), the body of accountants concerned shall be guilty of an offence.

Definitions

'auditor': this is not defined in the Companies Acts; but see the UK case *R. v. Shacter* [1960] 2 QB 252.

'company': Companies Act, 1963, section 2.

'Minister': Companies Act, 1990, section 3.

'registrar of companies': Companies Act, 1963, section 2.

General Note

This section sets out the requirement of keeping the Registrar of Companies notified of new persons who are entitled to act as auditors.

(1) A recognised body of accountants is obliged to notify the Registrar of Companies within one month of the names and addresses of persons becoming qualified to act as auditors.

(2) A recognised body of accountants whose members wish to practise must notify the Registrar of any new person qualified to act as auditor within one month of their becoming so qualified.

(3) Any person who is granted an authorisation by the Minister must give his name and address to the Registrar of Companies within one month after such grant.

(4) Any person in default of subsection (1) will be guilty of an offence.

SECTION 201

Power to make supplementary regulations.

(1) The Minister may make such supplementary regulations as he considers necessary for the proper and effective implementation of the Council Directive.

(2) Without prejudice to the generality of subsection (1), if, in any respect, any difficulty arises in regard to the implementation of the Directive, the Minister may by regulations do anything which appears to him to be necessary or expedient for removing that difficulty, and any such regulations may modify any provision of this Part so far as may be necessary or expedient to implement the Directive but no regulations shall be made under this subsection in relation to any provision of this Part after the expiration of 3 years commencing on the day on which the relevant provision of this Part came into operation.

(3) Every regulation made by the Minister under this section shall be laid before each House of the Oireachtas as soon as may be after it is made and, if a resolution annulling the regulation is passed by either House within the next 21 days on which that House has sat after the regulation is laid before it, the regulation shall be annulled accordingly, but without prejudice to the validity of anything previously done thereunder.

Definitions

'*Council Directive*': Companies Act, 1990, section 182.
'*Minister*': Companies Act, 1990, section 3.

General Note

This section gives the Minister a general power to make supplementary regulations for the proper and effective implementation of the EC directive. For example, the directive provides that member-states may approve firms of auditors that satisfy specified conditions. In Ireland at present only nationals can be approved as auditors, and the question of allowing auditors to form companies has yet to be addressed.

(1) The Minister may make such supplementary regulations as he considers necessary for the proper and effective implementation of the EC directive.

(2) This is a transitional provision that would allow the Minister to modify by regulations any of the provisions of part X of the Act introduced to implement the EC directive. Any such modification must be made within three years of the commencement of this part of the Act.

(3) Every regulation made by the Minister under this section must be laid before each house of the Oireachtas as soon as possible after it is made and will come into force unless there is a resolution passed by either house within twenty-one days following the laying of the regulations before that house.

SECTION 202
Keeping of books of account.

(1) Every company shall cause to be kept proper books of account, whether in the form of documents or otherwise, that—

(*a*) correctly record and explain the transactions of the company,
(*b*) will at any time enable the financial position of the company to be determined with reasonable accuracy,
(*c*) will enable the directors to ensure that any balance sheet, profit and loss account or income and expenditure account of the company complies with the requirements of the Companies Acts, and
(*d*) will enable the accounts of the company to be readily and properly audited.

(2) The books of account of a company shall be kept on a continuous and consistent basis, that is to say, the entries therein shall be made in a timely manner and be consistent from one year to the next.

(3) Without prejudice to the generality of subsections (1) and (2), books of account kept pursuant to those subsections shall contain—

(*a*) entries from day to day of all sums of money received and expended by the company and the matters in respect of which the receipt and expenditure takes place,

(*b*) a record of the assets and liabilities of the company,

(*c*) if the company's business involves dealing in goods—

(i) a record of all goods purchased, and of all goods sold (except those sold for cash by way of ordinary retail trade), showing the goods and the sellers and buyers in sufficient detail to enable the goods and the sellers and buyers to be identified and a record of all the invoices relating to such purchases and sales,

(ii) statements of stock held by the company at the end of each financial year and all records of stocktakings from which any such statement of stock has been, or is to be, prepared, and

(*d*) if the company's business involves the provision of services, a record of the services provided and of all the invoices relating thereto.

(4) For the purposes of subsections (1), (2) and (3), proper books of account shall be deemed to be kept if they comply with those subsections and give a true and fair view of the state of affairs of the company and explain its transactions.

(5) Subject to subsection (6), the books of account shall be kept at the registered office of the company or at such other place as the directors think fit.

(6) If books of account are kept at a place outside the State, there shall be sent to and kept at a place in the State and be at all reasonable times open to inspection by the directors such accounts and returns relating to the business dealt with in the books of account so kept as will disclose with reasonable accuracy the financial position of that business at intervals not exceeding 6 months and will enable to be prepared in accordance with the Companies Acts the company's balance sheet, its profit and loss account or income and expenditure account and any document annexed to any of those documents giving information which is required by the said Acts and is thereby allowed to be so given.

(7) Books of account required by this section to be kept, and accounts and returns referred to in subsection (6), shall be kept either in written form in an official language of the State or so as to enable the books of account and the accounts and returns to be readily accessible and readily convertible into written form in an official language of the State.

(8) A company shall make its books of account, and any accounts and returns referred to in subsection (6), available in written form in an official language of the State at all reasonable times for inspection without charge by the officers of the company and by other persons entitled pursuant to the Companies Acts to inspect the books of account of the company.

(9) A record, being a book of account required by this section to be kept or an account or return referred to in subsection (6), shall be preserved by the company concerned for a period of at least 6 years after the latest date to which it relates.

(10) A company that contravenes this section and a person who, being a director of a company, fails to take all reasonable steps to secure compliance by the company with the requirements of this section, or has by his own wilful act been the cause of any default by the company thereunder, shall be guilty of an offence:

Provided, however, that—

(*a*) in any proceedings against a person in respect of an offence under this section consisting of a failure to take reasonable steps to secure compliance by a company with the requirements of this section, it shall be a defence to prove that he had reasonable grounds for believing and did believe that a competent and reliable person was charged with the duty of ensuring that those requirements were complied with and was in a position to discharge that duty, and

(*b*) a person shall not be sentenced to imprisonment for such an offence unless, in the opinion of the court, the offence was committed wilfully.

Definitions

'company': Companies Act, 1963, section 2.
'director': Companies Act, 1963, section 2.
'financial year': Companies Act, 1963, section 2.

General Note

This section, which deals with the keeping of books of account by companies, expands on the existing provisions and gives more specific guidelines on the matters to be dealt with in the company's books, and is intended to make for a better standard of account-keeping generally.

(1) Every company is required to keep proper books of account that correctly record and explain the transactions of the company, enable the financial position of the company to be determined with reasonable accuracy, and enable the accounts to be properly audited.

(2) The books of account must be kept on a continuous and consistent basis from one year to the next.

(3) This subsection sets out what the books of account must contain.

(4) Proper books will be deemed to have been kept if they give a true and fair view of the state of affairs of the company and explain its transactions.

(5) The books of account must be kept at the registered office or such other place as the directors think fit.

(6) If the books are kept outside the state, accounts and returns that show with reasonable accuracy the state of affairs of the company must be sent to and kept at a place in the state and be open for inspection by the directors.

(7) Books of account must be kept in written form in one of the official languages of the state or in a form that is readily accessible and easily convertible into written form in one of the official languages of the state.

(8) A company must make its accounts in written form available for inspection to the officers of the company without charge at all reasonable times.

(9) Books of account must be preserved for a period of at least six years after the latest date to which they relate.

(10) If a company contravenes this section and fails to take reasonable steps to secure compliance it will be guilty of an offence.

(11) A person in respect of whom proceedings have been commenced under this section can provide as a defence that he had reasonable grounds for believing that a competent and reliable person was given the duty of ensuring that the requirements were complied with.

SECTION 203

Liability of officers of company to penalty where proper books of account not kept.

(1) If—

(*a*) a company that is being wound up and that is unable to pay all of its debts, has contravened section 202, and

(*b*) the court considers that such contravention has contributed to the company's inability to pay all of its debts or has resulted in substantial uncertainty as to the assets and liabilities of the company or has substantially impeded the orderly winding up thereof,

every officer of the company who is in default shall be guilty of an offence and liable—

(i) on summary conviction, to a fine not exceeding £1,000 or to imprisonment for a term not exceeding 6 months or to both, or
(ii) on conviction on indictment, to a fine not exceeding £10,000 or to imprisonment for a term not exceeding 5 years or to both.

(2) In a prosecution for an offence under this section it shall be a defence for the person charged with the offence to show that—

(*a*) he took all reasonable steps to secure compliance by the company with section 202, or

(*b*) he had reasonable grounds for believing and did believe that a competent and reliable person, acting under the supervision or control of a director of the company who has been formally allocated such responsibility, was charged with the duty of ensuring that that section was complied with and was in a position to discharge that duty.

Definitions
'company': Companies Act, 1963, section 2.
'court': Companies Act, 1990, section 235.
'director': Companies Act, 1963, section 2.
'officer': Companies Act, 1963, section 2.

General Note
This section imposes a criminal penalty on officers of companies before they are wound up for failing to keep proper books of account.

(1) If a company is being wound up and is unable to pay its debts and is in contravention of section 202 and the court considers that the contravention of section 202 has contributed to the company's inability to pay all its debts, every officer of the company who has been in default will be guilty of an offence. Any officer found guilty on summary conviction will be liable to a fine not exceeding £1,000 and/or a term of imprisonment not exceeding six months and on conviction on indictment to a fine not exceeding £10,000 and/or a term of imprisonment of not more than five years.

(2) It will be a defence for a person in such a prosecution to show that he took all reasonable steps to comply with section 202 or had reasonable grounds for believing and did believe that a competent and reliable person acting under the supervision or control of a company director was charged with the duty of ensuring that the section was complied with.

SECTION 204

Personal liability of officers of company where proper books of account not kept.

(1) Subject to subsection (2), if—

(a) a company that is being wound up and that is unable to pay all of its debts has contravened section 202, and

(b) the court considers that such contravention has contributed to the company's inability to pay all of its debts or has resulted in substantial uncertainty as to the assets and liabilities of the company or has substantially impeded the orderly winding up thereof,

the court, on the application of the liquidator or any creditor or contributory of the company, may, if it thinks it proper to do so, declare that any one or more of the officers and former officers of the company who is or are in default shall be personally liable, without any limitation of liability, for all, or such part as may be specified by the court, of the debts and other liabilities of the company.

(2) On the hearing of an application under this subsection, the person bringing the application may himself give evidence or call witnesses.

(3) (a) Where the court makes a declaration under subsection (1), it may give such directions as it thinks proper for the purpose of giving effect to the

declaration and in particular may make provision for making the liability of any such person under the declaration a charge on any debt or obligation due from the company to him, or on any mortgage or charge or any interest in any mortgage or charge on any assets of the company held by or vested in him or any company or other person on his behalf, or any person claiming as assignee from or through the person liable under the declaration or any company or person acting on his behalf, and may from time to time make such further order as may be necessary for the purpose of enforcing any charge imposed under this subsection.

(*b*) In paragraph (*a*) "assignee" includes any person to whom or in whose favour, by the directions of the person liable, the debt, obligation, mortgage or charge was created, issued or transferred or the interest created, but does not include an assignee for valuable consideration (not including consideration by way of marriage) given in good faith and without notice of any of the matters on the ground of which the declaration is made.

(4) The court shall not make a declaration under subsection (1) in respect of a person if it considers that—

(*a*) he took all reasonable steps to secure compliance by the company with section 202, or

(*b*) he had reasonable grounds for believing and did believe that a competent and reliable person, acting under the supervision or control of a director of the company who has been formally allocated such responsibility, was charged with the duty of ensuring that that section was complied with and was in a position to discharge that duty.

(5) This section shall have effect notwithstanding that the person concerned may be criminally liable in respect of the matters on the ground of which the declaration is to be made.

(6) In this section "officer", in relation to a company, includes a person who has been convicted of an offence under section 194, 197 or 242 in relation to a statement concerning the keeping of proper books of account by the company.

Definitions

'*assignee*': Companies Act, 1990, section 204.

'*company*': Companies Act, 1963, section 2.

'*contributory*': Companies Act, 1963, section 2.

'*court*': Companies Act, 1990, section 235.

'*director*': Companies Act, 1963, section 2.

'*officer*': Companies Act, 1990, section 204.

General Note

This section imposes a civil liability on company officers who have contravened the provisions concerning the keeping of proper books of account. In such circumstances any one or more of the officers or former officers of the company in default may be made personally liable for all or part of the debts and other liabilities of the company.

(1) If a company is being wound up and is unable to pay its debts and is in contravention of section 202 and the court considers that the contravention of section 202 has contributed to the company's inability to pay its debts, the court may on the application of the liquidator or any creditor or contributory of the company if it considers it proper declare that any one or more officers and former officers are personally liable, without limitation on liability, for all or part of the debts and other liabilities of the company.

(2) At the hearing of the application the person making the application may himself give evidence or call witnesses.

(3) 'Assignee' is defined for the purposes of the section, which states that where the court makes a declaration it may give such directions as it thinks proper and may make provision for making the liability of any person under the declaration a charge on any debt or obligation or mortgage as the case may be.

(4) The court will not make a declaration under subsection (1) if it considers that a person has taken all reasonable steps to secure compliance by the company under section 202 or had reasonable grounds for believing and did believe that a competent and reliable person was charged with the duty of keeping proper books and was in a position to discharge that duty.

(5) This section will apply irrespective of the fact that the person may be criminally liable in respect of matters on which the declaration is made.

(6) 'Officer' is defined for the purposes of the section.

SECTION 205
Commencement of Part X.

Each of the following provisions, that is to say sections 202 to 204 shall apply as respects the accounts of a company for each financial year of the company beginning or ending after such date after the commencement of the provision as may be specified by the Minister by order.

Definitions
'*company*': Companies Act, 1963, section 2.
'*financial year*': Companies Act, 1963, section 2.
'*Minister*': Companies Act, 1990, section 3.

General Note
This section empowers the Minister to order that sections 202–204 apply as regards the accounts of a company from a specific date after the commencement of the sections themselves.

11

ACQUISITION OF OWN SHARES AND SHARES IN HOLDING COMPANY

This part of the Act permits a company to purchase back its own shares or shares in a holding company, and imposes safeguards to avoid the procedure being abused to the detriment of the shareholder, who would not be privy to the company's affairs. The provisions also permit the company to reissue the shares bought back under certain conditions.

This part will now permit limited companies to issue redeemable shares of any class and not just preference shares. On the redemption of shares the redemption or purchase price must be satisfied at the time of redemption or purchase, and must normally be met out of distributable profits. This will apply not only to the nominal value of the shares purchased or redeemed but also to any premium that is paid on purchase or redemption. Previously on redemption of shares a premium could be met out of a share premium account.

Where a subsidiary company purchases shares in its holding company and within six months the subsidiary goes into liquidation and is unable to pay its debts in full, the court may be asked to make the directors personally liable to refund the purchase price to the subsidiary.

SECTION 206

Interpretation.

In this Part—

"the Act of 1983" means the Companies (Amendment) Act, 1983;

"company" means a company to which section 207 relates;

"distribution" has the meaning assigned to it by section 51 (2) of the Act of 1983 (as amended by section 232 (*d*) and (*e*) of this Act);

"redeemable shares" includes shares which are liable at the option of the company or the shareholder to be redeemed.

Definitions
'*Act of 1983*': Companies Act, 1990, section 206.
'*company*': Companies Act, 1990, section 206.

Acquisition of own shares

'*distribution*': Companies Act, 1990, section 206.
'*redeemable shares*': Companies Act, 1990, section 206.
'*share*': Companies Act, 1963, section 2.

General Note
This section sets out the definitions for this part of the Act.

SECTION 207

Power to issue redeemable shares.

(1) Subject to the provisions of this Part, a company limited by shares or limited by guarantee and having a share capital may, if so authorised by its articles, issue redeemable shares and redeem them accordingly.

(2) The issue and redemption of shares by a company pursuant to subsection (1) shall be subject to the following conditions—

(*a*) No redeemable shares shall be issued or redeemed at any time when the nominal value of the issued share capital which is not redeemable is less than one tenth of the nominal value of the total issued share capital of the company.
(*b*) No such shares shall be redeemed unless they are fully paid.
(*c*) The terms of redemption must provide for payment on redemption.
(*d*) (i) Subject to subparagraph (ii), no such shares shall be redeemed otherwise than out of profits available for distribution.
(ii) Where the company proposes to cancel shares on redemption pursuant to section 208, such shares may also be redeemed out of the proceeds of a fresh issue of shares made for the purposes of redemption.

(*e*) The premium, if any, payable on redemption, must, subject to paragraph (*f*), have been provided for out of the said profits of the company.
(*f*) Where the shares were issued at a premium, any premium payable on their redemption (being a redemption to which paragraph (*d*) (ii) applies) may be paid out of the proceeds of a fresh issue of shares made for the purposes of the redemption, up to an amount equal to—

(i) the aggregate of the premiums received by the company on the issue of the shares redeemed, or
(ii) the current amount of the company's share premium account (including any sum transferred to that account in respect of premiums on the new shares),

whichever is the less, and in any such case the amount of the company's share premium account shall, notwithstanding anything in section 62 (1) of the Principal Act, be reduced by a sum corresponding (or by sums in the aggregate corresponding) to the amount of any payment made by virtue of this paragraph out of the proceeds of the issue of the new shares.

(3) Subject to the provisions of this Part, the redemption of shares may be effected on such terms and in such manner as may be provided by the articles of the company.

Definitions
'*company*': Companies Act, 1990, section 206.
'*Principal Act*': Companies Act, 1990, section 3.

'*redeemable shares*': Companies Act, 1990, section 206.
'*share*': Companies Act, 1963, section 2.

General Note

This section enables companies limited by shares or limited by guarantee and having a share capital to issue redeemable shares and to redeem such shares accordingly, if so permitted by their articles of association.

(1) Companies limited by shares and companies limited by guarantee having a share capital are permitted, if allowed by their articles of association, to issue redeemable shares and to redeem such shares, subject to the provisions of part XI of the Act.

(2) The conditions for the issue and redemption of redeemable shares are as follows:

- no redeemable shares can be issued or redeemed where there are no shares issued that are not redeemable;
- no shares can be redeemed unless fully paid;
- the terms of redemption must provide for payment on redemption;
- no shares may be redeemed otherwise than out of profits available for distribution;
- where it is proposed to cancel shares on redemption, such shares may be redeemed out of the proceeds of a fresh issue made for the purposes of the redemption;
- the premium, if any, payable on redemption must have been provided for out of the profits of the company;
- where the shares were issued at a premium, any premium payable on redemption may be paid out of the proceeds of a fresh issue of shares made for the purposes of the redemption to the aggregate of the premiums received on the issue of the shares redeemed.

(3) The redemption of shares may be made on such terms and in a manner provided by the articles of the company but subject to the provisions of this part of the Act.

SECTION 208
Cancellation of shares on redemption.

Shares redeemed pursuant to this Part may be cancelled on redemption, in which case the following provisions shall apply as respects those shares:

(a) The amount of the company's issued share capital shall be reduced by the nominal value of the shares redeemed but no such cancellation shall be taken as reducing the amount of the company's authorised share capital.

(b) Where the shares are—

(i) redeemed wholly out of the profits available for distribution, or

(ii) redeemed wholly or partly out of the proceeds of a fresh issue and the aggregate amount of those proceeds (disregarding any part of those proceeds used to pay any premium on redemption) is less than the aggregate nominal value of the shares redeemed ("the aggregable difference"),

then a sum equal to, in the case of subparagraph (i), the nominal amount of the shares redeemed and, in the case of subparagraph (ii), the aggregable difference shall be transferred to a reserve fund ("the capital redemption reserve fund") and the provisions of the Principal Act relating to the reduction of the share capital of a company shall, except as provided in this section, apply as if the capital redemption reserve fund were paid-up share capital of the company.

(c) Where a company—

(i) has redeemed and cancelled shares, or

(ii) is about to redeem shares and cancel them upon redemption,

it shall have the power to issue shares up to the nominal amount of the shares redeemed or to be redeemed as if those shares had never been issued and for the purposes of section 68 of the Finance Act, 1973, shares issued by a company in place of shares redeemed under this Part shall constitute a chargeable transaction if, but only if, the actual value of the shares so issued exceeds the actual value of the shares redeemed at the date of their redemption and, where the issue of shares does constitute a chargeable transaction for those purposes, the amount on which stamp duty on the relevant statement relating to that transaction is chargeable under section 69 of the Finance Act, 1973, shall be the difference between—

(I) the amount on which the duty would be so chargeable if the shares had not been issued in place of shares redeemed under this section, and

(II) the value of the shares redeemed at the date of their redemption.

(d) Where new shares are issued before the redemption of the old shares, the new shares shall not, so far as relates to stamp duty, be deemed to have been issued in pursuance of paragraph (c) unless the old shares are redeemed within one month after the issue of the new shares.

(e) The capital redemption reserve fund may, notwithstanding anything in this section, be applied by the company in paying up unissued shares of the company (other than redeemable shares) to be allotted to members of the company as fully paid bonus shares.

Definitions

'company': Companies Act, 1990, section 206.

'Principal Act': Companies Act, 1990, section 3.

'redeemable shares': Companies Act, 1990, section 206.

'share': Companies Act, 1963, section 2.

General Note

This section sets out the procedure for cancellation of shares redeemed in accordance with this part of the Act. In particular it stipulates that shares redeemed may be cancelled and the amount of the company's issued share capital reduced by the nominal value of the shares redeemed, but the authorised capital will remain unchanged.

Where shares are redeemed out of profits available for distribution and/or the proceeds of a fresh issue of shares, a sum equal to the nominal amount of the shares redeemed must be transferred to a capital redemption reserve fund. Furthermore, where a company has redeemed and cancelled shares it has the power to issue shares up to the nominal amount of the shares redeemed as if the shares had never been issued, and the share capital will not be deemed to have been increased for stamp duty purposes. Where new shares are issued before the redemption of the old shares they will be deemed to have been issued in pursuance of paragraph (*c*) of this section for stamp duty purposes unless redeemed within one month after the issue of the new shares. The capital redemption reserve fund may be applied by the company in paying up unissued shares to be allotted to members as fully paid bonus shares.

SECTION 209
Treasury shares.

(1) Subject to the provisions of this section, a company may instead of cancelling shares upon their redemption hold them (as "treasury shares") and shares so held may be dealt with by the company in the manner provided for in subsection (4) but not otherwise.

(2) (*a*) The nominal value of treasury shares held by a company may not, at any one time, exceed ten per cent of the nominal value of the issued share capital of the company.

(*b*) For the purposes of paragraph (*a*), the following shall also be deemed to be shares held by the company—
(i) shares held in the company by any subsidiary in pursuance of section 224, and
(ii) shares held in the company by any subsidiary in pursuance of section 9 of the Insurance Act, 1990, and
(iii) shares held in the company by any person acting in his own name but on the company's behalf.

(3) For so long as the company holds shares as treasury shares—

(*a*) the company shall not exercise any voting rights in respect of those shares and any purported exercise of those rights shall be void; and

(*b*) no dividend or other payment (including any payment in a winding up of the company) shall be payable to the company in respect of those shares.

(4) Treasury shares may either be—

(*a*) cancelled by the company in which case the provisions of section 208 shall apply as if the shares had been cancelled on redemption, or

(*b*) subject to subsections (5) and (6), may be re-issued as shares of any class or classes.

(5) A re-issue of shares under this section shall be deemed for all the purposes of the Companies Acts to be an issue of shares but the issued share capital of the company shall not be regarded for any purpose (including the purposes of any enactments relating to stamp duties) as having been increased by the re-issue of the shares.

(6) (*a*) The maximum and minimum prices at which treasury shares may be re-issued off-market ("the re-issue price range") shall be determined in advance by the company in general meeting in accordance with paragraphs (*b*), (*c*) and (*d*) and such determination may fix different maximum and minimum prices for different shares.

(*b*) Where the treasury shares to be re-issued are derived in whole or in part from shares purchased by the company in accordance with the provisions of this Part the re-issue price range of the whole or such part (as the case may be) of those shares shall be determined by special resolution of the company passed at the meeting at which the resolution authorising the said purchase has been passed and such determination shall, for the purposes of this subsection, remain effective with respect to those shares for the requisite period.

(*c*) Where the treasury shares to be re-issued are derived in whole or in part from shares redeemed by the company in accordance with the provisions of this Part the re-issue price range of the whole or such part (as the case may be) of those shares shall be determined by special resolution of the company passed before any contract for the re-issue of those shares is entered into and such determination shall, for the purposes of this subsection, remain effective with respect to those shares for the requisite period.

(*d*) The company may from time to time by special resolution vary or renew a determination of re-issue price range under paragraph (*b*) or (*c*) with respect to particular treasury shares before any contract for re-issue of those shares is entered into and any such variation or renewal shall, for the purposes of this subsection, remain effective as a determination of the re-issue price range of those shares for the requisite period.

(*e*) (i) For the purposes of determining in this subsection whether treasury shares are re-issued off-market, the provisions of section 212 (off-market and market purchases) shall have effect with the substitution of the words "re-issue", "off-market re-issue" and "re-issued" respectively for the words "purchase", "off-market purchase" and "purchased" in subsection (1) (*a*) of that section.

(ii) In this subsection, "the requisite period" means the period of eighteen months from the date of the passing of the resolution determining the re-issue price range or varying or renewing (as the case may be) such determination or such lesser period of time as the resolution may specify.

(7) A re-issue by a company of treasury shares in contravention of any of the provisions of subsection (6) shall be unlawful.

Definitions

'company': Companies Act, 1990, section 206.

'share': Companies Act, 1963, section 2.

'subsidiary': Companies Act, 1963, section 155.

'treasury share': Companies Act, 1990, section 209.

General Note

This section provides that a company that purchases its own shares may hold them instead of cancelling them. Such shares will be called 'treasury shares', and the section sets out certain conditions regarding these shares.

(1) A company may hold the shares purchased back under this part of the Act, and such shares will be known as treasury shares and will be subject to the provisions of this section.

(2) A limit of 10 per cent of the issued share capital is imposed on the number of treasury shares that can be held at one time. The calculation of the number of treasury shares will include those held by subsidiary companies.

(3) The company may not vote on the treasury shares for so long as it holds such shares, nor pay any dividend on the shares in question, and any attempt to exercise rights under the treasury shares will be void.

(4) Treasury shares may be either cancelled or reissued as shares of any class.

(5) A reissue of shares will be regarded as an issue of shares, and the company will not be regarded as having increased its issued share capital.

(6) The technical provisions concerning the treatment of reissued shares are set out in this subsection.

(7) Any reissue of treasury shares in contravention of subsection (6) is unlawful.

SECTION 210

Power to convert shares into redeemable shares.

(1) Subject to subsections (2), (3), (4) and (5) and the provisions of the Companies Acts governing the variation of right attached to classes of shares and the alteration of a company's memorandum or articles, a company may convert any of its shares into redeemable shares.

(2) A conversion of shares under subsection (1) shall not have effect with respect to any shares, the holder of which notifies the company, before the date of conversion, of his unwillingness to have his shares converted but, subject to that and the other provisions of this section, the conversion shall have effect according to its terms.

(3) Subsection (2) shall not, where a shareholder objects to a conversion, prejudice any right he may have under the Companies Acts or otherwise to invoke the jurisdiction of the court to set aside the conversion or otherwise provide relief in respect thereof.

(4) No shares shall be converted into redeemable shares if as a result of the conversion the nominal value of the issued share capital which is not redeemable would be less than one tenth of the nominal value of the total issued share capital of the company.

(5) The provisions of sections 207, 208 and 209 shall apply to shares which have been converted into redeemable shares under this section.

Definitions

'company': Companies Act, 1990, section 206.
'court': Companies Act, 1990, section 235.
'redeemable share': Companies Act, 1990, section 206.
'share': Companies Act, 1963, section 2.

General Note

This section enables a company to convert any of its shares into convertible shares.

(1) A company is permitted to convert any of its shares into redeemable shares.

(2) A conversion of shares will not have effect if the holder notifies the company before the date of conversion of his unwillingness and withholds his consent or votes against a resolution.

(3) Where a shareholder objects to a conversion, subsection (2) will not prejudice his right under the Companies Acts to apply to the court to set aside the conversion or provide other relief.

(4) No shares can be converted into redeemable shares if as a result of the conversion there are no non-redeemable shares in the company.

(5) Sections 207–209 of the Act apply to shares converted under this section.

SECTION 211

Power of company to purchase own shares.

(1) Subject to the following provisions of this Part, a company may, if so authorised by its articles, purchase its own shares (including any redeemable shares).

(2) Sections 207 (2), 208 and 209 shall apply in relation to the purchase by a company under this section of any of its own shares as those sections apply in relation to the redemption of shares by a company under section 207.

(3) A company shall not purchase any of its shares under this section if as a result of such purchase the nominal value of the issued share capital which is not redeemable would be less than one tenth of the nominal value of the total issued share capital of the company.

Definitions

'*company*': Companies Act, 1990, section 206.
'*redeemable shares*': Companies Act, 1990, section 206.
'*share*': Companies Act, 1963, section 2.

General Note

This section enables a company to purchase back its own shares.

(1) A company may purchase its own shares if permitted to do so by its articles of association.

(2) Sections 207 (2), 208 and 209 of this Act apply to this section.

(3) A company may not purchase back its own shares if as a result of the purchase there would be no member holding shares other than redeemable shares.

SECTION 212
Off-market and market purchases.

(1) For the purposes of sections 213 and 215, a purchase by a company of its own shares is—

(*a*) an "off-market purchase" if the shares are purchased either—
(i) otherwise than on a recognised stock exchange, or
(ii) on a recognised stock exchange but are not subject to a marketing arrangement on that stock exchange,
(*b*) a "market purchase" if the shares are purchased on a recognised stock exchange and are subject to a marketing arrangement.

(2) For the purposes of subsection (1), a company's shares are subject to a marketing arrangement on a recognised stock exchange if either—

(*a*) they are listed on that stock exchange, or
(*b*) the company has been afforded facilities for dealings in those shares to take place on that stock exchange without prior permission for individual transactions from the authority governing that stock exchange and without limit as to the time during which those facilities are to be available.

Definitions

'*company*': Companies Act, 1990, section 206.
'*market purchase*': Companies Act, 1990, section 212.
'*off-market purchase*': Companies Act, 1990, section 212.
'*recognised stock exchange*': Companies Act, 1990, section 3.
'*share*': Companies Act, 1963, section 2.

General Note

The purchase by a company of its own shares under section 211 above can be effected by different procedures, depending on whether it is a purchase by private agreement or by listed shares.

Acquisition of own shares

Which procedure is used will depend on whether it is a 'market' or 'off-market' purchase of shares.

(1) 'Off-market purchase' and 'market purchase' are defined for the purpose of sections 213 and 215.

(2) A company can purchase its own shares only if they are listed on the stock exchange or if the company has been afforded facilities for dealings in the shares to take place on the stock exchange.

SECTION 213

Authority for off-market purchase.

(1) A company shall not make an off-market purchase of its own shares otherwise than in pursuance of a contract authorised in advance in accordance with this section.

(2) The terms of the proposed contract of purchase shall be authorised by special resolution before the contract is entered into and any such authority may be varied, revoked or from time to time renewed by special resolution.

(3) A special resolution under subsection (2) shall not be effective for the purposes of this section if any member of the company holding shares to which the resolution relates exercises the voting rights carried by any of those shares in voting on the resolution and the resolution would not have been passed if he had not done so.

(4) Notwithstanding anything contained in section 137 of the Principal Act or in a company's articles, any member of the company may demand a poll on a special resolution under subsection (2).

(5) A special resolution under subsection (2) shall not be effective unless a copy of the proposed contract of purchase or, if the contract is not in writing, a written memorandum of its terms is available for inspection by members of the company both—

(a) at the registered office of the company for not less than the period of 21 days ending with the date of the meeting at which the resolution is passed, and
(b) at the meeting itself.

(6) Any memorandum of the terms of the contract of purchase made available for the purposes of this section must include the names of any members holding shares to which the contract relates, and any copy of the contract made available for those purposes must have annexed to it a written memorandum specifying any such names which do not appear in the contract itself.

(7) A company may agree to a variation of an existing contract of purchase approved under this section only if the variation is authorised by special resolution of the company before it is agreed to, and subsections (2) to (5) shall apply in relation to that authority save that a copy or memorandum (as the case may require) of the existing contract must also be available for inspection in accordance with subsection (5).

Definitions

'company': Companies Act, 1990, section 206.
'off-market purchase': Companies Act, 1990, section 212.
'Principal Act': Companies Act, 1990, section 3.
'share': Companies Act, 1963, section 2.

General Note

This section imposes a stringent procedure for the purchase of shares by private agreement. It applies to off-market purchases, and in essence requires prior approval of the contract of purchase, within eighteen months of the purchase by a public company, by a special resolution passed by votes other than those attaching to the shares in question. Disclosure of the contract terms must be made fifteen days before the passing of the special resolution.

(1) Off-market purchases require by way of special resolution the prior approval of the contract of purchase, whether a simple contract under this section or a contingent purchase contract. It is not the purchase itself that requires the approval.

(2) The terms of the proposed contract must be approved in advance by a special resolution.

(3) The holder of the shares in question will invalidate the resolution if he votes either on a show of hands or on a poll with the voting rights attached to those shares and the resolution would not have been passed if he had not so voted. He may abstain with those votes, and does not have to vote against the resolution. See *Re Gee* (1948), ch. 284.

(4) Any member of the company can demand a poll on a special resolution under subsection (2).

(5) A copy of the contract or a memorandum of its terms must be made available for inspection at the company's registered office for not less than twenty-one days ending with the date of the meeting, and at the meeting itself.

(6) The memorandum setting out the terms of purchase must include the names of any members holding shares to which the contract relates, and any copy of the contract made available must have included in it a written memorandum of any names that do not appear in the contract itself.

(7) Any proposed variation to a contract of purchase must be authorised in the same way as the original contract, and both the original contract and the terms of the contract varying it must be available for inspection as required by subsection (5).

SECTION 214
Contingent purchase contract

(1) In this section "contingent purchase contract" means a contract entered into by a company and relating to any of its shares which does not amount to a contract to purchase those shares but under which the company may become entitled or obliged to purchase those shares.

(2) A company shall only make a purchase of its own shares in pursuance of a contingent purchase contract if the terms of the contract have been authorised by a special resolution of the company before the contract is entered into and subsections (2) to (7) of section 213 shall apply to such contract and resolution.

Definitions

'*company*': Companies Act, 1990, section 206.
'*contingent purchase contract*': Companies Act, 1990, section 214.
'*share*': Companies Act, 1963, section 2.

General Note

This section applies the off-market purchase procedure to purchases by companies in pursuance of an option to purchase and other forms of contingent purchase contract. As a result each such purchase requires prior disclosure and specific approval by a special resolution. One effect of this is to prevent the purchase of an option on the stock exchange. It will facilitate private companies in negotiating with individual shareholders the right or obligation to acquire shares at a certain time in the future without the need to create a separate class of redeemable shares.

(1) 'Contingent purchase contract' is defined.

(2) A company may only make a purchase of its own shares pursuant to a contingent purchase contract if this has been authorised by a special resolution entered into before the contract is entered into.

SECTION 215
Authority for market purchase.

(1) A company shall not make a market purchase of its own shares unless the purchase has first been authorised by the company in general meeting and any such authority may be varied, revoked or from time to time renewed by the company in general meeting. This subsection shall not be construed as requiring any particular contract for the market purchase of shares to be authorised by the company in general meeting and for the purposes of this Part where a market purchase of shares has been authorised in accordance with this section any

contract entered into pursuant to that authority in respect of such a purchase shall be deemed also to be so authorised.

(2) Section 143 of the Principal Act shall apply to a resolution under subsection (1).

(3) In the case of a public limited company, any authority granted under subsection (1) shall—

(*a*) specify the maximum number of shares authorised to be acquired; and
(*b*) determine both the maximum and minimum prices which may be paid for the shares.

(4) A resolution to which subsection (3) applies may determine either or both the prices mentioned in paragraph (*b*) of that subsection by—

(*a*) specifying a particular sum; or
(*b*) providing a basis or formula for calculating the amount of the price in question without reference to any person's discretion or opinion.

Definitions

'*company*': Companies Act, 1990, section 206.
'*market purchase*': Companies Act, 1990, section 212.
'*Principal Act*': Companies Act, 1990, section 3.
'*public limited company*': Companies (Amendment) Act, 1983, section 2.

General Note

This section sets out the procedure to be adopted by companies exercising the power to purchase their own shares on the stock exchange. Such purchases are known as market purchases.

(1) A company may not purchase its own shares unless it has first obtained authority in general meeting, such authority being capable of being varied or revoked from time to time by general meeting. The company can obtain a general authorisation to purchase its own shares.

(2) Section 143 of the Companies Act, 1963 (Registration of, and obligation of company to supply copies of, certain resolutions and agreements), will apply to this section.

(3) Any authority granted to a public limited company will specify the maximum number of shares authorised to be acquired, together with the maximum and minimum prices to be paid for such shares.

(4) A resolution to which subsection (3) applies may determine either or both the prices to be paid for the shares by setting out a particular sum or formula for calculating the price.

SECTION 216
Duration of authority granted by public limited companies to purchase own shares.

(1) Without prejudice to the generality of sections 213, 214 and 215, in the case of a public limited company, any authority granted under those sections shall specify the date on which the authority is to expire which shall not be later than 18 months after the date on which the special resolution or ordinary resolution, as the case may be, granting the authority is passed.

(2) A public limited company may make a purchase after the expiry of any time limit imposed by virtue of subsection (1) in any case where the contract of purchase was concluded before the authority expired and the terms of the authority permit the company to make a contract of purchase which would or might be executed wholly or partly after the authority expired.

Definitions

'*company*': Companies Act, 1963, section 2.

'*public limited company*': Companies (Amendment) Act, 1983, section 2.

General Note

This section sets out the criteria for specifying the duration of any authority to purchase a company's own shares.

(1) The period during which a company is permitted to purchase its own shares must be specified in the authority given to public limited companies and must not exceed eighteen months from the date on which the resolution is passed.

(2) Where the contract was concluded before the expiry of the specified duration a company may make a purchase even though the shares were purchased after the expiry of the duration period.

SECTION 217
Assignment or release of company's right to purchase own shares.

(1) Any purported assignment of the rights of a company under any contract authorised under section 213, 214 or 215 shall be void.

(2) Nothing in subsection (1) shall prevent a company from releasing its right under any contract authorised under section 213, 214 or 215 provided that, in the case of a contract authorised under section 213 or 214, the release has been authorised by special resolution of the company before the release is entered into, and any such purported release by a company which has not been authorised as aforesaid shall be void.

(3) Subsections (2) to (7) of section 213 shall apply to a resolution under subsection (2).

Definitions

'*company*': Companies Act, 1990, section 206.

General Note

This section prohibits the assignment of a right of a company under any contract to purchase the company's own shares.

(1) Any purported assignment of a right of a company to purchase its own shares is void.

(2) The release of any right is allowed if the purchase was authorised by the off-market procedure or as a contingent purchase contract. Such a release must, however, be approved before the release by a special resolution of the company.

(3) Section 213 (2–7) (Authority for off-market purchase) applies to special resolutions under subsection (2) above.

SECTION 218

Incidental payments with respect to purchase of own shares.

(1) Any payment made by a company in consideration of—

(*a*) acquiring any right with respect to the purchase of its own shares in pursuance of a contract authorised under section 214, or
(*b*) the variation of a contract authorised under section 213 or 214, or
(*c*) the release of any of the company's obligations with respect to the purchase of any of its own shares under a contract authorised under section 213, 214 or 215

shall be unlawful if any such payment is made otherwise than out of distributable profits of the company.

(2) If the requirements of subsection (1) are not satisfied in relation to a contract—

(*a*) in a case to which paragraph (*a*) of that subsection applies, no purchase by the company of its own shares in pursuance of that contract shall be lawful under this Part;
(*b*) in a case to which paragraph (*b*) of that subsection applies, no such purchase following the variation shall be lawful under this Part; and
(*c*) in a case to which paragraph (*c*) of that subsection applies, the purported release shall be void.

Definitions

'*company*': Companies Act, 1990, section 206.

General Note

This section requires any payment made by a company in consideration of acquiring any option to purchase its own shares under a contingent purchase contract, any variation for off-market purchase contract or contingent purchase contract or release from any of its obligations with respect to any authorised purchase to be found from distributable profits. If this requirement is not satisfied the section makes the consequent purchase of shares or release void.

SECTION 219 **Effect of company's failure to redeem or purchase.**	(1) This section applies to—

(*a*) redeemable shares issued after the coming into operation of this Part;

(*b*) shares which have been converted into redeemable shares pursuant to section 210; and

(*c*) shares which a company has agreed to purchase pursuant to section 213, 214 or 215.

(2) Without prejudice to any other right of the holder of any shares to which this section applies a company shall not be liable in damages in respect of any failure on its part to redeem or purchase any such shares.

(3) The court shall not grant an order for specific performance of the terms of redemption or purchase of the shares to which this section applies if the company shows that it is unable to meet the cost of redeeming or purchasing the shares out of profits available for distribution.

(4) Where at the commencement of the winding up of a company any shares to which this section applies have not been redeemed or purchased then, subject to subsections (5), (6) and (7), the terms of redemption or purchase may be enforced against the company and the shares when so redeemed or purchased under this subsection shall be treated as cancelled.

(5) Subsection (4) shall not apply if—

(*a*) the terms of redemption or purchase provided for the redemption or purchase to take place at a date later than that of the commencement of the winding-up, or

(*b*) during the period beginning with the date on which the redemption or purchase was to have taken place and ending with the commencement of the winding-up the company could not at any time have lawfully made a distribution equal in value to the price at which the shares were to have been redeemed or purchased.

(6) There shall be paid in priority to any amount for which the company is liable by virtue of subsection (4) to pay in respect of any shares—

(*a*) all other debts and liabilities of the company other than any due to members in their character as such, and

(*b*) if other shares carry rights, whether as to capital or to income, which are preferred to the rights as to capital attaching to the first mentioned shares, any amount due in satisfaction of those preferred rights,

but subject as aforesaid, any such amount shall be paid in priority to any amounts due to members in satisfaction of their rights (whether as to capital or income) as members.

(7) Where by virtue of the application by section 284 of the Principal Act of the rules of bankruptcy in the winding-up of insolvent companies a creditor of a company is entitled to payment of any interest only after payment of all other debts of the company, the company's debts and liabilities shall for the purposes of subsection (6) include the liability to pay that interest.

Definitions

'company': Companies Act, 1990, section 206.
'court': Companies Act, 1990, section 235.
'Principal Act': Companies Act, 1990, section 3.
'redeemable shares': Companies Act, 1990, section 206.
'share': Companies Act, 1963, section 2.

General Note

This section applies whenever a company fails to implement an agreement to purchase its shares or fails to redeem its shares. It covers such a failure both before a liquidation and on the liquidation of a company.

(1) The section applies to redeemable shares issued after the coming into operation of this part, shares that have been converted into redeemable shares, and shares that a company has agreed to purchase in accordance with sections 213, 214, or 215.

(2) A company is not liable in damages in respect of any failure to redeem or purchase its shares, without prejudice to any other right the holder of the shares may have.

(3) The court will not grant an order of specific performance if the company can show that it is unable to meet the cost of redeeming or purchasing the shares out of profits available for distribution.

(4) If the company is wound up and the date for redemption or purchase has passed, the terms of redemption may be enforced in the liquidation.

(5) Subsection (4) will not apply if the terms of purchase or redemption provide for purchase or redemption to take place at a date later than that of the commencement of the winding up or if between the date of purchase or redemption and the commencement of the winding up the company could not have fulfilled its obligation out of the distributable profits.

(6) Where there is a failure to purchase or redeem in accordance with subsection (4), the amount so claimed is a deferred debt in the liquidation beyond all other creditors and any preference shares' rights, although in priority to other amounts payable to members.

(7) The amount claimed in the winding up of the company is deferred beyond all other debts, even interest on the deferred debt referred to in subsection (6) above.

SECTION 220
Redemption of existing redeemable preference shares.

Section 64 of the Principal Act is hereby repealed but any redeemable preference shares issued by a company limited by shares before the coming into operation of this Part which could but for the repeal of section 64 have been redeemed under that section shall be subject to redemption in accordance with the provisions of this Part save that any premium payable on redemption may, notwithstanding section 207 (2) (*e*) and (*f*), be paid out of the share premium account instead of out of profits or may be paid partly out of that account and partly out of profits available for distribution.

Definitions

'Principal Act': Companies Act, 1990, section 3.

General Note

This section repeals section 64 of the Companies Act, 1963 (Power to issue redeemable preference shares), and provides for the treatment of redeemable preference shares issued before the commencement of this part of the Act.

SECTION 221

Construction of references to redeemable preference shares.

A reference to redeemable preference shares in—

(*a*) section 69 (1) (*e*) of, and the Second, Third, Fourth and Sixth Schedules to, the Principal Act, and
(*b*) section 55 (1) (*h*) of the Act of 1983,

shall be construed as a reference to redeemable shares.

Definitions

'Principal Act': Companies Act, 1990, section 3.
'redeemable shares': Companies Act, 1990, section 206.

General Note

This is a technical section regarding the references to redeemable shares under the Companies Acts, 1963 and 1983.

SECTION 222
Retention and inspection of documents.

(1) Every company which enters into a contract under section 213, 214 or 215 shall, until the expiration of ten years after the contract has been fully performed, keep at its registered office a copy of that contract or, if it is not in writing, a memorandum of its terms.

(2) Every document required to be kept under subsection (1) shall during business hours (subject to such reasonable restrictions as the company in general meeting may impose, so that not less than 2 hours in each day be allowed for inspection) be open to the inspection of any member and, if the company is a public limited company, of any other person.

(3) If a company fails to comply with this section, the company and every officer of the company who is in default shall be guilty of an offence.

(4) In the case of a refusal of an inspection of a document required under subsection (2), the court may, on the application of a person who has requested an inspection and has been refused, by order require the company to allow the inspection of that document.

Definitions

'company': Companies Act, 1990, section 206.

'court': Companies Act, 1990, section 235.

'officer': Companies Act, 1963, section 2.

'public limited company': Companies (Amendment) Act, 1983, section 2.

General Note

This section sets out the period for which contracts and documents must be retained by the company and the conditions for the inspection of such documents.

(1) Every company that enters into a contract under sections 213, 214 or 215 must keep at its registered office a copy of the contract or, if that is not in writing, a memorandum of the terms, for a period of ten years after the completion of performance under the contract.

(2) Every document required to be kept under subsection (1) must be available for a minimum of two hours each business day for inspection by members. In the case of public limited companies such documents are also open for inspection by any other person.

(3) If a company fails to comply with this section the company and every officer in default will be guilty of an offence.

(4) If a company has failed to permit an applicant to inspect the relevant documents the court may require the company to permit inspection by the applicant.

SECTION 223
Application of section 108 (6) to dealings by company in its own securities.

Subsection (6) of section 108, in its application to dealings by a company in its own securities, shall not preclude a company from dealing in its own shares at any time by reason only of information in the possession of an officer of that company if—

(a) the decision to enter into the transaction was taken on its behalf by a person other than the officer, and

(b) the information was not communicated to that person and no advice relating to the transaction was given to him by a person in possession of the information.

Definitions

'company': Companies Act, 1990, section 206.
'officer': Companies Act, 1963, section 2.
'share': Companies Act, 1963, section 2.

General Note

This section stipulates that section 108 (6) (Unlawful dealing in securities by insiders) shall not prevent a company from dealing in its own shares by reason of the fact that an officer of the company had information, if the decision to enter into the transaction was taken on its behalf by another officer and the information was not communicated to that person and no advice relating to the transaction was given to him by someone in possession of the information.

SECTION 224
Holding by subsidiary of shares in its holding company.

(1) Notwithstanding sections 32 and 60 of the Principal Act a company may, subject to the provisions of this section, acquire and hold shares in a company which is its holding company.

(2) The acquisition and holding by a subsidiary under subsection (1) of shares in its holding company shall be subject to the following conditions:

(*a*) The consideration for the acquisition of such shares shall be provided for out of the profits of the subsidiary available for distribution.

(*b*) Upon the acquisition of such shares and for so long as the shares are held by the subsidiary—

(i) the profits of the subsidiary available for distribution shall for all purposes be restricted by a sum equal to the total cost of the shares acquired;

(ii) the shares shall, for the purposes of the consolidated accounts prepared by the holding company in accordance with sections 150 to 152 of the Principal Act, be treated in the same manner as is required in respect of shares held as treasury shares under section 43A of the Act of 1983 (inserted by section 232 (*c*) of this Act); and

(iii) the subsidiary shall not exercise any voting rights in respect of the shares and any purported exercise of those rights shall be void.

(3) A contract for the acquisition (whether by allotment or transfer) by a subsidiary of shares in its holding company shall not be entered into without being authorised in advance both by the subsidiary and its holding company and the provisions of sections 212 to 217 shall apply, with the necessary modifications, to the granting, variation, revocation and release of such authority.

(4) For the purposes of this section, a subsidiary's profits available for distribution shall not include the profits attributable to any shares in the subsidiary for the time being held by the subsidiary's holding company so far as they are profits for the period before the date on or from which the shares were acquired by the holding company.

(5) This section shall not apply to shares held by a subsidiary in its holding company in the circumstances permitted by section 32 of the Principal Act.

(6) This section, except subsection (2) (*b*) (iii), shall not apply to shares subscribed for, purchased or held by a subsidiary in its holding company pursuant to section 9 (1) of the Insurance Act, 1990.

Definitions

'*company*': Companies Act, 1990, section 206.

'*holding company*': Companies Act, 1963, section 155.

'*Principal Act*': Companies Act, 1990, section 3.

'*share*': Companies Act, 1963, section 2.

'*subsidiary*': Companies Act, 1963, section 155.

'*treasury share*': Companies Act, 1990, section 209.

General Note

This section deals with the circumstances where a company acquires and holds shares in its holding company.

(1) A company is permitted to acquire and hold shares in its holding company, subject to sections 32 (Membership of holding company) and 60 (Giving of financial assistance by a company for the purchase of its shares) of the Companies Act, 1963.

(2) The conditions under which a subsidiary may acquire shares in its holding company are set out in this subsection, and include a provision that the consideration for the acquisition of the shares must be provided for out of the subsidiary's profits available for distribution.

(3) A contract for the acquisition of shares by a subsidiary in its holding company must be authorised in advance both by the subsidiary and the holding company.

(4) The subsidiary's profits available for distribution must not include profits attributable to any shares in the subsidiary held by the holding company so far as they are profits for a period before the date on which the shares were acquired by the holding company.

(5) This section does not apply to shares held by a subsidiary in its holding company as permitted by section 32 of the Companies Act, 1963.

(6) This section does not apply to shares subscribed for, purchased or held by a subsidiary in its holding company under section 9 of the Insurance Act, 1990, with the exception of subsection (2) (*b*) (iii) above.

SECTION 225
Civil liability for
improper
purchase in
holding company.

(1) Where the winding-up of a company which has acquired shares in its holding company in accordance with section 224 commences within six months after such acquisition and the company is at the time of the commencement of the winding-up unable to pay its debts (taking into account the contingent and prospective liabilities), the court, on the application of a liquidator, creditor, employee or contributory of the company, may subject to subsection (2), declare that the directors of the company shall be jointly and severally liable to repay to the company the total amount paid by the company for the shares.

(2) Where it appears to the court that any person in respect of whom a declaration has been sought under subsection (1) believed on reasonable grounds that the said purchase was in the best interests of the company, the court may relieve him, either wholly or in part, from personal liability on such terms as it may think fit.

Definitions

'*company*': Companies Act, 1990, section 206.
'*contributory*': Companies Act, 1963, section 2.
'*court*': Companies Act, 1990, section 235.
'*director*': Companies Act, 1963, section 2.
'*holding company*': Companies Act, 1963, section 155.

General Note

This section provides that there may be an action in civil liability where the winding up of a company that has acquired shares in its holding company occurs within six months after the purchase of the shares and the company is unable to pay its debts.

(1) Where a company that has acquired shares in its holding company goes into liquidation within six months of the purchase and is unable to pay its debts, the court may declare that the directors of the company shall be jointly and severally liable to repay to the company the total amount paid by the company for the shares purchased.

(2) The court may grant relief to any person where the person believed on reasonable grounds that the purchase was in the best interests of the company.

SECTION 226
Return to be
made to registrar.

(1) Every company which has purchased shares pursuant to this Part shall, within 28 days after delivery to the company of those shares, deliver to the registrar for registration a return in the prescribed form stating with respect to shares of each class purchased the number and nominal value of those shares and the date on which they were delivered to the company.

(2) In the case of a public limited company, the return shall also state—

(*a*) the aggregate amount paid by the company for the shares, and

(*b*) the maximum and minimum prices paid in respect of each class purchased.

(3) Particulars of shares delivered to the company on different dates and under different contracts may be included in a single return to the registrar, and in such a case the amount required to be stated under subsection (2) (*a*) shall be the aggregate amount paid by the company for all the shares to which the return relates.

(4) If a company fails to comply with the requirements of this section, the company and every officer who is in default shall be guilty of an offence.

(5) Summary proceedings in relation to an offence under this section may be brought and prosecuted by the registrar of companies.

Definitions

'*company*': Companies Act, 1990, section 206.

'*officer*': Companies Act, 1963, section 2.

'*public limited company*': Companies (Amendment) Act, 1983, section 2.

'*registrar of companies*': Companies Act, 1963, section 2.

'*share*': Companies Act, 1963, section 2.

General Note

Every company that purchases or redeems its own shares must submit a return to the Registrar of Companies.

(1) Every company must within twenty-eight days of a purchase of its own shares deliver a statement to the Registrar of Companies on the prescribed form with details of the transaction.

(2) In the case of public limited companies additional information is required.

(3) Particulars of shares delivered on different dates may be included in a single return, and the amount required to be stated will be the aggregate amount paid for the shares.

(4) If a company fails to comply with this section the company and every officer in default will be guilty of an offence.

(5) The Registrar of Companies may bring and prosecute summary proceedings under this section.

SECTION 227

Amendment of section 89 of the Principal Act.

The following section is hereby substituted for section 89 of the Principal Act:

"89.—(1) If a company has created or issued shares in its capital, or acquired any of its shares by a redemption or purchase in purported compliance with Part XI of the Companies Act, 1990, and if there is reason to apprehend that such shares were invalidly created, issued or acquired as aforesaid, the court may, on the application of the company, any holder or former holder of such shares or any member or former member or creditor, or the liquidator, of the company, declare that such creation, issue or acquisition shall be valid for all purposes if the court is satisfied that it would be just and equitable to do so and thereupon such shares shall from the creation, issue or acquisition thereof, as the case may be, be deemed to have been validly created, issued or acquired.

(2) Where shares have been redeemed or purchased in contravention of paragraph (*d*), (*e*) or (*f*) of section 207 (2) or section 207 (3) of the Companies Act, 1990, then the court shall not make a declaration under subsection (1) above in respect of those shares.

(3) The grant of relief by the court under this section shall, if the court so directs, not have the effect of relieving the company or its officers of any liability incurred under section 41 (3) of the Companies (Amendment) Act, 1983.".

Definitions

'*company*': Companies Act, 1990, section 206.

'*court*': Companies Act, 1990, section 235.

'*officer*': Companies Act, 1963, section 2.

'*Principal Act*': Companies Act, 1990, section 3.

'*share*': Companies Act, 1963, section 2.

General Note

This section amends section 89 of the Companies Act, 1963 (Validation of invalid issue, redemption or purchase of shares), so as to take into account the provisions under this part of the Act.

SECTION 228

Regulations as to purchase of shares.

(1) The Minister may make regulations governing the purchase by companies of their own shares or of shares in their holding company and the sale by companies of their own shares held as treasury shares and such regulations may relate to companies in general or to a particular category or class of company.

(2) Without prejudice to the generality of subsection (1), regulations under this section may provide for in particular—

(*a*) the class or description of shares which may (or may not) be purchased or sold,

(*b*) the price at which they may be purchased or sold,

(*c*) the timing of such purchases or sales,

(*d*) the method by which the shares may be purchased or sold, and

(*e*) the volume of trading in the shares which may be carried out by companies.

(3) If a company fails to comply with the provisions of regulations made under this section, the company and every officer who is in default shall be guilty of an offence.

Definitions

'*company*': Companies Act, 1990, section 206.
'*holding company*': Companies Act, 1963, section 155.
'*Minister*': Companies Act, 1990, section 3.
'*officer*': Companies Act, 1963, section 2.
'*share*': Companies Act, 1963, section 2.

General Note

This section enables the Minister for Industry and Commerce to make regulations governing the purchase of its own shares by a company.

(1) The Minister may make regulations governing the purchase by companies of their own shares or of shares in their holding companies.

(2) The specific areas in which the Minister may make regulations are set out.

(3) Where a company fails to comply with the regulations, the company and every officer who is in default will be guilty of an offence.

SECTION 229

Duty of company to notify stock exchange.

(1) Whenever shares for which dealing facilities are provided on a recognised stock exchange have been purchased either by the company which issued the shares or by a company which is that company's subsidiary, the company whose shares have been purchased shall be under an obligation to notify that stock exchange of that matter; and the stock exchange may publish, in such manner as it may determine, any information received by it under this subsection.

(2) An obligation imposed by subsection (1) shall be fulfilled before the end of the day next following that on which it arises.

(3) If default is made in complying with this section, the company and every officer of the company who is in default shall be guilty of an offence.

Definitions

'*officer*': Companies Act, 1963, section 2.
'*recognised stock exchange*': Companies Act, 1990, section 3.
'*share*': Companies Act, 1963, section 2.
'*subsidiary*': Companies Act, 1963, section 155.

Acquisition of own shares

General Note

This section sets out the duty of a company whose shares are dealt in on a recognised stock exchange to notify the stock exchange.

(1) Where a company's shares are dealt in on a recognised stock exchange there is an obligation on the company to notify the stock exchange.

(2) The obligation to notify the stock exchange under subsection (1) must be fulfilled before the end of the day following that on which it arises.

(3) The company and every officer in default of this section will be guilty of an offence.

SECTION 230

Duty of stock exchange in relation to unlawful purchases.

(1) If it appears to a relevant authority of a recognised stock exchange that a company in the case of whose shares dealing facilities have been provided on that stock exchange has committed an offence under section 228 or 229, such authority shall forthwith report the matter to the Director of Public Prosecutions and shall furnish to the Director of Public Prosecutions such information and give to him such access to and facilities for inspecting and taking copies of any documents, being information or documents in the possession or under the control of such authority and relating to the matter in question, as the Director of Public Prosecutions may require.

(2) Where it appears to a member of a recognised stock exchange that any person has committed an offence under section 228 or 229, he shall report the matter forthwith to a relevant authority of the recognised stock exchange concerned, who shall thereupon come under the duty referred to in subsection (1).

(3) If it appears to a court in any proceedings that any person has committed an offence as aforesaid, and that no report relating to the matter has been made to the Director of Public Prosecutions under subsection (1), that court may, on the application of any person interested in the proceedings concerned or of its own motion, direct a relevant authority of the recognised stock exchange concerned to make such a report, and on a report being made accordingly, this section shall have effect as though the report had been made in pursuance of subsection (1).

(4) If, where any matter is reported or referred to the Director of Public Prosecutions under this section, he considers that the case is one in which a prosecution ought to be instituted and institutes proceedings accordingly, it shall be the duty of a relevant authority of the recognised stock exchange concerned, and of every officer of the company whose shares are concerned, and of any other person who appears to the Director of Public Prosecutions to have relevant information (other than any defendant in the proceedings) to give all assistance in connection with the prosecution which he or they are reasonably able to give.

(5) If it appears to the Minister, arising from a complaint to a relevant authority of a recognised stock exchange concerning an alleged offence under section 228 or 229, that there are circumstances suggesting that—

(*a*) the relevant authority ought to use its powers under this section but has not done so, or

(*b*) that a report ought to be made to the Director of Public Prosecutions under subsection (1), but that the relevant authority concerned has not so reported,

he may request the relevant authority to use such powers or make such a report, and on a report being made accordingly, this section shall have effect as though the report had been made in pursuance of subsection (1).

(6) Where the Minister makes a request under subsection (5), the relevant authority concerned shall communicate the results of its investigations, or a copy of its report under subsection (1), as the case may be, to the Minister.

(7) A relevant authority of a recognised stock exchange shall not be liable in damages in respect of anything done or omitted to be done by the authority in connection with the exercise by it of its functions under this section unless the act or omission complained of was done or omitted to be done in bad faith.

(8) For the purposes of this section each of the following shall be a "relevant authority" in relation to a recognised stock exchange—

(i) its board of directors, committee of management or other management body,

(ii) its manager, however described.

(9) A relevant authority shall have the same powers and duties for the purposes of this section as it has under sections 117 and 120.

(10) Where the Minister considers it necessary or expedient to do so for the proper and effective administration of this section, he may make such regulations as he thinks appropriate in relation to—

(*a*) the powers of authorised persons, or

(*b*) the matters in respect of which, or the persons from whom, authorised persons may require information under section 117, as applied by subsection (9).

Definitions

'*company*': Companies Act, 1990, section 206.

'*court*': Companies Act, 1990, section 235.

'*Minister*': Companies Act, 1990, section 3.

'*officer*': Companies Act, 1963, section 2.

'*recognised stock exchange*': Companies Act, 1990, section 3.

'*relevant authority*': Companies Act, 1990, section 230.

'*share*': Companies Act, 1963, section 2.

General Note

This section requires the authorities of the stock exchange to report to the Director of Public Prosecutions if they have reason to believe that the notification requirements have not been complied with.

Acquisition of own shares

(1) The authorities of the stock exchange will notify the Director of Public Prosecutions of any company that it believes has committed an offence under sections 228 or 229 of the Act and will provide access to such documents and information as are in its possession.

(2) Stockbrokers are obliged to notify the stock exchange of any breaches under sections 228 or 229.

(3) If it appears to the court that a person has committed an offence and no report relating to the matter has been made to the Director of Public Prosecutions, the court may direct the authorities of the stock exchange to prepare and submit a report.

(4) The stock exchange and every officer of the company whose shares are concerned must give all reasonable assistance in connection with the institution of proceedings.

(5) Arising from a complaint to the relevant authority of the stock exchange the Minister may request the authorities of the stock exchange to use their powers to make a report covering an alleged offence under sections 228 or 229 of the Act.

(6) Where the Minister has made a request under subsection (5) the authorities of the stock exchange will submit a copy of the report to the Minister.

(7) The authorities of the stock exchange will not be liable for damages for any act done in connection with the exercise of their functions unless the act or omission was done in bad faith.

(8) 'Relevant authority' is defined.

(9) A relevant authority will have the same powers as under sections 117 and 120 of the Act.

(10) The Minister may make regulations concerning the powers of appropriate persons in the effective administration of the section.

SECTION 231

Amendments to the Principal Act in respect of share capital.

(1) The Principal Act is hereby amended—

(a) in section 62 (1) by the insertion after "except as provided in this section" of "and section 207 (2) of the Companies Act, 1990,";
(b) in section 62 (2) by the deletion of "preference" where it first appears and the insertion after "on redemption of any redeemable preference shares" of "in pursuance of section 220 of the Companies Act, 1990,"; and
(c) in section 72 (1) by the deletion of "to purchase any of its shares or".

(2) The Sixth Schedule to the Principal Act is hereby amended by the substitution of the following subparagraph for subparagraph (d) of paragraph 12:

"(d) the amounts respectively provided for purchase of the company's share capital, for redemption of share capital and for redemption of loans;".

Definitions

'Principal Act': Companies Act, 1990, section 3.

General Note

This section makes two technical amendments to section 62 (Application of premiums on issue of shares) of the Companies Act, 1963, which are necessary to take account of the new situation allowing for companies to purchase their own shares provided for by this part of the Act.

SECTION 232

Amendments to the Act of 1983.

The Act of 1983 is hereby amended—

(a) by the substitution in section 41 (4) of the following paragraph for paragraph (a):

"(a) the redemption of preference shares in pursuance of section 65 of the Principal Act or the redemption or purchase of shares in pursuance of Part XI of the Companies Act, 1990;";

(b) by the deletion of section 43 (13);

(c) by the insertion after section 43 of the following new section:

43A.—Where a company or a nominee of a company holds shares in the company or an interest in such shares, such shares shall not be shown in the balance sheet of the company as an asset, but—

(a) the deduction of the cost of the acquired shares from the profits available for distribution, and

(b) the nominal value of such shares,

shall be disclosed in the notes to the accounts and the profits available for distribution shall accordingly be restricted by the amount of such deduction. ";

(d) by the substitution in section 51 (2) of the following paragraph for paragraph (b):

"(b) the redemption of preference shares pursuant to section 65 of the Principal Act out of the proceeds of a fresh issue of shares made for the purposes of redemption;"; and

(e) by the addition of the following paragraph after the paragraph inserted by paragraph (d):

"(bb) the redemption or purchase of shares pursuant to Part XI of the Companies Act, 1990 out of the proceeds of a fresh issue of shares made for the purposes of the redemption or purchase and the payment of any premium out of the company's share premium account on a redemption pursuant to section 220 in the said Part;".

Definitions

'*company*': Companies Act, 1990, section 206.
'*Principal Act*': Companies Act, 1990, section 3.
'*share*': Companies Act, 1963, section 2.

General Note

This section amends the Companies (Amendment) Act, 1983, to make it consistent with the provisions of part XI. Section 41 (4) of the 1983 Act prohibits companies from purchasing their own shares, with certain exceptions. The new section 232 ensures that redemption and purchase of shares are included in the exceptions.

Section 43 (13) of the 1983 Act provides for the accounting treatment of shares held by a public limited company in the company itself, which is necessary to amend the section to provide for part XI.

SECTION 233

Amendments to the Companies (Amendment) Act, 1986.

(1) Section 14 of the Companies (Amendment) Act, 1986, is hereby amended—

(*a*) in paragraph (vi) by the substitution of "acquisition or disposal" for "disposal"; and

(*b*) by the insertion of the following paragraph after paragraph (vi):

"(vii) the reasons for the acquisition, lien or charge, as the case may be.".

(2) Part I of the Schedule to the Companies (Amendment) Act, 1986, is hereby amended—

(*a*) by the deletion in Format 1 of the balance sheet formats of items A.III.7, B. III. 2 and H.IV. 2;

(*b*) by the deletion in Format 2 of the balance sheet formats—
(i) under "Assets", of items A.III.7 and B.III.2 (Assets), and
(ii) under "Liabilities", of item A.IV.2; and

(*c*) by the deletion of note (3) in the notes on the balance sheet formats following the aforesaid formats.

(3) Part IV of the Schedule to the Companies (Amendment) Act, 1986, is hereby amended—

(*a*) by the insertion of the following paragraph after paragraph 32:

"32A. Particulars of any restriction on profits available for distribution by virtue of section 224 (2) (*b*) (i) of the Companies Act, 1990, must also be stated."; and

(*b*) by the substitution of the following subparagraph for subparagraph (3) of paragraph 39:

"(3) The amounts respectively provided for the purchase of the company's share capital, for redemption of share capital and for redemption of loans.".

General Note

This section amends the Companies (Amendment) Act, 1986, to reflect the changes introduced in part XI of the Act to ensure that the annual directors' report includes information on the amounts paid for shares acquired. It also introduces a new requirement that the directors' report show the reasons for the acquisition of the company's own shares or the subjection of shares to a lien or charge.

SECTION 234
Offences under this Part.

(1) A company which contravenes any of the following provisions shall be guilty of an offence, namely sections 207 to 211, 218 and 222 to 224.

(2) Section 241 shall apply to an offence under this Part.

Definitions

'company': Companies Act, 1990, section 206.

General Note

This section makes contraventions of sections 207–211, 218 and 222–224 an offence.

12
GENERAL

This part of the Act deals with a number of miscellaneous provisions, such as ensuring that the company secretary of a public limited company is suitably qualified to carry out the task. There are also amended provisions concerning the qualifications of liquidators and receivers.

This part also deals with penalties that may be imposed for offences committed under the Act, and the liabilities for furnishing false information and for the destruction, falsification or mutilation of documents.

SECTION 235
Amendment of section 2 of the Principal Act.

(1) Unless the context otherwise requires, "the court", used in any provision of the Companies Acts in relation to a company, means—

(a) the High Court, or
(b) where another court is prescribed for the purposes of that provision, that court.

(2) The definition of "the court" in subsection (1) is in substitution for the definition in section 2 (1) of the Principal Act.

Definitions
'court': Companies Act, 1990, section 235.
'Principal Act': Companies Act, 1990, section 3.

General Note
This section amends the definition of 'the court' in section 2 of the Companies Act, 1963, by extending it to include any other court that may be prescribed.

SECTION 236
Qualifications of secretary of public limited company.

It shall be the duty of the directors of a public limited company to take all reasonable steps to secure that the secretary (or each joint secretary) of the company is a person who appears to them to have the requisite knowledge and experience to discharge the functions of secretary of the company and who—

(a) on the commencement of this section held the office of secretary of the company; or
(b) for at least three years of the five years immediately preceding his appointment as secretary held the office of secretary of a company; or
(c) is a member of a body for the time being recognised for the purposes of this section by the Minister; or

(*d*) is a person who, by virtue of his holding or having held any other position or his being a member of any other body, appears to the directors to be capable of discharging those functions.

Definitions

'*director*': Companies Act, 1963, section 2.

'*Minister*': Companies Act, 1990, section 3.

'*public limited company*': Companies (Amendment) Act, 1983, section 2.

General Note

This section imposes a duty on the directors of public limited companies to ensure that the secretary is a person who appears to them to have the requisite knowledge and experience to discharge the functions. The secretary should be a person who held the office at the commencement of this section, or who had been employed as secretary of another company for at least three of the five preceding years, or is a member of a body recognised by the Minister for Industry and Commerce, or is a person whom the directors consider capable of discharging the functions of secretary.

SECTION 237

Qualifications of liquidators and receivers.

(1) The Minister may, if he considers it necessary or expedient to do so in the interests of the orderly and proper regulation of the winding-up of companies generally, by regulations add to the list of persons in section 300A of the Principal Act (inserted by section 146) who shall not be qualified for appointment as liquidator of a company.

(2) The Minister may, if he considers it necessary or expedient to do so in the interests of the orderly and proper regulation of receiverships generally, by regulations add to the list of persons in section 315 of the Principal Act (inserted by section 170) who shall not be qualified for appointment as receiver of the property of a company.

(3) Every regulation made by the Minister under this section shall be laid before each House of the Oireachtas as soon as may be after it is made and, if a resolution annulling the regulation is passed by either House within the next 21 days on which that House has sat after the regulation is laid before it, the regulation shall be annulled accordingly, but without prejudice to the validity of anything previously done thereunder.

Definitions

'*company*': Companies Act, 1963, section 2.

'*Minister*': Companies Act, 1990, section 3.

'*Principal Act*': Companies Act, 1990, section 3.

General Note

This section permits the Minister to amend the list of persons who shall not be qualified for appointment as a liquidator or receiver of a company or of the property of a company. It also sets out the procedure for enabling the Minister to enact any regulations made by him.

SECTION 238
Amendment of section 61 of the Principal Act.

Section 61 of the Principal Act is hereby amended by the insertion after subsection (2) of the following subsection:

"(3) As respects debentures which, under the terms of issue, must be repaid within five years of the date of issue, an offer for subscription or sale to a person whose ordinary business is to buy or sell shares or debentures (whether as principal or agent) shall not be deemed an offer to the public for the purposes of this Part.".

Definitions
'debenture': Companies Act, 1963, section 2.
'Principal Act': Companies Act, 1990, section 3.
'share': Companies Act, 1963, section 2.

General Note

The Companies Act, 1963, adopts different approaches to the requirements for the issue of prospectuses, depending on whether the company concerned is incorporated in or outside the state. In the case of Irish companies section 44 (4) (*b*) provides that the requirements regarding prospectuses need not be complied with in relation to shares or debentures that are not offered to the public. Section 61 goes on to define what constitutes offering shares or debentures to the public.

Section 367 (2) provides that in the case of foreign companies any offer of shares or debentures to any person whose ordinary business is to buy or sell shares or debentures will not be deemed to be an offer to the public. The need for this protection does not arise in respect of certain short-term debentures that are issued to investment professionals, such as the various investment institutions operating from the International Financial Services Centre.

The amendment provides that debentures will include short-term commercial negotiable certificates of deposit and similar instruments.

SECTION 239
Power to make regulations for transfer of securities.

(1) The Minister may make provision by regulations for enabling title to securities to be evidenced and transferred without a written instrument.

(2) In this section—

(*a*) "securities" means shares, stock, debentures, debenture stock, loan stock, bonds, units in undertakings for collective investments in transferable securities within the meaning of the European Communities (Undertakings for Collective Investment in Transferable Securities) Regulations, 1989 (S.I. No. 78 of 1989), and other securities of any description;

(*b*) references to title to securities include any legal or equitable interest in securities; and

(*c*) references to a transfer of title include a transfer by way of security.

(3) The regulations may make provision—

(*a*) for procedures for recording and transferring title to securities, and

(*b*) for the regulation of those procedures and the persons responsible for or involved in their operation, and

(*c*) for dispensing with the obligations of a company under section 86 of the Principal Act to issue certificates and providing for alternative procedures.

(4) The regulations shall contain such safeguards as appear to the Minister appropriate for the protection of investors and for ensuring that competition is not restricted, distorted or prevented.

(5) (*a*) The regulations may for the purpose of enabling or facilitating the operation of the new procedures make provision with respect to the rights and obligations of persons in relation to securities dealt with under the procedures.

(*b*) The regulations shall be framed so as to secure that the rights and obligations in relation to securities dealt with under the new procedures correspond, so far as practicable, with those which would arise apart from any regulations under this section.

(6) (*a*) The regulations may include such supplementary, incidental and transitional provisions as appear to the Minister to be necessary or expedient.

(*b*) In particular, provision may be made for the purpose of giving effect to—
(i) the transmission of title of securities by operation of law;
(ii) any restriction on the transfer of title to securities arising by virtue of the provisions of any enactment or instrument, court order or agreement;
(iii) any power conferred by any such provision on a person to deal with securities on behalf of the person entitled.

(7) The regulations may for the purposes mentioned in this section make provision with respect to the persons who are to be responsible for the operation of the new procedures and for those purposes may empower the Minister to delegate to any person willing and able to discharge them any functions of his under the regulations.

(8) The regulations may make different provision for different cases.

(9) Every regulation made under this section shall be laid before each House of the Oireachtas as soon as may be after it is made and if a resolution annulling the regulation is passed by either such House within the next twenty-one days on which that House has sat after the regulation is laid before it, the regulation shall be annulled accordingly, but without prejudice to the validity of anything previously done thereunder.

Definitions

'*company*': Companies Act, 1963, section 2.
'*debenture*': Companies Act, 1963, section 2.
'*Minister*': Companies Act, 1990, section 3.
'*Principal Act*': Companies Act, 1990, section 3.
'*securities*': Companies Act, 1990, section 239.
'*share*': Companies Act, 1963, section 2.

General Note

This section was introduced on the basis of representations from the stock exchange to facilitate the 'dematerialisation' on the Dublin and London stock exchanges. This is part of the process to reduce the paperwork involved in share transactions of listed companies under the Taurus project.

(1) The Minister may make such regulations as are necessary to enable title to securities to be transferred without a written instrument.

(2) 'Securities' is defined for the purposes of this section.

(3) The regulations made by the Minister may provide for the procedures for recording and transferring title to securities, regulations relating to their operation, and the issue of certificates and alternative procedures.

(4) The Minister may provide such safeguards as are appropriate so as to protect the investors.

(5) This is a technical provision regarding the rights and obligations of persons in relation to the securities to be dealt with under the procedures.

(6) The Minister may make supplementary regulations under this section.

(7) The regulations may make provision regarding the persons who are responsible for operating the new procedures.

(8) The regulations may make different provisions for different circumstances.

(9) This subsection sets out the procedure for the enactment of the regulations published by the Minister under this section.

SECTION 240
Offences.

(1) A person guilty under any provision of the Companies Acts of an offence for which no punishment is specifically provided shall be liable—

(*a*) on summary conviction, to a fine not exceeding £1,000 or, at the discretion of the court, to imprisonment for a term not exceeding 12 months or to both, or

(*b*) on conviction on indictment, to a fine not exceeding £10,000 or, at the discretion of the court, to imprisonment for a term not exceeding 3 years or to both.

(2) A person guilty under any provision of the Companies Acts of an offence made punishable by a fine of an unspecified amount shall be liable—

(*a*) on summary conviction to a fine not exceeding £1,000, or

(*b*) on conviction on indictment, to a fine not exceeding £10,000.

(3) Every offence under the Companies Acts made punishable by a fine not exceeding £1,000 or by imprisonment for a term not exceeding 12 months, or by both, may be prosecuted summarily.

(4) Summary proceedings in relation to an offence under the Companies Acts may be brought and prosecuted by the Director of Public Prosecutions or the Minister.

(5) Notwithstanding section 10 (4) of the Petty Sessions (Ireland) Act, 1851, summary proceedings for an offence under the Companies Acts may be instituted within 3 years from the date of the offence.

(6) Where, in relation to a contravention of any provision of the Companies Acts, it is provided that for continued contravention a person shall be liable to a daily default fine, he shall be guilty of contravening the provision on every day on which the contravention continues after conviction of the original contravention and for each such offence he shall be liable to a fine not exceeding the amount specified in the provision, instead of the penalty specified for the original contravention.

Definitions

'*court*': Companies Act, 1990, section 235.

'*daily default fine*': Companies Act, 1990, section 3.

'*Minister*': Companies Act, 1990, section 3.

General Note

This section deals with offences generally. In addition to the usual provisions this section also stipulates that where it is provided in the Companies Acts that for continued contravention a person will be liable to a daily default fine, he will be guilty of contravening the provision on every day on which the contravention continues after conviction for the original contravention.

SECTION 241
Offences by certain bodies.

(1) Where an offence under section 19, 21, 79 or 242 which is committed by a body to which any such section applies is proved to have been committed with

the consent or connivance of or to be attributable to any neglect on the part of any person being a director, manager, secretary or other officer of the body, or any person who was purporting to act in any such capacity, that person shall also be guilty of an offence under that section.

(2) Where the affairs of a body are managed by its members, subsection (1) shall apply in relation to the acts and defaults of a member in connection with his functions of management as if he were a director or manager of the body.

Definitions

'director': Companies Act, 1963, section 2.

'officer': Companies Act, 1963, section 2.

General Note

This section provides that where offences by a body under certain sections of the Act are proved to have been committed with the consent or connivance of or to be attributable to any neglect on the part of the directors or other officers, such persons will also be guilty of the offence.

SECTION 242
Furnishing false information.

(1) A person who, in purported compliance with any provision of the Companies Acts, answers a question, provides an explanation, makes a statement or produces, lodges or delivers any return, report, certificate, balance sheet or other document false in a material particular, knowing it to be false, or recklessly answers a question, provides an explanation, makes a statement or produces, lodges or delivers any such document false in a material particular shall be guilty of an offence.

(2) Where a person is guilty of an offence under subsection (1) and the court is of opinion that any act, omission or conduct which constituted that offence has—

(*a*) substantially contributed to a company being unable to pay its debts;

(*b*) prevented or seriously impeded the orderly winding-up of the company; or

(*c*) substantially facilitated the defrauding of the creditors of the company or creditors of any other person,

that person shall be liable on conviction on indictment to imprisonment for a term not exceeding 7 years or to a fine not exceeding £10,000 or to both.

Definitions

'company': Companies Act, 1963, section 2.

'court': Companies Act, 1990, section 235.

General note

This section provides that it will be an offence for a person to knowingly or recklessly give false information on the various forms required under the Companies Acts.

Subsection (2) sets out the penalties imposed on a person convicted of an offence under this section.

SECTION 243
Penalisation of destruction, mutilation or falsification of documents.

(1) A person, being an officer of any such body as is mentioned in paragraphs (*a*) to (*e*) of section 19 (1) who destroys, mutilates or falsifies, or is privy to the destruction, mutilation or falsification of any book or document affecting or relating to the property or affairs of the body, or makes or is privy to the making of a false entry therein, shall, unless he proves that he had no intention to defeat the law, be guilty of an offence.

(2) Any such person who fraudulently either parts with, alters or makes an omission in any such book or document, or who is privy to fraudulent parting with, fraudulent altering or fraudulent making of an omission in, any such book or document, shall be guilty of an offence.

Definitions

'*officer*': Companies Act, 1963, section 2.
'*book or document*': Companies Act, 1990, section 3.

General Note

It is an offence to destroy, mutilate or falsify any document relating to a company or to be privy to such an act unless it can be proved that there was no intention to defeat the law. It will also be an offence to fraudulently part with, alter or make an omission in a company's books.

SECTION 244
Increase of penalties.

Sections 125 (2), 126 (4), 127 (2) and 128 (3) of the Principal Act shall have effect as if for the sums mentioned therein there were substituted "£1,000" in each case.

Definitions

'*Principal Act*': Companies Act, 1990, section 3.

General Note

This section revises the fine payable for failure to make the annual return or failure to annex accounts to the annual return. The fine is now increased to £1,000 in each case.

SECTION 245
Amendment of section 12 of Companies (Amendment) Act, 1982.

Section 12 (1) of the Companies (Amendment) Act, 1982 (which relates to failure to make annual returns) is hereby amended by the substitution for "three consecutive years" of "two consecutive years".

General Note

Section 12 (1) of the Companies (Amendment) Act, 1982, is designed to tackle the problem of companies that ignore the requirement to file annual returns. The provision was that if returns were not filed for three consecutive years the Registrar of Companies could have the company struck off the register. This time limit is now changed to two consecutive years.

SECTION 246
Restoration to register of company struck off.

The Principal Act is hereby amended by the insertion after section 311 of the following section—

"311A.—(1) Without prejudice to the provisions of section 311 (8) of this Act and section 12 (6) of the Companies (Amendment) Act, 1982, if a company feels aggrieved by having been struck off the register, the registrar of companies, on an application made in the prescribed form by the company before the expiration of twelve months after the publication in *Iris Oifigiúil* of the notice striking the company name from the register, and provided he has received all annual returns outstanding, if any, from the company, may restore the name of the company to the register.

(2) Upon the registration of an application under subsection (1) and on payment of such fees as may be prescribed, the company shall be deemed to have continued in existence as if its name had not been struck off.

(3) Subject to any order made by the court in the matter, the restoration of the name of a company to the register under this section shall not affect the rights or liabilities of the company in respect of any debt or obligation incurred, or any contract entered into by, to, with or on behalf of, the company between the date of its dissolution and the date of such restoration.".

Definitions

'company': Companies Act, 1963, section 2.
'court': Companies Act, 1990, section 235.
'Principal Act': Companies Act, 1990, section 3.
'registrar of companies': Companies Act, 1963, section 2.

General Note

Section 311 of the Companies Act, 1963, and section 12 of the Companies (Amendment) Act, 1982, provide that the Registrar of Companies may strike off the register dormant companies and companies that fail to make annual returns for two consecutive years, respectively. To reinstate a company requires an application to be made to the High Court. This amendment introduces a new procedure allowing the Registrar to restore companies to the register, provided the application is made within twelve months of the company being struck off and on the payment of the relevant fees.

SECTION 247
System of classification of information.

(1) Where, under the Companies Acts, any information relating to any person is required to be delivered to the registrar of companies and is so received by him, the registrar may apply such system of classification as he considers appropriate to such information and may assign symbols of identification to persons or classes of persons to whom any such information relates.

(2) The Minister may make regulations requiring that the symbol assigned under subsection (1) to any person or persons of any class shall be entered on all documents which, under any provision of the Companies Acts, are required to contain the name of that person.

(3) Regulations under subsection (2) may, in particular, specify particular persons whose duty it shall be to comply or ensure compliance with the regulations.

(4) A person who makes default in complying with regulations under subsection (2) shall be guilty of an offence and liable to a fine.

Definitions

'Minister': Companies Act, 1990, section 3.

'registrar of companies': Companies Act, 1963, section 2.

General Note

This section empowers the Registrar of Companies to classify the information he receives in whatever form he considers desirable. Subsection 2 enables the Minister to make regulations requiring certain forms of classification or symbols of identification to be entered on any relevant company documents.

SECTION 248
Delivery to the registrar of documents in legible form.

(1) This section applies to the delivery to the registrar under any provision of the Companies Acts of documents in legible form.

(2) The document must—

(*a*) state in a prominent position the registered number of the company to which it relates,

(*b*) satisfy any requirements prescribed for the purposes of this section as to the form and content of the document, and

(*c*) conform to such requirements as may be prescribed for the purpose of enabling the registrar to copy the document.

(3) If a document is delivered to the registrar which does not comply with the requirements of this section, he may serve on the person by whom the document was delivered (or, if there are two or more such persons, on any of them) a notice indicating the respect in which the document does not comply.

(4) Where the registrar serves such notice, then, unless a replacement document—

(*a*) is delivered to him within 14 days after the service of the notice, and

(*b*) complies with the requirement of this section or is not rejected by him for failure to comply with those requirements,

the original document shall be deemed not to have been delivered to him.

(5) For the purposes of any provision imposing a penalty for failure to deliver a document, so far as it imposes a penalty for continued contravention, no account shall be taken of the period between the delivery of the original document and the end of the period of 14 days after the service of the registrar's notice under subsection (3).

(6) Regulations made for the purposes of this section may make different provision as to the form and content of the document with respect to different descriptions of document.

(7) Every regulation made under this section shall be laid before each House of the Oireachtas as soon as may be after it is made and if a resolution annulling the regulation is passed by either such House within the next twenty-one days on which that House has sat after the regulation is laid before it, the regulation shall be annulled accordingly, but without prejudice to the validity of anything previously done thereunder.

(8) In this section, "document" includes any periodic account, abstract, statement or return required to be delivered to the registrar.

Definitions
'document': Companies Act, 1990, section 248.
'registrar of companies': Companies Act, 1963, section 2.

General Note
This section allows the Registrar of Companies some control over the delivery of documents to him under the various requirements of the Companies Acts.

(1) The section applies to documents being delivered to the Registrar of Companies in legible form.

(2) The document in legible form must comply with the requirements as set out.

(3) The Registrar may serve a notice on the person who delivers a document if the document does not comply with subsection (2).

(4) Where notice is served and the replacement document is not delivered within fourteen days it will be deemed not to have been delivered.

(5) This is a technical provision concerning penalties.

(6) This is a technical requirement concerning form and content of documents.

(7) This is a technical provision for the enactment of regulations made under this section.

(8) 'Document' is defined for the purposes of this section.

SECTION 249

Delivery to the registrar of documents otherwise than in legible form.

(1) This section applies to the delivery to the registrar under any provision of the Companies Acts of documents otherwise than in legible form (whether by electronic means or otherwise).

(2) Any requirement to deliver a document to the registrar, or to deliver a document in the prescribed form, shall be satisfied by the communication to the registrar of the requisite information in any non-legible form prescribed for the purposes of this section.

(3) Where any document is required to be signed or sealed, it shall instead be authenticated in such manner as may be prescribed for the purposes of this section.

(4) The document must—

(a) contain in a prominent position the registered number of the company to which it relates,

(b) satisfy any requirements prescribed for the purposes of this section, and

(c) be furnished in such manner and conform to such requirements as may be prescribed for the purposes of enabling the registrar to read and copy the document.

(5) If a document is delivered to the registrar which does not comply with the requirements of this section, he may serve on the person by whom the document was delivered (or if there are two or more such persons, on any of them) a notice indicating the respect in which the document does not comply.

(6) Where the registrar serves such notice, then, unless a replacement document—

(a) is delivered to him within 14 days after the service of the notice, and

(b) complies with the requirement of this section or is not rejected by him for failure to comply with those requirements,

the original document shall be deemed not to have been delivered to him.

(7) For the purposes of any provision imposing a penalty for failure to deliver a document, so far as it imposes a penalty for continued contravention, no account shall be taken of the period between the delivery of the original document and the end of the period of 14 days after the service of the registrar's notice under subsection (5).

(8) The Minister may by regulations make further provision with respect to the application of this section in relation to instantaneous forms of communication.

(9) Regulations made for the purpose of this section may make different provision with respect to different descriptions of documents and different forms of communication.

(10) Every regulation made under this section shall be laid before each House of the Oireachtas as soon as may be after it is made and if a resolution annulling the regulation is passed by either such House within the next twenty-one days on which that House has sat after the regulation is laid before it, the regulation shall be annulled accordingly, but without prejudice to the validity of anything previously done thereunder.

(11) In this section, "document" includes any periodic account, abstract, statement or return required to be delivered to the registrar.

Definitions

'document': Companies Act, 1990, section 249.
'Minister': Companies Act, 1990, section 3.
'registrar of companies': Companies Act, 1963, section 2.

General Note

This section sets out the procedure for the delivery of documents in a form other than in writing.

(1) The section applies to documents in a form other than writing.

(2) The requirement for delivering a document is that it be in a form with which the Registrar is satisfied.

(3) Where documents are required to be signed or sealed it must be in a manner prescribed by the Registrar.

(4) The information that must be contained in a document for filing with the Registrar of Companies is set out.

(5) If a document does not comply with the Registrar's requirements he will serve a notice that it does not comply.

(6) Where such a notice is served by the Registrar and a replacement document is not filed within fourteen days it will be deemed not to have been filed.

(7) This is a technical provision regarding penalties.

(8) The Minister may make regulations concerning this section.

(9) The regulations may provide for different forms of communication.

(10) This subsection sets out the procedure for the enactment of the regulations made under this section.

(11) 'Document' is defined for the purposes of this section.

SECTION 250

Amendment of section 377 of, and Ninth Schedule to, the Principal Act.

(1) The Principal Act is hereby amended—

(*a*) by the substitution for section 377 (1) of the following subsection—
"(1) The provisions specified in the Ninth Schedule shall apply to all bodies corporate incorporated in and having a principal place of business in the State, other than those mentioned in subsection (2), as if they were companies registered under this Act and subject to such adaptations and modifications (if any) as may be prescribed.", and

(*b*) by the substitution for the Ninth Schedule of the provisions set out in the Schedule to this Act.

(2) The Minister may, if he considers it necessary to do so in the interests of the orderly and proper regulation of the business of unregistered companies, make regulations adding to, or subtracting from, the list of the provisions of the Companies Acts specified in the Ninth Schedule to the Principal Act.

(3) Every regulation made by the Minister under this section shall be laid before each House of the Oireachtas as soon as may be after it is made and, if a resolution annulling the regulation is passed by either House within the next 21 days on which that House has sat after the regulation is laid before it, the regulation shall be annulled accordingly, but without prejudice to the validity of anything previously done thereunder.

Definitions

'Principal Act': Companies Act, 1990, section 3.

General Note

This section amends the Companies Act, 1963, as regards unregistered companies by imposing certain provisions on such companies.

SECTION 251
Application of certain provisions to companies not in liquidation.

(1) This section applies in relation to a company that is not being wound up where—

(*a*) execution or other process issued on a judgment, decree or order of any court in favour of a creditor of the company is returned unsatisfied in whole or in part; or
(*b*) it is proved to the satisfaction of the court that the company is unable to pay its debts, taking into account the contingent and prospective liabilities of the company, and

it appears to the court that the reason or the principal reason for its not being wound up is the insufficiency of its assets.

(2) The following sections, with the necessary modifications, shall apply to a company to which this section applies, notwithstanding that it is not being wound up—

(*a*) sections 139,140, 203, and 204 of this Act, and
(*b*) the provisions of the Principal Act mentioned in the Table to this section.

(3) References in the sections mentioned in subsection (2) to the commencement of the winding-up of a company, the appointment of a provisional liquidator or the making of a winding up order and to the "relevant date" shall, for the purposes of this section, be construed as references to the date—

(*a*) of the judgment, decree or order mentioned in subsection (1) (*a*); or
(*b*) on which the court determines that the company is unable to pay its debts.

(4) Where, by virtue of this section, proceedings are instituted under section 139, 140 or 204 of this Act or section 245A, 297A or 298 of the Principal Act, section 297A (7) (*b*) of the Principal Act shall apply in relation to any order made as a result of those proceedings.

(5) Where section 295 of the Principal Act is applied by virtue of this section, it shall apply as if the words "which is subsequently ordered to be wound up or

subsequently passes a resolution for voluntary winding-up" were deleted therefrom.

TABLE

Sections of Principal Act to which this section applies

Section	Subject	Comment
243	Inspection of books by creditors and contributories	
245	Power of court to summon persons for examination	Inserted by section 126 of this Act
245A	Order for payment or delivery of property against person examined under section 245	Inserted by section 127 of this Act
247	Power to arrest absconding contributory	
295	Frauds by officers of companies which have gone into liquidation	
297	Criminal liability for fraudulent trading	Inserted by section 137 of this Act
297A	Civil liability for fraudulent trading	Inserted by section 138 of this Act
298	Power of court to assess damages against directors	Amended by section 142 of this Act

Definitions

'company': Companies Act, 1963, section 2.
'court': Companies Act, 1990, section 235.
'Principal Act': Companies Act, 1990, section 3.
'relevant date': Companies Act, 1990, section 251.

General Note

This section applies certain provisions of the Act to companies in respect of which there is an unsatisfied judgment or where it is proved to the court that the company is unable to pay its debts. The provisions to be applied include those on examination of officers and on fraudulent and reckless trading.

13
INVESTMENT COMPANIES

Part XIII of the Act introduces updated legislation concerning investment companies and UCITS, and clarifies the position of the Central Bank in relation to the authorisation of investment companies to commence dealings in shares.

SECTION 252

Interpretation of this Part.

(1) In this Part—

"the Bank" means the Central Bank of Ireland;

"investment company" means a company to which this Part applies and "company" shall be construed accordingly;

"property" means real or personal property of whatever kind (including securities);

"the UCITS Regulations" means the European Communities (Undertakings for Collective Investment in Transferable Securities) Regulations, 1989 (S.I. No. 78 of 1989).

(2) For the purposes of the application by this Part of certain provisions of the UCITS Regulations to investment companies, the said provisions shall be construed as one with the Companies Acts.

Definitions
'Bank': Companies Act, 1990, section 252.
'company': Companies Act, 1990, section 252.
'investment company': Companies Act, 1990, section 252.
'property': Companies Act, 1990, section 252.
'UCITS regulations': Companies Act, 1990, section 252.

General Note
This section defines certain terms for the purpose of this part of the Act.

SECTION 253

Share capital of investment companies

(1) Notwithstanding anything in the Companies Acts, the memorandum of a company to which this Part applies may in respect of the share capital of the company state in lieu of the matters specified in paragraph (a) of section 6 (4) of the Principal Act—

  (a) that the share capital of the company shall be equal to the value for the time being of the issued share capital of the company, and
  (b) the division of that share capital into a specified number of shares without assigning any nominal value thereto,

and the form of memorandum set out in Table B of the First Schedule to the Principal Act or Part I of the Second Schedule to the Companies (Amendment) Act, 1983, as may be appropriate, shall have effect with respect to such company with the necessary modifications.

(2) This Part applies to a company limited by shares (not being a company to which the UCITS Regulations apply)—

(*a*) the sole object of which is stated in its memorandum to be the collective investment of its funds in property with the aim of spreading investment risk and giving members of the company the benefit of the results of the management of its funds; and

(*b*) the articles or memorandum of which provide—

(i) that the actual value of the paid up share capital of the company shall be at all times equal to the value of the assets of any kind of the company after the deduction of its liabilities, and

(ii) that the shares of the company shall, at the request of any of the holders thereof, be purchased by the company directly or indirectly out of the company's assets.

(3) For the purposes of subsection (2) (*b*) (ii), action taken by a company to ensure that the stock exchange value of its shares does not deviate from its net asset value by more than a percentage specified in its articles (which deviation shall not be so specified as greater than 5 per cent) shall be regarded as the equivalent of purchase of its shares by the company.

(4) The memorandum or articles of a company shall be regarded as providing for the matters referred to in paragraphs (*a*) and (*b*) of subsection (2) notwithstanding the inclusion in the memorandum or articles with respect thereto of incidental or supplementary provisions.

(5) In the Companies Acts—

(*a*) a reference to a company limited by shares shall be construed as including an investment company within the meaning of this Part and a reference to a share in, or the share capital of, a company limited by shares shall be construed accordingly, and

(*b*) a reference to the nominal value of an issued or allotted share in, or of the issued or allotted share capital of, a company limited by shares shall be construed, in the case of an investment company, as a reference to the value of the consideration for which the share or share capital (as the case may be) has been issued or allotted.

Definitions

'company': Companies Act, 1990, section 252.

'investment company': Companies Act, 1990, section 252.

'Principal Act': Companies Act, 1990, section 3.

'property': Companies Act, 1990, section 252.

'share': Companies Act, 1963, section 2.

'UCITS regulations': Companies Act, 1990, section 252.

General Note

This section sets out the criteria concerning the share capital of investment companies.

(1) The memorandum of a company to which this part applies may state that the share capital of the company shall be equal to the value for the time being of the issued share capital of the company and that the share capital shall be divided into a specified number of shares without assigning any value to them.

(2) The requirements for a company limited by shares whose object is to be a collective investment company are set out in this subsection.

(3–4) These are technical provisions to comply with the Companies Acts.

SECTION 254
Power of company to purchase own shares.

(1) Subject to subsection (2), the purchase by an investment company of its own shares shall be on such terms and in such manner as may be provided by its articles.

(2) An investment company shall not purchase its own shares unless they are fully paid.

(3) For the avoidance of doubt, nothing in the Companies Acts shall require an investment company to create any reserve account.

Definitions

'*investment company*': Companies Act, 1990, section 252.
'*share*': Companies Act, 1963, section 2.

General Note

This section enables an investment company to purchase its own shares, and there is no obligation on such a company to create any reserve account.

SECTION 255
Treatment of purchased shares.

(1) Shares of an investment company which have been purchased by the company shall be cancelled and the amount of the company's issued share capital shall be reduced by the amount of the consideration paid by the company for the purchase of the shares.

(2) (*a*) Where a company has purchased or is about to purchase any of its own shares, it shall have the power to issue an equal number of shares in place of those purchased and for the purposes of section 68 of the Finance Act, 1973, the issue of those replacement shares shall constitute a chargeable transaction if, but only if, the actual value of the shares so issued exceeds

the actual value of the shares purchased at the date of their purchase and, where the issue of shares does constitute a chargeable transaction for those purposes, the amount on which stamp duty on the relevant statement relating to that transaction is chargeable under section 69 of the Finance Act, 1973, shall be the difference between—

(i) the amount on which the duty would be so chargeable if the shares had not been issued in place of shares purchased under this section, and
(ii) the value of the shares purchased at the date of their purchase.

(*b*) Where new shares are issued before the purchase of the old shares, the new shares shall not, so far as relates to stamp duty, be deemed to have been issued in pursuance of paragraph (*a*) unless the old shares are purchased within one month after the issue of the new shares.

Definitions

'company': Companies Act, 1990, section 252.
'investment company': Companies Act, 1990, section 252.
'share': Companies Act, 1963, section 2.

General Note

This is a technical provision concerning the treatment of shares by an investment company in itself.

(1) An investment company that purchases shares in itself must cancel such shares, and the issued share capital will be reduced by the amount of the consideration paid for the purchase of the shares.

(2) Where a company has purchased or is about to purchase shares in itself it has the power to issue an equal number of shares. Capital duty will only be payable on the new shares issued if the actual value of the shares issued exceeds the actual value of the shares purchased at the date of their purchase.

SECTION 256
Authorisation by Bank.

(1) An investment company shall not carry on business in the State unless it has been authorised to do so by the Bank on the basis of criteria approved by the Minister.

(2) A person shall not carry on business on behalf of an investment company, insofar as relates to the purchase or sale of the shares of the investment company, unless the investment company has been authorised in the manner referred to in subsection (1).

(3) The Bank shall not authorise an investment company to carry on business in the State unless the company has paid up share capital which, in the opinion of the Bank, will be sufficient to enable it to conduct its business effectively and meet its liabilities.

(4) An application by an investment company for the authorisation referred to in subsection (1) shall be made in writing to the Bank and contain such information as the Bank may specify for the purpose of determining the application (including such additional information as the Bank may specify in the course of determining the application).

(5) Where the Bank proposes to grant an authorisation to an investment company under this section and the Bank is satisfied that the company will raise capital by promoting the sale of its shares to the public, the Bank shall, in granting the authorisation, designate the company as an investment company which may raise capital in that manner, and "designated company" in this section and section 257 shall be construed accordingly.

(6) In the event that a designated company does not promote the sale of its shares to the public within a period, not greater than six months, which shall be specified in the authorisation under this section, the company shall, on the expiry of the period so specified, be deemed to have ceased to be a designated company.

(7) An investment company which is not a designated company shall not raise capital by promoting the sale of its shares to the public.

(8) A company incorporated outside the State which, if it were incorporated in the State, would be a company to which this Part applies shall not advertise or market its shares in any way in the State without the approval of the Bank, which approval may be subject to such conditions as the Bank considers appropriate and prudent for the purposes of the orderly and proper regulation of so much of the business of companies of that type as is conducted in the State.

(9) This section is without prejudice to sections 6 and 19 of the Companies (Amendment) Act, 1983.

Definitions

'*Bank*': Companies Act, 1990, section 252.
'*designated company*': Companies Act, 1990, section 256.
'*investment company*': Companies Act, 1990, section 252.
'*Minister*': Companies Act, 1990, section 3.

General Note

This section stipulates that an investment company must not carry on business in the state unless it has been authorised to do so by the Central Bank and that if it is to do so it must have such paid-up share capital as in the opinion of the Central Bank will be sufficient to enable it to conduct its business and meet its liabilities.

(1) An investment company must obtain the approval of the Central Bank before carrying on business in the state.

(2) A person must not carry on business on behalf of an investment company in relation to the purchase or sale of shares of an

investment company unless the investment company has been authorised under subsection (1) above.

(3) The Central Bank will not authorise an investment company to carry on business unless it is of the opinion that the paid-up share capital is sufficient to enable it to conduct its business effectively and to meet its liabilities.

(4) An application for authorisation must be made to the Central Bank in writing and must include such information as may be required by the bank.

(5) This is a technical provision on the granting of the authorisation by the Central Bank.

(6) The investment company must promote the sale of its shares within six months of the authorisation or it will be deemed to have ceased to be a designated company.

(7) An investment company that is not a designated company must not promote the sale of its shares to the public.

(8) An investment company incorporated outside the state must not advertise or market its shares unless authorised to do so by the Central Bank.

(9) This section is without prejudice to sections 6 (Restriction on commencement of business by a public limited company) and 19 (Meaning of 'authorised minimum') of the Companies (Amendment) Act, 1983.

SECTION 257
Powers of Bank.

(1) Notwithstanding any other powers which may be available to the Bank under any other enactment, order or regulation, the Bank may impose such conditions for the granting of an authorisation to a company under section 256 as it considers appropriate and prudent for the purposes of the orderly and proper regulation of the business of investment companies.

(2) Conditions imposed under subsection (1) may be imposed generally, or by reference to particular classes of company or business (including, but not limited to, whether or not an investment company is a designated company), or by reference to any other matter the Bank considers appropriate and prudent for the purposes of the orderly and proper regulation of the business of investment companies.

(3) The power to impose conditions referred to in subsection (1) shall include a power to impose such further conditions from time to time as the Bank considers appropriate and prudent for the purposes of the orderly and proper regulation of the business of investment companies.

(4) Without prejudice to the generality of subsections (1), (2) and (3), conditions imposed by the Bank on an investment company may make provision for any or all of the following matters—

(*a*) the prudential requirements of the investment policies of the company,
(*b*) prospectuses and other information disseminated by the company,
(*c*) the vesting of the assets or specified assets of the company in a person nominated by the Bank with such of the powers or duties of a trustee with regard to the company as are specified by the Bank,
(*d*) such other supervisory and reporting requirements and conditions relating to its business as the Bank considers appropriate and prudent to impose on the company from time to time for the purposes referred to in the aforesaid subsections.

(5) A company shall comply with any conditions relating to its authorisation or business imposed by the Bank.

Definitions

'Bank': Companies Act, 1990, section 252.
'company': Companies Act, 1990, section 252.
'investment company': Companies Act, 1990, section 252.

General Note

This section allows the Central Bank to impose conditions for the granting of an authorisation to investment companies. Under subsection (2) the bank can impose conditions generally or by reference to specific classes of company or business; this can enable it to discriminate between different types of investment company.

(1) The Central Bank has the power to impose additional conditions other than those in section 256 on the authorisation of investment companies.

(2) Conditions imposed under subsection (1) may be imposed generally or by reference to particular circumstances.

(3) The Central Bank has the power to impose conditions in addition to those imposed under subsection (1) if it is considered appropriate and prudent.

(4) This subsection sets out a list of matters the Central Bank will have regard to in considering the imposition of conditions on an investment company.

(5) An investment company must comply with the conditions imposed by the Central Bank.

SECTION 258
Adaptation of certain provisions of UCITS Regulations.

Regulations 14, 30, 63, 83 (2) to (7), and 99 to 105 of the UCITS Regulations shall apply to an investment company as they apply to the bodies to which those Regulations relate subject to the following modifications—

(*a*) a reference in those Regulations to a term or expression specified in the second column of the Table to this section at any reference number shall be construed, where the context admits, as a reference to the term or expression specified in the third column of the said Table at that reference number, and

(*b*) references to cognate terms or expressions in those Regulations shall be construed accordingly.

TABLE

Ref. No. (1)	Term or expression referred to in UCITS Regulations (2)	Construction of term or expression for purposes of this section (3)
1.	"repurchase"	"purchase"
2.	"these Regulations"	"Part XIII of the Companies Act, 1990"
3.	"UCITS"	"investment company"
4.	"unit"	"share"
5.	"unit-holder"	"shareholder"

Definitions

'investment company': Companies Act, 1990, section 252.
'UCITS regulations': Companies Act, 1990, section 252.

General Note

This section is designed to adapt certain of the UCITS regulations to the investment company requirements under the provisions of this part of the Act.

SECTION 259
Default of investment company or failure in performance of its investments.

An authorisation by the Bank under section 256 of an investment company shall not constitute a warranty by the Bank as to the creditworthiness or financial standing of that company and the Bank shall not be liable by virtue of that authorisation or by reason of its exercise of the functions conferred on it by this Part (or any regulations made under this Part) in relation to investment companies for any default of the company unless the Bank acted in bad faith in exercising such functions.

Definitions

'Bank': Companies Act, 1990, section 252.
'investment company': Companies Act, 1990, section 252.

General Note

This section stipulates that the granting of an authorisation does not constitute a warranty by the Central Bank as to the creditworthiness of an investment company and that the Central Bank will not be liable for the default of any company unless the bank had acted in bad faith.

SECTION 260
Restriction of certain provisions of Companies Acts.

(1) None of the following provisions of the Principal Act shall apply to an investment company, namely sections 60, 69, 70, 72, 119 and 125.

(2) None of the following provisions of the Companies (Amendment) Act, 1983, shall apply to an investment company, namely sections 5 (2), 23 to 25, 40, 41 and Part IV.

(3) Section 14 of the Companies (Amendment) Act, 1986, shall not apply to an investment company.

(4) None of the following provisions of this Act shall apply to an investment company, namely Chapters 2 to 4 of Part IV, and Part XI.

Definitions

'investment company': Companies Act, 1990, section 252.

General Note

This section clarifies which sections of the Companies Acts are applicable to investment companies.

SECTION 261
Power to make supplementary regulations.

The Minister may make such regulations as he considers necessary for the purposes of giving full effect to the provisions of this Part.

Definitions

'Minister': Companies Act, 1990, section 3.

General Note

This section allows the Minister for Industry and Commerce to make supplementary regulations in connection with investment companies.

SECTION 262
Offences.

Where a company contravenes—

(*a*) any of the provisions of this Part, or
(*b*) any regulations made in relation thereto (whether under this Part or under any other enactment), or
(*c*) any condition in relation to its authorisation or business imposed by the Bank under section 257,

the company and every officer thereof who is in default shall be guilty of an offence.

Definitions

'Bank': Companies Act, 1990, section 252.
'company': Companies Act, 1990, section 252.
'officer': Companies Act, 1963, section 2.

General Note

This section sets out the offences that apply to investment companies in this part of the Act.

SCHEDULE

"NINTH SCHEDULE

PROVISIONS APPLIED TO UNREGISTERED COMPANIES

PRINCIPAL ACT

Subject matter	Provisions applied
Acts done by company (*ultra vires* rule).	Section 8.
Pre-incorporation contracts.	Section 37 (1) and (2).
Prospectuses and allotments.	Sections 43 to 52, 56, 57, 61 and the Third Schedule.
Registered office .	Section 113 (inserted by the Companies (Amendment) Act, 1982).
Annual Return.	Sections 125 to 129 and the Fifth Schedule.
Accounts and Audit.	Sections 148 to 153, 155 to 161, 191 and the Sixth Schedule (except subparagraphs (*a*) to (*d*) of paragraph 2, sub-paragraphs (*c*) to (*e*) of paragraph 3 and subparagraph (*d*) of paragraph 8), as amended by the Companies (Amendment) Act, 1986
Validity of acts of directors.	Section 178.
Register of directors and secretaries. Particulars relating to directors to be shown on all business letters of the company.	Sections 195 (inserted by the Companies Act, 1990) and 196.
Registration of documents, enforcement and other supplemental matters.	Sections 2, 193, 369 to 371, 378, 379, 383, 384, 386, 387, 395 (1) and the Eighth Schedule.
Liability of officers and others for negligence etc.	Sections 200 and 391.

COMPANIES (AMENDMENT) ACT, 1977

Subject matter	Provisions applied
Share certificates.	Sections 2 and 3.
Company records.	Section 4.

COMPANIES (AMENDMENT) ACT, 1983

Subject matter	Provisions applied
Maintenance of capital. Restrictions on distribution of profits and assets.	Sections 40 to 42, 45, 45A (inserted by the Companies (Amendment) Act, 1986) and 49 to 51.
	Sections 43, 44, 46 and 47, with the modification that those sections shall apply to all bodies corporate to which section 377 (1) of the Principal Act applies other than those which, if they were registered, would be private companies.

EUROPEAN COMMUNITIES (STOCK EXCHANGE) REGULATIONS, 1984
(S.I. No. 282 of 1984)

Provisions applied
All of the Regulations.

COMPANIES (AMENDMENT) ACT, 1986

Subject matter	Provisions applied
Power to alter form of accounts.	Section 24.

EUROPEAN COMMUNITIES (MERGERS AND DIVISIONS OF COMPANIES) REGULATIONS, 1987
S.I. No. 137 of 1987)

Provisions applied
All of the Regulations.

COMPANIES (AMENDMENT) ACT, 1990

Provisions applied
The whole Act.

COMPANIES ACT, 1990

Provisions applied

Parts I to III.

Part IV, with the modification that Chapter 2 of that Part shall apply to all bodies corporate to which section 377 (1) of the Principal Act applies other than those which if they were registered, would be private companies and Chapter 3 of that Part shall apply to all such bodies corporate which, if they were registered, would be private companies.

Part V.

Part VI, except sections 122, 128 to 131 and 133.

Parts VII, IX, X and XII.

THE COMPANIES (AMENDMENT) ACT, 1990

This Act introduces into company law a new legal mechanism for the rescue or reconstruction of ailing but potentially viable companies. The central feature of this new concept is the appointment by the court of an examiner and the placing of the particular company or group of companies under the protection of the court for a period of three months. For as long as the company is so protected it may not be wound up, a receiver may not be appointed, debts cannot be executed against it, and no security can be enforced against it.

If the examiner considers that the company or group of companies or part of it can be saved and that this would be more advantageous than a winding up, he is required to prepare a draft rescue plan. This rescue plan will be put to the appropriate meetings of members and creditors and, if agreed, put to the court for confirmation. Should the court approve the plan it will become binding on those concerned, and the examiner's appointment will be terminated.

SECTION 1

Definitions.

In this Act, unless the context otherwise requires—

"the Companies Acts" means the Principal Act, and every enactment (including this Act) which is to be construed as one with that Act;

"examiner" means an examiner appointed under section 2;

"interested party", in relation to a company to which section 2 (1) relates, means—

(a) a creditor of the company,
(b) a member of the company;

"the Minister" means the Minister for Industry and Commerce;

"the Principal Act" means the Companies Act, 1963.

Definitions

'Companies Acts': Companies (Amendment) Act, 1990, section 1.
'company': Companies Act, 1963, section 2.
'examiner': Companies (Amendment) Act, 1990, section 1.
'interested party': Companies (Amendment) Act, 1990, section 1.
'Minister': Companies (Amendment) Act, 1990, section 1.
'Principal Act': Companies (Amendment) Act, 1990, section 1.

The Companies (Amendment) Act, 1990

General Note

This section defines various terms used in this Act.

SECTION 2

Power of court to appoint examiner.

(1) Where it appears to the court that—

(a) a company is or is likely to be unable to pay its debts, and
(b) no notice of a resolution for the winding-up of the company has been given under section 252 of the Principal Act more than 7 days before the application hereinafter referred to, and
(c) no order has been made for the winding-up of the company,

it may, on application by petition presented, appoint an examiner to the company for the purpose of examining the state of the company's affairs and performing such duties in relation to the company as may be imposed by or under this Act.

(2) Without prejudice to the general power of the court under subsection (1), it may, in particular, make an order under this section if it considers that such order would be likely to facilitate the survival of the company, and the whole or any part of its undertaking, as a going concern.

(3) For the purposes of this section, a company is unable to pay its debts if—

(a) it is unable to pay its debts as they fall due,
(b) the value of its assets is less than the amount of its liabilities, taking into account its contingent and prospective liabilities, or
(c) section 214 (a) or (b) of the Principal Act applies to the company.

(4) In deciding whether to make an order under this section the court may also have regard to whether the company has sought from its creditors significant extensions of time for the payment of its debts, from which it could reasonably be inferred that the company was likely to be unable to pay its debts.

Definitions

'company': Companies Act, 1963, section 2.
'court': Companies Act, 1990, section 235.
'examiner': Companies (Amendment) Act, 1990, section 1.
'Principal Act': Companies (Amendment) Act, 1990, section 1.

General Note

This section sets out the powers of the High Court in the appointment of an examiner for the purpose of examining the state of a company's affairs and performing such other duties as may be imposed on him in this part of the Act.

(1) The High Court has discretion in the appointment of an examiner, and it may appoint one where it appears that

(a) the company is or is likely to be unable to pay its debts,
(b) no notice has been inserted in *Iris Oifigiúil* under section 252 of the Companies Act, 1963, more than seven days before the application for the appointment of an examiner, and

(*c*) no winding-up order has been made.

(2) The court may make an order for the appointment of an examiner for the purpose of examining the state of a company's affairs and performing such other duties as may be imposed by the Act if it considers that this would be likely to facilitate the survival of the company as a going concern. Section 181 (1) (*a*) of the Companies Act, 1990, amended this subsection by providing that the examiner should not be capable of being appointed once an actual resolution to wind up a company has been passed.

(3) A company is considered to be unable to pay its debts if it is unable to pay them as they fall due, or if the value of the assets is less than the amount of its liabilities, taking into account prospective or contingent liabilities, or if section 214 (*a*) or (*b*) of the Companies Act, 1963 (Circumstances in which a company is unable to pay its debts), applies.

(4) The court will take into consideration whether the company has sought arrangements or extensions from its creditors from which it could be inferred that the company was unable to pay its debts: see *Crowley* v. *Northern Bank Finance Corp.* [1981] IR 353.

SECTION 3

Petition for protection of the court.

(1) Subject to subsection (2), a petition under section 2 may be presented by—

(*a*) the company, or
(*b*) the directors of the company, or
(*c*) a creditor, or contingent or prospective creditor (including an employee), of the company, or
(*d*) members of the company holding at the date of the presentation of a petition under that section not less than one tenth of such of the paid-up capital of the company as carries at that date the right of voting at general meetings of the company,

or by all or any of those parties, together or separately.

(2) (*a*) Where the company referred to in section 2 is an insurer, a petition under that section may be presented only by the Minister, and subsection (1) of this section shall not apply to the company.
(*b*) Where the company referred to in section 2 is the holder of a licence under section 9 of the Central Bank Act, 1971, or any other company supervised by the Central Bank under any enactment, a petition under section 2 may be presented only by the Central Bank, and subsection (1) of this section shall not apply to the company.

(3) A petition presented under section 2 shall—

(*a*) nominate a person to be appointed as examiner, and
(*b*) be supported by such evidence as the court may require for the purpose of showing that the petitioner has good reason for requiring the appointment of an examiner, and

(*c*) where the petition is presented by any person or persons referred to in subsection (1) (*a*) or (*b*), include a statement of the assets and liabilities of the company (in so far as they are known to them) as they stand on a date not earlier than 7 days before the presentation of the petition.

(4) A petition presented under section 2 shall be accompanied—

(*a*) by a consent signed by the person nominated to be examiner, and
(*b*) if proposals for a compromise or scheme of arrangement in relation to the company's affairs have been prepared for submission to interested parties for their approval, by a copy of the proposals.

(5) The court shall not give a hearing to a petition under section 2 presented by a contingent or prospective creditor until such security for costs has been given as the court thinks reasonable, and until a *prima facie* case for the protection of the court has been established to the satisfaction of the court.

(6) The court shall not give a hearing to a petition under section 2 if a receiver stands appointed to the company the subject of the petition and such receiver has stood so appointed for a continuous period of at least 14 days prior to the presentation of the petition.

(7) On hearing a petition under this section, the court may dismiss it, or adjourn the hearing conditionally or unconditionally, or make any interim order, or any other order it thinks fit.

(8) Without prejudice to the generality of subsection (7), an interim order under that subsection may restrict the exercise of any powers of the directors or of the company (whether by reference to the consent of the court or otherwise).

(9) (*a*) Where it appears to the court that the total liabilities of the company (taking into account its contingent and prospective liabilities) do not exceed £250,000, the court may, after making such interim or other orders as it thinks fit, order that the matter be remitted to the judge of the Circuit Court in whose circuit the company has its registered office or principal place of business.
(*b*) Where an order is made by the court under this subsection the Circuit Court shall have full jurisdiction to exercise all the powers of the court conferred by this Act in relation to the company and every reference to the court in this Act shall be construed accordingly.
(*c*) Where, in any proceedings under this Act which have been remitted to the Circuit Court by virtue of this subsection, it appears to the Circuit Court that the total liabilities of the company exceed £250,000, it shall make, after making such interim orders as it thinks fit, an order transferring the matter to the court.

Definitions

'*company*': Companies Act, 1963, section 2.

'*court*': Companies Act, 1990, section 235.

'*director*': Companies Act, 1963, section 2.

'*examiner*': Companies (Amendment) Act, 1990, section 1.

'*Minister*': Companies (Amendment) Act, 1990, section 1.

General Note

Where an examiner is appointed the company will be deemed to be under the protection of the court for a period of three months from the date of the presentation of the petition. For so long as the company has this protection no proceedings may be commenced and no resolution passed for winding up, no receiver may be appointed, no execution may be put into force against the company, and no action may be taken to realise any security against the company or other person who may be liable for the debts of the company. In addition no order for relief may be made under section 205 of the Companies Act, 1963, and no proceedings in relation to the company may be commenced except by leave of the court.

(1) A petition for protection may be presented by any or all of the following:
- the company;
- the directors of the company (it is worth noting that under the Companies Act, 1963, the directors as such do not have power to petition for the winding up of a company);
- a creditor, contingent creditor, or prospective creditor;
- members of the company holding at the date of the presentation of the petition 10 per cent or more of the shares carrying voting rights at general meetings.

(2) Where a company that is the subject of an application is an insurer, a petition may be presented only by the Minister for Industry and Commerce or, in the case of a body holding a licence under section 9 of the Central Bank Act, only by the Central Bank.

(3) The petition must nominate an examiner and must be supported by evidence to demonstrate to the court that an examiner should be appointed. This could be difficult in the case of an unsecured creditor, who would not normally know much of the company's affairs.

(4) The petition must be accompanied by the consent in writing of the examiner and proposals for a compromise or scheme of arrangement if one has been prepared.

(5) The court will not give a hearing to a petition presented by a contingent or prospective creditor until security for such court costs as the court shall consider reasonable has been given and a prima facie case for court protection has been established to the court's satisfaction.

The Companies (Amendment) Act, 1990

(6) The court will not hear a petition under section 2 if a receiver has been appointed for a continuous period of at least three days before the presentation of the petition. The period within which an examiner could be appointed after a company had gone into receivership was fourteen days but this was reduced to three days under section 180 of the Companies Act, 1990.

(7) The court may dismiss, adjourn or make an interim order on a petition or any other order as it thinks fit.

(8) The court may grant an interim order restricting the exercise of any powers of the directors.

(9) The court may order the matter to be referred to the Circuit Court after making an interim or other order where the total liabilities do not exceed £250,000. In such a case the Circuit Court will have full jurisdiction to exercise the powers conferred under the Act.

SECTION 4
Related companies.

(1) Where the court appoints an examiner to a company, it may, at the same or any time thereafter, make an order—

(*a*) appointing the examiner to be examiner for the purposes of this Act to a related company, or

(*b*) conferring on the examiner, in relation to such company, all or any of the powers or duties conferred on him in relation to the first-mentioned company.

(2) In deciding whether to make an order under subsection (1), the court shall have regard to whether the making of the order would be likely to facilitate the survival of the company, or of the related company, or both, and the whole or any part of its or their undertaking, as a going concern.

(3) A related company to which an examiner is appointed shall be deemed to be under the protection of the court for the period beginning on the date of the making of an order under this section and continuing for the period during which the company to which it is related is under such protection.

(4) Where an examiner stands appointed to two or more related companies, he shall have the same powers and duties in relation to each company, taken separately, unless the court otherwise directs.

(5) For the purposes of this Act, a company is related to another company if—

(*a*) that other company is its holding company or subsidiary; or

(*b*) more than half in nominal value of its equity share capital (as defined in section 155 (5) of the Principal Act) is held by the other company and companies related to that other company (whether directly or indirectly, but other than in a fiduciary capacity); or

(*c*) more than half in nominal value of the equity share capital (as defined in section 155 (5) of the Principal Act) of each of them is held by members of the other (whether directly or indirectly, but other than in a fiduciary capacity); or (*d*) that other company or a company or companies related to that other company or that other company together with a company or companies related to it are entitled to exercise or control the exercise of more than one half of the voting power at any general meeting of the company; or

(*e*) the businesses of the companies have been so carried on that the separate business of each company, or a substantial part thereof, is not readily identifiable; or

(*f*) there is another company to which both companies are related;

and "related company" has a corresponding meaning.

(6) For the purposes of this section "company" includes any body which is liable to be wound up under the Companies Acts.

Definitions

'*body corporate*': Companies Act, 1963, section 2 (3).
'*company*': Companies (Amendment) Act, 1990, section 4.
'*court*': Companies Act, 1990, section 235.
'*examiner*': Companies (Amendment) Act, 1990, section 1.
'*holding company*': Companies Act, 1963, section 155.
'*related company*': Companies (Amendment) Act, 1990, section 4.
'*subsidiary*': Companies Act, 1963, section 155.

General Note

The purpose of this section was to simplify the petitioning process where a company that is the subject of a petition is a member of a group of companies by giving the court flexibility at the outset. The court will make an order protecting the related company when it is of the opinion that such an order would 'facilitate the survival of the company, or of the related company, or both, and the whole or any part of its or their undertaking, as a going concern.' Thus all of a group of companies can benefit from court protection.

(1) Where an examiner has been appointed to a company the court may appoint the examiner to be examiner of a related company or confer on the examiner with regard to the related company all the powers and/or duties he possesses regarding the company to which he had been appointed examiner.

(2) In deciding whether to make an order under subsection (1) the court will take into account whether it would facilitate the survival of the company or a related company and the undertaking of the whole group or part of the group as a going concern.

(3) If a related company has an examiner appointed by the court it will be deemed to be under court protection from the making of the order and for the period during which the first company is under protection.

(4) Where an examiner is appointed to two or more related companies he will have the same powers and duties in relation to each company taken separately unless otherwise directed by the court.

(5) This subsection sets out a wide definition for a 'related company'. Section 181 (1) (*b*) of the Companies Act, 1990, amended this subsection by substituting the term 'body corporate' for 'company'. The purpose of the amendment is to enable a relationship to be shown between two Irish companies whose parent is registered abroad.

(6) 'Company' is defined for the purposes of this section.

SECTION 5
Effect of petition to appoint examiner on creditors and others.

(1) During the period beginning with the presentation of a petition for the appointment of an examiner to a company and (subject to section 18 (3) or (4)) ending on the expiry of three months from that date or on the withdrawal or refusal of the petition, whichever first happens, the company shall be deemed to be under the protection of the court.

(2) For so long as a company is under the protection of the court in a case under this Act, the following provisions shall have effect—

(*a*) no proceedings for the winding-up of the company may be commenced or resolution for winding-up passed in relation to that company and any resolution so passed shall be of no effect;

(*b*) no receiver over any part of the property or undertaking of the company shall be appointed, or, if so appointed before the presentation of a petition under section 2, shall, subject to section 6, be able to act;

(*c*) no attachment, sequestration, distress or execution shall be put into force against the property or effects of the company, except with the consent of the examiner;

(*d*) where any claim against the company is secured by a charge on the whole or any part of the property, effects or income of the company, no action may be taken to realise the whole or any part of such security, except with the consent of the examiner;

(*e*) no steps may be taken to repossess goods in the company's possession under any hire-purchase agreement (within the meaning of section 11 (8)), except with the consent of the examiner; ·

(*f*) where, under any enactment, rule of law or otherwise, any person other than the company is liable to pay all or any part of the debts of the company—

(i) no attachment, sequestration, distress or execution shall be put into force against the property or effects of such person in respect of the debts of the company, and

(ii) no proceedings of any sort may be commenced against such person in respect of the debts of the company.

(3) Subject to subsection (2), no other proceedings in relation to the company may be commenced except by leave of the court and subject to such terms as the court may impose and the court may on the application of the examiner make such order as it thinks proper in relation to any existing proceedings including an order to stay such proceedings.

(4) Complaints concerning the conduct of the affairs of the company while it is under the protection of the court shall not constitute a basis for the making of an order for relief under section 205 of the Principal Act.

Definitions

'*company*': Companies Act, 1963, section 2.

'*court*': Companies Act, 1990, section 235.

'*examiner*': Companies (Amendment) Act, 1990, section 1.

'*Principal Act*': Companies (Amendment) Act, 1990, section 1.

General Note

This section restricts the rights of the creditors once a petition for protection has been presented to the court. From that point no petition can be presented for the winding up of the company and no sequestration of property or repossession of goods etc. put into force.

(1) From the time of the presentation of a petition to appoint an examiner to a company and for a period of three months from that date, or on the withdrawal or refusal of the petition, whichever occurs first, such company will be deemed to be under the protection of the court.

(2) The restrictions imposed on creditors for the time during which the company is under court protection are set out. Section 180 (1) (*b*) of the Companies Act, 1990, amended this subsection by the addition of paragraph (*g*), which provides that no act may be taken by shareholders under section 205 of the Companies Act, 1963, while the company is under court protection for anything done by the directors before the appointment of the examiner. Section 181 (1) (*c*) of the Companies Act, 1990, amended this subsection by the addition of paragraph (*h*), which is intended to tackle the means by which creditors, particularly banks, could bypass the restrictions imposed by section 5 (2) of the Act by using the practice of 'set-off'.

This would arise where customers operated separate accounts and agreed to the bank using the funds in one account to offset on an automatic basis the shortfall in another.

(3) Subject to the provisions of subsection (2), no other proceedings may be commenced in relation to the company except by leave of the court and subject to the terms imposed by it. The court may also make such orders as it thinks proper in relation to any existing proceedings.

(4) Any complaints concerning the conduct of the affairs of a company while under examination will not be a basis for relief under section 205 of the Companies Act, 1963 (Remedies in case of oppression).

SECTION 6
Effect on receiver or provisional liquidator of order appointing examiner.

(1) Where the court appoints an examiner to a company and a receiver stands appointed to the whole or any part of the property or undertaking of that company the court may make such order as it thinks fit including an order as to any or all of the following matters—

(a) that the receiver shall cease to act as such from a date specified by the court,

(b) that the receiver shall, from a date specified by the court, act as such only in respect of certain assets specified by the court,

(c) directing the receiver to deliver all books, papers and other records, which relate to the property or undertaking of the company (or any part thereof) and are in his possession or control, to the examiner within a period to be specified by the court,

(d) directing the receiver to give the examiner full particulars of all his dealings with the property or undertaking of the company.

(2) Where the court appoints an examiner to a company and a provisional liquidator stands appointed to that company, the court may make such order as it thinks fit including an order as to any or all of the following matters—

(a) that the provisional liquidator be appointed as examiner of the company,

(b) appointing some other person as examiner of the company,

(c) that the provisional liquidator shall cease to act as such from the date specified by the court,

(d) directing the provisional liquidator to deliver all books, papers and other records, which relate to the property or undertaking of the company or any part thereof and are in his possession or control, to the examiner within a period to be specified by the court,

(e) directing the provisional liquidator to give the examiner full particulars of all his dealings with the property or undertaking of the company.

(3) In deciding whether to make an order under subsection (1) (a) or (b), or subsection (2) (c), the court shall have regard to whether the making of the order would be likely to facilitate the survival of the company, and the whole or any part of its undertaking, as a going concern.

(4) Where the court makes an order under subsection (1) or (2), it may, for the purpose of giving full effect to the order, include such conditions in the order and make such ancillary or other orders as it deems fit.

(5) Where a petition is presented under section 2 in respect of a company at a date subsequent to the presentation of a petition for the winding-up of that company, but before a provisional liquidator has been appointed or an order made for its winding-up, both petitions shall be heard together.

Definitions

'company': Companies Act, 1963, section 2.

'court': Companies Act, 1990, section 235.

'examiner': Companies (Amendment) Act, 1990, section 1.

General Note

This section applies to a situation where either a receiver or a provisional liquidator has been appointed to a company and the company is subsequently put under the protection of the court.

(1) Where a receiver has been appointed to a company and subsequently the court appoints an examiner, the court may order that the receiver

(*a*) cease to act from a date specified by the court (this seems to freeze the receivership for the duration of the examination),

(*b*) act only in relation to certain assets,

(*c*) deliver books, records etc. to the examiner within a period specified by the court, or

(*d*) give full details of his dealings with the assets of the company.

The appointment of the receiver will have given rise to the crystallisation of a relevant floating charge, and preferential creditors will have been triggered. The appointment of an examiner as such does not create a class of preferential creditors.

(2) Where a provisional liquidator has been appointed to a company, and subsequently the court appoints an examiner, the court may order that the provisional liquidator be appointed the examiner, or that he cease to act from a specified date and/or pass all books and documents to the examiner and/or give full details of all his dealings with the property to the examiner.

(3) In deciding whether to make an order the court will take into account matters that are likely to facilitate the survival of the company. The phrase 'likely' is used on a regular basis in this legislation. It also appears in similar legislation in the UK; and in *Re*

Primlaks (U.K.) Ltd. [1989] 5 BCC 710 it was held that the word meant that 'there was a real prospect of survival'.

(4) In making an order the court will include such conditions as it thinks fit.

(5) If there is an existing petition to wind up the company when the protection petition is filed, both petitions will be heard together.

SECTION 7
Powers of an
examiner.

(1) Any provision of the Companies Acts relating to the rights and powers of an auditor of a company and the supplying of information to and co-operation with such auditor shall, with the necessary modifications, apply to an examiner.

(2) Notwithstanding any provision of the Companies Acts relating to notice of general meetings, an examiner shall have power to convene, set the agenda for, and preside at meetings of the board of directors and general meetings of the company to which he is appointed and to propose motions or resolutions and to give reports to such meetings.

(3) An examiner shall be entitled to reasonable notice of, to attend and be heard at, all meetings of the board of directors of a company and all general meetings of the company to which he is appointed.

(4) For the purpose of subsection (3) "reasonable notice" shall be deemed to include a description of the business to be transacted at any such meeting.

(5) Where an examiner becomes aware of any actual or proposed act, omission, course of conduct, decision or contract, by or on behalf of the company to which he has been appointed, its officers, employees, members or creditors or by any other person in relation to the income, assets or liabilities of that company which, in his opinion, is or is likely to be to the detriment of that company, or any interested party, he shall, subject to the rights of parties acquiring an interest in good faith and for value in such income, assets or liabilities, have full power to take whatever steps are necessary to halt, prevent or rectify the effects of such act, omission, course of conduct, decision or contract.

(6) The examiner may apply to the court to determine any question arising in the course of his office, or for the exercise in relation to the company of all or any of the powers which the court may exercise under this Act, upon the application to it of any member, contributory, creditor or director of a company.

(7) The examiner shall, if so directed by the court, have power to ascertain and agree claims against the company to which he has been appointed.

Definitions

'auditor': this is not defined in the Companies Acts; but see the UK case *R.* v. *Shacter* [1960] 2 QB 252.

'company': Companies Act, 1963, section 2.

'contributory': Companies Act, 1963, section 2.

'court': Companies Act, 1990, section 235.

'director': Companies Act, 1963, section 2.

'*examiner*': Companies (Amendment) Act, 1990, section 1.
'*interested party*': Companies (Amendment) Act, 1990, section 1.
'*officer*': Companies Act, 1963, section 2.
'*reasonable notice*': Companies (Amendment) Act, 1990, section 7.

General Note

This section provides that the examiner shall have all the powers of a company inspector and company auditor as regards the obtaining of information. He has the power to convene, set the agenda for and preside at board meetings and general meetings of the company and to propose motions or resolutions to such meetings. He has power to take the necessary steps to halt, prevent or rectify the effects of any act, omission, course of conduct or decision that he considers likely to be to the detriment of the company. He also has power to make changes in the direction and management of the company.

(1) The examiner has the same powers as the company auditor and inspector.

(2) The examiner has power to convene board and general meetings, set the agenda, preside at such meetings, propose motions or resolutions, and give reports to such meetings.

(3) The examiner is entitled to reasonable notice to attend, and to be heard at, all board meetings and general meetings of the company to which he is appointed.

(4) 'Reasonable notice' is defined for the purposes of the section.

(5) The examiner has power, subject to certain conditions, to take the necessary steps to halt, prevent or rectify the effects of any act, omission, course of conduct or decision, actual or proposed, that in his opinion is or is likely to be to the detriment of the company or any interested party.

(6) The examiner may apply to the court for directions in relation to the exercise of powers or to determine any question arising in the course of his office.

(7) The examiner, if directed by the court, has the power to ascertain and agree claims against the company.

SECTION 8
Production of documents and evidence.

(1) It shall be the duty of all officers and agents of the company or a related company to produce to the examiner all books and documents of or relating to any such company which are in their custody or power, to attend before him when required so to do and otherwise to give to him all assistance in connection with his functions which they are reasonably able to give.

(2) If the examiner considers that a person other than an officer or agent of any such company is or may be in possession of any information concerning its affairs, he may require that person to produce to him any books or documents in his custody or power relating to the company, to attend before him and otherwise to give him all assistance in connection with his functions which he is reasonably able to give; and it shall be the duty of that person to comply with the requirement.

(3) If the examiner has reasonable grounds for believing that a director, or past director, of any such company maintains or has maintained a bank account of any description, whether alone or jointly with another person and whether in the State or elsewhere, into or out of which there has been paid—

(*a*) any money which has resulted from or been used in the financing of any transaction, arrangement or agreement particulars of which have not been disclosed in the accounts of any company for any financial year as required by law; or

(*b*) any money which has been in any way connected with any act or omission, or series of acts or omissions, which on the part of that director constituted misconduct (whether fraudulent or not) towards that company or its members;

the examiner may require the director to produce to him all documents in the director's possession, or under his control, relating to that bank account; and in this subsection "bank account" includes an account with any person exempt by virtue of section 7 (4) of the Central Bank Act, 1971, from the requirement of holding a licence under section 9 of that Act.

(4) An examiner may examine on oath, either by word of mouth or on written interrogatories, the officers and agents of such company or other person as is mentioned in subsection (1) or (2) in relation to its affairs and may—

(*a*) administer an oath accordingly,

(*b*) reduce the answers of such person to writing and require him to sign them.

(5) If any officer or agent of such company or other person refuses to produce to the examiner any book or document which it is his duty under this section so to produce, refuses to attend before the examiner when required so to do or refuses to answer any question which is put to him by the examiner with respect to the affairs of the company, the examiner may certify the refusal under his hand to the court, and the court may thereupon enquire into the case and, after hearing any witnesses who may be produced against or on behalf of the alleged offender and any statement which may be offered in defence, punish the offender in like manner as if he had been guilty of contempt of court.

(6) In this section, any reference to officers or to agents shall include past, as well as present, officers or agents, as the case may be, and "agents", in relation to a company, shall include the bankers and solicitors of the company and any persons employed by the company as auditors, whether those persons are or are not officers of the company.

Definitions

'agent': Companies (Amendment) Act, 1990, section 8.

'auditor': this is not defined in the Companies Acts; but see the UK case *R.* v. *Shacter* [1960] 2 QB 252.

'bank account': Companies (Amendment) Act, 1990, section 8.

'books and documents': Companies Act, 1990, section 3.

'company': Companies Act, 1963, section 2.

'court': Companies Act, 1990, section 235.

'director': Companies Act, 1963, section 2.

'examiner': Companies (Amendment) Act, 1990, section 1.

'officer': Companies Act, 1963, section 2.

General Note

This section imposes an obligation on all officers and agents of a company to produce all books and documents to the examiner so as to enable him to undertake the examination.

(1) It is a duty of all officers and agents of a company (including bankers and solicitors to the company) to produce all books and documents relating to the company when required to do so and to give all assistance as may be reasonably required.

(2) If the examiner considers that a person other than an officer or agent is or may be in possession of information concerning the company's affairs he may require that person to produce the documents or to attend before him so as to assist him in the examination.

(3) On having reasonable grounds for believing that any director or past director ('past director' was inserted by section 180 (1) (*c*) of the Companies Act, 1990) maintains or has maintained a bank account, whether alone or in association with someone else, used for transactions that were not disclosed in the accounts of the company or into or out of which any money that has been in any way connected with any act or omission that constituted misconduct towards the company or its members was paid, the examiner may require the director to produce all documents in his possession or control relating to the bank account. This provision was amended by section 180 (1) (*d*) of the Companies Act, 1990, to widen the scope of the enquiry to ensure that full information could be obtained in relation to bank accounts operated not only by directors but also by people connected with them and by shadow directors.

(4) An examiner has power to examine on oath, either orally or in writing, the officers and agents of the company or other person.

(5) If any person, including an agent or officer, refuses to produce to the examiner any documents or books or refuses to attend or answer questions put to him in respect of the affairs of the company the examiner may certify the refusal to the court, and after a hearing the court may hold such person to be in contempt of court.

(5A) This subsection was inserted by section 180 (1) (*e*) of the Companies Act, 1990, and covers a situation where the examiner fails to obtain the information or the responses to questions and reports the matter to the court. It enables the court to make an order that the person attend the court to answer questions or produce the books required.

(6) The terms 'officer' and 'agent' are defined for the purpose of this section.

SECTION 9
Further powers of court.

(1) Where it appears to the court, on the application of the examiner, that, having regard to the matters referred to in subsection (2), it is just and equitable to do so, it may make an order that all or any of the functions or powers which are vested in or exercisable by the directors (whether by virtue of the memorandum or articles of association of the company or by law or otherwise) shall be performable or exercisable only by the examiner.

(2) The matters to which the court is to have regard for the purpose of subsection (1) are—

(*a*) that the affairs of the company are being conducted, or are likely to be conducted, in a manner which is calculated or likely to prejudice the interests of the company or of its employees or of its creditors as a whole, or
(*b*) that it is expedient, for the purpose of preserving the assets of the company or of safeguarding the interests of the company or of its employees or of its creditors as a whole, that the carrying on of the business of the company by, or the exercise of the powers of, its directors or management should be curtailed or regulated in any particular respect, or
(*c*) that the company, or its directors, have resolved that such an order should be sought, or
(*d*) any other matter in relation to the company the court thinks relevant.

(3) Where the court makes an order under subsection (1), it may, for the purpose of giving full effect to the order, include such conditions in the order and make such ancillary or other orders as it sees fit.

(4) Without prejudice to the generality of subsections (1) and (3), an order under this section may provide that the examiner shall have all or any of the powers that he would have if he were a liquidator appointed by the court in respect of the company and, where such order so provides, the court shall have all the powers that it would have if it had made a winding-up order and appointed a liquidator in respect of the company concerned.

Definitions

'*company*': Companies Act, 1963, section 2.

'*court*': Companies Act, 1990, section 235.

'*director*': Companies Act, 1963, section 2.

'*examiner*': Companies (Amendment) Act, 1990, section 1.

General Note

This section gives further powers to the court in relation to the examiner. In particular, the examiner may apply to the court to have the powers and/or functions of the directors vested in the examiner. The court may grant such powers if it considers it just and equitable to do so.

(1) The examiner may apply to the court to have the powers and/or functions of the directors vested in himself. The court may grant such powers if it considers it just and equitable to do so having regard to the circumstances of the case.

(2) Among the circumstances the court will have regard to for the purpose of subsection (1) are

(*a*) that the affairs of the company are being conducted in a manner likely to prejudice the interests of the company or employees or creditors as a whole,

(*b*) that it is expedient that the powers of the directors or management be curtailed in order to preserve the assets or safeguard the interests of the company, employees, or creditors, or

(*c*) that the company or directors seek a court order.

(3) The court may make such order as it sees fit.

(4) The court is empowered to give the examiner all the powers of a court-appointed liquidator. If it so orders, the court will have all the powers it would have if it made a winding-up order and appointed a liquidator.

SECTION 10
Incurring of certain liabilities by examiner.

(1) Where an order is made under this Act for the winding-up of the company or a receiver is appointed, any liabilities incurred by the company during the protection period which are referred to in subsection (2) shall be treated as expenses properly incurred, for the purpose of section 29, by the examiner.

(2) The liabilities referred to in subsection (1) are those certified by the examiner at the time they are incurred, to have been incurred in circumstances where, in the opinion of the examiner, the survival of the company as a going concern during the protection period would otherwise be seriously prejudiced.

(3) In this section, "protection period" means the period, beginning with the appointment of an examiner, during which the company is under the protection of the court.

Definitions

'company': Companies Act, 1963, section 2.

'court': Companies Act, 1990, section 235.

'examiner': Companies (Amendment) Act, 1990, section 1.

'protection period': Companies (Amendment) Act, 1990, section 10.

General Note

This section is designed to ensure that a company under the protection of the court will be able to continue to trade while it is under protection. It ensures the continuity of supply by ranking any post-protection debts certified by the examiner as essential for the survival of the company as an expense of the examiner, which must be paid before any other debts, even preferential ones, in the event of the company being subsequently wound up or a receiver being appointed, subject to a minor amendment under section 180 (1) (*f*) of the Companies Act, 1990.

(1) Any liabilities incurred by the company during the protection period as referred to in subsection (2) will be treated by the examiner as being properly incurred under section 29 where an order is made for the winding up or on the appointment of a receiver.

(2) The liabilities referred to in subsection (1) are those incurred where otherwise the survival of the company would have been seriously prejudiced.

(3) 'Protection period' is defined for the purpose of this section.

SECTION 11
Power to deal with charged property, etc.

(1) Where, on an application by the examiner, the court is satisfied that the disposal (with or without other assets) of any property of the company which is subject to a security which, as created, was a floating charge or the exercise by the examiner of his powers in relation to such property would be likely to facilitate the survival of the whole or any part of the company as a going concern, the court may by order authorise the examiner to dispose of the property, or exercise his powers in relation to it, as the case may be, as if it were not subject to the security.

(2) Where, on an application by the examiner, the court is satisfied that the disposal (with or without other assets) of—

(*a*) any property of the company subject to a security other than a security to which subsection (1) applies, or

(*b*) any goods in the possession of the company under a hire-purchase agreement,

would be likely to facilitate the survival of the whole or any part of the company as a going concern, the court may by order authorise the examiner to dispose of the property as if it were not subject to the security or to dispose of the goods as if all rights of the owner under the hire-purchase agreement were vested in the company.

(3) Where property is disposed of under subsection (1), the holder of the security shall have the same priority in respect of any property of the company directly or indirectly representing the property disposed of as he would have had in respect of the property subject to the security.

(4) It shall be a condition of an order under subsection (2) that—

(*a*) the net proceeds of the disposal, and

(*b*) where those proceeds are less than such amount as may be determined by the court to be the net amount which would be realised on a sale of the property or goods in the open market by a willing vendor, such sums as may be required to make good the deficiency,

shall be applied towards discharging the sums secured by the security or payable under the hire-purchase agreement.

(5) Where a condition imposed in pursuance of subsection (4) relates to two or more securities, that condition requires the net proceeds of the disposal and, where paragraph (*b*) of that subsection applies, the sums mentioned in that paragraph to be applied towards the sums secured by those securities in the order of their priorities.

(6) An office copy of an order under subsection (1) or (2) in relation to a security shall, within 7 days after the making of the order, be delivered by the examiner to the registrar of companies.

(7) If the examiner without reasonable excuse fails to comply with subsection (6), he shall be liable to a fine not exceeding £1,000.

(8) References in this section to a hire-purchase agreement include a conditional sale agreement, a retention of title agreement and an agreement for the bailment of goods which is capable of subsisting for more than 3 months.

Definitions

'*company*': Companies Act, 1963, section 2.

'*court*': Companies Act, 1990, section 235.

'*examiner*': Companies (Amendment) Act, 1990, section 1.

'*registrar of companies*': Companies Act, 1963, section 2.

General Note

This section, based on section 15 of the UK Insolvency Act, 1986, permits the examiner with the approval of the court to dispose of property subject to a fixed charge as if it were not so subject, but to account to the chargeholder for the proceeds.

(1) Where the court agrees with the examiner that the disposal or other treatment by the examiner of property that is subject to a floating charge would be likely to lead to the survival of the company as a going concern, it may allow the examiner to do so as if the property were not the subject of a charge.

(2) Where the court agrees with the examiner that the disposal of any property that is the subject of a fixed security or goods in possession under a hire purchase agreement would be likely to lead to the survival of the company as a going concern, the court may allow the examiner to do so as if the property were not the subject of a charge.

(3) Where property is disposed of under subsection (1) the holder of the floating charge will nevertheless retain his priority rights over the property involved.

(4) The net proceeds of the disposal and the deficiency between the net proceeds and the price on the 'open market' under subsection (2) will be applied towards discharging the sums secured by the security or payable under the hire purchase agreement.

(5) Where there are two or more securities the sums will be applied to the securities in the order of their priorities. Section 181 (1) (*d*) of the Companies Act, 1990, amended this subsection by inserting the word 'discharging' after 'towards' in line 4.

(6) A copy of the order made under subsection (1) or (2) must be delivered by the examiner to the Registrar of Companies within seven days of the making of the order.

(7) If the examiner fails to comply with subsection (6) without reasonable excuse he will be liable to a fine not exceeding £1,000.

(8) Hire purchase agreements are defined for the purpose of the section.

SECTION 12
Notification of appointment of examiner.

(1) Where a petition is presented under section 2, notice of the petition in the prescribed form shall, within 3 days after its presentation, be delivered by the petitioner to the registrar of companies.

(2) (*a*) An examiner shall, within the time limits specified in paragraph (*b*), cause to be published in *Iris Oifigiúil* and in at least two daily newspapers circulating in the district in which the registered office or principal place of business of the company is situate a notice of—
(i) his appointment and the date thereof, and

(ii) the date, if any, set for the hearing of the matters arising out of the report to be prepared by the examiner under section 15.

(*b*) The time limits referred to in paragraph (*a*) are—

(i) twenty-one days after his appointment in the case of *Iris Oifigiúil*, and

(ii) three days after his appointment in the other case referred to in that paragraph.

(3) An examiner shall, within three days after his appointment, deliver to the registrar of companies a copy of the order appointing him.

(4) Where a company is, by virtue of section 5, deemed to be under the protection of the court, every invoice, order for goods or business letter issued by or on behalf of the company, being a document on or in which the name of the company appears, shall contain the statement "under the protection of the court".

(5) A person who fails to comply with the provisions of this section shall be guilty of an offence and shall be liable, on summary conviction, to a fine not exceeding £1,000 and, on conviction on indictment, to a fine not exceeding £10,000.

Definitions

'company': Companies Act, 1963, section 2.

'court': Companies Act, 1990, section 235.

'examiner': Companies (Amendment) Act, 1990, section 1.

'registrar of companies': Companies Act, 1963, section 2.

General Note

This section sets out the publicity requirements concerning the appointment of an examiner.

(1) The Registrar of Companies must be notified of the presentation of a petition to appoint an examiner within three days after its presentation.

(2) When the examiner has been appointed he must insert a notice of his appointment in *Iris Oifigiúil* and at least two daily newspapers circulating in the district where the registered office or principal place of business is situated. In the case of *Iris Oifigiúil* the notice must be published within twenty-one days and in the case of newspapers within three days.

(3) An examiner must notify the Registrar of Companies within three days of his appointment

(4) The phrase 'under the protection of the court' must appear on every invoice, order for goods, and business letter.

(5) The penalties for failure to comply with the section are set out.

SECTION 13

General provisions as to examiners.

(1) An examiner may resign or, on cause shown, be removed by the court.

(2) If for any reason a vacancy occurs in the office of examiner, the court may by order fill the vacancy.

(3) An application for an order under subsection (2) may be made by—

(*a*) any committee of creditors established under section 21, or
(*b*) the company or any interested party.

(4) An examiner shall be described by the style of "the examiner" of the particular company in respect of which he is appointed and not by his individual name.

(5) The acts of an examiner shall be valid notwithstanding any defects that may afterwards be discovered in his appointment or qualification.

(6) An examiner shall be personally liable on any contract entered into by him in the performance of his functions (whether such contract is entered into by him in the name of the company or in his own name as examiner or otherwise) unless the contract provides that he is not to be personally liable on such contract, and he shall be entitled in respect of that liability to indemnity out of the assets; but nothing in this subsection shall be taken as limiting any right to indemnity which he would have apart from this subsection, or as limiting his liability on contracts entered into without authority or as conferring any right to indemnity in respect of that liability.

(7) A company to which an examiner has been appointed or an interèsted party may apply to the court for the determination of any question arising out of the performance or otherwise by the examiner of his functions.

Definitions

'company': Companies Act, 1963, section 2.
'court': Companies Act, 1990, section 235.
'examiner': Companies (Amendment) Act, 1990, section 1.
'interested party': Companies (Amendment) Act, 1990, section 1.

General Note

This section allows an examiner to resign or be removed from office and the resulting vacancy to be filled by the court. The company concerned or an interested party may apply to the court for determination of any matters arising from the performance by the examiner of his functions.

(1) The examiner may resign or be removed by the court.

(2) The court may fill any vacancy in the office of examiner.

(3) An application for an order under subsection (2) may be made by the company, a committee of creditors, or any interested party.

(4) The examiner must be described as such and not by his individual name.

(5) The acts of an examiner are valid even though defects in his appointment are later discovered.

(6) An examiner may be personally liable on any contract entered into by him in the performance of his duties unless the contract provides that he is not so liable, but he is entitled in respect of that liability to indemnity out of the assets.

(7) A company to which an examiner was appointed may apply to the court for the determination of any question arising from the performance of his functions.

SECTION 14
Information to be given when examiner appointed.

(1) The directors of a company to which an examiner has been appointed shall, within 7 days of the appointment, cause to be made out, verified by affidavit and submitted to the examiner a statement in accordance with this section as to the affairs of the company.

(2) The statement shall, in so far as is reasonably possible to do so, show as at the date of the examiner's appointment particulars of the company's assets, debts and liabilities (including contingent and prospective liabilities), the names and addresses of its creditors, the securities held by them respectively, the dates when the securities were respectively given and such further information as may be prescribed or as the court may direct.

(3) A person to whom subsection (1) applies who makes default in complying with the requirements of this section shall be guilty of an offence and shall be liable, on summary conviction, to a fine not exceeding £1,000 and, on conviction on indictment, to a fine not exceeding £10,000.

Definitions
'*company*': Companies Act, 1963, section 2.
'*director*': Companies Act, 1963, section 2.
'*examiner*': Companies (Amendment) Act, 1990, section 1.

General Note
This section requires directors to have a statement of affairs prepared for the examiner on his appointment.

(1) The directors of a company must cause the statement of affairs to be made out and arrange for it to be verified by affidavit and to be submitted to the examiner within seven days of his appointment. There is no provision, however, for the costs in the preparation of a statement of affairs.

(2) The statement must show, as far as reasonably possible, details of the assets, debts and liabilities (including contingent and prospective) of the company and the name and addresses of creditors and the securities held by them, together with the dates on which the securities were given.

(3) The penalties that may be imposed for default of the section are set out.

SECTION 15 **Examination of** **affairs of** **company.**	(1) It shall be the duty of an examiner to conduct an examination of the affairs of the company to which he is appointed and report to the court, within 21 days of his appointment or such longer period as the court may allow, the results of his examination in accordance with section 16. (2) Notwithstanding any other provision of this Act the court may impose on the examiner such other duties as it deems appropriate. (3) The examiner shall deliver a copy of his report under this section to the company on the same day as his delivery of such report to the court. (4) The examiner shall also supply a copy of his report under this section to any interested party on written application, provided that such supply may, if the court so directs, be subject to the omission of such parts of the report as the court thinks fit. (5) The court may, in particular, give a direction under subsection (4) if it considers that the inclusion of certain information in the report to be supplied under that subsection would be likely to prejudice the survival of the company, or the whole or any part of its undertaking.

Definitions

'*company*': Companies Act, 1963, section 2.

'*court*': Companies Act, 1990, section 235.

'*examiner*': Companies (Amendment) Act, 1990, section 1.

'*interested party*': Companies (Amendment) Act, 1990, section 1.

General Note

This section sets out the basic duties of the examiner. It provides that he shall ascertain the financial state of the company and form an opinion as to whether the company is capable of being rescued.

(1) An examiner must conduct an examination of the company's affairs and make a report within twenty-one days of his appointment. The court may extend the period during which he may make his report. (In the case of the Goodman Group the court extended the period within which the examiner had to report, having regard to the complexity and size of the case: see *Re Goodman International Ltd* (1990).)

(2) The court may impose such other duties on the examiner as it considers fit.

(3) The examiner must deliver a copy of his report to the company on the same day as it delivers it to the court.

(4) The examiner must also provide a copy of his report to any interested party on written application. However, on the direction of the court it may be subject to the omission of such parts as directed by the court.

(5) The court may give a direction under subsection (4) if it considers that the inclusion of certain information may prejudice the survival of the company.

SECTION 16

Examiner's report.

The examiner's report under section 15 shall comprise the following—

(*a*) the names and permanent addresses of the officers of the company and, in so far as the examiner can establish, any person in accordance with whose directions or instructions the directors of the company are accustomed to act,

(*b*) the names of any other bodies corporate of which the directors of the company are also directors,

(*c*) a statement as to the affairs of the company, showing, insofar as is reasonably possible to do so, particulars of the company's assets, debts and liabilities (including contingent and prospective liabilities) as at the latest practicable date, the names and addresses of its creditors, the securities held by them respectively and the dates when the securities were respectively given,

(*d*) whether in the opinion of the examiner any deficiency between the assets and the liabilities of the company has been satisfactorily accounted for or, if not, whether there is evidence of a substantial disappearance of property that is not adequately accounted for,

(*e*) a statement of opinion by the examiner as to whether the company, and the whole or any part of its undertaking, would be capable of survival as a going concern and a statement of the conditions which he feels are essential to ensure such survival, whether as regards the internal management and controls of the company or otherwise,

(*f*) his opinion as to whether the formulation, acceptance and confirmation of proposals for a compromise or scheme of arrangement would facilitate such survival,

(*g*) whether, in his opinion, an attempt to continue the whole or any part of the undertaking of the company would be likely to be more advantageous to the members as a whole and the creditors as a whole, than a winding-up of the company,

(*h*) recommendations as to the course he thinks should be taken in relation to the company including, if warranted, draft proposals for a compromise or scheme of arrangement,

(*i*) his opinion as to whether the facts disclosed would warrant further enquiries under sections 33 and 34,

(*j*) such other matters as the examiner thinks relevant or the court directs, and

(k) his opinion as to whether his work would be assisted by a direction of the court extending the role or membership of any creditors' committee referred to in section 21.

Definitions

'*body corporate*': Companies Act, 1963, section 2 (3).

'*company*': Companies Act, 1963, section 2.

'*court*': Companies Act, 1990, section 235.

'*director*': Companies Act, 1963, section 2.

'*examiner*': Companies (Amendment) Act, 1990, section 1.

'*officer*': Companies Act, 1963, section 2.

General Note

This section sets out the contents of the first report of the examiner, which must include data on the directors and officers of the company, a statement of affairs, the opinion of the examiner as to whether the company and the whole or part of its undertaking is capable of survival, his opinion as to whether an attempt to continue the whole or part of the undertaking is likely to be advantageous to the members and creditors, and recommendations as to the future of the company.

This section was subject to a minor change by section 180 (1) (g) of the Companies Act, 1990, to tidy up the provisions of the section.

SECTION 17
Hearing of matters arising from examiner's report.

(1) Where, in a report made under section 15, the examiner expresses the opinion that—

(a) the whole or any part of the undertaking of the company to which he has been appointed would not be capable of survival as a going concern, or

(b) the formulation, acceptance, or confirmation of proposals for a compromise or scheme of arrangement would not facilitate such survival, or

(c) an attempt to continue the whole or part of the undertaking of the company would not be likely to be more advantageous to the members as a whole, or the creditors as a whole, than a winding-up of the company, or

(d) there is evidence of a substantial disappearance of property that is not adequately accounted for, or of other serious irregularities in relation to the company's affairs,

the court shall, as soon as may be after the receipt of the examiner's report, hold a hearing to consider matters arising out of the report.

(2) The following parties shall be entitled to appear and be heard at a hearing under subsection (1)—

(a) the examiner,

(b) the company,

(c) any interested party,

(d) any person who is referred to in the report in relation to the matters mentioned in subsection (1) (d).

(3) Following a hearing under this section, the court may make such order or orders as it deems fit.

(4) Without prejudice to the generality of subsection (3), an order under that subsection may include an order for—

(*a*) the discharge from the protection of the court of the whole or any part of the assets of the company,

(*b*) the imposition of such terms and conditions as it sees fit for the continuance of the protection of the court,

(*c*) the winding-up of the company,

(*d*) the sale of the whole or any part of the undertaking of the company on such terms and conditions, including terms and conditions relating to the distribution of the proceeds of such sale, as the court sees fit, and, if necessary for that purpose, the appointment of a receiver,

(*e*) the formulation by the examiner of proposals for a compromise or scheme of arrangement,

(*f*) the summoning of the meetings mentioned in this Act for the purpose of considering proposals for a compromise or scheme of arrangement,

(*g*) the calling, holding and conduct of a meeting of the board of directors, or a general meeting of the company, to consider such matters as the court shall direct.

(5) On the making of an order under this section, the examiner or such other person as the court may direct shall deliver an office copy of the order to the registrar of companies for registration.

(6) Where the court makes an order for the winding-up of a company under this Act, such a winding-up shall be deemed to have commenced on the date of the making of the order, unless the court otherwise orders.

Definitions

'company': Companies Act, 1963, section 2.

'court': Companies Act, 1990, section 235.

'examiner': Companies (Amendment) Act, 1990, section 1.

'interested party': Companies (Amendment) Act, 1990, section 1.

'registrar of companies': Companies Act, 1963, section 2.

General Note

This section provides for a court hearing where the examiner's '21-day report' under section 15 expresses the view that the company is not capable of survival, or where he has discovered serious irregularities in relation to its affairs. Having considered the examiner's report the court can make whatever order it deems fit, which could include orders for the winding up of the company, its partial sale, or the appointment of a receiver.

(1) Where the examiner concludes in his report that the company is not capable of survival, or reports evidence of substantial

disappearance of properties not adequately accounted for or other serious irregularities, the court will hold a hearing to consider matters arising out of the report.

(2) At the hearing certain parties are entitled to attend and be heard, including the examiner, the company, the creditors, the members of the company, and any person referred to in the report regarding irregularities.

(3) The court may make such orders as it deems fit.

(4) In the making of an order the court may

(*a*) discharge from the protection of the court all or part of the assets,

(*b*) impose such conditions for continued protection as it sees fit,

(*c*) order that the company be wound up,

(*d*) direct the sale of the whole or part of the undertaking on such terms as it sees fit,

(*e*) direct the examiner to formulate proposals for a compromise or scheme of arrangement,

(*f*) summon meetings to consider proposals for a compromise or scheme of arrangement, or

(*g*) order the holding of a board or general meeting of the company to consider such matters as the court directs.

(5) The examiner or such other person directed by the court must deliver a copy of the court order to the Registrar of Companies.

(6) If the court orders a winding up, the liquidation commences on the date of the order, unless the court directs otherwise.

SECTION 18

Further report by examiner.

(1) Where, in the opinion of the examiner—

(*a*) the whole or any part of the undertaking of the company would be capable of survival as a going concern, and

(*b*) an attempt to continue the whole or any part of the undertaking of the company would be likely to be more advantageous to the members as a whole, and to the creditors as a whole, than a winding-up of the company, and

(*c*) the formulation, acceptance and confirmation of proposals for a compromise or scheme of arrangement would facilitate such survival,

the examiner shall formulate proposals for a compromise or scheme of arrangement.

(2) Notwithstanding any provision of the Companies Acts relating to notice of general meetings, (but subject to notice of not less than three days in any case) the examiner shall convene and preside at such meetings of members and creditors as he thinks proper, to consider such proposals and report thereon to the court within 42 days of his appointment or such longer period as the court may allow, in accordance with section 19.

(3) Where, on the application of the examiner, the court is satisfied that the examiner would be unable to report to the court within the period of three months referred to in section 5 (1) but that he would be able to make a report if that period were extended, the court may by order extend that period by not more than 30 days to enable him to do so.

(4) Where the examiner has submitted a report under this section to the court and, but for this subsection, the period mentioned in section 5 (1) (and any extended period allowed under subsection (3) of this section) would expire, the court may, of its own motion or on the application of the examiner, extend the period concerned by such period as the court considers necessary to enable it to take a decision under section 24.

(5) The examiner shall deliver a copy of his report under this section—

(*a*) to the company on the same day as his delivery of such report to the court, and

(*b*) to any interested party on written application,

provided that such delivery under paragraph (*b*) may, if the court so directs, be subject to the omission of such parts of the report as the court thinks fit.

(6) The court may, in particular, give a direction under subsection (5) (*b*) if it considers that the inclusion of certain information in the report to be delivered under that paragraph would be likely to prejudice the survival of the company, or the whole or any part of its undertaking.

Definitions

'company': Companies Act, 1963, section 2.

'court': Companies Act, 1990, section 235.

'examiner': Companies (Amendment) Act, 1990, section 1.

'interested party': Companies (Amendment) Act, 1990, section 1.

General Note

Where the examiner's report expresses the view that the company could be wholly or partly saved by reaching agreement on a rescue plan with its creditors, members etc. and that this would be more advantageous than a winding up, he must formulate proposals for such a plan and put them to the creditors and members and report back to the court within forty-two days of his appointment or such longer period as may be allowed by the court.

(1) If the examiner reports that the undertaking or part of it is capable of survival he must formulate proposals for a compromise or scheme of arrangement.

(2) In these circumstances the examiner must convene and preside at meetings of members and creditors and report back to the court within forty-two days of his appointment or such longer period as may be allowed by the court.

(3) Where the court is satisfied that the examiner would be unable to report back within the three-month period referred to in section 5 it may extend the period in which to report by not more than a further thirty days.

(4) If the court needs extra time to consider the result of the meetings, the protection period can be extended accordingly.

(5) A copy of the second report must be given to the company and any interested party on written application, with possible deletions as may be decided by the court.

(6) The court may allow certain information to be deleted from the report if it is likely to prejudice the survival of the company or part of the undertaking.

SECTION 19

Examiner's report under section 18.

An examiner's report under section 18 shall include—

(a) the proposals placed before the required meetings,
(b) any modification of those proposals adopted at any of those meetings,
(c) the outcome of each of the required meetings,
(d) the recommendation of the committee of creditors, if any,
(e) a statement of the assets and liabilities (including contingent and prospective liabilities) of the company as at the date of his report,
(f) a list of the creditors of the company, the amount owing to each such creditor, the nature and value of any security held by any such creditor, and the priority status of any such creditor under section 285 of the Principal Act or any other statutory provision or rule of law,
(g) a list of the officers of the company,
(h) his recommendations,
(i) such other matters as the examiner deems appropriate or the court directs.

Definitions

'*company*': Companies Act, 1963, section 2.
'*court*': Companies Act, 1990, section 235.
'*examiner*': Companies (Amendment) Act, 1990, section 1.
'*officer*': Companies Act, 1963, section 2.
'*Principal Act*': Companies (Amendment) Act, 1990, section 1.

General Note

This section sets out the contents of the second report of the examiner required under section 18. In particular the report must include details of the proposals placed before the required meetings and of the outcome of the meetings, with recommendations, if any, and a statement of assets and liabilities, together with a list of creditors with details of the amounts owing. In addition a list of the officers of the company must be included.

SECTION 20
Repudiation of certain contracts.

(1) Where proposals for a compromise or scheme of arrangement are to be formulated in relation to a company, the company may, subject to the approval of the court, affirm or repudiate any contract under which some element of performance other than payment remains to be rendered both by the company and the other contracting party or parties.

(2) Any person who suffers loss or damage as a result of such repudiation shall stand as an unsecured creditor for the amount of such loss or damage.

(3) In order to facilitate the formulation, consideration or confirmation of a compromise or scheme of arrangement, the court may hold a hearing and make an order determining the amount of any such loss or damage and the amount so determined shall be due by the company to the creditor as a judgement debt.

(4) Where the examiner is not a party to an application to the court for the purposes of subsection (1), the company shall serve notice of such application on the examiner and the examiner may appear and be heard on the hearing of any such application.

(5) Where the court approves the affirmation or repudiation of a contract under this section, it may in giving such approval make such orders as it thinks fit for the purposes of giving full effect to its approval including orders as to notice to, or declaring the rights of, any party affected by such affirmation or repudiation.

Definitions
'company': Companies Act, 1963, section 2.
'court': Companies Act, 1990, section 235.
'examiner': Companies (Amendment) Act, 1990, section 1.

General Note
Where the court has ordered proposals to be prepared and considered, the company may, subject to court approval, affirm or repudiate certain contracts. However, any person who suffers loss or damage as a result will stand as an unsecured creditor for the amount involved.

(1) The company may, with court approval, affirm or repudiate any contract with some element of performance other than payment to be rendered both by the company and other contracting parties.

(2) In the event of any loss or damage suffered as a result of repudiation of a contract the person who suffers will stand as an unsecured creditor for the amount of loss or damage.

(3) The court may hold a hearing and make an order determining the amount of damage and the amount due by the company to the creditor.

(4) Where the examiner is not a party to the application the court will serve notice of the application on the examiner, who may appear and be heard at the hearing.

(5) Where the court approves the affirmation or repudiation of a contract it will make such orders as it thinks fit to give full effect to its approval.

SECTION 21
Appointment of creditors' committee.

(1) An examiner may, and if so directed by the court shall, appoint a committee of creditors to assist him in the performance of his functions.

(2) Save as otherwise directed by the court, a committee appointed under subsection (1) shall consist of not more than five members and shall include the holders of the three largest unsecured claims who are willing to serve.

(3) The examiner shall provide the committee with a copy of any proposals for a compromise or scheme of arrangement and the committee may express an opinion on the proposals on its own behalf or on behalf of the creditors or classes of creditors represented thereon.

(4) As soon as practicable after the appointment of a committee under subsection (1) the examiner shall meet with the committee to transact such business as may be necessary.

Definitions
'court': Companies Act, 1990, section 235.
'examiner': Companies (Amendment) Act, 1990, section 1.

General Note
This section allows for the possibility of the appointment of a committee of creditors to assist the examiner.

(1) An examiner may appoint a committee of creditors to assist him in the performance of his functions. The court may also order the formation of such a committee.

(2) The committee will consist of a maximum of five members, unless otherwise directed by the court, and must include representatives of the three largest unsecured creditors who are willing to serve.

(3) The examiner must give a copy of the proposals for a compromise or scheme of arrangement to the committee, who may express an opinion on them.

(4) The committee must meet the examiner as soon as possible after their appointment to transact any business as may be necessary.

SECTION 22

Contents of proposals

(1) Proposals for a compromise or scheme of arrangement shall—

(a) specify each class of members and creditors of the company,

(b) specify any class of members and creditors whose interests or claims will not be impaired by the proposals,

(c) specify any class of members and creditors whose interests or claims will be impaired by the proposals,

(d) provide equal treatment for each claim or interest of a particular class unless the holder of a particular claim or interest agrees to less favourable treatment,

(e) provide for the implementation of the proposals,

(f) if the examiner considers it necessary or desirable to do so to facilitate the survival of the company, and the whole or any part of its undertaking, as a going concern, specify whatever changes should be made in relation to the management or direction of the company,

(g) if the examiner considers it necessary or desirable as aforesaid, specify any changes he considers should be made in the memorandum or articles of the company, whether as regards the management or direction of the company or otherwise,

(h) include such other matters as the examiner deems appropriate.

(2) A statement of the assets and liabilities (including contingent and prospective liabilities) of the company as at the date of the proposals shall be attached to each copy of the proposals to be submitted to meetings of members and creditors under section 23.

(3) There shall also be attached to each such copy of the proposals a description of the estimated financial outcome of a winding-up of the company for each class of members and creditors.

(4) The court may direct that the proposals include whatever other provisions it deems fit.

(5) For the purposes of this section and sections 24 and 25, a creditor's claim against a company is impaired if he receives less in payment of his claim than the full amount due in respect of the claim at the date of presentation of the petition for the appointment of the examiner.

(6) For the purposes of this section and sections 24 and 25, the interest of a member of a company in a company is impaired if—

(a) the nominal value of his shareholding in the company is reduced,

(b) where he is entitled to a fixed dividend in respect of his shareholding in the company, the amount of that dividend is reduced,

(c) he is deprived of all or any part of the rights accruing to him by virtue of his shareholding in the company,

(d) his percentage interest in the total issued share capital of the company is reduced, or

(e) he is deprived of his shareholding in the company.

Definitions

'company': Companies Act, 1963, section 2.

'court': Companies Act, 1990, section 235.

'examiner': Companies (Amendment) Act, 1990, section 1.

General Note

This section sets out the matters that proposals for a compromise or scheme of arrangement must contain.

(1) The compromise or scheme of arrangement proposals must contain the specific details set out in this subsection.

(2) A statement of the assets and liabilities of the company on the date of the proposals must accompany each copy of the proposals.

(3) Each copy of the proposals must also contain a description of the estimated financial outcome of a winding up of the company for each class of members and creditors.

(4) The court may direct that the proposals include whatever matters it deems fit.

(5) A person's claim is impaired if he receives less in payment of his claim than the full amount due in respect of the claim on the date of presentation of the petition to appoint the examiner.

(6) The circumstances when the interest of a member of a company in the company is impaired are set out in this subsection.

SECTION 23

Consideration by members and creditors of proposals.

(1) This section applies to a meeting of members or creditors or any class of members or creditors summoned to consider proposals for a compromise or scheme of arrangement.

(2) At a meeting to which this section applies a modification of the proposals may be put to the meeting but may only be accepted with the consent of the examiner.

(3) Proposals shall be deemed to have been accepted by a meeting of members or of a class of members if a majority of the votes validly cast at that meeting, whether in person or by proxy, are cast in favour of the resolution for the proposals.

(4) Proposals shall be deemed to have been accepted by a meeting of creditors or of a class of creditors when a majority in number representing a majority in value of the claims represented at that meeting have voted, either in person or by proxy, in favour of the resolution for the proposals.

(5) (*a*) Where a State authority is a creditor of the company, such authority shall be entitled to accept proposals under this section notwithstanding—
(i) that any claim of such authority as a creditor would be impaired under the proposals, or
(ii) any other enactment.
(*b*) In this subsection, "State authority" means the State, a Minister of the Government or the Revenue Commissioners.

(6) Section 144 of the Principal Act shall apply to any resolution to which subsection (3) or (4) relates which is passed at any adjourned meeting.

(7) Section 202, subsections (2) to (6), of the Principal Act shall, with the necessary modifications, apply to meetings held under this section.

(8) With every notice summoning a meeting to which this section applies which is sent to a creditor or member, there shall be sent also a statement explaining the effect of the compromise or scheme of arrangement and in particular stating any material interests of the directors of the company, whether as directors or as members or as creditors of the company or otherwise and the effect thereon of the compromise or arrangement, insofar as it is different from the effect on the like interest of other persons.

Definitions

'*company*': Companies Act, 1963, section 2.

'*director*': Companies Act, 1963, section 2.

'*examiner*': Companies (Amendment) Act, 1990, section 1.

'*Principal Act*': Companies (Amendment) Act, 1990, section 1.

'*State authority*': Companies (Amendment) Act, 1990, section 23.

General Note

This section deals with the consideration of the examiner's proposals by meetings of creditors and members of the company.

In *Re Coombe Importers Ltd.* (1990) the Revenue Commissioners refused to accept the scheme put forward, as they were not satisfied with the amount they would receive under the scheme of arrangement and objected to the proposals under section 25 below.

(1) The section applies to a meeting of members or creditors or class of members or creditors to consider proposals for a compromise or scheme of arrangement.

(2) Any modification put to the meeting may only be accepted with the consent of the examiner.

(3) Proposals will be deemed to have been accepted by the particular class of members when accepted by a majority of the votes validly cast in favour of the resolution for the proposals.

(4) Proposals will be deemed to have been accepted by the particular class of creditors when a majority in number representing a majority in value of the claims have voted in favour of the proposals, either in person or by proxy.

(5) Where a state authority (including the Revenue Commissioners) is a creditor such authority will be entitled to accept the proposals even though the claim of the authority as creditor would be impaired. This allows the Revenue Commissioners to participate in compromises and schemes of arrangement; in the past, under certain circumstances the Revenue Commissioners could not agree to waive or write off any part of their debt, and this resulted in serious difficulties for proposals. This subsection was amended by section 180 (1) (*b*) of the Companies Act, 1990, to allow a local authority to accept a scheme of arrangement, for example for rates or other local charges.

(6) Section 144 of the Companies Act, 1963 (Resolutions passed at adjourned meetings), applies to this section.

(7) Section 202 (2–6) of the Companies Act, 1963 (Information as to compromises between members and creditors), applies to this section.

(8) Every notice summoning a meeting must include a statement setting out details of the effect of the compromise or scheme of arrangement as well as providing details of any material interests of the directors of the company.

SECTION 24
Confirmation of proposals.

(1) The report of the examiner under section 18 shall be set down for consideration by the court as soon as may be after receipt of the report by the court.

(2) The following persons may appear and be heard at a hearing under subsection (1)—

(*a*) the company,
(*b*) the examiner,
(*c*) any creditor or member whose claim or interest would be impaired if the proposals were implemented.

(3) At a hearing under subsection (1) the court may, as it thinks proper, subject to the provisions of this section and section 25, confirm, confirm subject to modifications, or refuse to confirm the proposals.

(4) The court shall not confirm any proposals—

(*a*) unless at least one class of members and one class of creditors whose interests or claims would be impaired by implementation of the proposals have accepted the proposals, or
(*b*) if the sole or primary purpose of the proposals is the avoidance of payment of tax due, or
(*c*) unless the court is satisfied that—
(i) the proposals are fair and equitable in relation to any class of members or creditors that has not accepted the proposals and whose interests or claims would be impaired by implementation, and

(ii) the proposals are not unfairly prejudicial to the interests of any interested party.

(5) Where the court confirms proposals (with or without modification), the proposals shall be binding on all the members or class or classes of members, as the case may be, affected by the proposal and also on the company.

(6) Where the court confirms proposals (with or without modification), the proposals shall, notwithstanding any other enactment, be binding on all the creditors or the class or classes of creditors, as the case may be, affected by the proposals in respect of any claim or claims against the company and any person other than the company who, under any statute, enactment, rule of law or otherwise, is liable for all or any part of the debts of the company.

(7) Any alterations in, additions to or deletions from the memorandum and articles of the company which are specified in the proposals shall, after confirmation of the proposals by the court and notwithstanding any other provisions of the Companies Acts, take effect from a date fixed by the court.

(8) Where the court confirms proposals under this section it may make such orders for the implementation of its decision as it deems fit.

(9) A compromise or scheme of arrangement, proposals for which have been confirmed under this section shall come into effect from a date fixed by the court, which date shall be not later than 21 days from the date of their confirmation.

(10) On the confirmation of proposals a copy of any order made by the court under this section shall be delivered by the examiner, or by such person as the court may direct, to the registrar of companies for registration.

(11) Where—

(*a*) the court refuses to confirm proposals under this section, or
(*b*) the report of an examiner under section 18 concludes that, following the required meetings of members and creditors of a company under this Act, it has not been possible to reach agreement on a compromise or scheme of arrangement,

the court may, if it considers it just and equitable to do so, make an order for the winding-up of the company, or any other order as it deems fit.

Definitions

'*company*': Companies Act, 1963, section 2.

'*court*': Companies Act, 1990, section 235.

'*examiner*': Companies (Amendment) Act, 1990, section 1.

'*interested party*': Companies (Amendment) Act, 1990, section 1.

'*registrar of companies*': Companies Act, 1963, section 2.

General Note

This section deals with the consideration by the court of the proposals contained in the examiner's second report. The court may confirm, modify or refuse to confirm the proposals, and guidelines are set down for the court in reaching its decision. Where the court confirms such proposals they will be binding on all creditors and members affected by the proposal and on the company or other person who may be liable for its debts. Any confirmed proposals will take effect not later than twenty-one days from the order of the court.

(1) The examiner's report under section 18 must be set down for court consideration as soon as possible after receipt of the report by the court.

(2) The company, the examiner and any creditor or member whose claim or interest may be impaired may appear and be heard at the hearing.

(3) The court may confirm, modify or refuse the proposals as it thinks fit.

(4) The court will only confirm the proposals under the following circumstances:
(*a*) if at least one class of members and creditors whose interests would be impaired by the implementation of such proposals has accepted the proposals;
(*b*) if the sole or primary aim of the proposals is not to avoid payment of tax that is due;
(*c*) if it is satisfied that the proposals are fair and equitable in relation to any class of members or creditors that would be impaired and the proposals are not unfairly prejudicial to the interest of any interested party.

(5) Where the court confirms proposals they are binding on all members or classes of members affected by the proposals.

(6) Where the court confirms the proposals they are binding on all creditors or classes of creditors affected by the proposals.

(7) Any alterations, additions or deletions in the memorandum and articles of association of the company must take effect from the date fixed by the court.

(8) Where the court confirms proposals it may make such orders as it deems fit to implement them.

(9) Any compromise or scheme of arrangement must come into effect from the date fixed by the court but not later than twenty-one days from the date of confirmation.

(10) A copy of any confirmation order must be delivered to the Registrar of Companies for registration.

(11) The court may make an order to wind up the company where it refuses to confirm the proposals under this section or where the examiner has reported that it has not been possible to reach agreement on a compromise or scheme of arrangement.

(12) Where the examiner forms the opinion that the company is able to survive as a going concern he may include in his report proposals requiring management changes that do not impair the interests of the creditors or members. This subsection was inserted by section 180 (1) (*i*) of the Companies Act, 1990.

SECTION 25
Objection to confirmation by court of proposals

(1) At a hearing under section 24 in relation to proposals a member or creditor whose interest or claim would be impaired by the proposals may object in particular to their confirmation by the court on any of the following grounds—

(*a*) that there was some material irregularity at or in relation to a meeting to which section 23 applies,

(*b*) that acceptance of the proposals by the meeting was obtained by improper means,

(*c*) that the proposals were put forward for an improper purpose,

(*d*) that the proposals unfairly prejudice the interests of the objector.

(2) Any person who voted to accept the proposals may not object to their confirmation by the court except on the grounds—

(*a*) that such acceptance was obtained by improper means, or

(*b*) that after voting to accept the proposals he became aware that the proposals were put forward for an improper purpose.

(3) Where the court upholds an objection under this section, the court may make such order as it deems fit, including an order that the decision of any meeting be set aside and an order that any meeting be reconvened.

Definitions

'*court*': Companies Act, 1990, section 235.

General Note

This section provides for objections to the confirmation of the plan to be considered by the court. The subsections set out the grounds on which a challenge may be entertained. In *Re Coombe Importers Ltd.* (1990) the Revenue Commissioners objected to the amount they would receive under the scheme proposed. As a result a binding agreement was not reached and an order to wind up the company was made.

(1) At a hearing a member or creditor may object to the proposals on the following grounds:

(*a*) that there was a material irregularity at or in relation to the meeting of members or creditors to which section 23 applies;

(*b*) that acceptance of the proposals was obtained by improper means;

(*c*) that the proposals were put forward for an improper purpose;

(*d*) that the proposals unfairly prejudice the interests of the objector.

(2) A person who voted in favour of the proposals may not object to their confirmation, except where acceptance was obtained by improper means or after the voting he became aware that the proposals were put forward for an improper purpose.

(3) If the objections are upheld the court may set aside the decision of any meeting and order that the meeting be reconvened.

SECTION 26
Cessation of protection of company and termination of appointment of examiner.

(1) Subject to section 5, the protection deemed to be granted to a company under that section shall cease—

(*a*) on the coming into effect of a compromise or scheme of arrangement under this Act, or

(*b*) on such earlier date as the court may direct.

(2) Where a company ceases to be under the protection of the court, the appointment of the examiner shall terminate on the date of such cessation.

Definitions

'*company*': Companies Act, 1963, section 2.

'*court*': Companies Act, 1990, section 235.

'*examiner*': Companies (Amendment) Act, 1990, section 1.

General Note

Where a plan comes into effect earlier than three months after the petition for the examiner's appointment the protection of the court will cease from the earlier date. The examiner will cease to operate when the protection ceases.

(1) The protection of the court will end

(*a*) when the compromise or scheme of arrangement comes into effect, or

(*b*) at an earlier date if so directed by the court.

(2) The examiner's appointment ceases on the cessation of protection.

SECTION 27
Revocation.

The company or any interested party may, within 180 days after the confirmation of the proposals by the court, apply to the court for revocation of that confirmation on the grounds that it was procured by fraud and the court, if satisfied that such was the case, may revoke that confirmation on such terms and conditions, particularly with regard to the protection of the rights of parties acquiring interests or property in good faith and for value in reliance on that confirmation, as it deems fit.

Definitions

'*company*': Companies Act, 1963, section 2.

'*court*': Companies Act, 1990, section 235.

'*interested party*': Companies (Amendment) Act, 1990, section 1.

General Note

If the court is satisfied that the compromise or scheme of arrangement was procured by fraud it can revoke the confirmation. An application to revoke the compromise or scheme of arrangement must be brought within 180 days from confirmation either by the company or by any interested party.

SECTION 28
Disqualification of examiners.

(1) A person shall not be qualified to be appointed or act as an examiner of a company if he would not be qualified to act as its liquidator.

(2) A person who acts as examiner of a company while disqualified under this section shall be guilty of an offence, and shall be liable, on summary conviction, to a fine not exceeding £1,000 and, on conviction on indictment, to a fine not exceeding £10,000.

Definitions

'*company*': Companies Act, 1963, section 2.

'*examiner*': Companies (Amendment) Act, 1990, section 1.

General Note

A person is not qualified to act as an examiner of a company unless he was qualified to act as its liquidator.

Any person who is guilty of an offence under this section is liable to a fine.

SECTION 29
Costs and remuneration of examiners.

(1) The court may from time to time make such orders as it thinks proper for payment of the remuneration and costs of, and reasonable expenses properly incurred by, an examiner.

(2) Unless the court otherwise orders, the remuneration, costs and expenses of an examiner shall be paid and the examiner shall be entitled to be indemnified in respect thereof out of the revenue of the business of the company to which he

has been appointed, or the proceeds of realisation of the assets (including investments).

(3) The remuneration, costs and expenses of an examiner which have been sanctioned by order of the court shall be paid in full and shall be paid before any other claim, secured or unsecured, under any compromise or scheme of arrangement or in any receivership or winding-up of the company to which he has been appointed.

(4) The functions of an examiner may be performed by him with the assistance of persons appointed or employed by him for that purpose provided that an examiner shall, insofar as is reasonably possible, make use of the services of the staff and facilities of the company to which he has been appointed to assist him in the performance of his functions.

(5) In considering any matter relating to the costs, expenses and remuneration of an examiner the court shall have particular regard to the proviso to subsection (4).

Definitions

'company': Companies Act, 1963, section 2.

'court': Companies Act, 1990, section 235.

'examiner': Companies (Amendment) Act, 1990, section 1.

General Note

This section deals with the costs, remuneration and expenses of examiners. These will be paid out of the company's revenue and, subject to the sanction of the court, will be paid in full before any other claim under any compromise or scheme of arrangement or in any receivership or winding up of the company. The section also provides that the examiner may employ persons to assist him in his functions.

(1) The court may sanction payment of the costs, remuneration and expenses reasonably incurred by the examiner.

(2) The examiner is entitled to be indemnified out of the revenue of the business or proceeds of the realisation of assets for his costs and expenses, unless otherwise decided by the court.

(3) The costs, remuneration and expenses of the examiner must be paid before any other claim under any compromise or scheme of arrangement or on the winding up or receivership of the company.

(4) The examiner may employ persons to assist him in carrying out his functions but must use the existing staff and facilities of the company as far as reasonably possible.

(5) The court will have regard to subsection (4) above in considering the costs, remuneration and expenses of the examiner.

SECTION 30
Publicity.

(1) An examiner or, where appropriate, such other person as the court may direct, shall, within 14 days after the delivery to the registrar of companies of every order made under section 17 or 24, cause to be published in *Iris Oifigiúil* notice of such delivery.

(2) Where a person fails to comply with this section, that person, and where that person is a company, the company and every officer of the company who is in default, shall be guilty of an offence and shall be liable to a fine not exceeding £1,000.

(3) Proceedings in relation to an offence under this section may be brought and prosecuted by the registrar of companies.

Definitions

'company': Companies Act, 1963, section 2.
'court': Companies Act, 1990, section 235.
'examiner': Companies (Amendment) Act, 1990, section 1.
'officer': Companies Act, 1963, section 2.
'registrar of companies': Companies Act, 1963, section 2.

General Note

The examiner or such other person as directed by the court must ensure that every order made under sections 17 (Hearing of matters arising from examiner's report) or 24 (Confirmation of proposals) is delivered to the Registrar of Companies and must publish a notice in *Iris Oifigiúil* within fourteen days of such delivery. Failure to do so may result in a fine.

Subsection (3) was repealed by section 181 (2) of the Companies Act, 1990.

SECTION 31
Hearing of proceedings otherwise than in public.

The whole or part of any proceedings under this Act may be heard otherwise than in public if the court, in the interests of justice, considers that the interests of the company concerned or of its creditors as a whole so require.

Definitions

'company': Companies Act, 1963, section 2.
'court': Companies Act, 1990, section 235.

General Note

This section provides that in the interests of justice, proceedings may be held in camera.

In the case of Goodman International the hearings were held in camera: see *Re Goodman International Ltd* (1990). The legal position in relation to hearings in camera was established by Mr Justice Walsh in *Re R. Ltd. and re the Companies Act, 1963*. In that case the Supreme Court would not allow a hearing to be held in camera simply on the grounds that a public hearing would 'be prejudicial to the legitimate interests of the company'.

SECTION 32
No lien over company's books, records etc.

Where the court has appointed an examiner, no person shall be entitled as against the examiner to withhold possession of any deed, instrument, or other document belonging to the company, or the books of account, receipts, bills, invoices, or other papers of a like nature relating to the accounts or trade, dealings or business of the company, or to claim any lien thereon provided that—

(*a*) where a mortgage, charge or pledge has been created by the deposit of any such document or paper with a person, the production of the document or paper to the examiner by the person shall be without prejudice to the person's rights under the mortgage or charge (other than any right to possession of the document or paper),

(*b*) where by virtue of this section an examiner has possession of any document or papers of a receiver or that a receiver is entitled to examine, the examiner shall, unless the court otherwise orders, make the document or papers available for inspection by the receiver at all reasonable times.

Definitions

'*company*': Companies Act, 1963, section 2.
'*court*': Companies Act, 1990, section 235.
'*examiner*': Companies (Amendment) Act, 1990, section 1.

General Note

Where the court has appointed an examiner no person can hold a lien over any of the company's books or records, and where any mortgage or pledge has been created by the deposit of documents, the production of such books to the examiner will be without prejudice to the person's rights under the mortgage, charge, or pledge.

This section was repealed by section 180 (3) of the Companies Act, 1990.

SECTION 33
Civil liability of persons concerned for fraudulent trading of company.

(1) If in the course of proceedings under this Act it appears that—

(*a*) any person was, while an officer of the company, knowingly a party to the carrying on of any business of the company in a reckless manner; or

(*b*) any person was knowingly a party to the carrying on of any business of the company with intent to defraud creditors of the company, or creditors of any other person or for any fraudulent purpose;

the court, on the application of the examiner, or any creditor or contributory of the company, may, if it thinks it proper to do so, declare that such person shall be personally responsible, without any limitation of liability, for all or any part of the debts or other liabilities of the company as the court may direct.

(2) Without prejudice to the generality of subsection (1) (*a*), an officer of a company shall be deemed to have been knowingly a party to the carrying on of any business of the company in a reckless manner if—

(*a*) he was a party to the carrying on of such business and, having regard to the general knowledge, skill and experience that may reasonably be expected of a person in his position, he ought to have known that his actions or those of the company would cause loss to the creditors of the company, or any of them, or

(*b*) he was a party to the contracting of a debt by the company and did not honestly believe on reasonable grounds that the company would be able to pay the debt when it fell due for payment as well as all its other debts (taking into account the contingent and prospective liabilities).

(3) Notwithstanding anything contained in subsection (1) the court may grant a declaration on the grounds set out in paragraph (*a*) of that subsection only if—

(*a*) paragraph (*a*), (*b*) or (*c*) of section 214 of the Principal Act applies to the company concerned, and

(*b*) an applicant for such a declaration, being a creditor or contributory of the company, or any person on whose behalf such application is made, suffered loss or damage as a consequence of any behaviour mentioned in subsection (1).

(4) In deciding whether it is proper to make an order on the ground set out in subsection (2) (*b*), the court shall have regard to whether the creditor in question was, at the time the debt was incurred, aware of the company's financial state of affairs and, notwithstanding such awareness, nevertheless assented to the incurring of the debt.

(5) On the hearing of an application under this section, the applicant may himself give evidence or call witnesses.

(6) Where it appears to the court that any person in respect of whom a declaration has been sought under subsection (1) (*a*) has acted honestly and responsibly in relation to the conduct of the affairs of the company or any matter or matters on the ground of which such declaration is sought to be made, the court may, having regard to all the circumstances of the case, relieve him either wholly or in part, from personal liability on such terms as it may think fit.

(7) Where the court makes any such declaration, it may—

(*a*) give such further directions as it thinks proper for the purpose of giving effect to the declaration and in particular make provision for making the liability of any such person under the declaration a charge on any debt or obligation due from the company to him, or on any mortgage or charge or any interest in any mortgage or charge on any assets of the company held by or vested in him or any company or person on his behalf, or any person claiming as assignee from or through the person liable or any company or person acting on his behalf, and may from time to time make such further orders as may be necessary for the purpose of enforcing any charge imposed under this subsection;

(b) provide that sums recovered under this section shall be paid to such person or classes of persons, for such purposes, in such amounts or proportions at such time or times and in such respective priorities among themselves as such declaration may specify.

(8) This section shall have effect notwithstanding that—

(a) the person in respect of whom the declaration has been sought under subsection (1) may be criminally liable in respect of the matters on the ground of which such declaration is to be made; or

(b) any matter or matters on the ground of which the declaration under subsection (1) is to be made have occurred outside the State.

(9) Subsection (1) (a) shall not apply during a period when the company is under the protection of the court.

(10) For the purposes of this section—

"assignee" includes any person to whom or in whose favour, by the directions of the person liable, the debt, obligation, mortgage or charge was created, issued or transferred or the interest created, but does not include an assignee for valuable consideration (not including consideration by way of marriage) given in good faith and without notice of any of the matters on the ground of which the declaration is made;

"company" includes any body which may be wound up under the Companies Acts; and

"officer" includes any auditor, liquidator, receiver, or any person in accordance with whose directions or instructions the directors of the company are accustomed to act.

Definitions

'assignee': Companies (Amendment) Act, 1990, section 33.

'company': Companies (Amendment) Act, 1990, section 33.

'contributory': Companies Act, 1963, section 2.

'court': Companies Act, 1990, section 235.

'officer': Companies (Amendment) Act, 1990, section 33.

General Note

This section deals with fraudulent trading by a company and the civil liabilities to be imposed. It introduces into Irish law the new concept of reckless trading.

This section was repealed by section 180 (3) of the Companies Act, 1990.

(1) If an officer of a company is found by the court to have been carrying on the business of the company in a reckless manner or was knowingly a party to the carrying on of business with intent to defraud its creditors he will be personally responsible for all or part of the debts and other liabilities of the company without limitation on liability.

(2) Reckless trading is likely to result

(*a*) where an officer of the company was a party to the carrying on of the business and ought to have known that his actions or those of the company would cause loss to the creditors, his state of knowledge being based on the general knowledge, skill and experience to be reasonably expected from a person in his position, or

(*b*) where he was a party to the contracting of a debt by the company and did not honestly believe on reasonable grounds that the company would be able to pay the debt when it fell due as well as paying all its other debts.

(3) The court will grant a declaration on the grounds of subsection (1) (*a*) only if section 214 (*a–c*) of the Companies Act, 1963 (Circumstances in which a company is unable to pay its debts), applies, and the applicant, being a creditor or contributory, has suffered loss or damage as a consequence of any behaviour mentioned in subsection (1).

(4) The court in making an order will take into consideration whether the creditor was aware of the company's financial state of affairs and despite the awareness consented to the incurring of the debt.

(5) The applicant may call witnesses in a hearing.

(6) Where it appears to the court that any person against whom a declaration is sought has acted honestly and reasonably in relation to the conduct of the affairs of the company the court may relieve him wholly or partly from personal liability, on such terms as it thinks fit.

(7) Where the court makes a declaration it may give further directions as it considers proper and may make provision for the making of a liability and provide that sums recovered shall be paid to such persons and priorities as the declaration shall specify.

(8) This section applies irrespective of whether the person is subject to criminal action or whether the matters occurred in or outside the state.

(9) Subsection (1) will not apply during a period when the company is under the protection of the court.

(10) The terms 'assignee', 'company' and 'officer' are defined for the purposes of this section.

SECTION 34

Criminal liability of persons concerned for fraudulent trading of company.

(1) If any person is knowingly a party to the carrying on of the business of the company with intent to defraud creditors of the company or creditors of any other person or for any fraudulent purpose, that person shall be guilty of an offence.

(2) Any person who is convicted of an offence under this section shall be liable—

(*a*) on summary conviction, to imprisonment for a term not exceeding 12 months or to a fine not exceeding £1,000 or to both, or

(*b*) on conviction on indictment, to imprisonment for a term not exceeding 7 years or to a fine not exceeding £50,000 or to both.

Definitions

'*company*': Companies Act, 1963, section 2.

General Note

Anyone who is knowingly carrying on a business with intent to defraud creditors of the company or for any fraudulent purpose will be guilty of an offence and be subject to the penalties set out in subsection (2).

This section was repealed by section 180 (3) of the Companies Act, 1990.

SECTION 35

Power of court to order the return of assets which have been improperly transferred.

(1) Where, on the application of an examiner of a company, it can be shown to the satisfaction of the court that—

(*a*) any property of the company of any kind whatsoever was disposed of either by way of conveyance, transfer, mortgage, security, loan, or in any way whatsoever whether by act or omission, direct or indirect, and

(*b*) the effect of such disposal was to perpetrate a fraud on the company, its creditors or members,

the court may, if it deems it just and equitable to do so, order any person who appears to have the use, control or possession of such property or the proceeds of the sale or development thereof to deliver it or pay a sum in respect of it to the examiner on such terms or conditions as the court sees fit.

(2) Subsection (1) shall not apply to any conveyance, mortgage, delivery of goods, payment, execution or other act relating to property made or done by or against a company to which section 286 (1) of the Principal Act applies.

(3) In deciding whether it is just and equitable to make an order under this section, the court shall have regard to the rights of persons who have *bona fide* and for value acquired an interest in the property the subject of the application.

Definitions

'company': Companies Act, 1963, section 2.
'court': Companies Act, 1990, section 235.
'examiner': Companies (Amendment) Act, 1990, section 1.
'Principal Act': Companies (Amendment) Act, 1990, section 1.

General Note

This section gives the court power to order the return of assets that have been improperly transferred to some other party.

This section was repealed by section 180 (3) of the Companies Act, 1990.

(1) The examiner may apply to the court, which, if it is satisfied that it is just and equitable, may order any person who appears to have the use, control or possession of assets that have been transferred or disposed of to perpetrate a fraud on the company, its creditors or members to return such property on such terms and conditions as the court sees fit.

(2) Subsection (1) does not apply to property that is the subject of section 286 (1) of the Companies Act, 1963 (Fraudulent preference).

(3) In deciding whether it is just and equitable to make an order under this section the court will consider the rights of persons who have in good faith and for value acquired an interest in the property that is the subject of the application.

SECTION 36
Enforcement of reconstruction orders made by courts outside the State.

(1) Any order made by a court of any country recognised for the purposes of this section and made for or in the course of the reorganisation or reconstruction of a company may be enforced by the High Court in all respects as if the order had been made by the High Court.

(2) When an application is made to the High Court under this section, an office copy of any order sought to be enforced shall be sufficient evidence of the order.

(3) In this section "company" means a body corporate incorporated outside the State, and "recognised" means recognised by order made by the Minister.

Definitions

'company': Companies (Amendment) Act, 1990, section 36.
'court': Companies Act, 1990, section 235.

General Note

Any order made by a court of any country recognised for the purposes of this section and made for or in the course of the reorganisation or reconstruction of a company may be enforced by the High Court as if it had been made in Ireland. When an application is made to the High Court an office copy of any order sought to be enforced will be sufficient evidence of the order.

SECTION 36A
Proceedings by registrar.

Proceedings in relation to an offence under 11 (6), 12 or 30 may be brought and prosecuted by the registrar of companies.

Definitions

'*registrar of companies*': section 2 of Companies Act, 1963, section 2.

General Note

Section 181 (1) (*e*) of the Companies Act, 1990, amended this Act by the insertion of this new provision. This section now gives the Registrar of Companies power to bring and prosecute summary proceedings for offences committed under sections 11 (6) (Power to deal with property charged), 12 (Notification of appointment of examiner) or 30 (Publicity) of this Act.

SECTION 37
Short title, collective citation and construction.

(1) This Act may be cited as the Companies (Amendment) Act, 1990.

(2) This Act and the Companies Acts, 1963 to 1986, may be cited together as the Companies Acts, 1963 to 1990.

(3) The Companies Acts, 1963 to 1986, and this Act shall be construed together as one Act.

General Note

This is a technical section setting out the titles of the statutes.

INDEX

Accounts
    disclosure of directors' interests, 61
    duty to keep books of account, 275
    liability where proper books not
        kept, 278
    particulars of directors' loans, 63
    particulars relating to licensed
        banks, 66
    purchase of own shares, 310
    substantial contract disclosure, 57
Agent
    definition, 12, 358
Agreement
    definition, 111
Amount outstanding
    definition, 63
Appropriate rate
    definition, 221
Arrangements
    excluded from disclosure, 68
Assignee
    definition, 195, 279, 385
Auditor
    appointment of, 249
    disqualification from acting, 224
    duty in breach of disclosure, 70
    duty of, where proper books not
        kept, 267
    duty to keep Registrar informed, 273
    extended notice on appointment or
        removal, 250
    penalty for false statement to, 271
    powers in relation to subsidiaries,
        269
    prohibition on acting, 268
    qualification for appointment, 256
    qualifications, approval of, 261
    qualifications, consultation with
        Minister, 262
    recognition of accounting bodies,
        262, 263
    register of, 272
    removal, 249
    report of, 265
    requisition of general meeting by
        resigning, 254
    resignation, 252
    training as, persons undergoing, 260
Authorised person
    definition, 171

Bank
    particulars of directors' loans, 66
Bank account
    definition, 12
Books and documents
    definition, 4
    duty of auditor where not kept, 267
    falsification or destruction, 320
Business transactions
    definition, 53

Charge
    circumstances where invalid, 193
    ship or aircraft, 177
Child
    definition, 4
Commencement
    definition, 2
Company
    contributing to related company
        debts, 200
    definition, 195, 200, 212, 223, 282,
        345, 385
    duty to keep books of account, 275
    power to purchase own shares, 289
    power to vary minimum share
        capital, 222
    relief on prohibited transactions,
        222,
    report to members of investigation,
        131
    restoration on register, 321
    restrictions regarding directors, 219,
    unregistered company, 325
    unsatisfied judgments, 326,
Company investigations, 127
    on requisition of members, 129
Competent authority
    definition, 31
Connected person
    definition, 4, 36, 191, 193
Contingent purchase contract
    definition, 293,
Contracts
    disclosure of interest by directors,
        70
    repudiation, 370
    retention and inspection, 299
Contravention
    definition, 4